Towards Reformed Multilateralism in the Era of Indo-Pacific

Towards Reformed Multilateralism in the Era of Indo-Pacific

Edited by

Sujan Chinoy
Smruti S Pattanaik

First published in 2026 by
PENTAGON PRESS LLP
206, Peacock Lane, Shahpur Jat
New Delhi-110049, India
Contact: 011-26490600

Typeset in AGaramond, 11.5 Point
Printed at
PRINTS 24X7, Quiinkit Infotech Pvt. Ltd., Gurugram

ISBN 978-81-997728-2-3

Disclaimer: The views expressed in this book are those of the authors and do not necessarily reflect those of the Manohar Parrikar Institute for Defence Studies and Analyses, or the Government of India.

www.pentagonpress.in

Contents

About the Editors *ix*

List of Contributors *xi*

Introduction 1
Towards Reformed Multilateralism in the Era of the Indo-Pacific
Sujan Chinoy and Smruti S Pattanaik

Towards Reformed Multilateralism:
Emerging Power Dynamics and Transforming Global Institutions

1. Revisionism: A Logical Must or A Negative Characteristic? 17
Alireza Khoda Gholipour

2. Inclusive Multipolarity Towards Reformed Multilateralism: Why are Reforms of Multilateral Institutions Important? 30
Emilio J. Zeca

3. A Way to New Multilateralism: From Money-Centrism to Mind-Centrism 40
Tsogbaatar Damdin

4. The Evolution of Vietnam's Multilateral Diplomacy and its Perspective on Multilateralism 58
Tu Anh Tuan

Geo-economics:
Reforming Global Financial Institutions

5. Reforming the Global Financial Architecture to Achieve the SDGs 73
Masahiro KAWAI

6. Crisis of Bretton Woods 2 and Global Financial Institutions 94
Stanislav L. Tkachenko

7. Awakening Sea Monster: Shifting Tides in the Indian Ocean in the Emergent and Emerging World 109
Manisha Dookhony

8. Geo-economics and the Reform of Multilateral Financial Institutions 129
Vova A Chikanda

9. The Evolution of Multilateral Development Banks' Missions and Operations 139
Samir Elsadek Mahmoudi

10. Connectivity and Emerging Initiatives in Asia: A Conceptual Framework 153
Dareskedar Taye

11 Policy Considerations to Advance the Strategic Partnership Between India and the Republic of Korea Based on the Framework of G20 165
Beeho Chun

12 Deepening Bangladesh-India Connectivity: Realising the Emerging Opportunities 191
Mustafizur Rahman

13 Connectivity and Trade, Boosting Investment, Incubating Resilient Supply Chains: Towards Interdependent independence 203
Herrick Mpuku

Multilateral Approach to Climate Adaptation and Mitigation

14. Nontraditional Security Challenges and True Multilateralism 215
Huang Yunsong and Li Linjie

15. Emerging Green Agendas and Multi-scalar Multilateralism in Asia 236
Medha Bisht

16. Climate-Security Nexus at the UN System: Implications for Integration in Eurasia 251
Anatoly Boyashov

17. Multilateral Approach to Non-Traditional Security Challenges: Climate Adaptation and Mitigation – The Case of Madagascar 263
Clara Randrianjara

18. Devising Multilateral Approach to Non-Traditional Security Challenges: Climate change, Mitigation and Governance 282
Felix Wandwe

Ensuring Water, Health, Food, Energy Security and Technology

19. Ensuring Water, Health and Food Security: Role of Multilateral STI Ecosystem 297
Umar Ibrahim Gaya

20. Strengthening Multilateralism for Peace and Sustainable Development 312
Diana Benoit

21. Intellectual Property in an Era of Great Technology Competition 329
Mohammed Soliman

Bibliography 346

Index 348

About the Editors

Amb Sujan Chinoy is the Director General of the Manohar Parrikar Institute for Defence Studies and Analyses (MP-IDSA), New Delhi since 2019. He is a member of the Executive Council of the Society of the Prime Ministers Museum and Library (PMML) and Member, Governing Council, Indian Council of World Affairs. He was a Member of the All-Party MPs Delegation to the UAE and West Africa in the context of OPERATION SINDOOR.

A career diplomat from 1981-2018, he was Ambassador to Japan and Mexico and the Consul General of India in Shanghai and Sydney. A specialist on China and politico-security-military issues, he headed the India-China Diplomatic and Military Expert Group negotiating the confidence-building measures (CBMs) dialogue with China on the boundary dispute from 1996-2000. At the National Security Council Secretariat (NSCS) from 2008-2012, he handled external and internal security policy issues.

During his public service spanning 45 years, he has dealt with political, security, defence, trade and economic issues. His Foreign Service career included postings at the UN in New York and Saudi Arabia. He was the Chair of the Think20 engagement group for India's G20 Presidency. Amb Chinoy has chaired the Mid-Term evaluation of the Modernisation Plans (III & IV) for Central Armed Police Forces (CAPFs).

He speaks fluent Mandarin and is conversant in Japanese, German, French and Spanish. He is the author of "World Upside Down: India Recalibrates Its Geopolitics" (HarperCollins) and "Global Tumult: India as a Pole Star" (Rupa Publications) and has edited several books on defence, security and IR issues.

Smruti S Pattanaik is a Research Fellow at the Manohar Parrikar Institute for Defence Studies and Analysis (MP-IDSA). She holds PhD in South Asian Studies from the School of International Studies, JNU. She was a visiting Asia Fellow at the department of International Relations, Dhaka University in 2004 and 2007, Kodikara Fellow in 1999, postdoctoral fellow at FMSH, Paris in 2008 and visiting fellow at PRIO in 2011, Fellow at the University of Hull in 2018, Visiting Professor on ICCR's India Chair in Colombo University in 2013. She attended the prestigious Symposium on the East Asian Security (SEAS) Program of the US State Department and USPACOM in 2011. She has lectured extensively in India and abroad on India's foreign policy and South Asia.

Dr Pattanaik has published more than 100 research articles and chapters on various aspects of politics in South Asia and have focused on India's relations with its neighbours. She is the author of "Elite Perception in Foreign Policy: Role of Print Media in influencing Indo-Pak relations, 1989-99" (2004) and has edited three books titled "South Asia: Envisioning a Regional Future" (2011) and "Four Decades of India-Bangladesh Relations: Historical Context and Future Direction (2012), "Recounting the Memories of Bangladesh's Liberation War: Why It Is Still Relevant" (Routledge, 2024) She has also authored a monograph "Afghanistan and its Neighbourhood: In Search of a Stable Future" (PRIO-IDSA, 2014).

About the Contributors

Dr. Alireza Khoda Gholipour is a career diplomat with a long background in think-tank business. He has a PhD in Political Science and International Relations. Dr. Gholipour has attended many international conferences and seminars and has written a few books and several articles. His studies have been mostly focused on developments in South Asia Region (namely Afghanistan and Pakistan) and Indo-Pacific Region (Emerging powers and their strategies). Currently, he is the Director, Group for Asian Studies at the Institute for Political and International Studies, based in Tehran, Iran.

Emílio Jovando Zeca Deputy Director, Centre for Strategic and International Studies, Mozambique. He holds PhD in Strategic and International Studies; Master in Conflict Resolution and Mediation; and Bachelor in International Relations and Diplomacy. He is a researcher at the Department of Peace and Security of the Centre for Strategic and International Studies – CEEI/UJC. Mr. Zeca is also a teacher of Security Studies and Maritime Security Regimes and a visiting professor at the Institute of Global Governance in China and Dakhla Open University in Morocco. Over the last decade, he attended several courses, conferences and workshops like Building Capacity for Effective Implementation of the Arms Trade Treaty at Geneva Centre for Security Policy – GCSP in 2019, Global Governance, Community of Human Destiny and Global Governance in Wuhan – China (2018), National Security at Galilee Collage in 2015 among other. His notable publications include "The Mozambican Foreign Policy and Diplomacy" (2021); "Mozambique: Maritime Security in Indian Ocean" (2020); "Mozambique: Energy Resources and International Policy" (2016); and "International Relations: Nature, Paradigms and Contemporary Issues" (2013). Dr. Zeca's research interests are International Relations and Diplomacy, International Security Studies; and Peace and Security Studies.

Mr. Tsogtbaatar Damdin is a diplomat and a politician. He is a Member of Parliament. He served as Mongolia's Minister for Foreign Affairs from 2017 to 2020. Prior to that he was the Chairman of the Parliamentary Subcommittee on

Human Rights between 2016 and 2017, and was elected twice to the National Parliament (2016 and 2020). He has also served as a foreign policy advisor to two Presidents of Mongolia. Mr. Tsogtbaatar Damdin started his diplomatic career as an attaché in the Asian Department of the Ministry of Foreign Affairs in 1994. He became State Secretary of the Ministry in 2008 and was later appointed as the Minister for Foreign Affairs of Mongolia in 2017. During his time at the Ministry of Foreign Affairs, he initiated a number of sweeping reforms both in the mind-set and practice of the Mongolian diplomacy. As a Member of Parliament, he drafted the Law on Legal Status of Human Rights Defenders, which made Mongolia the first country in Asia to legislate such a law and was a big step forward in the Mongolian legislative system, especially in the area of human rights promotion.

Tu Anh Tuan is a Senior Researcher at the Institute for Foreign Policy and Strategic Studies (IFPSS), Diplomatic Academy of Vietnam. He has extensive experience in multilateral and economic diplomacy, including roles with APEC, ASEAN, and ASEM. He served as Program Director at the APEC Secretariat (2010–2014), First Secretary at the Viet Nam Embassy in the Netherlands overseeing multilateral organisations and economic diplomacy. He holds a Master's degree in American Studies from the University of East Anglia (2003).

Masahiro Kawai is Representative Director, Economic Research Institute for Northeast Asia, Professor Emeritus University of Tokyo. Prof. Kawai began his professional career as a Research Fellow at the Brookings Institution (1977-78). He then served as an Associate Professor in the Department of Political Economy of the Johns Hopkins University (1978-86), Professor of Economics at the Institute of Social Science of the University of Tokyo (1986-2008). Prof. Kawai also served as Chief Economist for the World Bank's East Asia and the Pacific Region (1998-2001), Deputy Vice Minister of Finance for International Affairs of Japan's Ministry of Finance (2001-03), and President of the Policy Research Institute of Japan's Finance Ministry (2003). Afterwards he was Special Advisor to the Asian Development Bank President in charge of regional economic cooperation and integration (2005-2007), and Dean and CEO of the Asian Development Bank Institute (2007 to 2014). Prof. Kawai assumed his current position in April 2014. In addition, Prof. Kawai has been President of the Japan Chapter of "Economists for Peace and Security" since 2002. He is also a Councilor of the Bank of Japan (since 2014), a Special Research Advisor to the Policy Research Institute of Japan's Ministry of Finance (since 2014), and Vice President of the Council on East Asia Community (since 2015).

Stanislav L Tkachenko is Founder and Director of the M.A. Programme, Diplomacy of Russian Federation and Foreign States, Saint-Petersburg State University. He has received his Ph.D. in History from the Saint-Petersburg State University and Doctoral Degree in Economics from the Saint-Petersburg State University of Economics. He is a Professor of International Political Economy at the Department of European Studies of Saint-Petersburg State University since 1994. In 2002-2007. Tkachenko was Vice-Rector of Saint-Petersburg State University for International Relations. He is the President of the International Studies Association's section on "Post-Communist Systems in International Relations" (2013-2023). He is visiting professor at the Bologna University (Italy) since 2004 and consultant to the Inter-Parliamentary Assembly of CIS since 2006. Professor Tkachenko has published extensively and edited 14 books, including: "European EMU and prospects for monetary integration among post-Soviet states" (in Russian), "La Russia, I BRICS e l'Ordine Internationale" (in Italian); "Political economy of ICT" (in Russian); "The Russian Challenge to the European Security Environment"; Institute of Presidential Power (in Russian). He is also a regular participant on TV and radio programs at Business FM, RBC TV, 5-th Channel, TV Sankt-Petersburg.

Ms. Manisha Dookhony is an economist, with double Master's degrees in economics and Public Administration from Harvard University. Ms Dookhony has very strong linkages across both Francophone and Anglophone Africa. With over 20 years of work experience in developing policies and strategies for business environment, she has extensive experience advising business leaders and high-level government officials at Presidential level. Her opinion is sought for economics, regulatory affairs, geo-political and business-related matters and she regularly provides expert opinion to international media. As a seasoned board director, she serves on a range of for-profit and non-profit institutions at the international level. Her latest board appointment is for the Africa Legal Support Facility under the aegis of the African Development Bank. At the professional level, Manisha co-manages Africa Rise, an EU funded regional facility that covers 25 countries in Eastern and South Africa. She is also the senior advisor for the Namibian Investment Promotion and Development Board. She is a graduate of prestigious Indian institutions - Lady Shri Ram College and Jawaharlal Nehru University. She is the co-author of the recent report on "New Players in the Indian Ocean".

Mr. Vova.A.Chikanda is the Founder, Executive Director and Principal Lecturer at Zimbabwe Institute of Diplomacy. He holds a Master of Arts degree in

International Relations and International Law from the Kiev State University and is currently pursuing a PhD in Diplomacy and International Affairs at Swiss Management Centre. Mr Chikanda was Deputy Ambassador and Minister Plenipotentiary at the United Nations Mission Vienna, Austria with multiple accreditations to the Czech Republic, Slovakia and Slovenia. He was also responsible for the UN Crime Commission; the UN International Atomic Energy Agency; the UN Industrial Development Organisation and as the Observer Representative at the OPEC Fund. Mr. Chikanda has won many awards including the Best Award for his contribution to Diplomacy. A motivational and public speaker he is fluent in English, Russian, Shona and Ndebele.

Samir Elsadek Mahmoudi is a career diplomat with a range of experiences across multilateral economic affairs, trade and development finance. He was adviser to Egypt's G20 Sherpa on the reform of Multilateral Development Banks, climate finance and global economic trends. Prior to that, he served on Egypt's COP27 organising committee and as a focal point in charge of UNDP's activities in Egypt. He contributed to various multilateral processes on financing for development, including the Paris Summit on the Financing of African Economies, the G8 Deauville Partnership in support of Arab Economies in transition and the Arab Economic Summit. Elsadek Mahmoudi served in Egypt's Embassy in Paris, where he contributed to development finance talks and represented Egypt in the OECD investment and regulatory policy committees.

Elsadek Mahmoudi earned his PhD in Economics at Georgia State University, where he conducted research on pensions, mortgage markets, and climate-related financial risks. He is currently an Emerging Climate Leaders Fellow with Yale University. His research was published in the Journal of Public Economics. His research was funded by an NBER pre-doctoral fellowship and was recognised by the National Academy of Social Insurance, BlackRock and the American Real Estate and Urban Economics Association. He also conducted a research internship with the IMF, where he contributed to the Fund's research on SMEs' access to finance.

Dareskedar Taye, is the Director General for the research department of Asia Pacific. He is also a lead researcher at the Institute of Foreign Affairs, Ethiopia. His recent publication is entitled "Redeeming the Ethio-US relations as the world is heading towards great power rivalry". His list of publications include a book in local language. Taye has a PhD in Political Science, an MA in International Relations, and BA in Political Science and International Relations. In the past seventeen years, he has worked as a university professor in different public universities and specialised training institutes in Ethiopia. He had worked as a political analyst for embassies and media outlets and an experience of intelligence analysis. Now, he is working as a researcher in the foreign policy research institute called Institute of Foreign Affairs.

Dr. Chun Beeho is the vice president of Korean Council on Foreign Relations and the distinguished professor of SKKU (Sungkyunkwan University) at Seoul, Republic of Korea. Prior to joining the University, He was a career diplomat serving as Korean ambassador plenipotentiary to Mexico and Bulgaria together with foreign services in France, Belgium, Spain, Costa Rica and the European Commission. He also served as ambassador of international relations at Gangwon Province, ROK. At the University, he served as the Director of International Cooperation Development Centre and participated as project manager in KDI's (Korea Development Institute) policy consultation project to Peru in the capacity development for Civil Service Reform and as coordinator in WCO's (World Customs Organization) scholarship program on data analysis for the customs officials of member countries. He holds a doctoral degree in Political Science and Sociology at the Complutense University of Madrid, Spain. He was endowed with a degree of doctor honoris causa in philology science by Sofia University of Bulgaria.

Mustafizur Rahman is a Distinguished Fellow at the Centre for Policy Dialogue (CPD), a leading think tank in South Asia. Prior to this he was the Executive Director of the CPD (2007-2017). Professor Rahman started his career as an Assistant Professor at the Department of Accounting and Information Systems (AIS) of the Faculty of Business Studies, University of Dhaka. Having taught for twenty-five years, he took voluntary early retirement from the University in 2012 to work full time at the CPD. He was awarded the prestigious Ibrahim Memorial Gold Medal by the University of Dhaka for excellence in research. Professor Rahman is a member of the Dhaka University Senate (2009-2013 and 2018-2024). He is a member of Board of Trustees and Syndicate member of the BRAC University. Professor Rahman has undertaken post-doctoral research at several reputed academic institutions including the University of Oxford, UK and the Institute of Southeast Asian Studies (ISEAS), Singapore. He has published widely in professional journals both in Bangladesh and abroad, and has authored books and monographs in his area of expertise.

Herrick C Mpuku is the Executive Director for the Zambia Institute for Policy Analysis and Research. He also have worked for the Southern African Development Community - Development Finance Resource Centre (SADC-DFRC) in Gaborone, Botswana as Programmes Manager for Capacity Building and Policy Research. He served as Permanent Secretary in the Ministry of Finance (2001) and Ministry of Transport and Communications (2003). He was Programme Economist at USAID Zambia. Dr. Mpuku was also the Director of the Zambia Institute of Management (ZAMIM).

He also served in various capacity at the Copperbelt University (CBU) holding positions of Head of Research and Consultancy and Acting Dean in the School of Business. He was the founding Director of the Institute of Consultancy, Applied Research and Extension Studies and contemporaneously serving as Director of the University Computer Centre at the Copperbelt University.

He holds a PhD in Economics from the University of Birmingham, an MBA from the University of Bradford, and an MSc in Development Economics from the University of Oxford. He also holds a Bachelor of Business Administration (B.B.A) from the University of Zambia (Ndola Campus) and a Bachelor of Laws (LL.B) from the University of South Africa.

He has served on several boards including Tanzania-Zambia Railways Authority, Zambia Railways Limited, National Airports Corporation, Zambia Telecommunications Corporations, National Council of Scientific Research, Presidents Citizenship College. He has several publications to his credit.

Huang Yunsong is Professor of Law, Coordinator of China Center for South Asian Studies, and Associate Dean at School of International Studies, Sichuan University. He has held research scholarships in Pakistan, India and the US. He did his postdoctoral research on international law at the University of Michigan Law School. His research focuses on international law and South Asian studies. His current research projects include improving regional cooperation between China and South Asia, and China-India relations.

Linjie Li is a doctoral researcher in International Relations at Sichuan University and a joint PhD trainee at the East Asian Institute, National University of Singapore. He also serves as a Researcher at the Sichuan Provincial Taiwan Studies Center and has been involved in policy-oriented and academic research across multiple institutions.

His research focuses on Cross-Strait relations, Sino–Indian relations, regional security dynamics and normative political theory with particular emphasis on peace-oriented political order, sovereignty, and responsibility. He has published extensively in peer-reviewed journals across mainland China, Taiwan, Hong Kong, and international outlets, and has presented his work at numerous national and international academic conferences.

Medha Bisht is Associate Professor at the South Asian University, Delhi. She is a Ph.D from Diplomatic Studies Division, Jawaharlal Nehru University, where she wrote her thesis on Multi-stakeholder negotiations on security and development. Her country expertise in South Asia is restricted to Bhutan and Pakistan. She also works at the intersection of strategy and philosophy and is particularly interested in non-western sources of diplomatic practices in Asia. Her book, 'Kautilya's Arthashastra: Philosophy of Strategy' is published by Routledge in 2020. Interested in the concept of water diplomacy, her research engagement has highlighted the micro and macro narratives related to water governance and water diplomacy in South Asia. She has conducted stakeholder engagements and dialogues in South Asia to identify the political, cultural and ecological perspectives pertaining to rivers and riparian communities. She was a consultant to IUCN-India in 2017, where she co-authored a course on 'Hydro-diplomacy in South Asia' in collaboration with Dhaka University. The course was pilot-tested in India and Bangladesh in 2017 with mid-level water professionals. She was also a lead investigator in India, for a project undertaken in collaboration with WWF-Pakistan, based in Lahore from 2016 to 2017.

Anatoly Boyashov is an Expert at Center for International Studies, Belarusian State University. Anatoly received his Ph.D. in political science from Bielefeld University in 2020. Having studied at Saint Petersburg State University, College of Europe, Anatoly has worked with the Center for Sociological and Internet Research in Russia, Bielefeld University in Germany, Interparliamentary Assembly of the Commonwealth of Independent States. Anatoly has regularly performed as an international electoral observer in Central Asia. Author of "Network Governance of the UN Human Rights Council" (Routledge, 2022), Anatoly publishes on the UN system, regional integration, and human rights.

Clara Randrianjara has been with the Ministry of Foreign Affairs (MFA) of Madagascar since 2004. She has served in the Malagasy Embassy in Ottawa (Canada) from 2007-2016 and has had Head Office assignments in the Regional

Integration Directorate where she dealt with the integration of Madagascar within the regional organisations such as the Indian Ocean Commission (IOC), Indian Ocean Rim Association (IORA) and the African Union (AU) from 2019-2022. Moreover, she has served at the MFA from 2016-2018 where she was a research officer at the Directorate of Regional Integration. Before her posting in Canada, she was the Head of Department of the United Nations and Specialized Agencies at the Directorate of Multilateral Cooperation from 2005-2007. Ms Randrianjara is currently a Senior Policy Analyst at the Centre for Strategic Studies and Analysis at the MFA since November 2022. Ms Randrianjara holds a BA (Hons) from the Ottawa University, Canada and MA from the University of Antananarivo, Madagascar. She attended the Consular and Diplomatic Agent Programme from 2001-2003 where she earned a Diploma in Diplomatic Studies (Hons). Ms. Randrianjata also holds a Certificate in International Civil Service from the International Organization of La Francophonie and the United Nations Institute for Training and Research (UNITAR). Besides, she has completed various professional training programmes in Diplomacy, Negotiation and Mediation.

Mr. Felix Wandwe is the Acting Director of The Tanzania-Mozambique Centre for Foreign Relations, Dar Es Salaam, Tanzania; One of the strategic training institutions under the Ministry of Foreign Affairs and East African Cooperation. With a proven experience in Accounting, Finance, Banking, Security and Strategic Studies, he has held various leadership, administrative and management roles in Tanzania. He has worked with Prevention and Combat Corruption Bureau of Tanzania heading Private sector Investigations, Public sector Investigations in different periods of time. He has led the Bureau in various regions in Tanzania. Mr. Wandwe has worked for the National Electoral Commission of Tanzania as a Director of the Zanzibar Office. He later headed the Planning Department and the Directorate of Planning Finance and Administration of the Tanzania-Mozambique Centre for Foreign Relations, before recently being appointed as the acting Director of the Centre. Mr. Wandwe professional career spans over more than 25 years with learning experience in various countries across the world including China, Vietnam, United States of America, United Kingdom, Namibia, Kenya, South Africa and India.

Umar Ibrahim Gaya is the Coordinating Director, Science Infrastructure and a principal officer at the National Agency for Science and Engineering Infrastructure (NASENI), Abuja Nigeria. He received PhD Catalysis from Universiti Putra Malaysia in 2009. Prof. Gaya has been a postdoctoral research fellow in the

Department of Chemistry, Universiti Putra Malaysia (2011), and later in the Department of Petroleum and Chemical Engineering, Sultan Qaboos University, Oman (2011-2012). He has published many articles in top tier high impact journals of Science and Technology. He has been the most cited author from NASENI and Bayero University and has published a book with the Springer Nature. He is a fellow of the Chemical Society of Nigeria (CSN) and the Institute of Chartered Chemists of Nigeria (ICCON). He is also a member of the American Chemical Society-Catalysis Division (ACS-CATL).

Diana Benoit is the Director of the James R. Mancham Peace and Diplomacy Research Institute at the University of Seychelles which is an academic research institute that focuses on eastern Africa and the western Indian Ocean region. She is a founding member of the institute and is actively involved in research projects on peacebuilding, conflict and security, transitional and restorative justice. Her recent projects are on the role of civil society actors in responding to gender-based violence in Seychelles; and the transitional justice processes in small island developing states. She is currently engaged in a doctoral study on the nexus between trauma healing and peacebuilding, which has an action research element.

Mohammed Soliman is the director of the Strategic Technologies and Cyber Security Program at the Middle East Institute and a Manager at McLarty Associates' Middle East and North Africa Practice. His work focuses on the intersection of technology, geopolitics, and business in emerging markets. A native of Cairo, Mohammed started his career as an engineer and worked as a consultant, providing strategic advisory services for local and international businesses. In Washington, DC, he has also served as a country analyst for the Peace Tech Lab at the US Institute of Peace, and as a Huffington Fellow at Georgetown's Institute for the Study of Diplomacy. Mohammed earned his Bachelor's Degree in engineering from the Egyptian Aviation Academy and graduated with a Master of Science in Foreign Service with distinction from Georgetown University.

Introduction

Towards Reformed Multilateralism in the Era of the Indo-Pacific

Sujan Chinoy and Smruti S Pattanaik

The world is undergoing transformational changes. The 'engine' of manufacturing and growth has shifted from the West to the East, primarily to East Asia in the last century. China's opening and its reform policy led it to emerge as a primary engine of economic growth and the world's largest trading nation. In recent years, growth and prosperity have spread to wider regions from East Asia to Southeast Asia, South Asia, and to the dynamic coast of Africa. The construct of the Asia-Pacific as a sphere of economic dynamism in the last century has given way to the notion of the Indo-Pacific, which has gained currency due to its inclusive nature, more reflective of the aspirations of people in a wider arc. Asia is a key plank of the Indo-Pacific and reflects the region's aspiration for growth and prosperity. The future of the Asian continent is not contingent on the rise of any single great power – rather on multiple civilisations and emerging powers that are striving to play a larger global role. India has been a great votary of reformed multilateralism. Prime Minister Modi alluded to this concept at the 2018 BRICS Summit held in Johannesburg. Reform of multilateral institutions remains India's key agenda as plurilateral initiatives are gaining ground where countries can collectively negotiate and bargain to protect their interests.

The global COVID-19 pandemic revealed the stresses and risks in critical supply chains as the world scrambled to deal with supply chain disruption. The phenomenon of globalisation has further fused trade and investment flows to geostrategic competition. Monopolisation of critical minerals and the recent trade wars reflects how disruption in supply due to policies adopted by countries impinge on domestic industries including countries' transition to green energy. The US and major European countries have long played a key role in Asia's trade and economic rise as well as stability. But with China's rise along with that of peer powers like India and Japan, the centrality of Asia in global geopolitics is visible. Yet, multilateral organisations like the G20 are forums most representative of the engagement between the US, Europe and developing countries, not just in Asia but also in Africa and Latin America.

The "Asian Age" or the "Asian Century" in the era of the Indo-Pacific is being redefined as a broader concept signalling the inevitable rise of different parts of Asia, which are home to some of the world's most ancient civilisations. For the past two decades, if not more, Asia has re-emerged to shape global dynamics by involving many stakeholders from the extended neighbourhood of Africa, West Asia, Eurasia as well as the great powers that have a long-standing economic and security stake in different parts of Asia. According to McKinsey, by 2040, Asia is expected to generate more than 50 per cent of the world's GDP, and could account for nearly 40 per cent of global consumption, ushering in the "Asian Age".

An Emerging Asia

The onset of the 'Asian Century' – Asianisation of world politics – has renewed focus on the continent and the promise it holds for the emerging global political order as Asia remains the main growth engine of the world. After all, Asia is today home to the world's second, fourth and fifth-largest economies, and it is, therefore, not surprising that the balance of power has shifted to Asia. There is, in fact, a repositioning of Asia, with China and India emerging as dominant actors in global politics. Japan, as the world's second-largest developed economy, is a potent power that is taking increasingly robust positions on defence and security issues and is involved in infrastructure development contributing to economic growth. India has also witnessed sustained economic growth for the last three decades and is poised for an even higher rate of growth. It has emerged as the fastest-growing major economy and is on track to become the world's third-largest economy with a projected GDP of $7.3 trillion by 2030. ASEAN too has emerged as one of the economically most dynamic regions in the world and the member states collectively boast of being the fourth largest economy in the world with a GDP of US$4.1 trillion. China's exponential economic growth together with its growing technological prowess, has aided its geopolitical rise. Overall, post-COVID-19 Asia is on the path of economic recovery and Asia's average growth stands at 6.9 per cent according to the Asian Development Bank. Asia is the biggest driver of global growth, contributing sixty per cent.

The continent's heterogeneity in terms of its diverse culture, skilled manpower and availability of cheap labour, has made it a manufacturing hub and demonstrated its economic success. Asia continues to remain a manufacturing hub with China in the lead followed by Vietnam, India, Malaysia and Singapore.

Economic growth has also brought in its own challenges in terms of ensuring macro-economic stability, and sustainable growth as trade and investment issues are linked to uncertain global supply chains. As the Indo-Pacific countries strive to achieve their Sustainable Development Goals (SDGs), there is a growing emphasis on climate adaptation initiatives and green growth powered by green energy. However, the technologies required for energy transition are expensive and the Global South needs to find a way to make the transition sustainable with help from the developed nations.

An emerging Asia would prioritise important agendas such as access to drinking water, securing health, preserving bio-diversity, water security and water conservation and exploring opportunities in the blue economy. As climate change impacts agriculture and consequently food security, countries in the Indo-Pacific region would be compelled to focus on sustainable consumption alongside green transition.

Investing in Infrastructure for Economic Development

In order to advance the UN-mandated Sustainable Development Goals (SDGs) in Asia, the existing digital divide needs to be bridged through uninterrupted, resilient and decentralised Digital Commons. China has taken a lead in offering 'green infrastructure' in its programme 'infrastructure for tomorrow' through its Asian Infrastructure and Investment Bank. It has an ambitious target of providing 'cumulative climate finance approvals of US$50 billion by 2030'. Moreover, competing for investment and market access, the rising economies of Asia, i.e., India, China and Japan, are keen to invest in mega infrastructural projects as a part of their geo-economic power projection. At the same time, Asian economies have been vying for greater connectivity in a bid to integrate economies of the region. China's ambitious and aggressive Belt and Road Initiative (BRI) has challenged the status quo. Connectivity has become a core facet of both competition and cooperation. While originally centred on a Eurasian connectivity construct, the BRI has pushed its geographical boundaries to incorporate the Arctic, Africa, South Asia, Southeast Asia and Latin America as well as parts of Oceania. It has now run into challenges of debt-traps and negative perceptions in some countries. Meanwhile, the US, EU and Japan are offering more transparent and sustainable alternatives to finance the infrastructure and connectivity deficit in the Indo-Pacific.

Asian infrastructure needs are estimated to be between US$ 22.6 trillion and US$ 26 trillion until 2030. The BRI is China's attempt to take advantage of the existing gap in investment in the infrastructure and connectivity sectors, thereby accruing strategic gains. This has led Asian economies like Japan to expand their investment in connectivity projects via the Expanded Partnership for Quality Infrastructure (EPQI). India, through its concept of Security and Growth for All (SAGAR) emphasises on an integrated future towards sustainable development. The forty states that are India's littoral, host nearly 40 per cent of the world's population. The concept of Mahasagar strengthens India's relationship with the Global South. The US too has launched multilateral ventures like the Blue Dot Network (BDN) and the Group of Seven (G7)-linked connectivity ventures, the Build Back Better World, the Millennium Challenge Corporation (MCC) and the Partners in the Blue Pacific with like-minded States. With the launch of its Global Gateway in 2021, the European Union (EU) has emerged as the latest player entering the infrastructure and connectivity race.

The COVID-19 pandemic has generated wide-ranging discussions among major powers on supply chain diversification and the challenges of relying on a single source of supply. As a result, Australia, Japan, and India launched the Supply Chain Resilience Initiative (SCRI) to diversify supply chains and build sustainable networks that are resistant to future shocks. Maritime trading nations such as India, Australia and Japan remain best placed to take the SCRI forward, along with the cooperation of the US and Europe. There also exists immense potential for these countries to work with new partners in Africa and ASEAN region. Meanwhile, China has reintroduced Health Silk Road as part of its vaccine diplomacy. As a manufacturing hub of pharmaceuticals, India has provided equitable access to vaccines to countries around the world as part of the QUAD Vaccine partnership.

A multilateral institutional framework for global digital governance architecture is needed with Asian countries as stakeholders. However, Asia's representation in the current multilateral organisations continues to be inadequate compared to its growing significance in world politics, It is pertinent to underline the need to transform global institutions like the United Nations by creating a new framework and reforming the existing multilateral fora to reflect the current international reality.

According to the Asian Development Bank (ADB), "by 2030, the prevalence of extreme poverty in the region [read Asia] is expected to drop below 1 per cent [and the same time] about 25 per cent of the population is projected to achieve at least middle-class status. With the shift of economic power towards Asia, Asian concerns need to be reflected in the global financial order. The dominant international financial institutions such as the IMF and World Bank, etc., need to be sensitive to the requirements of the developing nations that are keen to meet the SDGs.

Need for Reformed Multilateralism

The United Nations created more than 80 years ago have become part of global power politics. Some of the multilateral Institutions are not aligned with the aspirations of rising powers with economic strength exerting political influence and boasting technological capacity. Many of the institutions are dominated by the Western countries, especially the United States is seen as perpetuation of power through global mechanisms. Reform of Security Council is being debated for years with 'Open-Ended Working Group on UNSC Reforms' and one does not see much progress as the P5 countries are reluctant to provide space to the rising powers to become part of global decision making body that has a dominant role in maintaining peace and security as part of global governance mechanism. As UN Secretary-General António Guterres in his message for the International Day of Multilateralism and Diplomacy for Peace said in April 2022, "The principles at the heart of multilateral cooperation are under the greatest strain since the founding of the United Nations.... We need to transform this moment of crisis into a moment for multilateralism."

Multilateralism on the other hand, would serve the interests of the Asian countries. This would call for the reordering of other UN-affiliated institutions like the World Trade Organisation (WTO), World Health Organisation (WHO), and International Labour Organisation (ILO) to reflect the essential character of the multipolar global order representing diverse interests. In addition, the reform of the international financial institutions in order to better provide finance for climate change adaptation and mitigation, infrastructure development and investments in the social sector would no doubt help the developing countries in Asia to meet the rising aspirations of their people as well as contribute responsibly to the global efforts to save the planet. The WHO initiated COVID-19 Tools Accelerator (ACT-Accelerator) in April 2020 which brought together brought together governments, scientists, businesses, NGOs for production and equitable distribution of COVID-19 vaccines and treatment needs to go beyond to meet any such health crisis in the future. India's Minister of Health and Family Welfare Mansukh Mandaviya said, "India will strive to build a consensus among member countries on the need for such a permanent institutional platform", to give voice to the Global South in the decision-making structure.

India has been a strong votary of UN reforms for many years. Speaking at the United Nations, Foreign Minister, Dr. S. Jaishankar said, "We not only need to increase stakeholdership but also enhance the effectiveness and credibility of multilateralism in the eyes of the international community and in the eyes of global public opinion. If this is to happen, member states from Latin America, Africa, Asia, and the Small Island Developing States should have credible and continuing representation in the Security Council. Decisions about their future can no longer be taken without their participation." As of now, a few veto-wielding countries in the Security Council have exercised disproportionate control over the global agenda. This has not served the interest of an equitable and level playing field for all. The current composition of the Council reflects, as Dr. Jaishankar stated, "the inequities and inadequacies of the way the world currently functions". The undemocratic structure of current multilateral organisations that privileges only a few countries who want to control global political order at the cost of the aspirations of the majority of the countries have given rise to 'mini-laterals' that reflect the diverse interests, which the current global structure is unable to address. India has, on numerous occasions, emphasised the need to have an honest conversation on the reform of various multilateral institutions created 80 years ago and has expressed its disappointment over the lack of progress in regard to Security Council reforms. It is also imperative that there should be policy coordination among various multilateral groupings without which it will be difficult to cater to the needs of developing and underdeveloped nations in a cohesive manner.

One of the ways developing economies have attempted to address their concerns is to focus on minilateralism. Minilateralism has shaped new cohorts of like-minded nations to focus on micro issues that are considered important for the participating countries. Smaller groupings with similar objectives have emerged as the new and preferred mediums of strategic cooperation to advance national interests. Minilateralism focuses more on shared values and convergent interests. Such cooperation, including at the regional level, is likely to reshape the post-pandemic geopolitical order. As the world waits for the reform of the UN system and emphasis on reforms, multilateralism is increasingly gaining ground to address several challenges that the world is facing today, like climate change, conflict, green energy transition and pandemics.

India has emphasised "One Earth, One Family, One Future" in the spirit of its ancient philosophy of "*Vasudhaiva Kutumbakam*". India has consistently championed the cause of the Global South and need for reforms. As a member of

BRICS, ASEAN, CICA, SCO, QUAD, IBSA and CELAC, India would centre its efforts on 'reformed multilateralism' as a part of its endeavour to transform global institutions to suit the changing international power configuration in the context of the rise of the Global South.

Asia is now increasingly situated in the unfolding paradigms of the Indo-Pacific region. It is clear that regional power politics in Asia as well as their interplay with external powers will be a critical factor in determining the future of the region. In an integrated world, Asian security issues impact on the wider Indo-Pacific, and vice-versa. Keeping these developments in context, this edited volume seeks to answer to the following questions through contributions from eminent scholars:

1. Why are reforms of multilateral institutions important? Two major developments are transforming the multilateral system. The first is the emergence of a number of key States as influential actors in the global political system. The second is a trend towards multi-polarity that is gaining momentum.
2. In the global power transition, how is Asia situated in the era of the Indo-Pacific? What role can India play in this evolving paradigm?
3. How are Asian powers responding to the New Supply Chain Resilience Initiative (SCRI)? What will be the impact of SCRI on the evolving geo-economics of Asia?
4. Will cooperation on non-traditional issues such as climate adaptability and energy transition strengthen multilateral actions? Can widely agreed-on general rules be formulated to cooperate on managing the global commons and in the provision of global public goods?
5. What level of policy coordination is required within the complex of global institutions – such as the WHO, WTO, and the ILO – and which of these institutions should and can be reformed substantially?
6. How will global Bretton Woods financial institutions adapt to the rise of Asia and alternative sources of finance for infrastructure and connectivity?
7. What would be the role of technology in bridging the digital divide? How could a framework be evolved, that will help in structuring an uninterrupted and resilient 'Digital Commons' and make technology affordable and accessible?
8. What mechanisms can like-minded countries in Asia and the G20 devise that will serve as solutions to the threats of an impending recession, high inflation, and interrupted supply chains?

This edited volume comprises twenty-one chapters.

Chapter 1 written by Alireza Khoda Gholipour titled "Revisionism: A Logical Must or a Negative Characteristic?" argues in the era of globalisation multilateralism is evolving with the nature of changing power dynamics. There is now a considerable unanimity that international organisations such as the United Nations, the World Trade Organisation (WTO), Bretton Woods Institutions and the international economic architecture need to be reformed in order to create the conditions for a much more just and sustainable world and to achieve greater collective and democratic governance to tackle the myriad of challenges facing the world. He raises question why revisionism or reform has always been considered a negative factor, especially for State actors, while most of emerging powers believe that the world needs structural reform.

Chapter 2 titled "Inclusive Multipolarity: Towards Reformed Multilateralism: Why Are Reforms of Multilateral Institutions Important", Emílio Jovando Zeca opines that the contemporary international system faces complex problems such as demographic, climate, energy and technological transition, that require multilateral initiatives for their resolution. He argues that multilateralism must be reformed through political-diplomatic cooperation institutional arrangements, dialogue, coordination, cooperation and mutual respect, because the contemporary international system is inclusive and multipolar, with several poles of power and different cooperation alternatives.

Chapter 3 titled "A Way to New Multilateralism: From Money Centricism to Mind Centricism" by Tsogbaatar Damdin focuses on how discontent and frustration is widespread throughout the world which stem from the intra-societal problems and is now spilling over to the realm of the international relations. Hence, diplomacy alone cannot handle the existing strife and solutions need to be searched within the societies. Understandably, such a situation complicates the resolution of modern international stand-offs. He argues that this needs to be solved on the basis of thorough cognition of the issues and design of new, novel and unorthodox approaches.

Chapter 4 by Tu Anh Tuan on "The Evolution of Vietnam's Multilateral Diplomacy and its Perspective on Multilateralism". Multilateralism was built to address global challenges, promote cooperation, and maintain peace, stability, and order. However, when major power competition escalates, there is a risk the multilateral platforms can be politicised and can consequently devolve into arenas for great powers' consolidation of force. He argues that India has the ability to play a significant role given its multicultural makeup and religious diversity that is its soft power. While many other powers want to impose their ideologies and values on small countries, India embraces pluralism, inclusivity, and respect for different cultures and religions.

Chapter 5 on "Reforming Global Financial Architecture to achieve SDGs" by Masahiro Kawai focuses on reforming global financial architecture. He argues that global financial institutions have been responding flexibly to the financial needs of developing countries affected by the invasion and sanctions and thinks that there is larger scope to do more.

Chapter 6 on "Crisis of Bretton Woods Two and Global Financial Institutions" by Stanislav L Tkachenko argues that Bretton Woods Two model of global financial institutions was based on US petrodollars and the regime of free floating of currencies. Today there is no such hegemonic state on the planet capable of imposing its will on the global community. A new or radically reformed monetary regime should take into account the opinion of all the states, regardless of their size. He points to the unwillingness of Washington to negotiate transition to multipolar international system, based on respect of sovereignty and "good old balance of power" model, and argues this attitude opens the door for BRICS states, including India, to reproduce individual elements of the former Bretton Woods System among BRICS as a group of genuine sovereign states.

Chapter 7 by Manisha Dookhony on "Shifting Tides and Ties in Indian Oceanin the Emergent and Emerging World", argues Geopolitical changes within Indian Ocean have led to evolving economic trends. Increasingly large crude and cargo carriers find it easier to pass through the region, enhancing the role of maritime routes. She further argues India Mauritius relationship has grown tremendously. However, there is a significant ramping up of competition between China and India in their bilateral relationships with Mauritius which has added to the geopolitical churning in the region.

Chapter 8 titled "Geoeconomics and the Reform of Global Multilateral Institutions" by V.A. Chikanda discusses the significance of The Indo-Pacific region and Africa to global economic multilateralism. The prevalence of geoeconomic unilateralism in Global Financial Institutions has disenfranchised Africa's place in the global economy. This chapter analyses paper will also analyse geoeconomics through the prism of the geopolitical role of actors in international relations viz states, international governmental and non-governmental organisations with an obvious bias to reform of multilateral institutions.

Chapter 9 on "The Evolution of Multilateral Development Banks' Missions and Operations" by Samir Elsadek Mahmoudi writes in response to a growing external financing gap, developing countries recognised the value of establishing new development finance institutions including the Asian Infrastructure Investment Bank (AIIB) and the New Development Bank (NDB). He argues the challenges facing the expansion of the financial footprint of MDBs is the limitations on their risk-capacity. This chapter discusses the points of strength that make Multilateral Development Banks efficient intermediaries between capital markets on the one hand and developing countries on the other.

Chapter 10 by Dareskedar Taye on "Connectivity and Emerging Initiatives in Asia: A Conceptual Framework" writes the shifting of economic power house to the global east and the emergence of alternative connectivity mechanisms by different states having different economic capability and regional/global perspective means the debate around connectivity is still alive. This chapter delves on the conceptual and theoretical debates related to connectivity, the emerging initiatives in Asia, and its possible advantage towards trade, investment and resilient supply chain in the changing global order.

Chapter 11 by Beeho Chun and Young-Shin Chun titled "Policy Considerations to Advance the Strategic Partnership between India and the Republic of Korea in the Framework of G20" writes since the Indo-Pacific region is the locomotive for the economic growth of world economy, key middle power states such as India, Republic of Korea, Australia, Indonesia and Mexico in the region should contribute to produce new global and regional opportunities. He argues the need for both the sides to deepen cooperation in trade and investment as well as science and new technology, cultural exchanges and security and defense.

Chapter 12 titled "Deepening Bangladesh-India Connectivity: Realising the Emerging Opportunities" by Mustafizur Rahman argues triangulation of transport, investment and connectivity by building production networks and regional value chains will become critically important for the transition from predominantly preferential market-access driven competitiveness to efficiency and market-seeking investment and productivity driven competitiveness.

Chapter 13 titled "Connectivity and Trade, Boosting Investment, Incubating Resilient Supply Chains: Towards Independent Interdependence" by Herrick Mpuku writes the globalisation agenda and its liberal philosophy was coming apart at the seams. The world was moving back to into economic depression, global tension and uncertainty. This spectre necessitated a review of existing alliances and their realignment as each party sought to swing international public opinion and resources in their favour. This raises the conundrum of interdependence, whereby countries seeking to capitalise on the efficiency of production by specialising, and the author argues that they however need to have their own independent facilities to attenuate the risk of disruption.

Chapter 14 by Huang Yunsong and Li Linjie titled "Non-traditional Security Challenges and True Multilateralism" looks at the issue of multilateralism conceptually to emphasise how non-tradition threats have taken centre stage in the security discourse. He argues that the practice genuine multilateralism would caters to the common interests of most countries in the world. By utilising global and regional multilateral mechanisms such as UN and ASEAN, and pooling financial and scientific and technological resources of all member states, we have better odds against the urgent NTS challenges.

Chapter 15 titled "Emerging Green Agendas and Multi-scalar Multilateralism in Asia" by Medha Bisht analyses terms such as sustainable energy infrastructure has paved way for discussions around energy and water corridors. While the political economy of ideas stemming from global discourses is primarily responsible for these terminologies and is shaping policies at the regional and national level, transboundary water resources have often been the missing link in such discourses. She argues how such discourses can be linked to adaptive water governance and management, can be thought through with the regional institutions in South and Southeast Asia. This could channelise interactions between donors from the Global North and Global South, in informing the green discourse.

Chapter 16 titled "Climate-Security Nexus at the UN System: Implications for Integration in Eurasia" by Anatoly Boyashov analyses how the UN Security Council has been more and more concerned with non-profile matters of climate change and environment protection. On the one hand, interrelation between security and non-profile issues (e.g. climate, elections, and human rights) can serve as a uniting agenda when there is little room for wide international consensus on international security. He analyses this in the context of Eurasian region.

Chapter 17 titled "Multilateral Approach to Non-Traditional Security Challenges: Climate Adaptation and Mitigation: The Case of Madagascar" authored by Clara Randrianjara analyses how environmental issues first raised in 1972 by the Stockholm Declaration on Environmental Protection have acquired a new dimension with the rise of challenges posed by climate change. She argues how multilateralism has limitations in terms of implementing its resolutions.

Consequently, there is a growing loss of interest in and marginalisation of multilateralism. Nevertheless, multilateral cooperation should be strengthened either through a reform of multilateral institutions to make it more effective or through South-South and Triangular cooperation.

Chapter 18 titled "Devising Multilateral Approach to Non-Traditional Security Challenges: Climate change, Mitigation and Governance" by Felix Wandwe analyses the shifting security paradigm since the end of cold war era which has increasingly accommodated non-military strategies namely 'non-traditional' – threats to the holistic security phenomenon. He argues the need for devising policy options to accommodate the climate change related disasters, taking on board both bilateral and multilateral strategic ties that are of a paramount importance without leaving societies behind. The fact that national solutions are often inadequate, the NTS threats require regional and multilateral cooperation, hence calling upon countries to join hands in devising climate change mitigation and governance strategies and policy options.

Chapter 19 titled "Ensuring Water, Health and Food Security Role of Multilateral STI Ecosystem" by Umar Ibrahim Gaya writes the Indo-Pacific region, recognised with 60 percent of the global GDP, is uniquely-placed as a global center of both economic dynamism and challenge. However, depending upon the member country, there is imminent challenge for sustainable management of water, sanitation and wellbeing, as well as food security threats. He analyses the perspective of impact of leveraging multilateral science, technology and innovation (STI) in ensuring water, health and food security for the benefit of human well-being in both the Indo-Pacific region and its partners from the G20.

Chapter 20 titled "Strengthening Multilateralism for Peace and Sustainable Development" by Diana Benoit argues that the global pandemic has exacerbated the fragile health, social and economic structures in many parts of the world. In addition, the current challenges such as violent conflict, proliferation of weapons of mass destruction, climate change, poverty, inequality and health crises continue to exert compelling pressure on the multilateral system to combine efforts to effectively tackle these challenges and future ones. She argues for an effective, democratic and sustainable multilateralism, there is an appeal for solidarity, global dialogues and international cooperation geared towards peace and sustainable development

Chapter 21 titled "Intellectual Property in the Era of Great Technology Competition" by Mohammed Soliman argues that the digitalisation of economies is a chief objective for governments that are looking to exact digital sovereignty in an age where increased global connectivity is levied by great power competition. He writes that the Governments utilising machine learning and other AI applications to automate processes in a number of sectors will be affected by volatile IP competition. Biotechnologies will also feel the impact of IP wars as great power competition extends into technologies that have been the basis for public health innovations.

Towards Reformed Multilateralism: Emerging Power Dynamics and Transforming Global Institutions

CHAPTER 1

Revisionism: A Logical Must or A Negative Characteristic?

Alireza Khoda Gholipour

Talking about multilateralism, one recalls some prevailing trends of this important phenomenon. Among the trends that are transforming the world currently, we can mention globalisation, which has led to incredible changes in recent decades. This multilateral, multi-layered and multi-faceted phenomenon has significant effects and consequences on the international system.

Some of those effects and consequences include: triggering the interdependence of countries, communication and cross-border links, change in the nature of power, diversity in the type and number of actors, expansion of fields and arenas of interactions, and transformation in how actors influence decision-making processes in International Relations.

Globalisation, in the words of Schwab Klaus is associated with four characteristics: Hyper-Connectivity, Hyper-Transparency, Hyper-Complexity and Hyper-Vulnerability.[1] While empowering people to interact and communicate in easier forms and also at the same time increasing transparency, multiple and diverse means of communication have their negative implications for the world and make human life much more vulnerable.

In the era of globalisation, the international system has entered a new stage in which a new great game is taking shape. Growing instabilities in different parts of the world, the competition of different discourses and narratives, the entry of regional and global powers into the game of power or discourse coalition, and their efforts to rebuild and reconstruct oneself in order to gain a greater share in the future international system, indicates that the world is expectant of a new order in this historical turn.

The rapid pace of events and developments and the key importance of time in the age of globalisation, cause fluidity in the international system. The characteristics of this transition and the speed of developments are such that the international system is constantly evolving. In addition, the dominance of the post-structuralist paradigm in International Relations and the predominance of relativism as an approach and the lack of certainty in the age of globalisation, lead to the continuation of the transitional period in the system. In fact, this fluidity in the "changing international system" is caused by the dialectic of apparently contradictory issues which have not, finally, led to the emergence of a certain and specified synthesis.

With these profound changes during the transition period, we are witnessing some newly emerging dimensions of power, authenticity of cultural, semantic, normative, discursive and asymmetric characteristics and the increasing importance of civilian means of power such as economic power, technological power and assertion of power through consensus building.[2]

Due to the speed of these changes and momentum in the processes, the transitional state of the international system seems to be continuing for a time. Some important reasons can be attributed for this.[3]

First, the nature of power has changed, but there is still a kind of fluctuation between what constitutes the fourth face of power, i.e. discursive power or soft power on the one hand, and smart power on the other.

But the bigger change is in the gradual transformation in the nature of power; the ascendancy of "power to" be based on a pluralistic approach to power (in the sense of using power as a means to achieve a higher goal) over "power over" which was based on a hierarchical approach to power (considering the acquisition of power and its application to citizens as the specific goal of governments). With the priority of the "power to", the concept of "power over" has moved backstage. This is a major evidence of the nature of the "changing international system".

Second, the type and number of actors have evolved in such a way that in addition to the great international powers, the regional actors also play an important role, and the number of these regional influential actors is increasing. The world is witnessing the rapid rise of Asian powers among the existing great powers. Besides, globalisation leads to the emergence of a multi-central and multi-nodal politics, in which governments no longer act as single actors in the international system and the role of civil institutions, international non-governmental organisations, international inter-governmental organisations, informal multilateral institutions, parties, media, ethnicities, unions, multinational companies, individuals and international public opinion, is increasing rapidly.

This, taken together, has caused the international system to become polygonal; therefore, due to the erosion of the sovereignty of the States, the blurring of borders is a witness to the continuous change in the activity and functioning of governments in the space of interaction and competition with multinational and transnational actors.

Third, the nature of interaction between State actors in the international system has changed to a model of competition-cooperation in which there is no definite order or arrangement that indicates the total dominance of one trend over other trends, or one actor over other actors.

In this "moderate international system", social-virtual networks provide "increasing transparency" and this gives priority to the processes rather than structures. These processes in the global decision-making system are mostly horizontal and "bottom-up" processes.

In its simplest definition, the current international order is a hierarchical political system that reflects the interests of the dominant government or governments.[4] A change in this system occurs when great powers are emerging or declining and there is a struggle over international rules and institutions. Change in the international order, in the texts of international politics, has been theorised under the title of "power transfer". What can be learnt from the theoretical topics of this title is that emerging powers should be upgraded to the level of status-quo powers, so that the necessary conditions required for change in the international system are provided.[5]

In the current situation, there is a relative consensus among theorists about the occurrence of a tectonic change in this area and the emergence of a new world. During the past five centuries, three tectonic changes of power in international politics can be identified, which created fundamental changes in the distribution of power and redesigned the international environment in all three areas – politics, economy and culture. The first change was the emergence of the Western world, which began in the 11th century and reached its peak in the 18th century. The Western world created modernity with all its features. The second change occurred at the end of the 19th century with the emergence of America. America in a short time after industrialisation, became the most powerful country since the Roman Empire and has maintained this position for the past few centuries. Now the third tectonic change is taking place, during which new powers are emerging.[6]

But there are differences over the description of the transfer of material and normative power and the future of the international order in general. Some circles argue that we have entered the "post-America" era; but the most important feature of this new era is not the decline of America, but the emergence of other players and consequently their role in the international system. During recent decades, many countries of the world have experienced rapid economic growth and this has caused power to get distributed. This means that the world is moving towards multi-polarisation. In the economic sphere, there is definitely a transfer of power, and economic power is divided among an increasing number of actors, especially in Asia. But it is clear that changing the centre of gravity of the world's economy does not in itself mean a change in power, because money and economic ability cannot be easily converted into military ability or other forms of power.

In such a fluid transitional period, different scholars have anticipated different kind of world orders for future. Some are talking about a multipolar world order, while a few are expecting a non-polar or even post-polar world. But what is clear is that in the upcoming world order, diplomacy will be more complicated, because there will be no specific definition of the global situation and the relations of countries in such a situation will be selective and transient. Naturally, in such a system, countries cannot be defined as allies or enemies, because they cooperate on some issues and may compete or even confront each other in others. This more complex and complicated world will require a more flexible and informal multilateralism with greater level of participation by all influential actors in international institutions.

What is important in the current discussion is that the existing international order is an institutional order. Institutional order is an order that is formed on the axis of agreed political and legal institutions that should be used in the direction of rights of all actors and limit the exertion of power by larger ones. In other words, institutional order is an order that limits the exercise of power through agreed rules, institutions and official-institutional authority. Such an order has three main features: (1) Agreement on the principles and rules of order or agreement on the rules of the game, which gives legitimacy to the order; (2) Established institutions and rules that impose authoritative restrictions on the exercise of power. This means that powerful actors can exercise power only through institutions; (3) In this order, rules and institutions are placed in the heart of a larger political system and cannot be changed easily.[7]

An important development is the possible changes in the institutional system due to the ongoing developments at different levels. The current order, which was formed through the logic of liberal peace in the post-Second World War era and spread throughout the world in the post-Cold War era, created a period of hegemonic stability in the global economy, and this caused new actors to emerge quickly. These actors naturally have new demands that, if not answered, will deepen the crisis of the existing order.

One of the most important parts of these demands is aimed at reforming international institutions. Many new actors, especially the emerging powers, argue that these institutions were formed based on the requirements of the 1950s and still operate on the same basis, while the distribution of power internationally has changed drastically. Therefore, they demand extensive reforms in these institutions and believe that if these institutions are not reformed, they will quickly lose their function and meaning. The response to this demand of merging powers is one of the most important influencing factors for the future of the international order.

Besides this main trend, the rapidly evolving global world order reflects the shift in power dynamics. The swings in the United States-China relationship over time and the gradual decline of influence of Europe which was revealed in the process of the first Trump administration's withdrawal from the JCPOA, along with rising Asia as one of power centres of the international system, have influenced international dynamics to a great extent. In addition, the disruptions in the global supply chains especially during the COVID-19 pandemic, revealed many weaknesses of multilateral organisations, which have been crippled further by the ongoing Russia-Ukraine crisis.

At the same time, there are other security crises that are looming such as energy and food security, climate change and growing disinformation campaigns. Different scholars have different ways of describing the current challenges, but in one comprehensive and interesting way, the world has been described to confront simultaneous challenges characterised by the "six Ts":[8]

1. **Trade:** Growing trends of protectionism, regionalism, tariff and non-tariff barriers are hampering trade among different nations which can play an outstanding role in their interdependence and consequently peace and stability in the world;
2. **Technology:** Increasing weaponisation of modern technologies like the internet – especially 5G internet – artificial intelligence, etc. are emerging and challenging human life with cyber-attacks, misinformation and

disinformation campaigns and the like;

3. **Territory and water:** Historical differences among nations leading to conflicts for territorial control and keeping more sources of water for themselves, is increasing in several regions and some experts believe that the future war can be an extensive war for water;
4. **Terrorism:** Continuation of traditional terrorist and extremist acts of State-sponsored or militia groups and propagation of extreme readings of different religions based on the negation of others and at the same time, emergence of modern terrorism and radicalisation which is absorbing the younger generation, are a very big challenge for the world;
5. **Tenets:** Friction between different socio-economic models of development is widening with increasing promotion of the Asian – especially the Chinese – model of development which is challenging the Western model;
6. **Trust:** Lack of trust where "no one is a permanent friend and there is only permanent interest" is a very bold reality now and this is shaking many coalitions and alliances at regional and international levels.

Given the historical perspective of the emergence of multilateral institutions such as the UN, its agencies, and other international finance and trade bodies formed following the Second World War, they had lost relevance in the emerging world order of the 21st century and the accompanying frictions mentioned above. The UN system was established in 1945 primarily to ensure global peace and stability but has increasingly suffered exceptionalism. Over the decades, some countries that have been the biggest beneficiaries of the UN system have been using this system to promote their own exclusive interests.

The said challenges show that the current international system does not have a proper answer to the transforming world and emphasises the necessity of a series of thoughtful reforms that can bring up a more just system based on more inclusiveness, greater participation and a wider range of voices. This is not an ideal, but a real goal which is already in process. Knowing this, and by relying on global awareness and consensus, now we have an exceptional opportunity to do a good and the right job this time.

In such a situation, multilateralism still continues to be the most influential approach for tackling the challenges facing the international community today. However, genuine multilateralism must be founded on inclusiveness rather than exclusion, collaboration rather than confrontation above all ideological contestation, and the rule of law instead of the rule of power.

The effective application of international law and strict adherence to the purposes and principles of the UN are two main pillars of multilateralism. Yet, today the international community is plagued by double standards in the application of international law and the UN Charter.

The Islamic Republic of Iran, like many other members of the international community, continues to believe that the United Nations must act as the main centre for coordinating activities because it is the foundation of the contemporary world order and hosts representation for all sovereign governments. Its distinctive validity and exceptional capabilities are especially required now.[9]

This requires all member states to adhere unwaveringly to the principles and purposes of the Charter, including respecting the sovereign equality of States, not interfering in their internal affairs, settling disputes by political and diplomatic means, and rejecting the threat or use of force.

Among all different international institutions, the United Nations Security Council (UNSC) deserves more scrutiny. An honest review of the Security Council's practices evinces that its increasing deficiencies have resulted in its legitimacy and credibility crisis as well as its serious trust and confidence deficit, making its reform inevitable. The ultimate goal of the Security Council's reform must be to address all its current challenges and deficiencies and to evolve the Council into a truly representative, effective, transparent, accountable and above all, rules-based body.

While supporting the Council's enlargement as a means of addressing the existing inequalities in regional representation, the Islamic Republic of Iran does not consider this an end in itself. Currently, there are attempts by several emerging powers to focus mostly on the Council's enlargement, equating it with the Council's efficiency. But we should be all aware that this cannot happen at the expense of neglecting or underestimating other issues. However important, the Council's enlargement is, and must remain as only one out of many objectives in the Council's reform. At the same time, improving the Council's working methods and accountability and ensuring that all its decisions are taken in full accordance with the purposes and principles of the United Nations and international law, are in no way less important than the Council's enlargement.

The Council's reform must be considered as a comprehensive process, in which all five core issues under consideration must be treated equally, discussed thoroughly, and addressed in a package, as they are interlinked and as a whole, are greater than the sum of their parts. Therefore, any selective approach must be avoided. Attaching great importance to ensuring "equitable representation" in an expanded Council, Iran strongly believes that this cannot be realised only through safeguarding "geographical representation". Currently, the West has a strong presence and influence in the Council. Three of its members have veto power, while the developing countries are poorly represented in terms of both the number as well as privileges, including veto power. This means there is inequality "among the regions".

Likewise, there are many States within a given region that have never found a chance to become a Council member, while there are States in the same region that each have served between 10-22 years in the Council. This means there is inequality "within a region". The existing inequalities must therefore be addressed both "among" and "within" the regions, as they are both necessary and complementary. This indeed is of utmost importance for 103 States, 63 of which have never served in the Council and 40 served only once in the past 78 years. It is also essential in ensuring both geopolitical and geographical balance of the composition in an expanded Council.

In ensuring equitable regional representation, Iran fully supports addressing historical injustice towards the developing world, particularly Africa. Iran also fully supports ensuring equal opportunities for each State within a given region, which, inter alia, can be done through limiting chances for those who have served more in the Council and instead, provide more advantages to those who have never served in the Council or served less. Even, a combination of factors like population, economic power and regional position can be considered to that end.[10]

A reform that serves the interests of only certain regions or a few States is not acceptable, and any proposal that would literally deepen the current imbalances or reduce the equal chance for States to become a Council member or contradict such intrinsic principles as sovereign equality and equal rights of States, transparency and accountability, must seriously be avoided.

Iran also attaches great importance to reforming the Council's working methods to ensure that it acts in full compliance with international law, particularly the UN Charter. Decisions of the Security Council must not be ultra vires and it must not resort, too frequently, hastily, excessively or expeditiously, to its Chapter VII functions. Enforcement measures must be applied only as a last resort. The use of sanctions as blunt and blind instruments has raised fundamental ethical questions about whether sufferings inflicted on vulnerable groups is a legitimate means of exerting pressure on the targeted country.[11]

In the past, certain Security Council sanctions have served only to collectively punish an entire nation, without any actual positive impact on the maintenance of international peace and security. Therefore, sanctions must be applied very rarely, in a smart and targeted manner, with limited scope and duration, and only when all "measures not involving the use of armed force" are exhausted and have truly "proven to be inadequate" to "maintain or restore international peace and security".

It is also critical to ensure that a reformed Council does not consider situations not constituting a threat to international peace and security, or issues that are related to the internal affairs of States. Additionally, transforming the Council into a truly rules-based and accountable body must remain a top priority. Article 24(2) of the Charter stresses that in discharging its duties, "the Security Council shall act in accordance with the Purposes and Principles of the United Nations". This means the Council's powers are not limitless, it is not above the law and cannot act arbitrarily or without due regard for international law.

Likewise, through Article 24(1), the member states have conferred on the Security Council, the "primary responsibility for the maintenance of international peace and security". This means the Council has a legal, political and moral responsibility to act properly and responsibly and members of the Council must take decisions based not on their own national interests or that of the geopolitical or geographical groups they belong to, but based on the common interests of the entire membership of the Organisation. The Council must never be used as a tool to pursue national political interests and agendas.

The Council is responsible before the member states on behalf of whom it acts, and must therefore remain accountable to them. This indeed is the *raison d'être* of the Charter's Article 24(3) in obliging the Council to submit annual or special Reports to the General Assembly where all member states are represented. The correlation between Articles 24 and 25 of the Charter also makes it clear that the Council shall act in accordance with law, avoid *ultra-vires* decisions, act timely and responsibly, and remain accountable to member states. The Council shall also not consider issues that do not fall within its purview or are conferred by the Charter to other UN organs, and in particular, it must stop encroaching upon the functions and powers of the General Assembly.

Procedurally, Iran supports the continuation of deliberations within the process of Intergovernmental Negotiations on UNSC reforms (IGN), which must remain open, transparent, inclusive and membership-driven. Taking hasty decisions or setting artificial deadlines for its work will be counter-productive, and any possible decision – procedural or substantive – at any stage must be adopted only by consensus. Iran does not support text-based negotiations at this stage. Moreover, changing the rules or format of the process or its informal nature seems to be destructive, and must therefore be avoided.[12]

Revisionism

It is clear that neither 'business as usual' nor the 'status quo ante' are acceptable options for the future. While respecting rules-based international order is very important, revising the processes and structures based on the needs of today's world is a rational act, but it is strange that Revisionism is mostly disapproved and blamed as a negative characteristic, especially for State actors.

Different types of classifications for Revisionism are identifiable today. Some scholars identify three types of Revisionism: competitive Revisionism that is transgressive of the legitimate means; creative Revisionism that is transgressive of the legitimate ends; and revolutionary Revisionism that is transgressive of legitimate ends and means. Some others have thematically identified four types of Revisionism: (1) Economic revisionists who ask for a bigger share from the cake of global economy; (2) Security- political revisionists who, besides the economy, want a bigger role in political-security arrangements; (3) Geopolitical/Geostrategic revisionists who pursue access (if not dominance) to strategic locations; (4) Radical/ Ideological revisionists who do not accept bases and principles of the international system at all. Some others divide revisionist States into Integrated Revisionists, Bridging Revisionists, Isolated Revisionists and Rogue Revisionists.[13]

But structural realist theories of international change invariably posit all rising powers and different types of Revisionists of international order as spoilers and see no distinction among them. This is an assumption rooted in the power-transition theory, the core logic behind "Hegemonic-War Cycle" notions of system change.[14] According to the power transition theory, the onset of war between a dominant and rising power grows more likely as the gap in relative strength and capabilities between them narrows, and as the latter's grievances with the existing order– grievances that expand in lockstep with its mounting capabilities– move beyond any hope of peaceful settlement of disturbing issues and finding some solutions within the existing order. From this perspective, eras of power transition present a heightened risk of conflict, as incumbents react to stave off relative decline in the face of confident challengers.[15]

Economic and military convergence introduces a greater risk of conflict and disorder, as rising powers allegedly aim to place their imprint on reconstructed global institutions and that stamp differs markedly from the established order supported by the incumbent powers. The seemingly straightforward logic of this pessimistic view of convergence has a certain appeal, a seductive power rooted, perhaps, in primal myths about the son overtaking the father. Little wonder, then, that rising powers are usually portrayed in both theory and practice as troublemakers, promoting a disruptive agenda of change; as actors who feel constrained, even cheated, by the status quo and struggle against it to take what they think is rightfully theirs.[16]

Not all rising powers are dangerous Revisionists, however, and Revisionism is not always dangerous. Not every Revisionist seeks to overthrow the existing order, to maximise its power, or to do so at the expense of others. Overlooking these nuances, the literature tends to discuss both rising powers and Revisionist States in excessively general terms. Rising powers are deemed Revisionists; and all States that seek any kind of change or reform are termed 'Revisionist' without further distinction, while incumbent, established powers are invariably labeled status quoist. But in fact, there are four dimensions to Revisionism that, taken together, determine whether the Revisionist State poses a dangerous threat to the established powers and to what degree: (1) the extent of the Revisionist State's aims; (2) the Revisionist State's resolve and risk propensity to achieve its aims; (3) the nature of its Revisionist aims (does it seek changes in international norms, or territory, or prestige); and (4) the means it employs to further its Revisionist aims (whether peaceful or violent).[17]

An issue between emerging powers and established ones is the legitimacy of the existing international order – its division of territory, its institutional arrangements and governing structures, its norms and values. Here, legitimacy does not necessarily mean justice per se but rather an international consensus, especially among the great powers, about the nature of workable arrangements and the permissible aims and methods of foreign policy. Such a consensus about what is legitimate in International Relations does not eliminate conflict but, but at least, limits its scope and introduces some more acceptable means to resolve the problems that will inevitably arise among nations in a competitive, self-help system. In a legitimate order, even the most dissatisfied States desire only changes within the system, not a change of system; and adjustments of the status quo are acceptable as long as they are made within the framework of existing institutional arrangements and not at their expense.

There are two types of dissatisfied States: limited-aims Revisionists and unlimited-aims Revisionists or revolutionary powers. The goal of revolutionary States is not the adjustment of differences within a given system which will be at issue, but the system itself. It is a quest for global domination and ideological supremacy. While all revolutionary States are dissatisfied, not all dissatisfied States are revolutionary. The key question is whether the rising power or powers view the protection and promotion of their essential values as dependent on fundamental changes in the existing international order, or whether they are merely dissatisfied with their prestige and portions of the status quo, e.g., their sphere of influence, certain international norms. If the former, then it is a revolutionary State that cannot be satisfied without destroying essential elements of the international order. If the latter, then its grievances can be satisfied, while preserving – and in some cases actually strengthening– the established order. These limited-aim Revisionists are typically regional powers that seek either compensatory territorial adjustments to reflect their increased power, recognition as an equal among the great powers, or changes in the rules and decision-making procedures within, but not the basic norms and principles of existing regimes.[18]

Thus, what matters most about rising powers – whatever their preferences regarding territorial revisions or the content and form of global governance – is the means by which they plan to press their grievances. Do they choose peaceful or violent methods? Even the most outspoken reformers can display a more assertive policy pursued through engagement and negotiation: pressing for reform but operating very much within the system. Such peaceful appeals for reform within the established order should be seriously addressed, if not wholeheartedly supported, by the status quo powers, or else they risk creating precisely the challengers they fear most: violent risk-accepting Revisionists.

There is now considerable unanimity to fix our broken or obsolete institutions and systems to achieve greater democratic governance to tackle the myriad challenges facing the world. Here, I should emphasise the role of Asian countries and regional organisations like ASEAN, ECO and of course, SCO in this reforming process.

India as an emerging power and at the same time as the representative of the Global South can play a very important role in this process, especially this year? in which she holds simultaneously the presidency of the G20 and the SCO. And the Asian Security Conference (ASC) is well placed to keep the momentum going to work together to achieve a common goal: a safer, healthier, better world, for all to enjoy and leave to our children.

NOTES

1 Klaus Schwab, "Address by Founder and Executive Chairman", World Economic Forum, 101st Session, International Labour Conference, Provisional Record, Geneva, May-June 2012.

2 James H. Mittleman. and Robert Johnston, "The Globalization of Organized Crimes, the Courtesan State, and the Corruption of Civil Society", *Global Governance*, 5 (1), January-March 1999, pp. 103-26.

3 Dehshiri Mohammadreza, "Globalization and the International System", *Strategic Studies of Public Policy*, 5 (14), August 2014, pp. 7-44.

4 John J. Ikenberry, *After Victory*, Stanford University Press, Chicago, 2006, pp. 36-40.

5 Robert Gilpin, *War and Change in World Politics*, Cambridge University Press, Cambridge, 1981, pp. 70-73.

6 Fareed Zakaria, "The Future of American Power: How America Can Survive the Rise of the Rest", *Foreign Affairs*, 87 (3), May-June 2008, pp. 18-43.

7 John J. Ikenberry, no. 4, pp. 57-63.

8 Sujan Chinoy, "Towards Reformed Multilateralism: Transforming Global Institutions and Frameworks", Lecture presented at the Think20 (T20) Core Group, University of Mumbai, 27 January 2023.

9 This statement and some of following paragraphs have been incorporated from the Islamic Republic of Iran's positions on UN reforms such as the Statement by Iran's Permanent Representative to the United Nations before the United Nations General Assembly on 16 November 2021 at https://newyork.mfa.ir/portal/product/8121/451/Statement-on-United-Nations-Security-Council-Reform-UNGA-Plenary (Accessed 23 July 2024).

10 Ibid.

11 Ibid.

12 Ibid.

13 Stacie E. Goddard, "Embedded Revisionism: Networks, Institutions, and Challenges to World Order", *International Organization*, 72 (4), 2018, pp. 763-797 at https://doi.org/10.1017/S0020818318000206 (Accessed 25 July 2024).

14 Randall L. Schweller, "Rising Powers and Revisionism in Emerging International Orders", *Valdai Papers*, No. 16, May 2015.

15 Jonathan M. DiCicco, and Jack S. Levy, "Power Shifts and Problem Shifts: The Evolution of the Power Transition Research Program", *The Journal of Conflict Resolution* 43 (6), December 1999, pp. 675-704.

16 Aaron L. Friedberg, "Hegemony with Chinese Characteristics", *The National Interest*, 114, July/August 2011, p. 18.

17 Randall L. Schweller, no. 14.

18 Ibid.

CHAPTER 2

Inclusive Multipolarity Towards Reformed Multilateralism: Why are Reforms of Multilateral Institutions Important?

Emilio J. Zeca

Introduction

This chapter discusses inclusive multipolarity towards reformed multilateralism and answers the question, why are reforms of multilateral institutions important in the contemporary international system. Multilateralism is a "system of coordinating relations between three or more States in accordance with certain principles of conduct and with defined objectives."[1] It reflects the recognition that problems on a global scale such as environmental crises, international control of drug trafficking and terrorism cannot be dealt with individually by each State, but require coordinated efforts and policies, developed collectively by several States.

Multilateralism gained its modern characteristics in the 19th century, after the end of the Napoleonic Wars (1803-1815) and the Conference of Berlin (1884-1885). But it was after the Second World War that contemporary multilateralism was structured as a mechanism to operationalise global governance.[2] During the Cold War period, Multilateralism solved problems of the reconstruction in Europe, but quickly gained ideological, political and discriminatory contours. The globalisation process and the end of the Cold War brought new challenges to multilateralism. The model of multilateralism created after the Second World War it is out of step with reality, with States and non-State voices calling for reforms.

This chapter is based on a qualitative methodology, supported by the historical and analytical methods, bibliographical research and desk review and process tracing approach about the different changes that multilateralism has experienced throughout the evolution of the modern international system. This chapter is structured in three parts preceded by this introduction and followed by final considerations and references. Part one discusses the polarity and international system; part two relates the global challenges and inclusive multipolarity; part three verses about the importance reforms of multilateral institutions and Mozambican perspectives.

Polarity and International System

Throughout history, the international system has been structured based on the balance of power and distribution of conventional and strategic capabilities current at the time. The balance of power represents the distribution of military and economic resources among States in the international system. The balance of power can be analysed in a systemic/global or regional way, depending on the poles of power. Polarity has been one of the important elements in the analysis of the structure, dynamics, functioning and possible or necessary reforms for the international system. According to, "the literature on polarity is often confusing and sometimes even contradictory."[3] However, there is a consensus that, in International Relations, polarity refers to the number of actors and the distribution of their conventional and strategic capacities in the international system. Thus, polarity is an indicator of the structure of the international system, based on the distribution of power among the actors.

As the extensive writings on polarity studies have pointed out, according to multifaceted phenomena, concept and distribution of power and capabilities of States, there are three types of systems: unipolarity, bipolarity, and multipolarity. Unipolarity is a condition in which a State, under a situation of international anarchy, enjoys a preponderance of power and does not face competition from other States. The unipolar State is not the same as an Empire or a hegemonic State, that can control the behaviour of all other States.[4] Bipolarity is a power distribution, which two States have a preponderance of power in the system. In bipolarity, spheres of influence and alliance systems often develop around two poles of power.[5] The Cold War period is an example of the bipolarity system. In the book *Theory of International Politics* (1979), Kenneth Waltz[6] argued that bipolarity tended towards greater stability because the two great powers would engage in rapid mutual adjustment, which would prevent inadvertent escalation and reduce the chance of power asymmetries. Bipolarity thus has the potential to create stability between the dominant hegemonies in the international system and inhibit direct large-scale confrontations between them.

Finally, multipolarity is a distribution of power in which more than two nation-states have nearly equal power. The classic Realist theorists such as Hans Morgenthau (1904-1980) or Edward Hallett Carr (1892-1982) argue that multipolar systems are more stable than bipolar systems, because great powers can gain power through alliances and small wars that do not directly challenge other powers. But, the neo-realists argue that multipolar systems are particularly unstable and prone to conflict, because there is greater complexity in managing alliance systems and a many chances of misjudging the intentions of other States.[7]

For offensive realism, represented by John Meishermer, author of *The Tragedy of Great Power Politics*,[8] the regional balance of power can assume the following configurations: unipolarity, a single power is superior and has the capacity to prevent the formation of a coalition that counterbalances the system; bipolarity, a system dominated by two powers with similar capabilities and stable equilibrium; balanced multipolarity, a system dominated by three or more powers; the power is nearly equitable; and there is no hegemony; and unbalanced multipolarity, a system dominated by three or more great powers, one of them being the potential hegemon.

In terms of theoretical approaches and practical studies, the discussions about polarity, in the international system, are intense and interesting. For example, William Wohlforth[9] and John Ikenberry[10] are among those arguing for the stabilising impact of unipolarity; Kenneth Waltz[11] and John Mearsheimer[12] are among those who argue that bipolarity tends to generate relatively more stability; and Karl Deutsch and J. David Singer,[13] argued that multipolarity is the most stable structure of the international system. In fact, we have an open and constructive debate, which depends on the contexts, situations, perspectives and dominant institutions.

After the end of Cold War period, in 1989, the liberal American political scientist, Francis Fukuyama, predicted a unipolar world dominated by the United States of America, in his article "The End of History" published in the *National Interest Journal*,[14] transformed in 1992 into a book *The End of History and the Last Man.* On the same wave, in 1993, the civilisational-realist Samuel Huntington predicted a unipolar world with a clash of civilisations and regional dominant States in the text "The Clash of Civilizations?" published by *Foreign Affairs.*[15]

Influenced by American theorists, a global euphoria emerged and consolidated in the 1990s that the international system was unipolar and dominated by the United States. This sensation resulted from the collapse of the Soviet Union and the end of Cold War bipolarity. However, Charles-Philippe David, teacher of Strategy, Diplomatic Studies and Political Science at the University of Quebec in Montreal, in the book *War and Peace: Contemporary Approaches to Security and Strategy*,[16] published in French and Portuguese, refers that, "we live in the American unipolar illusion, due to the inexorable dynamics of the redistribution of power among States, which transforms the global strategic order."[17] In this perspective, we are in the multipolar international system, which sometimes tends to be balanced, and at other times, to be unbalanced. So, the global problems, challenges and threats demonstrate that the international system is multipolar and diffused, with their respective variants.

Global Challenges and Inclusive Multipolarity

The contemporary international system faces complex problems, threats, risks and vulnerabilities, such as demographic, climate, energy and technological transition that require multilateral initiatives for their solution. So there is no State that will be able to solve these problems alone. Several global aspects configure and reconfigure the current multipolarity of the international system. In this context, we can highlight, for example, Russia's resurgence and reorganisation as an assertive player in Europe, Asia and Africa; the rise of China as an economic, technological and military power; the economic and political unification of Europe around the European Union, despite the impacts of Brexit; the emergence of revisionist and inclusive economic blocs such as G20 and BRICS that claim a new international economic order; and the emergence of global challenges with their risks and threats related by demographic, climate, energy and technological transition.

Also, we have the recurrent economic and financial crises, mistrust and the revolt of those forgotten by globalisation; the emergence of Populism in Europe, the Trump era in the United States of America and that of Bolsonaro in Brazil; the mistrust in the United Nations system, that demand for reform in the United Nations Security Council; the mistrust in multilateralism and option in unilateralism. In October 1999, the US Senate refused to ratify the Comprehensive Test Ban Treaty signed by Bill Clinton in 1996; during the Bush Administration, the United States rejected the Kyoto Protocol, the International Criminal Court, the Ottawa Treaty and the Draft Protocol of the Biological Weapons Convention; and the Bush Administration withdrew from the Anti-Ballistic Missile Treaty, which Nixon signed with the USSR in 1972.

From 1990, the US became the main defender of multilateralism and included it in its Grand Strategy. However, post-9/11 invasion of Iraq and Afghanistan, the United States abandoned multilateralism and embraced unilateral realism. In recent years, economic crises in the States, the distrust and anger among those forgotten by globalisation and the rise of populist and far-right regimes put multilateralism in crisis. So, the unipolar illusion of the 1990s[18] and the return to multilateralism created after the end of the Second World War are in crisis and an inclusive multipolarity has emerged. After the Second World War, multilateralism had a relevant role to solve the post-War reconstruction problems. In this context, the Marshall Plan, the United Nations, the International Monetary Fund, the World Bank, the General Agreement on Tariffs and Trade (GATT) and other multilateral institutions emerged as mechanisms for global cooperation.

Currently there are demands for reforms and new models of multilateralism that are more adequate for the objective realities of the contemporary international system, to solve the current problems, risks, threats and vulnerabilities. The apparent unipolarity of the Post-Cold War, which gave rise to an unbalanced multipolarity, degenerated into an inclusive multipolarity. According to Paulo Wache and his former colleagues from the Higher Institute of International Relations of Mozambique (ISRI), in the book entitled "*As Potências Emergentes e a Construção da Multiporalidade Inclusiva: Uma Abordagem Comparativa das Políticas Externas dos BRICs*",[19] the international system is configured on an inclusive multipolarity, because it is not just the West that is powerful, we have Brazil, Russia, China and South Africa, which are emerging powers.

The multilateral system has encountered mounting challenges since the end of the Cold War; the United States became increasingly dominant in terms of military and economic power; and countries such as Brazil, Iran, China and India began to question the relevance of the United Nations.[20] So, according to inclusive multipolarity, in the contemporary international system, States, International Organisations and non-State actors claim their participation in the current balance of power equation. The contemporary global and regional threats, problems, challenges, vulnerabilities, issues and phenomena, require a more inclusive, holistic and integrated model of multilateralism.

Importance of Multilateral Institutions Reforms and the Mozambican Perspectives

In International Relations Studies, multilateralism refers to processes and joint initiatives of States around a certain subject or objective of common interest, because small and medium powers rarely have the resources to act alone in global affairs.[21] The multilateralism gained greater prominence with the end of the Second World War and the problems brought by globalisation and transnationalism. In this context, the international organisations emerged as operational mechanisms for multilateral initiatives, where the United Nations gained prominence. The multilateral system created after the Second World War, was based on the model of the United Nations, but this model needs structural, creative, constructive and integrative reforms.

Contemporary multilateralism must be reformed through political-diplomatic concertation, institutional arrangements, dialogue, coordination, cooperation and mutual respect, because the contemporary international system is multipolar and inclusive, with several poles of power and different cooperation alternatives. For example, the United Nations Security Council needs deep renovations in terms of categories of membership; the question of veto held by the five permanent members; the regional representation; the size of an enlarged Council and its working methods; and the Security Council-General Assembly relationship. The global issues require a more inclusive, holistic and integrated model of multilateralism. The emerging powers, non-State actors and small States need to be included in all equations for the stability of the international system.

At present, the multilateralism is based on global governance that is defined as "collective actions to establish norms and institutions capable of controlling the causes and adverse effects of national, transnational and supranational problems",[22] through institutional cooperation and coordination. Multilateralism is relevant for resolving the global political, economic, societal, environmental and other issues. However, it must be operationalised based on holistic and integrated models and approaches, which do not marginalise any State or non-State actor. This objective can be achieved with reforms in the multilateral model that was built on assumptions from the past.

Issues such as coronavirus, climate change, the environment and global warming, extreme events such as cyclones, droughts and floods, nuclear weapons and weapons of mass destruction, financial crises, international trade, migrations and rise of autocratic regimes, demonstrate that they need joint initiatives. These are disruptive threats that have effects on a global scale. Consequently, they need global and multilateral responses. The contemporary multilateral system has faced increasing challenges in recent decades. It needs to be calibrated and adapted to the new structure and dynamics of the international system.

The principles of Mozambique's Foreign Policy are in the Constitution of the Republic of Mozambique (2018) approved by a Resolution of the Council of Ministers – Resolution No. 32/2010 – of 30 August. These instruments contain general aspects of Foreign Policy and specific aspects of multilateralism. According to the principles of foreign policy contained in the Constitution of the Republic of Mozambique (2018), Mozambique values multilateralism, through initiatives from international organisations. Since the liberation struggle against the Portuguese, Mozambique has adopted "*making friends, avoiding enemies and diversifying partnerships*" as its foreign policy principle (Resolution No. 32/2010, 30 August). This principle has facilitated its participation in international multilateral forums.

Resolution No. 32/2010, of 30 August states that Mozambique's foreign policy focuses on the bilateral, regional, and multilateral relationship among Mozambican communities abroad. At the regional level, Mozambique postulates the development and consolidation of special relations of friendship, good neighbourliness and multifaceted cooperation with the States of Southern Africa and the African continent, within the scope of strengthening SADC and the African Union. At the multilateral level, Mozambique defends active participation in the activities of international organisations of which the country is a full member, as well as in other relevant forums, taking into account the importance of multilateralism in contemporary international relations and the need to mobilise resources for national development (Resolution No. 32/2010, 30 August).

Mozambique's foreign policy principles postulate that multilateralism[23] serves to promote independence and national sovereignty; to project the image of an internationally prestigious State, lover of peace and freedom of peoples, defender of multilateralism, that observes the principles and objectives established by the Charter of the United Nations, the African Union, the Southern Africa Development Community (SADC) and others organisations. The message from the President of the Republic alluded to the inauguration of Mozambique as a non-permanent member of the United Nations Security Council, and that the Mozambican State sees multilateralism as a space for developing countries to participate in decisions on global affairs. The message advocates reform of multilateral institutions and Mozambique makes an unconditional and determined effort to influence other States to bet on multilateralism to resolve global problems and promote peace, security and development.[24]

For the Mozambican State, the international organisations are instruments of multilateralism and an important component of contemporary international life. Multilateralism allows States to combine efforts and share a common view to solve problems and challenges that go beyond the individual dimension of States. Thus, Multilateralism creates a necessary environment for expanding dialogue and establishing international consensus on common and global challenges. Mozambique attaches great importance to the United Nations system as the most privileged forum of Multilateralism and recognises the central role of the United Nations as the universal forum for debate and consensus for peace, stability, security and progress of peoples and States. It also advocates greater democratisation and transparency in the functioning of the United Nations system, in particular the Security Council. The respect for human rights, disarmament and the fight against transnational terrorism and organised crime, are some of the priorities for Mozambique at the United Nations.

Conclusion

The new poles of power in the contemporary international system demand reforms in the multilateral system. Now, polarity has become multipolar and inclusive. The Cold War created a bipolar international system, which was marked by ideological confrontation between the West and the East, where multilateral initiatives took on strong ideological hues and encountered territorial discontinuity, politics and protectionism. The end of the Cold War raised several speculations about how the international system would be configured. The emergence of the G20 in 1999, and the BRICS in 2009, created the possibility of building an inclusive multipolarity. With complex global problems, it becomes clear that it is necessary to adopt a deep "reformed multilateralism", to solve common present and future problems, in an international system that is increasingly complex and competitive in economic, social and security terms.

We live in an inclusive multipolar international system where global and regional problems must be solved through multilateral institutional arrangements. The model of multilateralism created after the end of the Second World War needs to be revised and reformed. The global governance issues need to be based on a more holistic, integrated, creative and progressive model and approach of multilateralism. This model must include the Great Powers, small States and non-State actors, because we live in an international system marked by incisive multipolarity and diffused elements.

Mozambique is a State that defends multilateralism, as one of its foreign policy principles. The Mozambican State gives great importance and privilege for multilateral mechanisms such as the United Nations, African Union, SADC, CPLP and other international forums, to resolve common problems through cooperation in a coordinated manner. At the United Nations, Mozambique advocates more democratisation and transparency in the functioning of the United Nations system, in particular the Security Council. All of Mozambique's actions related to reforms of United Nations and other global organisations such as the World Trade Organisation, the International Monetary Fund, or the World Bank, are conducted based the principle of making more friends, avoiding enemies and diversifying partnerships.

NOTES

1 Sousa, Fernando de, Dicionário de Relações Internacionais (Dictionary of International Relations), CEPESE. Edições Afrontamento, Coimbra, 2025, p. 121.

2 Adogame, Afe, "The Berlin-Congo Conference 1884: The Partition of Africa and Implications for Christian Mission Today", *Journal of Religion in Africa*, 34(1-2), nos 1-2, 2004, p. 188.

3 James E Dougherty and Robert L Pfaltzgraff, "Contending Theories of International Relations: A Comprehensive Survey", Harper and Row, 1981, pp. 157-158.

4 Kenneth Waltz, "Structural Realism after the Cold War", *International Security*, 25(1), no 1, 2000, pp. 5-41, Daniel Nexon and Thomas Wright, "What's at Stake in the American Empire Debate", *American Political Science Review*, 101, no 2, 2007, pp. 253-271; Robert Jervis, "Unipolarity: A Structural Perspective", *World Politics*, 61(1), no 1, 2009, pp. 188-231 and Yuan-Kang Wang, "The Durability of a Unipolar System: Lessons from East Asian History", *Security Studies*, 29(5), no 5, 2021, pp. 832-863.2021:832-863).

5 Kenneth N Waltz, "The Stability of a Bipolar World", Daedalus, no 3, 1964, pp. 881-909.

6 Kenneth Neal Waltz, *Theory of International Politics*, McGraw-Hill, Boston, 1979.

7 Randall L. Schweller, "Tripolarity and the Second World War", *International Studies Quarterly*, 37(1), 1993, pp. 73-103; Manus I. Midlarsky and Ted Hopf, "Polarity and International Stability", *The American Political Science Review*, 87(1), 1993, pp. 171-180, Sullivan, A. 2001. "Cultural Capital and Educational Attainment", *Sociology* 35(4), pp. 893-912; Richard N. Haass and Charles Kupchan "The New Concert of Powers, How to Prevent Catastrophe and Promote Stability in a Multipolar World", *Foreign Affairs*, March 23, 2021.

8 Combining structure and war, the dimensions of power produces four possible kinds of systems: Unbalanced Bipolarity; Balanced Bipolarity; Unbalanced Multipolarity; and Balanced Multipolarity. Unbalanced bipolarity is not a useful category, because this kind of system is unlikely to be found in the real world. John Mearsheimer, "The Tragedy of Great Power Politics, W.W. Norton, New York and London, 2001, p. 337.

9 William Wohlforth, "The Stability of a Unipolar World", *International Security*, 24(1), 1999, pp. 5-41.

10 G. John Ikenberry, *After Victory: Institutions, Strategic Restraint, and the Rebuilding of Order After Major Wars*, Princeton University Press, Princeton, 2001.

11 Kenneth Neal Waltz, *Theory of International Politics*, McGraw-Hill, Boston, 1979.

12 John Mearsheimer, *The Tragedy of Great Power Politics*, W.W. Norton, New York and London, 2001.

13 Karl W. Deutsch, J. David Singer, (1964). "Multipolar Power Systems and International Stability", *World Politics*, 16(3), pp. 390-406.

14 Francis Fukuyama, "The End of History?" *The National Interest*, 16, 1989, pp. 3-18.

15 Samuel P. Huntington, "The Clash of Civilizations?" *Foreign Affairs*, 72 (3), 1993, pp. 22-49.

16 Charles-Philippe David, *A Guerra e a Paz: Abordagens Contemporâneas da Segurança e da Estratégia*. (War and Peace: Contemporary Approaches to Security and Strategy), Instituto Piaget, Lisboa, 2001.

17 Ibid, p. 69.

18 Ibid.

19 Paulo M. Wache, Iraê Baptista Lundin, Valter Fainda and Sérgio Gomes ed, "Emerging Powers and the Construction of Inclusive Multipolarity: A Comparative Study of the BRICS Foreign Policies", Book Review, *International Affairs*, 92(1), January 2016, https://doi.org/10.1111/1468-2346.12533

20 Steven Hook and John Spanier, "American Foreign Policy Since World War II", CQ Press, Washington, D.C., 2007, p. 305.

21 Victor D Cha, "Power play: Origins of the US Alliance System in Asia", *International Security*, 34(3), no 3, 2010, pp. 165-166.

22 Raimo Vayrynen, "Globalisation and Global Governance", Rowman and Littlefield Publishers, 1999, New York, p. 25.

23 In the spirit of multilateralism, Mozambique participates in the United Nations (UN) and other multilateral forums such as: African Union (AU); Southern Africa Development Community (SADC); Portuguese-Speaking African Countries (PALOP's); Community of Portuguese Language Countries (CPLP); African, Caribbean and Pacific Countries (ACP); the Non-Aligned Movement; the Organisation of the Islamic Conference (OCI); the Commonwealth; the Indian Ocean Rim Association for Regional Cooperation (IOR-ARC); the Organization Internationale de la Francophonie; among others (Resolution No. 32/2010, 30 August).

24 Nyusi, Filipe Jacinto, Mensagem do PR alusiva a tomada de posse de Mocambique como Membro Não Permanente no Conselho de Segurança das Nações Unidas. PresidÊncia da República, (Message from the President of the Republic alluding to Mozambique's inauguration as a Non-Permanent Member of the United Nations Security Council. Presidency of the Republic), Maputo, 2023.

CHAPTER 3

A Way to New Multilateralism: From Money-Centrism to Mind-Centrism

Tsogbaatar Damdin

Introduction

The world today is experiencing serious challenges and a painful process of polarisation. Though with the end of the Cold War the world entered the era of the globalisation that brought progress and prosperity of an unprecedented scale, yet International Relations stumbled over certain anomalies that prevented the further unfolding of good times.

The search for the roots of the degeneration could go along two directions. One could delve deep into history, throughout which the civilisational divides were forming, transfusing, transforming, crumbling and re-appearing. The other is focused on the more recent developments of immediate impact that actually led to the parting of the once partnering global actors. The earlier approach may not offer a clear and full explanation as to why we humans, re-entered into the trend of the clash of civilisations at this time of history, because these deep-rooted long-term dividing factors were always there, and irrespective or even despite their presence the Post-Cold War partnership-based globalisation began to take roots over the age-old divides. Therefore, alongside the study of the earlier approach, a focused analysis of the recent developments would provide a more explicable picture as to why we ended up in the conflict-ridden world, where we are today.

Although many would trace the immediate causes of modern rifts to the events of 2014, the roots of global disruptions could be attributed to the crisis of 2008. The property market collapse of 2008 shook the global system, serving cracks and early scratches that compromised the trust and confidence that had been solidly built by that time. The crisis sent a signal to many that the overly interconnected and globalised economy had globalised the risks and detriments as well. The author observing such developments was still hopeful and optimistic about the future of the global order. The reason for such a positive outlook was based on the hope that, although the world we had known by 2008 might have been collapsing, we, would make intelligent and rational choices leading to the building of a new world order, better and more sophisticated in structure and design, in place of the existing system.

However, by 2014 those expectations began to fade due to the increased regional military conflicts covering the vast stretches from the Maghreb to the Middle East, which eventually ended up spreading to Eastern Europe. From that time, the author of this chapter has been raising concerns consistently on the issue of irrational urges and calls coming from within communities and nation-states across the board at the international level, which could later lead to a conflict of a global nature.[1] The anger, frustration and distancing of the global community cannot not be fully explained by reason. From the perspective of technological progress and their direct effect on the individuals' lives on an average, the modern world would be an incomparably better place than any civilisation at any time in the past that the humanity had ever witnessed, no matter how dire and complicated the modern life could appear to be in the end. Unfortunately, emotions, sentiments, an indoctrinated approach to ideologies, glorification of bravery, heroism, which seemed to have been left behind in the Cold War era or in the era preceding it, were becoming the main drivers of the global psychological atmosphere. The whole broth was amplified by the ICT and the social media, operating with the speed of light, leaving no time for thorough reasoning and analysis. Therefore, the danger of a bigger conflict was imminent to the author from numerous arenas.[2]

Against such a background of weakening belief in the good of the globalised world community and its unprecedentedly inter-related economy, the more proactive attempt to rebuild trust in the modern world architecture needed to be raised, for it was, as described above, a much better system than any that preceded the 1990s. However, the aim of rebuilding the trust was not for the sake of preserving the post-Cold War globalisation model that rested on romantic, euphoric ideas and beliefs, but rather to encourage the intellectual search for an improved system with more complex and diverse mechanisms of cooperation which would prevent the backsliding of humanity into the Cold War era, or even worse, to the era of a real world war.

This chapter is another attempt at contributing to the global discussion to find a better option of a global system of international relations which could ensure additional perspectives on the discussion on the ways to prevent military conflicts on a global scale, while promoting new approaches to building an upgraded world order that corresponds to new realities, featuring an increased number of States with weapons of mass destruction or with such potential of an imminent nature and with more technologically empowered populations.

I

Opulence versus Discontent

The globalisation as it unfolded in the Post-Cold War era, made the world as affluent as it had never been before. It freed the world from the cut throat ideological divide that was programmed for the 'zero-sum' outcome arrangement where the 'mutually assured destruction' was the only barrier stopping the use of force between the global powers. Just to imagine that in the Cold War era the security, the very existence of humanity rested on the total destruction that was assured is indicative of the meagre realities and extreme danger of the times. Nevertheless, with the dismantling of the Berlin wall symbolising the iron curtain and the change for unlimited friendship and partnership seemed to have come to stay. Although the nuclear parity assuring mutual destruction remained throughout the Post-Cold War period as the major mechanism of security, the real focus on the guaranteed mutuality of the annihilation moved backstage. It seemed to have become obvious that given such vast opportunities of mutually beneficial commerce and growth, which turned yesterday's foes into friends, the prospect of nuclear war has become unimaginably distant. The likelihood of any major actor resorting to military power for global gain at that time appeared to have dropped so low, that no reasonable person then would expect that the nuclear weapon's use would ever become an issue of imminent risk. Hence, disarmament, that had intensified since the mid-1980s went on uninhibitedly. Consequently, military planning and preparedness became secondary issues which in turn, facilitated cuts across the board in the military budgets throughout the world. All this eventually led to the liberalisation and integration of the global economy that produced the dynamism in economic progress at the global level. In other words, from the mercantilist perspective, the human family collectively reached the point of wealth no previous generations had ever experienced.

A few statistics could amply represent the above proposition.

(a) Post-Cold War Mercantile Success

(i) Global GDP

The global economy and growth of wealth are assessed through the dynamics of the GDP, foreign trade and direct investment indicators. These indicators, though being criticised for overlooking the issues of equitable distribution and fairness, undoubtedly constitute important indicators displaying the humanity's growth and development through the use of measurable figures and data. Thus, once the dynamics of the global GDP growth are assessed in the period between 1960 to 2018, one can see that it had grown from US$ 1.3 trillion to US$ 87.5 trillion (Fig. 1). But if one divides the period into two parts as approximately 30 years before the Cold War and 30 years after it, taking 1990 as the turning point, then the situation would look like this:

- The global economy has grown 17 times from US$ 1.3. trillion within 30 years from 1960 to 1990 to US $ 22.5 trillion.
- In the 30 years after the 1990s if the Cold War had not ended, one can presume that the global economy would have continued its growth rate of the last 30 years of the Cold War. Then one can assume that in 60 years since 1960, the global economy would have grown 34 times. In this case, the world GDP would have reached US$ 44.2 trillion. But in reality, as of 2018, this indicator equaled US $ 87.5 trillion that exceeds the level expected in case of the continuation of the Cold War, by nearly 100 per cent. This may be the benefit and dividend of post-Cold-War globalisation and cooperation.

The sudden upward leap can be clearly seen in the graph shown in Fig. 1.

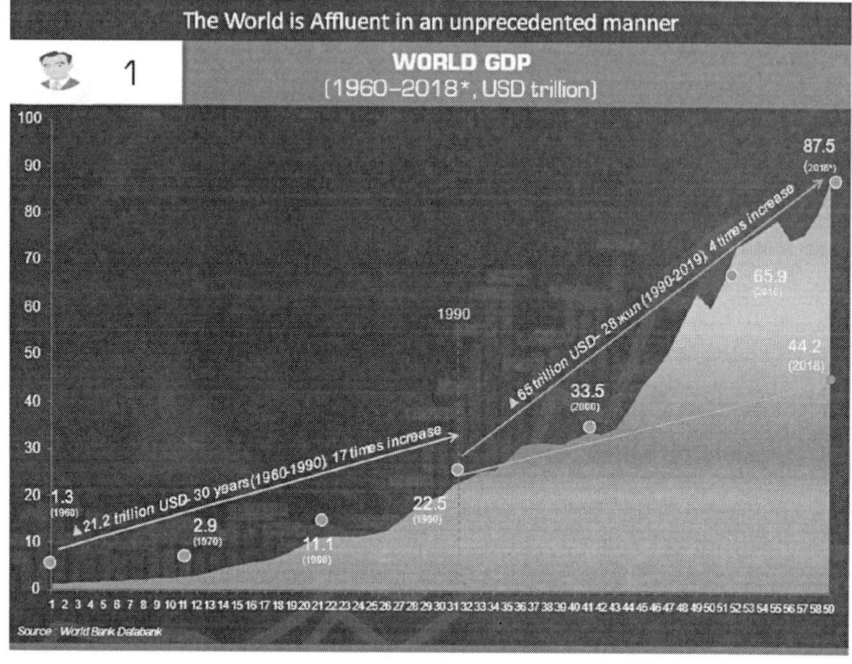

Fig. 1

(ii) Trade

- In 1960-1990 global trade increased 20 times from US$ 0.1 trillion to US$ 2 trillion.
- If the Cold War continued in the 30 years after the 1990s, global trade, would presumably, have increased by its pre-Cold War period rate. Then one can assume that in 60 years since 1960, global trade would have enlarged by 40 times. In this case, the trade turnover in 2020 would have reached US$ 4 trillion at the global level. But in reality, as of 2017, this indicator reached US$ 17.7 trillion (Fig. 2) and has exceeded the level expected in case of the continuation of the Cold War by four times or by over 300 per cent. This may be attributed to the end of the Cold War as the dividend of free globalisation.
- By comparing Fig. 1 and Fig. 2, it could clearly be seen that the end of the Cold War had a more favourable effect on the expansion of international trade than on the world's GDP growth. In other words, this fact clearly shows how seriously the global trade depends on the architecture, the system of international relations and on the international

political atmosphere. And it also demonstrates how fragile the international trade is being susceptible to the earlier factors of the international relations.

(iii) Investment

- One can see that global foreign direct investment, once measured in the scale of trillions, stood at a negligibly small (nearly zero) level during the Cold War period and reached US$ 0.2 trillion by the end of it (Fig. 2).
- In an analogy of the two graphs on the global GDP and trade in Figs. 1 and 2, it is observed that if the Cold War had not ended, then in the 30 years after the 1990s, the FDI inflow would have doubled. In that case, it would have reached US$ 0.4 trillion by 2020. However, in reality, by 2017, this indicator had already reached US$ 1.95 trillion which exceeded the would-be level by nearly five times or by 400 per cent. This is again another dividend and advantage achieved due to the end of the Cold War.

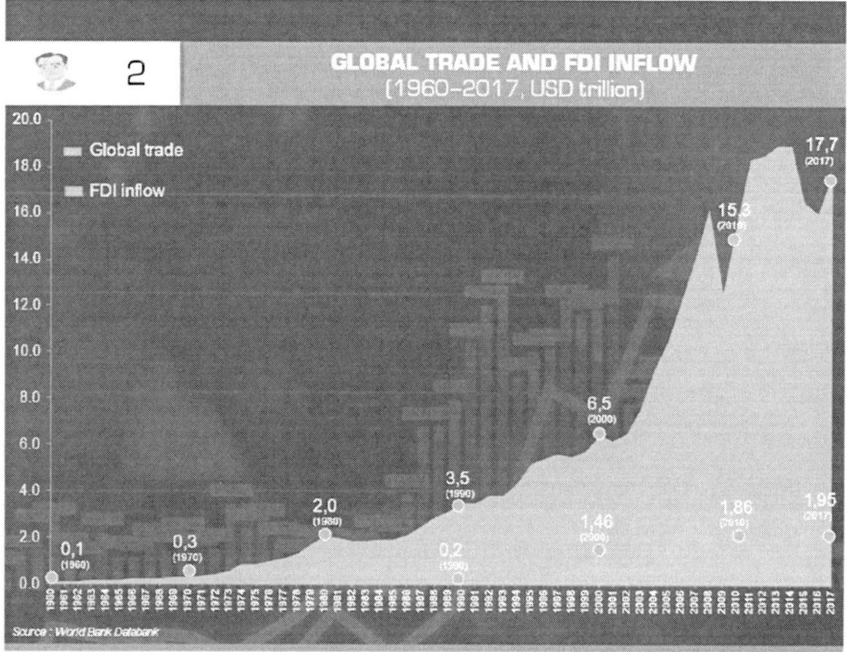

Fig. 2

(iv) GDP per capita

In terms of the GDP per capita, the rapid growth that is triggered by the end of the Cold War has impacted the indicator in a more modest way (Fig. 3). The world's population grew by 1.7 times between 1960-1990, whereas its growth since 1990 has been 1.5 times. As for the GDP per capita, it has been growing steadily without upward hikes and booms following the pattern of the previous 30 years development. Compared to the other economic indicators, the modest growth of the per capita GDP could be one of the subliminal reasons for the current world-wide frustration and dissatisfaction based on the difference of what an individual has received or could have received (which is short of the expected benefits) vis-à-vis the visible increase in wealth and accumulated capital. However, the rapid growth of the economy, trade and investment has clearly had a positive impact on the livelihood of people by considerably advancing social development, and improving their access to social welfare/support, healthcare and education services as well as the advantages offered by the ICT innovations.

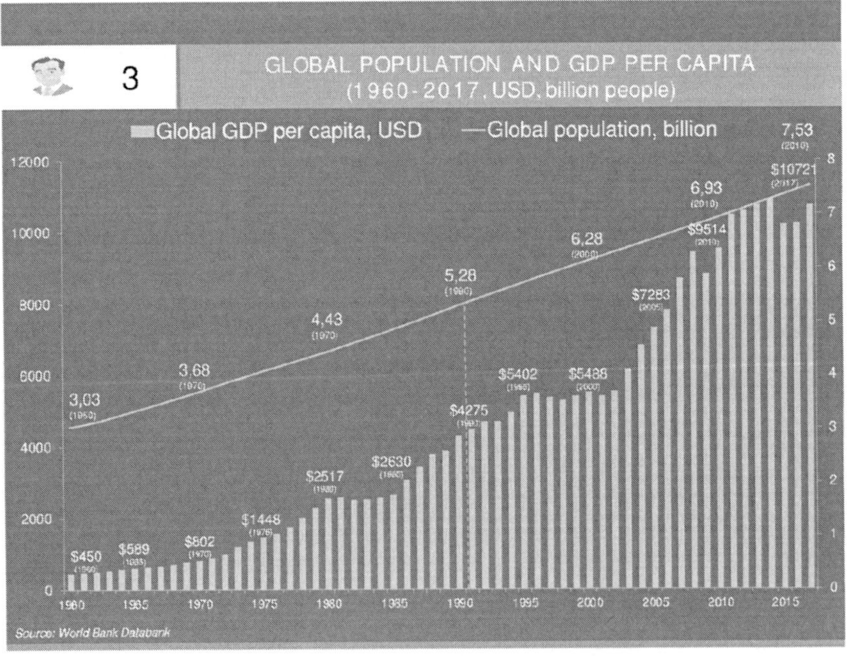

Fig. 3

(b) Reflection of the Global Trends on Individual Countries: The Case of Mongolia

If we compare the global trade and economic growth rate indicators with that of Mongolia, as a member country of the world community, then, one can see a similarly correlated pattern (Fig. 4). However, Mongolia's economic growth did not start outright from 1990, when the Cold War ended, as is the case with the global economy as shown in Fig. 1 and 2. On the contrary, in the 1990s, Mongolia's economy experienced a sharp fall and started to grow gradually from the beginning of the new century. From 2003-2004, however, it began to experience exponential growth. If we consider that in 2005-2006 Mongolia's economy regained its 1990s level (US$ 2.5 billion), then during the subsequent 6 to 7 years up to 2012, the growth increased by 5 times against the level that was achieved in previous 70-80 years (since the restoration of independence in 1921). From these facts, one can see the favourable effect of the end of the Cold War, as well as the constructive impact of globalised growth, democracy, market economy and cooperation.

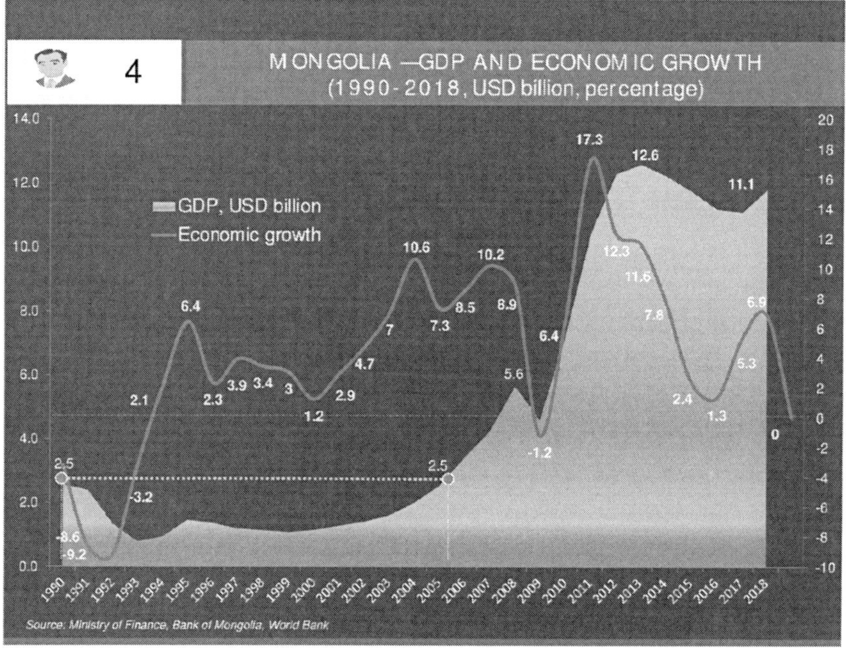

Fig. 4

A conclusion could be drawn from the above analysis that the world's economic progress and development, despite its imperfection, has had an unprecedented pace. With Cold War competition gone and the emergence of the international community with no irreconcilable foes, with the formation of the global pattern of collaboration envisaging partnership if not friendship, one would expect from a rational viewpoint that intensified global development would even further encourage and promote partnership and mutually beneficial cooperation. This should have facilitated international relations that support pragmatic and conducive approaches for economic progress. Yet, the populists (both at the national and international levels) have dismissed and downplayed these achievements, saying that there is room for more, and claiming that the more wealth produced could be distributed in a fairer, more equitable manner and further act in a misleading manner as if they knew the "secret mantra' for such distribution, thus, successfully triggering dissatisfaction and frustration at both the national and global levels. In such a world of irrational frustration, it has become evidently clear that the rational approach of increasing the "common pie" of the global economy through the promotion of cooperation and partnership is stalled and stuck.

(c) Discontent

(i) Over-expectations versus Delivery of Promises

As was argued earlier, today there should be no reason for serious discontent that requires fundamental revolution-like changes of an abrupt nature. Of course, good is never enough and therefore, there is always room for improvement. That in democratic societies, for example, could be achieved with the usual election mechanisms, as well as through nurturing fair competition in the free market systems, without having to resort to frequent changes of governments between elections. However, in today's social media-dominated environment of super intensity and high speed, where patience and the attention span has been sinking to a minimum, the above mechanisms seem to have become too slow to wait for and too simple to enjoy the confidence of the public. As a result, the global community has unreasonable expectations from everything with an unreasonably intense delivery speed.

Indeed, in the wake of an era of unbound globalisation, the world was overwhelmed with the euphoria caused by the openness and the possibility of free unrestrained exchange of ideas, cultures, goods, services and capital. The sudden expansion of markets and opportunities gave hope to businesses and entrepreneurs around the world. All these factors gave a profound opportunity to politicians to be optimistic and thus, to promise benefits to the people. Globalisation became the buzzword and anyone who raised doubts about it labeled backward or outdated. The further globalisation advanced the bigger the figures grew. In businesses millionaires were less visible, marking the start of a new era of billionaires, which could be termed as the period of transition. The trend is still continuing, which, in fact, may have a social effect that would, in a sense, resemble a shock wave.

The establishment of the WTO, the advent of e-commerce and the exponential progress in the ICT sector, made the statistics of the world economic pie even more astronomical, making the figure of a trillion dollars the routine for use by the global academia, media, businesses and politicians. However, as time went by, the overinflated expectations, oversold to the public by the politicians, began to hit reality. Then, even though the common pie of global wealth indeed had grown much bigger, benefiting everyone to a certain extent, the frustration and disillusionment gradually began to settle-in as the true results of global growth understandably fellshort of the trumpeted expectations. The scholarly community, corporate executives, the well-informed few may have known about the impossibility of achieving the hyped outcome, but the general public with naïve innocence and sincerity came to believe it, constantly being fed by politicians, the media and international financial institutions, as well as multinational investors, who supported the market's confidence for their security. The bitterly betrayed expectations unleashed the frustration-triggered indignation of the people throughout the world.

This mismatch seems to be a fairly sensible contributing factor to the general discontent observed worldwide, adding fuel to many protests in the industrialised countries with solid economic bases, where such continuous unrests are least expected. The 'Yellow Vests' protests, the 'Black Lives Matter' movement, the removal of monuments and memorials, the Capitol Hill attack, the multiplicity of anti-immigrant protests throughout the developed world were taking place partially due to this expanding general sense of dissatisfaction sparked by the frustration felt subliminally by the public.

In today's world an increase of suicides is another irrational phenomenon. This phenomenon is registered mostly in developed countries with high living standards. At present someone is leaving the world every 40 seconds at her/his own choice, and developed countries take the lead by this indicator. This means that every day by the time a person leaves his or her office after the completion of the working hours, almost one thousand people would have left the world. There is also no reasonable explanation for this. If it is explained by a difficult life and poverty, then, why is this indicator much lower in countries with much lower living standards, (than in the developed world) and why do people there (in countries with difficult life) not give up on life and continue to struggle?. Thus, it is impossible to explain the issue by a simple argument as life difficulties. Frustration and discontent could offer a partial explanation, though their root cause could hardly be explained in simple terms.

From Internal Frustration to International Frictions: With the end of the Cold War, which, at first sight, appeared to have heightened the threshold of the use of force to a prohibitively high level due to the spiking increase of the economic cost of military conflicts (in addition to the nuclear parity), peace and stability, the top achievements of the 1990s, began to be taken for granted. May be for the first time in history humanity had entered the era of international relations without the deadly confrontation of major adversarial camps. The world was almost without enemies! This sent the nations into an off-guard mode, where the world became careless about preserving peace, for it became unthinkably irrational and costly to start a conflict. Such an overly relaxed attitude to foreign interactions worked as if it relieved the actors from the discipline and diplomatic restraint in dealing with each other. As a result, the boundaries between internal political battles – where there are usually no rules of engagements– and international interactions blurred. In such circumstances, the politicians, in confronting their opponents in the international arena, almost seized to exercise sufficient prudence, for they apparently had the perception that since the countries were not enemies after all, then, ultimately – irrespective of the bitter verbal exchanges of a political nature– they would somehow in the end, resolve the differences. Consequently, during the political debates, the politicians prioritised being bold and tough in the eyes of their respective electorate. Often their concern about internal public opinion, which was (and is) never fully positive and always charged with emotion due to the discontent and frustration, overshadowed the risks of international rift. In so downplaying international affairs, politicians frequently presumed that the international problems created thus, could eventually always be cured through diplomacy, once solid internal popular support is secured. Unfortunately, however, since the invention of the nuclear weapons, humanity has been uninterruptedly living in the security system of mutually assured destruction, no matter how friendly the world became in the post-Cold War era. The major difference between the internal political battle and international confrontation was that the former was not (or unlikely to become) fatal, whereas the latter could be terminally fatal to the world. However, over-reliance on the reason that (against the risk of assured total destruction and/or unthinkably high economic costs of conflicts) no verbal squabbles of a political nature would spiral into all-out war, was, as it turns out, a miscalculation. In the modern world, the anger – globalised and empowered by social media – could trigger 'nuclear fusion' of an unprecedented extent in the minds, which could lead to unanticipated results. In such a case, no risk of loss of enormous wealth or even lives may stop the unfolding of global violence. Regrettably, a laidback approach to the existential issues led to the seriously confrontational military situation that the world has found itself in now. And once the international relations revealed their savage property, the system, relaxed by the 30 years' calm, was not ready to quickly respond in a preventive, non-escalatory manner. In short, often the internal frustration and the subsequent discontent urged politicians to re-address the problems to external factors, which triggered the 'witch hunt' overseas. Against the naïve presumption that the peace is undisturbable due to high costs and/or existential threats of large conflicts, such provocative actions were apparently thought to be tolerable, as no one in his/her right mind would start a real conflict merely over verbal exchanges. However, in diplomacy verbal communication (open or confidential) is the fundamental tool of interaction. Therefore, the impact of verbal communication is far more consequential than such communications in the internal politics. Consequently, the national level problems of today, triggered by local discontent and frustration, have transformed into international discontent, which, in turn, facilitates the creation of a conflict-prone international environment.

Response of politicians: The above deliberations demonstrate that wealth and prosperity do not guarantee content and satisfaction in human society. Sometimes, wanting more may actually exacerbate the spiritual condition. However, the policy and decision-makers keep to the old recipe of soothing nerves of the public by attempting to increase the common pie, with the view that everyone would benefit. Clearly, this is not wrong, but is not nearly enough in the modern world. Ensuring economic growth, thereby laying the foundation for the increased income, is merely one solution to the problem. Though money solves many difficulties, in the present it creates challenges as well. Especially, if there is no sense of inclusivity, equity and fairness in the distribution of wealth, the astronomical figures on economic progress turn into unfulfillable expectation provoking factors, which cause even more discontent than satisfaction.

Regrettably, political inertia at times does not allow a reformed approach; thus, the politicians and decision-makers resort to the old school method of offering economic and income growth to cure the discontent. Whenever, they encounter street rallies and sharp criticism of the public, they offer economic expansion solutions. Of course, they solve the problems to a large extent, but still create new issues and challenges.

Therefore, working with the minds and straightening the pro-monetary twist, through pursuit of inner peace may offer a more effective solution to many social problems that we are facing today. Also enhancing the critical thinking approach through nurturing analytical and reflective skills, while preserving the freedoms of speech and expression, may prevent the risks of affection by misleading, propaganda-driven false data and information distributed through numerous viral news-seeking media sources.

However, in a world with an acute attention span shortage that we are living in today, global politics is programmed to advocate for more money and wealth in order to overcome social crises and difficulties. There is no time for a pause to reflect. With such aggressive rush for having everything right now, and the culture of blaming others– including other countries– for economic failures, we have ended up sliding back into the confrontational mode in the international affairs. Such a confrontational mode, as time went by, began to influence more and more spheres of socio-political life, ending up degrading to the level of the Cold War. But, there must be better ways to build our global community in a manner that is more efficient than the fairly good post-Cold War globalisation system, instead of the retreat we are experiencing. In order to explore more scrupulously the avenues and possibilities for creating a better international order, a short excursion into the history of the models of the International Relations should be entertained.

Search for a Better Global Architecture Versus Reality

(a) Glimpse of the History of the Changes of the International Architecture

The international relations have seen various models, ranging from anarchic interaction between various actors, such as tribes, City-States to more orderly systems with major powers as gravitational centres surrounded by satellite States, etc. The major pattern of the evolution was that it was transforming from anarchic arrangements to more orderly ones, and from simple structures to more complex ones. As the system developed to a more complex one the epicentres of global power were geographically changing, and a number of power-nucleuses were also changing. It saw mono-centric models, like *Pax Romana* or *Pax Mongolica* (which did not rule out the existence of other centres, but those others were not nearly as dominant), as well as polycentric architectures. The collapse of each system involved its own Bing Bang with the subsequent entropy leading to the formation of multiple autonomous or separate constellations and gravitational centres. Throughout the history of the International Relations the selfish Machiavellian approach was a substantial influence and the relations were subject to hierarchical arrangements. From the Westphalian system through to the two World Wars, the institution of sovereignty was being augmented, irrespective of the size and influence of a nation in international affairs. With the strengthening of the concept of sovereignty and independence, the institution of international law was further progressively developing. With the end of the Second World War and the beginning of the UN era, the explicitly bipolar Cold War decades began. The review of the systems' various transformations and transfusion of the systems as described above, could be visualised as the figure below (Fig. 5).

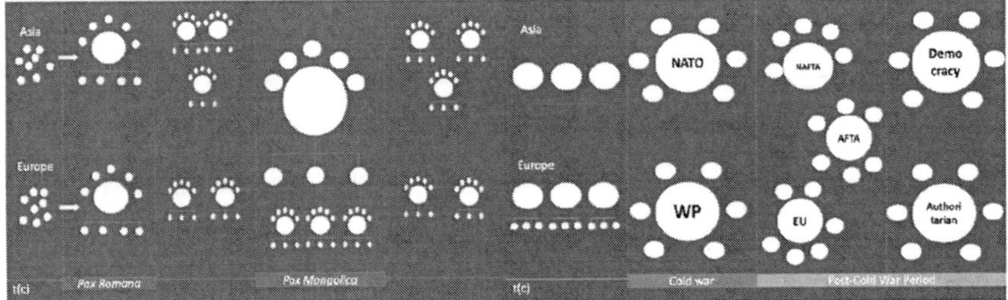

Fig. 5

With the collapse of the Soviet Union and the Warsaw Pact, communist ideology went bankrupt. As a result, the 'zero sum' ideological divide ended and a new era of amity was born. The new system had begun with the Trans-Atlantic Mono-Axis arrangement with the multipolar centres. The vibrant economic growth of the world helped develop additional Trans-Pacific Axes, which turned it into a double-axis system. This complex international architecture, free of confrontation and busy with commerce, trade and cross-border investment, served as a fertile ground for unprecedented progress of humanity. In fact, it apparently was too good a system to last. The humanity grew complacent, decadent and fell hostage to their success. As the Mongolian saying "the trouble of maldigestion of excessive happiness' goes, the humanity choked over the sudden success that ensued pursuant to the accelerated globalisation".

(b) Pluripolar, Multi-Axis World Architecture

If post-Cold War globalisation were to crumble and if it were to transform into a new system, then, desirably it should upgrade into a more progressive and complex system. Beginning from 2014, this author was hoping that the model of International Relations would fuse into the Pluripolar, Multi-Axis system (Fig. 6), where there would be plural, but not unlimited, number of gravitational centres, which would not be just States, but also non-State actors. Also, it was imagined, that there would be multiple axes such as the Indian Ocean, the Arctic Ocean, digital axis, space axis, transcontinental trade routes, such as the silk Road (Belt and Road), etc. With the development of new technologies, the axes could have any imaginary form, which is why its number could be unlimited. Hence, the term 'multi' is applied in relation to the axes. In other words, the system was to reflect the growing complexity of the global world. Moreover, in terms of the model, it would be somewhat analogous with the complex nature of the build-up of the Universe.

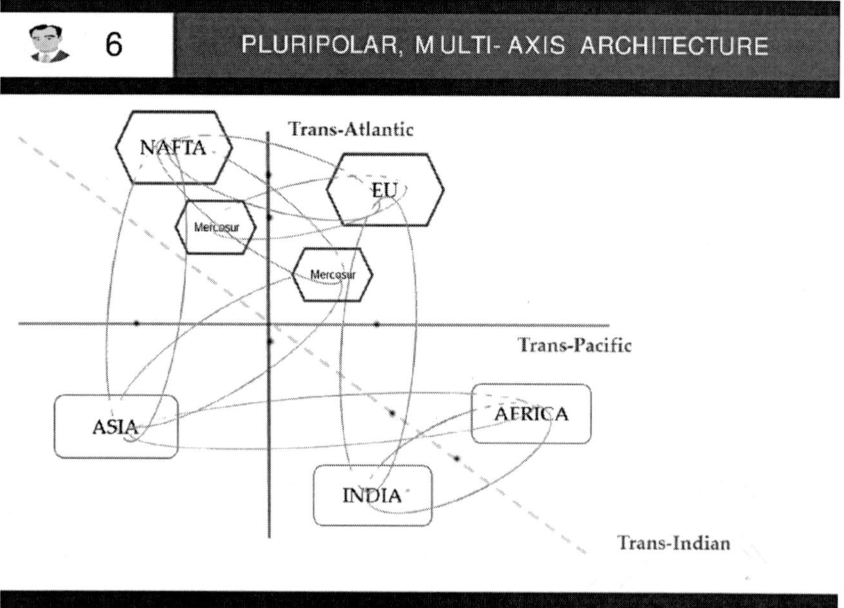

Fig. 6

Cold War II

At the time when such an approach was being developed, it was hoped by the author that, as intelligent beings, we could proactively engineer and build the architecture that is better than the good one (the post-Cold War globalisation) that was crumbling and thus, had to go. This would have been a better option, than the option of going backwards. However, in these times of irrationality, we precisely began to backslide into the past, unfortunately. Thus, if we are back in the Cold War system, then, it had to be termed as Cold War II.

Changing the Approach: Mercantilism versus Mind-Centrism

The re-entry into another Cold War, no matter how disappointing it is, should not discourage the modern generation from taking another chance to close it to begin a new attempt to consciously construct a better international system that corresponds to the complex realities of the present world. In fact, the post-Second World War, UN-centric system was, and still is a negotiated and yet collectively well-calculated system. This serves as a good indication that we ought not to live in a system of International Relations that is formed objectively because of the natural balance of powers with only some elements of consciously negotiated/built institutions. It is possible to build a well-thought architecture. Now, with the accumulated collective wisdom, experience of the contemporary generation, amplified with IT and AI capacities, we can build an intelligent system of our choice. Such a system should also entail mechanisms to respond to the unknown, unexpected as well. In other words, it would not, and cannot, have all the answers; however, it can factor in itself, programmes and mechanisms that would ready the system for comprehending and embracing new objectively forming realities and phenomena that life always ingenuously creates for us, challenging our intellect.

Since it is not too late to wind up the slide back into the confrontational set up and it is possible to enter a new system, then, one of the options could be the Multi-Axis Pluripolarity. However, one element should be added to the system now, i.e. multi-dimensionality. Multi-dimensionality means the respect and tolerance for multiplicity and difference in cultures, customs, traditions, perceptions, etc. It also takes into consideration something similar to the relativity of time in the historical development of various communities. As time is relative, is quantum physics, and as there are multiple worlds co-existing in the Universe, individual societies may have different historical time perceptions in terms of their evolution. Understandably, through interaction, these realities of individual societies may change as always, in the natural Universe, because of interactions between different systems. But such changes should happen with the awareness of cultural and traditional differences and with the clear consent of the actors involved. Also, multi-dimensionality entails awareness of the given complexity of the world that prevents oversimplified approaches to such a comprehensively sophisticated system.

In summary, this is the mind-centric dimension of Multi-Axis Pluripolarity. Hence, in the Multi-Axis, Multi-Dimensional Pluripolar architecture of the world, the power of cognition, analysis, sentience, intellect will be equally important as monetary, financial, mercantile values. Therefore, such a system would recognise the importance of fixing the mind, attaining inner peace by appreciating what has already been achieved, gained, and learning to control the otherwise unstoppable want for more. An intellectual return to age-old religious values, without over-reliance on superstitious reverence, would show and remind us of the deep philosophies embedded in them, that teach us the value of humility, gratefulness and forgiveness. Thousands of years ago, our predecessors already revealed that one cannot attain contentment through material wealth. Sometimes, mere reflection and appreciation may fix many problems that trillions of dollars cannot solve. The creation of such a comprehensive, complex system in the end may offer global peace and better coherence.

Conclusion

The purpose of proposing Multi-Axis, Multi-Dimensional Pluripolarity is an attempt to have the world recognise its arch-complexity. The complex nature gets even more sophisticated when spiritual realities and those of the mind are factored in; for they are as unlimited as the Universe itself. Moreover, they are not static and are always in motion and change mode, which is why they get more complicated for cognition. Yet the complexity is not a justification for not attempting to address it through a system that isbuilt to be aware and reflective of such complexity. Therefore, our generation has the duty to figure out a next level system of International Relations where security, freedom and liberties along with the material well-being, are guaranteed in a balanced way. The most important task is to strengthen the nuclear disaster risk prevention system beyond doubt. And such a security mechanism cannot be achieved only on the strength of money. It cannot be achieved without morality, spirituality and the wisdom of mind. If it were at all attainable, all the best minds, the total capacity of the modern AI had better be employed for scouring the data in order to develop the international affairs model of the comprehensive 21st century and beyond world. Then, probably all the dimensions and walks of life, big and small, could be incorporated into the research with their subsequent reflection in the international architecture. In short, the power of mind healing is not to be underestimated and overlooked in global problem solving, whose ultimate goal is giving peace a chance.

NOTES

1 For details see, Д.Цогтбаатар. (2014.05.11). "Хүйтэн дайн II" http://www.24tsag.mn/a/55200
Tsogtbaatar Damdin – Дамдины Цогтбаатар. (2017.02.07.). 2017 + БУЮУ ИРЭЭДҮЙ ЯМАР БАЙХ БОЛ ? https://www.facebook.com/tsogtbaatar.damdin/photos/a.300495723336850/1220328924686854
Tsogtbaatar Damdin's statement at the General debate 74th session of the United Nations General Assembly. (2019.09.28). https://www.un.int/mongolia/statements_speeches/statement-his-excellency-mr-tsogtbaatar-damdin-mp-minister-foreign-affairs
Tsogtbaatar Damdin's statement at the 76th session of ESCAP. (2020.05.28.). https://mfa.gov.mn/old/?p=50983&lang=en
Tsogtbaatar Damdin's Valdai annual meeting statement. (2021.10.19.). https://valdaiclub.com/multimedia/video/18th-annual-meeting-of-the-valdai-discussion-club-day-1/
Tsogtbaatar Damdin. (2023). *"Irrationalism and International Relations"*. Indian Council of World Affairs.

2 Ibid.

CHAPTER 4

The Evolution of Vietnam's Multilateral Diplomacy and its Perspective on Multilateralism

Tu Anh Tuan

> *"Since wars begin in the minds of men, it is in the minds of men that the defences of peace must be constructed".* (Constitution of the United Nations Educational, Scientific and Cultural Organisation - 1946)

The current global landscape witnesses various unprecedented challenges and crises, including the polarisation and decoupling between the United States and China, the West's economic sanctions on Russia, the growing trend of de-dollarisation, and the growing competition among groups and alliances formed around major powers. These perilous trends seem to imply the emergence of a new Cold War in different manifestations.

Multilateralism was built to address global challenges, promote cooperation, and maintain peace, stability, and order. However, when major power competition escalates, there is a risk the multilateral platforms can be politicised and can consequently devolve into arenas for great powers' consolidation of force. This can lead to a breakdown in trust, increased tensions, and the erosion of the principles of multilateralism. In this context, the solidarity of developing countries is much needed to promote true multilateralism with strong commitments to constructive dialogue, cooperation, and collective problem solving. They should actively work towards finding common ground, resolving conflicts through dialogue, and not through bandwagoning which further divides the world. By doing so, they can help push the multilateral institutions to fulfill their intended functions rather than allowing them to be hijacked by power struggles and political agendas.

Vietnam's approach to multilateralism consistently emphasises promoting strategic trust, pursuing peace, and maintaining strategic autonomy via nonalignment. Through a complicated history of war, sanctions, and political isolation, Vietnam's multilateral diplomacy has contributed greatly to the development of the country under the Renovation Process (Doi Moi) with historic achievements. After nearly 40 years of Doi Moi and international integration, the national economy has expanded 12-fold, exceeding $400 billion and per capita income has increased by 8.3-per cent. Additionally, import and export volumes have increased almost 30 times, and foreign direct investment capital has increased 22 times. Vietnam can therefore be seen as a success story of how a developing country can effectively leverage multilateralism to promote security, development, and influence.

VIETNAM TODAY: MAGIC STORY OF GROWTH

THANKS TO DOMESTIC STABILITY AND ACTIVE MULTILATERAL INTEGRATION

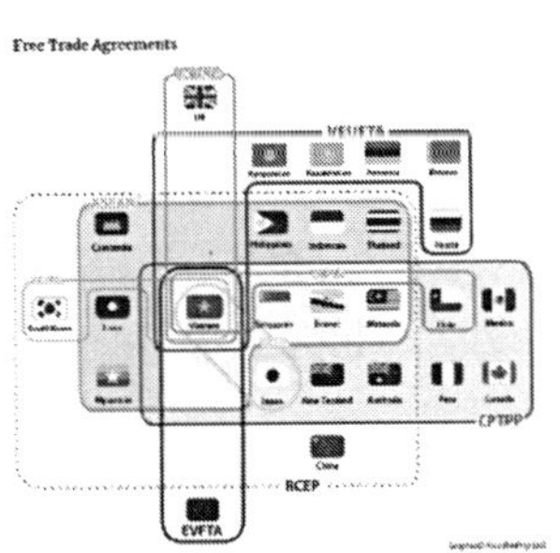

AMONG THE MOST MULTI-CONNECTED ECONOMIES IN THE WORLD

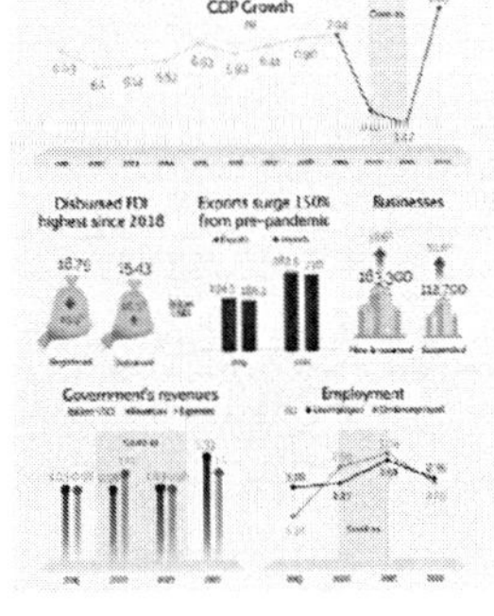

2022: GROW HIGHEST IN 12 YEAR, EXPECTED > 8% (TOP ASIA) INFLATION LESS THAN 3%

RATED BY MOODY'S AS STABLE (2022)

This chapter analyses the three phases of Vietnam's multilateral diplomacy as well as its view on how multilateralism should be from a developing country's vantage point. The reflections and lessons derived from Vietnam's experiences, as well as its aspirations in multilateralism, may serve as a reference for other developing countries seeking to formulate strategies that optimise their advantages, navigate challenges, and identify niche areas where they can lead when feasible and appropriate.

From 1986-1991: Striving for "More Friends, Fewer Enemies"

In the 1980s, Vietnam encountered numerous difficulties and challenges, including economic recession, production stagnation, budget shortages, high inflation, and political isolation stemming from misunderstandings surrounding the Cambodia issue. These circumstances compelled Vietnam to recognise that limiting the relations within a single bloc would not contribute to economic growth. There was also a growing trend of international engagement and cooperation among countries with institutional differences, driven by a common aspiration for prosperity.

Therefore, the 6th National Congress of the Communist Party of Vietnam, held in Hanoi in 1986, defined that the top task in foreign affairs is "... taking advantage of favorable international conditions for the cause of building socialism and defending the Fatherland", and securing "peace for economic development." The 6th Congress not only laid the foundation for a comprehensive reform process but also represented a crucial turning point in the perspective of "expanding relations with international organisations and all countries based on the principle of peaceful coexistence." Reflecting on this milestone, it was a breakthrough in thinking that innovates and develops the economy and simultaneously creates a foundation for foreign affairs, transitioning to the stage where Vietnam can be friends with other countries with ideological differences.

Subsequently, the 13th Conference of the Central Committee of CPV in 1988, for the first time, explicitly defined the goal of diversifying relations based on the principle of "adding friends, reducing enemies." This concept of multilateralism, which emphasised the significance of cultivating more friendships and minimising adversaries marked a substantial departure from the Cold War period, characterised by a confrontational stance and alignment within a particular bloc. With a changing mindset, Vietnam made several historic moves to diversify its international relations.

First, Vietnam's involvement in the Non-Aligned Movement (NAM) since 1976 showcased its commitment to multilateralism and the desire to "add friends". The NAM, composed of nations pursuing independent foreign policies, provided Vietnam a platform to engage with countries beyond traditional ideological alliances. By actively participating in the NAM, Vietnam sought to enhance its international standing, gain support for its cause, and cultivate economic and political ties with non-aligned nations. Through this movement, Vietnam demonstrated its willingness to develop friendships beyond conventional alliances and reduce the number of adversaries it faced on the global stage. NAM's membership allowed Vietnam to engage with a diverse range of countries, strengthening its diplomatic network and positioning itself as a constructive and cooperative player in international affairs.

Second, Vietnam's engagement in multilateral fora, such as the United Nations, exemplified its dedication to building friendships and forging alliances across the globe. Vietnam's admission to the United Nations in 1977 offered a platform for the country to participate in diplomatic negotiations, advocate for its interests, and establish connections with other nations. Through active involvement in the UN's multilateral initiatives, Vietnam has fostered cooperative relationships with various countries, regardless of their political or ideological orientations. Moreover, Vietnam's engagement in multilateral fora enabled it to shape international agendas, promote its perspectives, and contribute to the development of international norms and standards.

Recognising the need for diversifying international engagement and pursuing multilateralism has been a crucial change in Vietnam's perception of diplomacy in this period. These engagements have allowed Vietnam to expand its diplomatic reach, cultivate friendships beyond traditional alliances and contribute to global peace, stability, and development. By embracing multilateralism, Vietnam has demonstrated a willingness to collaborate with diverse nations, promote dialogue, and work towards common solutions to global challenges.

From 1991-2006: Building Trust to Advance Multilateral Integration

In the early 1990s, the collapse of the Socialist Bloc in Eastern Europe affected Vietnam briefly. However, this momentary disruption prompted Vietnam to continue the revival of its foreign policy in a multilateral direction. Aligned with this new perspective, the 7th National Congress of the Communist Party of Vietnam in 1991 affirmed Vietnam's desire "to befriend all countries in the international community, striving for peace, independence, and development" This shift fundamentally changed the Cold War mentality of categorising nations as "friends" or "enemies". Instead, relationships were now assessed on the basis of convergence or divergence of interests. This new understanding laid the groundwork for a multilateral approach to diplomacy, seeking to expand economic relations with all countries, regardless of their political regime or level of development. Committed to integration, Vietnam recognised the importance of building trust and successfully resolved the Cambodia problem in 1993, addressing all misunderstandings. Subsequently, Vietnam focused on establishing relations with multilateral mechanisms, starting with the Asia-Pacific region and primarily the Association of Southeast Asian Nations (ASEAN)

The 8th National Party Congress in 1995 continued to elevate the policy stance from "want to be friends" to "ready to be friends." This shift indicated a welcoming disposition and open-mindedness toward new relationships. Vietnam's position was well received by the international community, leading to several noteworthy milestones on the multilateral front. Vietnam became a member of ASEAN in 1995. This event holds historic implications. First, it marked the transformation of a polarised and confrontational ASEAN into a cohesive, peaceful, stable, and developed ASEAN. Second, it symbolised Vietnam's liberation from isolation through diplomacy. Third, it initiated a process of adapting and adjusting Vietnam's economy to being a regional economy. The accession into the Common Effective Preferential Tariff (CEPT) programme and the integration of the ASEAN Free Trade Area (AFTA) was the first stepping stone to prepare Vietnam's economy to integrate into the global economy.

The 9th Party Congress in 2001 marked a further step forward in the thinking on multilateral diplomacy when it decided to replace the phrase "want to be friends" with the phrase "ready to be friends, reliable partners of countries in the international community... .[1] This replacement demonstrated proactiveness and reflected Vietnam's increasingly affirmed position and role in international relations. It served as the foundation for Vietnam to renew its domestic economy and deepen its integration with the world, preparing the ground for joining the World Trade Organisation (WTO). These accomplishments exemplified Vietnam's commitment to active regional engagement and highlighted its growing significance on the international stage.

In summary, Vietnam's multilateral diplomacy during this period transcended the limits of ideological blocs. Vietnam's commitment to cooperation and integration was deepened through high-level political statements and concrete action aimed at building strategic trust. Multilateral diplomacy helped Vietnam integrate profoundly and widely, break through isolation, and pave the way for further advancements. During this period, the thinking on multilateral foreign relations primarily focused on the economic dimension and people-to-people diplomacy, characterised by international economic integration and the development of people-oriented foreign relations.

From 2006-Present: Delivering Public Goods, Deploying Niche Diplomacy

The 10th National Congress of the Party in 2006 marked a notable shift in the leadership's thinking on multilateral foreign policy. The Congress introduced the "international economic integration" concept and emphasised the need to expand international cooperation in all other areas. This expansion highlighted the country's confidence in integration without compromising its identity.

The 11th National Congress in 2011 represented a turning point in Vietnam's approach to multilateral foreign affairs. The Congress set the orientation of consistently implementing a foreign policy based on independence, self-reliance, peace, and cooperation for development. It stressed the importance of multilateralisation and diversification of relations, and proactive international integration. The Congress also underscored the significance of multilateral international cooperation in defence and security, as evidenced by the country's first-ever participation in a UN peacekeeping operation in 2014. This marked a historic milestone in Vietnam's expanded role in global peace and security efforts, demonstrating its commitment to international cooperation and willingness to contribute to peace and stability in conflict areas worldwide. Vietnam's involvement in various UN peacekeeping operations in Africa – particularly in South Sudan and the Central African Republic– highlights its growing importance as a responsible member of the international community.

The inclusion of the concept of "multilateral diplomacy" in the official document of the 12th National Congress of the Party in January 2016 further solidified its strategic significance in Vietnam's foreign policy. Not merely as a tool for foreign affairs, multilateral diplomacy became an orientation. The document emphasised the need to improve the quality of multilateral foreign affairs and actively participate in and promote Vietnam's role in multilateral mechanisms, extending beyond mere participation in negotiations. Vietnam is trusted and recommended by international friends to undertake many critical international responsibilities, such as serving on the Human Rights Council for the terms 2014-2016 and 2023-2025, the UNESCO World Heritage Committee for the term 2013-2017, and the United Nations Economic and Social Council (ECOSOC) for the term 2016-2018. Based on a strengthened position and better capability, Vietnamese diplomacy embraces a new vision and aspiration, not only "participating" as a positive and responsible partner but also striving to play a "core, leading, and mediating[2] role in multilateral fora, in line with specific capabilities and conditions. On many important international issues, Vietnam has put forward initiatives and solutions that are rational, fair, humane, based on law and justice, which enjoy the support of the international community, thereby enhancing Vietnam's position and reputation on the international stage. Vietnam's capacity for chairing, managing, and leading roles is increasingly affirmed, especially with the successful assumption of global responsibilities such as the Chair of ASEAN for two terms (2010 and 2020), hosting the APEC summit in 2006 and 2017, serving as a non-permanent member of the United Nations

Security Council for 2008-2009, and hosting the second US-North Korea Summit in February 2019. Notably, in 2020, Vietnam successfully fulfilled all three significant responsibilities: a non-permanent member of the United Nations Security Council, ASEAN Chair, and AIPA Chair, contributing to enhancing Vietnam's prestige and position in the region and the world. Vietnam's victory in the election for the UN Security Council for the term 2020-2021 with a record number of votes (192 out of 193 votes), on 7 June 2020, affirmed her position and reputation among the five non-permanent members.

At the 13th Party Congress in 2021, the foreign policy was formulated for the period 2021-2030. The Congress emphasised the continuation of the foreign policy of independence, self-reliance, multilateralism, and diversification, while proactively integrating into the world. In terms of multilateral diplomacy, the Congress outlined the need to build comprehensive and modern diplomacy framework with three pillars: Party diplomacy, State diplomacy, and People-to-People diplomacy. This new vision underscores an integrated and comprehensive approach to multilateral diplomacy that includes not only professional diplomats but also encompasses the entire society. It recognises the need to adapt to the modern landscape, where an individual can act as a messenger and utilise social media tools to disseminate messages.

Vietnam's multilateral diplomacy today is characterised by its commitment to contributing public good and readiness to deploy niche diplomacy, assuming leadership where it is capable. Vietnam actively voices the shared concerns of small and medium-sized countries, promoting the greater involvement of developing nations in shaping the rules of multilateral institutions, which will contribute to more democratic and equitable international frameworks.

Reflections and Recommendations

Multilateralism remains the indispensable path forward in solving the challenges of our time

Although it may sound cliched, this statement needs to be reiterated in the current context of major power confrontation, with widespread implications for global politics and multilateralism. Vietnam and many developing countries, continue to feel the pain of the divisions and coercion by the major powers, as victims of Cold War divisions and power politics, and treasure multilateralism.

The ever-increasing magnitude and complexity of today's issues, such as climate change, pandemics, terrorism, poverty, and inequality, transcends national boundaries, necessitating collaborative solutions that surpass the capacity of any single nation. Multilateralism serves as a platform for countries to pool their resources, knowledge, and expertise, empowering them to collectively address these complex challenges.

The increasingly globalised nature of our economies and societies underscores the interdependence among nations. Developments in one country, be they economic, political, or social, have profound impacts on others. Multilateralism recognises this interconnectedness and encourages cooperation among nations to tackle shared concerns. Through multilateral platforms, countries engage in dialogue, negotiate agreements, and coordinate policies to effectively manage common challenges. Embracing multilateralism allows countries to harness the benefits of interconnectedness while minimising risks and conflicts.

To remain effective, multilateralism must also be flexible and adaptable to evolving global realities. Regular reviews, assessments, and necessary reforms of multilateral initiatives are vital to enhance their efficacy and ensure their continued relevance in addressing contemporary challenges. By promoting a dynamic and responsive multilateral framework, nations can navigate the complexities of the interconnected world more effectively, advancing cooperation, stability, and progress for all.

Maintaining peace and stability should remain the highest priority for multilateralism today

Throughout history, peace and stability have been the aspirations of humanity, particularly for developing countries like Vietnam, which has experienced the horrors of devastating wars. The concept of multilateralism emerged as a response to the catastrophic consequences of the Second World War and the urgent need to prevent future global conflicts. Recognising the interconnectedness and interdependence of nations, it became clear that a new approach to international relations was necessary. Multilateralism, with its emphasis on collaboration, cooperation, and collective decision-making, offers a potential solution to counter the destructive tendencies of unilateralism and isolationism.

Multilateralism plays a crucial role in establishing norms, rules, and standards that govern international behaviour, which contributes greatly towards safeguarding peace and stability. This rules-based order fosters predictability, stability, and fairness in global relations. By adhering to multilateral agreements, countries can ensure that their actions align with global norms and contribute to a more just and orderly world.

Moreover, multilateralism serves as a vital avenue for diplomatic engagement and conflict resolution. By bringing countries together in neutral and inclusive settings, multilateral forums provide opportunities for dialogue, negotiation, and mediation. This diplomatic approach helps to de-escalate tensions, build trust, and find mutually beneficial solutions. International organisations, such as the United Nations, and regional bodies play a critical role in facilitating negotiations, peacekeeping efforts, and mediation processes to prevent and resolve conflicts.

By upholding the principles of multilateralism, nations can work together to foster worldwide peace, stability, and harmony. This requires a collective commitment to dialogue, cooperation, and the pursuit of common interests. Multilateralism provides a framework for countries to address shared challenges, resolve disputes peacefully, and build a more peaceful and prosperous future for all.

Building trust is vital for the effectiveness of multilateralism

Trust serves as the foundation upon which multilateral relationships are built, allowing nations to work together to address global challenges and pursue shared goals. The journey of Vietnam's integration with multilateral institutions has also been a trust-building process. There are two key conditions for fostering trust within multilateral settings:

(i) Constructive and peaceful dialogue is essential in multilateral settings, as it facilitates the exchange of perspectives, enhances understanding, and promotes collaboration and problem solving. It allows countries to express their concerns, find common ground, and negotiate mutually beneficial solutions. Constructive dialogue builds trust by fostering transparency and honesty, encouraging respect and empathy, and demonstrating consistency and reliability. Through open and meaningful discussions, nations can develop a shared understanding and build confidence in each other's intentions and capabilities.

(ii) Costly actions: Trust is also built through costly actions that demonstrate a nation's commitment to the principles, agreements, and decisions made within multilateral frameworks. Governments must back up their words with concrete steps and deliver on their commitments. By fulfilling financial obligations, implementing agreed-upon policies, contributing to peacekeeping operations, promoting sustainable development, and complying with international norms and regulations, nations establish a track record of reliability and credibility. These actions showcase a nation's willingness to act in good faith and contribute to the collective effort, strengthening trust among their peers.

Additionally, transparency and accountability play crucial roles within multilateralism. Openness in sharing information, including data, resources, and intentions, helps foster trust among nations. Moreover, establishing mechanisms for monitoring and evaluating progress, as well as holding nations accountable for their actions, ensures that commitments are upheld.

The Global South should raise their voice and find their niches to lead

The Global South constitutes a significant portion of the world's population and is home to many emerging economies. However, the region often faces unique challenges such as poverty, underdevelopment, and the adverse impacts of climate change. The history of multilateralism is marked by the dominance of developed countries, perpetuating a persistent North-South divide. Vietnam's experiences prove that there are opportunities for developing countries to deliver public goods and elevate their positions.

If developing countries fail to assert themselves and do not actively participate in shaping global agendas, the gap between developed and developing nations will continue to widen, resulting in an imbalanced global order. By raising their voices and assuming leadership roles in multilateral forums, developing countries have the opportunity to bridge this divide and contribute to the development of global policies that address the challenges they face. The experiences and insights of developing countries offer valuable perspectives and solutions to global issues. By actively participating in multilateral discussions, they can ensure that the global agenda is more responsive to the needs and aspirations of the most vulnerable populations.

Furthermore, developing countries can utilise multilateral platforms to foster South-South cooperation and solidarity. By collaborating with other developing nations, they can form minilateral groups to take a lead on certain issues that are important for those countries, for example: Like-Minded Group of Developing Countries (LMDC) that is playing important role in the UN system. This collaborative approach not only strengthens the collective voice of developing countries but also facilitates the emergence of new development models, innovative solutions, and mutually beneficial partnerships that are essential for achieving global progress.

India should play a leading role in the Global South to promote multilateralism

It appears that India has not fully utilised its potential to enhance its engagement in multilateralism. With its projected trajectory to become the world's third-largest economy by 2027, surpassing Japan and Germany, as well as possessing the third-largest stock market by 2030,[3] India has benefited from global trends and strategic investments in technology and energy. From the perspectives of many developing countries, India is a benevolent power capable of advocating the interests of the Global South, which further strengthens its case to assume a prominent position and advocate multilateralism. There are numerous compelling arguments supporting India's leading role, outlined as follows:

India has a long tradition of peaceful co-existence and non-aggression. India's commitment to democratic values, pluralism, and a rules-based international order has made her a power that can be trusted to uphold the principles of multilateralism.

As the largest democracy in the world and a significant regional power, India has played a key leading role in regional fora such as the South Asian Association for Regional Cooperation (SAARC) and the Indian Ocean Rim Association (IORA), demonstrating her determination to promote regional cooperation and address common challenges.

India's development experiences, challenges, and aspirations are closely aligned with those of many countries in the Global South. Given its large population, socio-economic diversity, and sustained development efforts, India understands the concerns and priorities of developing countries. It can effectively articulate and represent the interests and aspirations of the Global South in multilateral fora.

India's multicultural makeup and religious diversity give it a unique flair of soft power in the world. While many other powers want to impose their ideologies and values on small countries, India embraces pluralism, inclusivity, and respect for different cultures and religions. With its ability to accommodate diverse interests and find common ground, India is a bridge within the Global South, fostering dialogue and cooperation among countries with diverse perspectives.

India has a long history of active participation in multilateral institutions and initiatives andhas consistently advocated reform in global governance structures to increase the representation of the Global South. India's contributions to peacekeeping, climate change negotiations, and global health efforts demonstrate its commitment to multilateralism and tackling common challenges.

By playing a leading role in the Global South, India can leverage its benign soft power status, regional leadership, and understanding of the development needs and aspirations of developing countries to promote multilateralism. Through active engagement, India can foster cooperation, bridge divides, and advocate for a just and inclusive international order that addresses the concerns and aspirations of the Global South.

Transactionalism to Functionalism - Striving for common goals than national gains

Vietnam and ASEAN's success has been the result of their commitment to prioritise the interests of the regional community before their respective national interests. To save multilateralism, it is important to have the right perspective and mentality. If, for example, a country looks at multilateral institutions from a transactionalist lens, it would focus on the pursuit of specific national interests and the negotiation of bilateral or multilateral agreements based on those interests, not on long-term cooperation or shared values. However, if the country adopts a functionalist approach, it would focus on addressing specific functional or technical issues that affect multiple countries and require collective action. The shift from transactionalism to functionalism is crucial in order to prioritise common goals over narrow national gains within multilateral institutions.

Currently, multilateral institutions are increasingly becoming arenas for power politics and geopolitical rivalries, derailing them from their goals and missions. As a consequence, the competition within multilateral institutions has contributed to polarisation and fragmentation among member states. Divisions arise along ideological, geopolitical, or economic lines, creating rifts that hinder effective collaboration and decision-making.

Moreover, the instrumentalisation and politicisation of multilateral institutions have eroded trust and credibility among member states. When these institutions are perceived as biased or manipulated by powerful actors, it undermines the faith and confidence that countries place in these platforms. This erosion of trust and credibility is detrimental to the functioning of multilateralism and hampers its potential to effectively address global challenges.

Multilateral institutions were established with noble intentions of solving problems collectively. It is important to continue to improve the current institutions, making them fulfill their intended functions. Therefore, it is essential for countries to redirect their efforts towards striving for the noble goals of these institutions rather than using them as platforms for power politics and competition for influence. Embracing functionalism entails shifting the focus from short-term gains and individual interests to the pursuit of common goals that benefit the international community as a whole. This requires a commitment to collaboration, compromise, and finding win-win solutions that serve the collective interests of all nations. By doing so, countries can foster an environment of trust, cooperation, and mutual respect within multilateral institutions, enabling them to fulfill their intended purpose of addressing global challenges effectively.

In conclusion, the challenges of our time necessitate the continued reliance on multilateralism as the essential path forward. While addressing a range of global issues, it is crucial to prioritise the maintenance of peace and stability. Central to the effectiveness of multilateralism is the cultivation of trust among nations, fostering an environment conducive to cooperation and collaboration. Moreover, it is imperative for the Global South to assert itself, find its voice, and identify its unique contributions to lead in the multilateral arena. In this context, India, with its growing influence and capabilities, should assume a leading role within the Global South, championing multilateralism and promoting the transition from transactionalism to functionalism, where the pursuit of common goals supersedes narrow national interests. By embracing this approach, nations can work together more effectively, surmounting global challenges and creating a more prosperous and peaceful future.

NOTES

1 *Document of the 11th National Congress,* Communist Party of Vietnam, National Political Publishing House, Hanoi, 2011, p. 138.

2 *Document of the 11th National Congress,* Communist Party of Vietnam, National Political Publishing House, Hanoi, 2016, p. 156.

3 "India's Impending Economic Boom", 8 November 2022 at https://www.morganstanley.com/ideas/investment-opportunities-in-india

Geo-economics: Reforming Global Financial Institutions

CHAPTER 5

Reforming the Global Financial Architecture to Achieve the SDGs

Masahiro Kawai

Introduction

The COVID-19 pandemic has significantly affected developing countries, soaring energy and food costs, climate emergencies such as floods, typhoons, and heat waves, and external debt distress in the face of tightening financial conditions. Many countries in the Global South have not been able to invest adequately in accelerating economic recovery, pursuing long-term sustainable development goals (SDGs), or taking climate action. The United Nations (UN) Secretary General António Guterres has claimed that today's global financial architecture (GFA) is too short-sighted, crisis-prone, and deeply unequal to tackle the polycrisis. He has proposed a global SDG Stimulus Plan of at least $500 billion annually to scale up long-term financing for countries in need through GFA reforms.[1]

The GFA represents the governance arrangements that safeguard the stability and functions of the global monetary and financial systems (UN 2023b). Created immediately after the Second World War, it has evolved over time, driven by the policy preferences of G7 countries in the Global North in response to the changing economic and financial landscape of the world. The GFA is made up of International Financial Institutions (IFIs) such as the International Monetary Fund [IMF] and multilateral development banks [MDBs] including the World Bank, frameworks and structures that includes inter-governmental fora such as the G7 and G20, policies and rules (set collectively by a group of countries), and markets where private financial firms and investors are main players.

Reforms of the GFA have long been discussed in response to major financial shocks and crises, such as the external debt crisis in Latin America and Africa in the 1980s, the Asian financial crisis of 1997-98, and the global financial crisis of 2007-09. The multiple threats of the recent pandemic, war, external debt distress, and the lack of progress on the SDGs and climate goals, which would require trillions of US dollars annually to address, are now calling for another reform of the GFA. Developed countries in the Global North are expected to increase their financial assistance to the Global South and the IFIs are encouraged to play a more critical role in funding the needs of developing countries.

Several questions emerge. What type of GFA reform are needed? What specific changes in the operations of the IFIs are needed, particularly the IMF and the World Bank? What is the incentive for the Global North to bear (at least partially) costs for the Global South?

This chapter is organised as follows: first section reviews past episodes of GFA reform and suggests how the reform agenda today is different from past ones. Section two explains the context of GFA debates, identifies the financing needs of developing countries to achieve the SDGs, including poverty elimination, inequality reduction, and climate goals, and summarises the actual financial flows to developing countries, including by the IMF and MDBs. Section three presents several GFA reform proposals, including the Bridgetown Initiative, the UN, and the G20 process. The last section offers assessments of these proposals, explains GFA reform incentives for the Global North, and concludes the chapter.

I. Past Episodes of GFA Reform

Past GFA reform debates were driven by a series of currency, banking, and debt crises in developing and emerging countries as well as the global financial crisis that originated in the United States. The scope of reforms focused on crisis management – how a country can effectively prevent, respond to, and resolve financial crisis – including the IMF's economic and financial surveillance, international liquidity support and conditionality, new lending facilities as well as international standards and codes and resolution of sovereign debt.

Latin American and African external debt crises in the 1980s

Many countries in Latin America and Africa accumulated external debt in the 1970s and experienced severe debt crises in the 1980s. Debt had accumulated because these countries ran large current account deficits due to governments' overspending for development purposes, which was financed by developed-country financial firms' syndicated loans to recycle abundant petrodollars. The steep increase in interest rates in the United States to combat inflation in the early

1980s, triggered debt crises in many countries of Latin America and Africa, which fell into sovereign defaults.

In response to the debt crises, the IMF and the World Bank often introduced adjustment policies aimed at stabilisation, liberalisation, and privatisation – known collectively as the "Washington Consensus"[2] – on developing countries as conditionality for debt relief and financial support.[3] Thus, developing countries in Africa and Latin America had to undertake drastic adjustment and austerity measures for fiscal consolidation, cutting social expenditure and public investment, which partly contributed to a prolonged recession and a lost decade of development in those regions.

The call for reform of the GFA, then dominated by the "Washington Consensus," came from the United Nations system.[4] The United Nations Children's Fund (UNICEF) expressed concerns about the social impact – especially the impact on children – of the Structural Adjustment Programmes led by the IMF and the World Bank, and argued for an alternative approach – called "adjustment with a human face" – to protect vulnerable groups in society and restore economic growth. This call had a profound impact on how international financial institutions should view the adjustment process. Both the IMF and the World Bank began to pay attention to the protection of human conditions, such as those of health, nutrition, and education, of the most vulnerable groups in their adjustment programmes. Thus, a newly emerging view was that while developing countries in serious fiscal and external imbalances would need economic adjustment to put the economy back on a sustained path of growth and development, they should avoid a "one-size-fits-all" approach of cutting back on social service expenditures in achieving fiscal balance.

There was also an important development in external debt resolution. In the initial phase of debt crises in the 1980s, governments in the developed countries promoted debt rescheduling at the Paris Club and applied Structural Adjustment Programmes of the IMF and the World Bank. As they were not successful in containing the crises, the US government pushed for the Brady Plan to cooperate with commercial bank creditors in restructuring and reducing the debt of those developing countries that were pursuing structural adjustments under the IMF and World Bank programmes. While the plan had some success for the participating countries, the developed countries introduced the Highly Indebted Poor Countries (HIPC) Initiative in 1996 and the Multilateral Debt Relief Initiative (MDRI) in 2005 in order to reduce the external debt of the poorest countries. The IFIs and bilateral and commercial creditors agreed to debt reduction to ensure that the HIPCs can restore debt sustainability. Through these two initiatives, 37 low-income countries (31 of which are sub-Saharan) received a total of $100 billion in public debt relief.[5]

Asian financial crisis in 1997-98

The next crisis that intensified discussions on GFA reform was the 1997-98 Asian financial crisis. The crisis not only devastated the crisis-hit Asian economies but also affected Russia, Brazil and even advanced economies, including the major US hedge fund, Long-Term Capital Management (LTCM). As the crisis originated from financial crises in emerging economies, the emphasis of reform was placed on strengthening macro-economic policies and financial systems in these economies. Key issues included the choice of appropriate exchange rate regimes, the liberalisation of international capital flows, and the development of financial markets in emerging economies. Issues also included reforms of IMF crisis management policies as some policy responses prescribed by the IMF, such as its programmes' optimistic growth projections, contractionary macro-economic (particularly fiscal) policy responses, and the wide nature of structural conditionality, were not appropriate in addressing the Asian financial crisis. Later, the IMF admitted these problems and decided to change the formulation of policy conditionality for financial assistance, prescribing more flexible macro-economic policy in response to the countries' specific economic conditions and focusing on only those structural issues considered critical from a macro-economic perspective.[6]

At the global level, the G7 countries led the initiatives of introducing several international fora, standards and codes, and policy instruments to promote international cooperation for the stability and growth of the global economy and finance. They established the G20 Finance Ministers' and Central Bank Governors' Meeting for international policy cooperation, with the participation of both advanced and emerging economies. They also created the Financial Stability Forum (FSF) to help stabilise the domestic financial systems of important countries and international financial markets through surveillance and supervision. They introduced international standards and codes, focusing on macro-economic policy transparency, financial sector regulation and supervision, and financial market integrity. The IMF and the World Bank introduced the Financial Sector Assessment Program (FSAP) to monitor and assess the financial systems of member countries. The IMF also introduced a new Contingent Credit Line (CCL) for crisis prevention purposes.

Global financial crisis in 2007-09

The third debate on GFA reform was triggered by the 2007-09 global financial crisis, caused by the subprime crisis originating in the United States, the centre of the world economy and finance. The subprime crisis culminated in the Lehman Shock, which not only severely damaged the US financial system but also greatly destabilised the global economy and finance by prompting rapid capital outflows from the rest of the world into the United States and creating global liquidity shortages. Several emerging economies, especially those in Eastern Europe and the Baltic region, encountered financial crises due to massive capital outflows. To respond to the impacts of the global financial crisis, the G20 Finance Ministers' and Central Bank Governors' Meeting was upgraded to the meeting of Heads of State (G20 Summit) so that the leaders of both major developed and developing countries can jointly decide policies for early, sustained economic recovery.[7]

As the crisis originated from the United States, the emphasis of GFA reform was placed on strengthening financial regulation and supervision mainly in developed countries. In particular, the international community strengthened regulations of the financial system, including through the Basel III framework for the banking sector. The FSF was reorganised as the Financial Stability Board (FSB) to include the views of more emerging economies. The IMF and the World Bank put pressure on the United States, which had not been covered by FSAP, to undergo an FSAP review every five years. As IMF surveillance failed to contribute to the early detection and warning of the global financial crisis, GFA reform also focused on improving IMF surveillance by expanding its coverage of surveillance to include the health and vulnerability of financial markets and macro-financial linkages.

To support developing countries, the IMF quota was doubled and its financial base was strengthened. The IMF implemented a general allocation of Special Drawing Rights (SDRs) equivalent to about $250 billion in 2009 to supplement its member countries' foreign exchange reserves. The World Bank and the regional MDBs also saw general capital increases to boost financial support for developing countries.[8] Indeed, the World Bank's loan disbursements increased dramatically from $17 billion in 2007 to $30 billion in 2009 and $34 billion in 2010, the largest annual amount ever committed and significantly exceeding the less than $20 billion it provided during the Asian financial crisis (World Bank, International Debt Statistics). The IMF introduced new Flexible Credit Lines (FCL) and Precautionary Credit Lines (PCL) to replace the CCL (which had expired in 2003).[9]

II. Context of the Current Debate on GFA Reform

The key context of the current debate on GFA reform is the need for scaling up external financing to support developing countries in recovering from the COVID-19 pandemic and the hikes in food, energy, and fertilizer prices and in achieving SDGs and climate goals (i.e., nationally determined contributions pledged under the Paris Agreement).

Impact of COVID-19, Russia-Ukraine war, and debt distress

The global economy has been severely affected by the global spread of COVID-19 since 2020. Although the world economy has been supported by large-scale monetary and fiscal policy responses by major developed countries and regions, the health, economic, and poverty impact on developing countries has been substantial. Developing countries with high external debts have faced difficulties in debt repayment. Russia's military invasion of Ukraine, which escalated food and energy crises and have triggered record-high inflation and tighter financial conditions exacerbated difficulties in developing countries. Overall, the socio-economic consequences of the pandemic and war have been more serious than the impact of the global financial crisis.

As vulnerable developing countries began to face difficulties in repaying public external debts due to the pandemic, the G20 process has adopted relief measures to address vulnerable countries' debt problems, starting with the Debt Service Suspension Initiative (DSSI) during April 2020 – December 2021, and moving to the "Common Framework for Debt Treatments beyond the DSSI" from 2022. After the pandemic hit, the IMF approved $306 billion in financing for 96 countries, including below-market rate loans to 57 low-income countries. It also increased interest-free lending four-fold to $24 billion and provided $964 million in grants to 31 of the most vulnerable members between April 2020 and 2022, so they could service their debts. In addition, the IMF operationalised the new Resilience and Sustainability Trust (RST) in October 2022, to help low-income and vulnerable middle-income countries in building resilience to external challenges, such as for climate change and pandemic preparedness. In 2021, the IMF allocated $650 billion in SDRs to all member countries to support vulnerable developing countries affected by the pandemic. G20 leaders have pledged to sub-lease up to $100 billion of their own SDRs to support vulnerable countries to significantly increase the effectiveness of SDR allocations, and by February 2023, $87 billion (and $1.4 billion in grants) had been pledged.[10]

The SDGs, climate goals, and financing needs for developing countries

All UN member states adopted the 2030 Agenda for Sustainable Development in 2015, which provided a shared blueprint for peace, prosperity, and partnership for people and the planet. The 2030 agenda explicitly shows 17 Sustainable Development Goals (SDGs), which call for action by both developed and developing countries in a cooperative way.[11] These include poverty eradication, improvements in health, sanitation, education, and the environment, and economic growth. In addition, each country participating in the Paris Agreement has made self-defined national climate action pledges, called nationally determined contributions (NDCs), in helping meet the global goal of pursuing 1.5°C. NDCs include efforts by each country to reduce national GHG emissions, adapt to climate impacts, and ensure sufficient financing to support these efforts. Achieving the SDGs and taking climate action require financing, which may be excessively high for many developing countries. Developed countries have made climate finance commitments of mobilising jointly $100 billion per year until 2025 to address the needs of developing countries in the context of meaningful mitigation actions and transparency on implementation, which unfortunately, has not been met.[12]

Significant investment is needed for achieving the SDGs. The cost estimates would have to consider various types of investment requirements, such as those for eradicating extreme poverty (SDG 1.1); implementing nationally appropriate social protection systems and measures for all (SDG 1.3); achieving universal health coverage (SDG 3.8); ensuring that all girls and boys complete free, equitable and quality primary and secondary education (SDG 4.1); achieving a 7 per cent annual GDP growth for least developed countries (LDCs) (SDG 8.1); promoting inclusive and sustainable industrialisation – a major form of structural transformation – as reflected in the target of doubling the share of industry (manufacturing) in GDP in LDCs (SDG 9.2); and ensuring the conservation, restoration and sustainable use of terrestrial and inland freshwater ecosystems and their services (SDG 15.1). Thus, developing countries have to invest significantly to eradicate poverty, reduce inequality, and improve other socio-economic conditions of their people, embedded in the SDGs, while at the same time contribute to global public goods (GPGs).[13]

Expecting the launch of the 2030 Agenda, the UNCTAD initially estimated that $5 trillion to $7 trillion per year would be needed between 2015 and 2030 to achieve a set of SDGs globally. Out of this, developing countries would need to spend $3.3 trillion to $4.5 trillion per year, mainly for basic infrastructure, food security, climate change mitigation and adaptation, health, and education.[14] Given the level of both public and private investment in SDG-related sectors at the time, developing countries faced an average annual funding gap of $2.5 trillion. The most recent UNCTAD estimates show that, as the COVID-19 pandemic has increased the funding gap for achieving the SDGs by an additional $2 trillion per year, developing countries now face a $4 trillion annual SDG investment gap.[15]

Financing flows to developing countries

These financing requirements are significantly large given the current financial flows to developing countries. For example, Figure 1 depicts annual disbursements on long-term external debt flows (loans, including disbursements by the IMF) that developing countries have received from the rest of the world during 2000-21, based on World Bank data.[16] Figure 1A shows that long-term debt flows to developing countries as a whole (low- and middle-income countries, including China) have been expanding as a trend for more than a decade since 2000, although there were temporary declines in 2009 and 2015. Despite the COVID-19 pandemic, the value of debt flows to developing countries was at a historical high of $1.2 trillion in 2019-21. However, the upper-middle income countries have received the largest debt flows, followed by lower-middle income countries. Low-income countries have received the least amount, recording only $23 billion in 2021, followed by least developed countries with $64 billion in the same year. Figure 1B shows that both public and publicly guaranteed (PPG) and private non-guaranteed (PNG) debt flows have risen over time, but the private flows have expanded the most. The share of PPG flows for low- and middle-income countries in total flows has declined as a trend from 60 per cent in 2000 to 40 per cent in 2021. Though not shown here, this share is much higher for LDCs, recording 65 per cent in 2021, suggesting that the role of public creditors such as bilateral donors and MDBs is much more important for these poorer countries.

1A. Long-term debt flows by income group

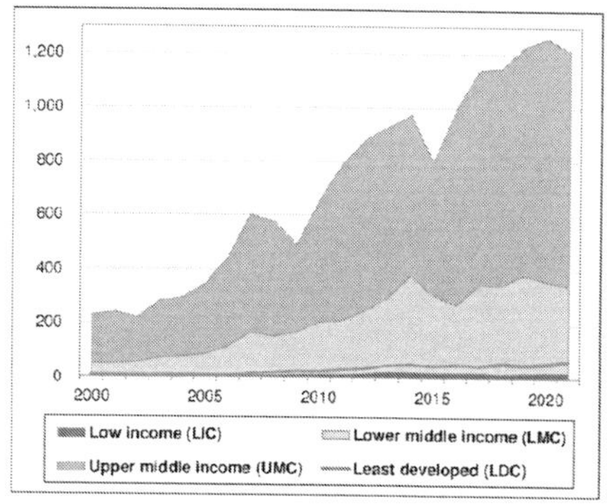

1B. Long-term debt flows by type

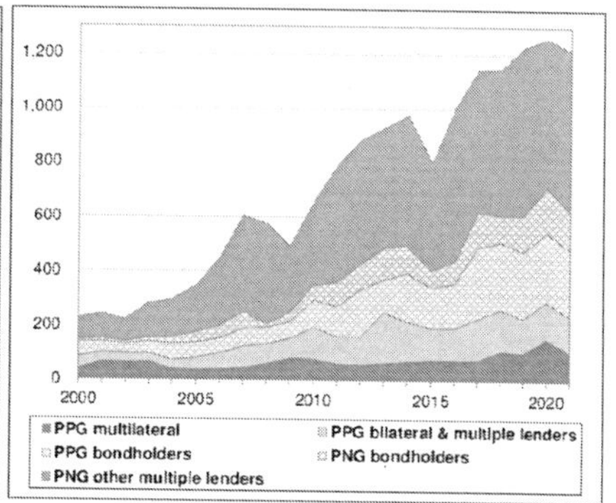

Figure 1: Disbursements on long-term external debt to developing countries (US$ Billion)

PNG = Private non-guaranteed; PPG = Public and publicly guaranteed.

Note: Long-term debt flows to developing countries from the world refer to disbursements on external debt, long-term (DIS, current US$), including disbursements by the IMF. In Figure 1B, PPG multilateral includes IMF disbursements.

Source: Compiled by author from World Bank, International Debt Statistics at https://databank.worldbank.org/source/international-debt-statistics# 08 June 2023

Figure 2 demonstrates resource flows to developing countries from Development Assistance Committee (DAC) member countries and multilateral development institutions. Figure 2A shows that total net flows from DAC countries to developing countries and multilateral institutions were on an upward trend between 2007-08 and 2013-14 and exhibited a downward trend from 2015-16 until 2020, although they recovered to $442 billion (at 2020 constant prices) in 2021, which was still below the peak level recorded in 2013-14. This fluctuation is largely due to private flows in market terms (direct investment plus bilateral and multilateral portfolio investment) as ODA flows (bilateral ODA and contributions to multilateral institutions) kept rising as a trend during the period covered. Bilateral ODA flows were $129 billion in 2021.

Figure 2B shows that multilateral development institutions' financing commitments to developing countries have risen as a trend since 2005 and 2020, reaching $230 billion in 2020. The World Bank Group and other MDBs accounted for 75-76 per cent ($127 billion and $175 billion) of the total multilateral commitments in 2019-2020 and 79 per cent of the total increase of $62 billion from 2019 to 2020. This demonstrates that the multilateral development system, strongly supported by the MDBs, has played a crucial role in the response to the COVID-19 crisis.

2A. Total net flows from DAC countries to developing countries and multilateral institutions, by type of flow

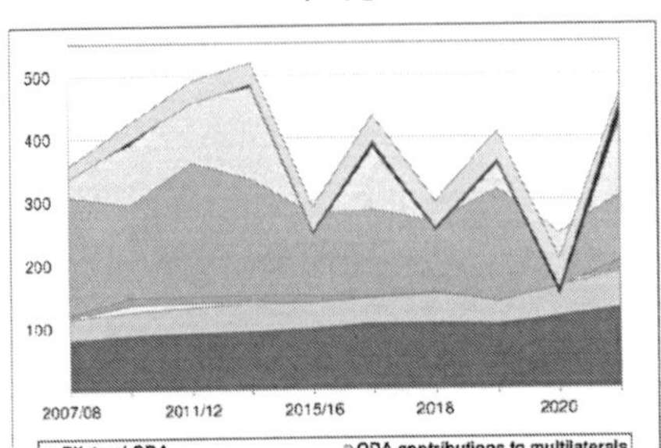

2B. Financing commitments made by multilateral development institutions

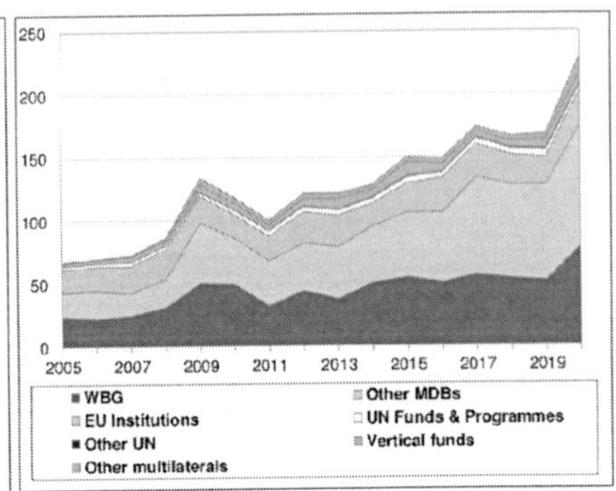

Figure 2: Resource flows to developing countries (US$ Billion at 2020 constant prices)

DAC = Development Assistance Committee; EU = European Union; MDBs = multilateral development banks; NGOs = non-governmental organisations; ODA = Official development assistance; UN = United Nations; WBG = World Bank Group

Note: ODA consists of bilateral ODA and contributions to multilateral institutions. Other official flows include bilateral and multilateral flows. Private flows at market terms include direct investment, bilateral portfolio investment, and multilateral portfolio investment. Data on private flows are obtained from DAC members' reporting to the annual DAC Questionnaire on total official and private flows.

Source: 2A: OECD statistics on resource flows to developing countries. https://www.oecd.org/dac/financing-sustainable-development/development-finance-data/statisticsonresourceflowstodevelopingcountries.htm

2B: OECD,[17] calculations based on the OECD Creditor Reporting System. https://www.oecd.org/development/multilateral-development-finance-2022-9fea4cf2-en.htm (Accessed 15 June 2023).

Figure 3 presents disbursements on long-term external debt made by the MDBs and those made by the IMF, thus excluding grants. Figure 3A is for all developing countries (low- and middle-income countries) and Figure 3B is for LDCs where the role of WB-IDA is more significant. Both figures show that MDB loans have risen over time in value and reached their peak in 2020, as a response to the COVID-19 crisis. IMF loans also rose sharply in 2020, particularly for LDCs. The IMF provided a large amount of concessional financing (currently at zero interest rates) to low-income countries through the PRGT.

3A. Disbursements for low- and middle-income countries

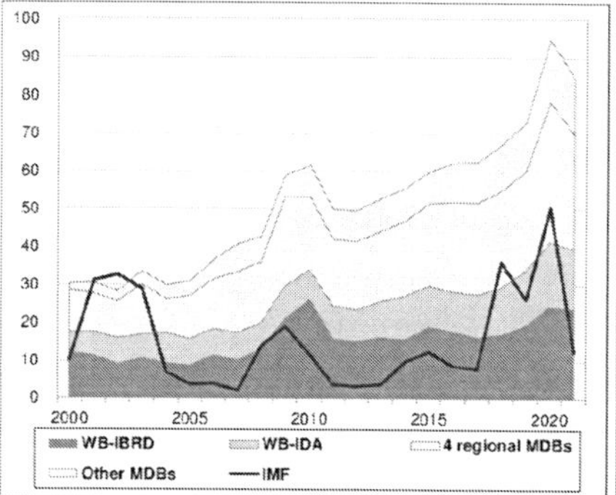

3B. Disbursements for least developed countries

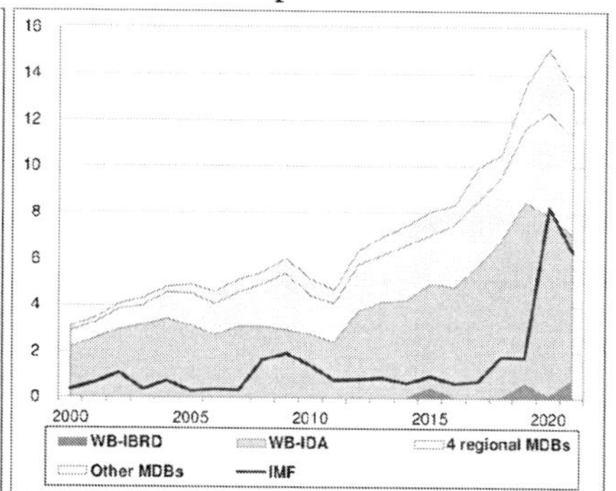

Figure 3: Disbursements by the IMF and MDBs (US$ Billion)

IMF = International Monetary Fund; MDBs = multilateral development banks; WB-IBRD = World Bank-International Bank for Reconstruction and Development; WB-IDA = World Bank-International Development Association

Note: Data are disbursements on external debt, long-term plus IMF. Four regional MDBs refer to the African Development Bank, Asian Development Bank, Inter-American Development Bank, and European Bank for Reconstruction and Development.

Source: Compiled by author from World Bank, International Debt Statistics. https://databank.worldbank.org/source/international-debt-statistics# (Accessed 17 June 2023).

III. GFA Reform Proposals to Scale up Financing Flows to Developing Countries

Until the 2010s, GFA reform was driven by the need to secure the stability of the international monetary and financial systems, given the frequent financial crises observed in various parts of the world. The reform debates today focus on the lack of adequate financing flows to developing countries willing to pursue the SDGs and climate action. This section takes up GFA reform proposals made by the Bridgetown Initiative, the UN, and the G20 process.

The Bridgetown Initiative

The Bridgetown Initiative is a one-page proposal, made by the Barbados government[18] that seeks to boost public and private financing for developing countries facing both development and climate, and transform the current GFA for this purpose. As a proposal offered by the Global South, the initiative has gained significant traction in the international community and affected debates on GFA reform. This initiative had three key proposals to: (i) provide emergency liquidity to stop the debt crisis; (ii) expand multilateral lending to governments by $1 trillion; and (iii) activate private sector savings for climate mitigation and fund reconstruction after a climate disaster through new multilateral mechanisms.

First, it suggested the IMF should: restore enhanced access limits established during the COVID pandemic for two emergency financial support instruments, the Rapid Credit Facility (RCF) and Rapid Financing Instruments (RFI); temporarily suspend its interest surcharges to reduce borrowing costs; re-channel at least $100 billion of unused SDRs that were allocated during the pandemic; and operationalise its new RST. It also called for an ambitious DSSI that includes all MDB loans to the poorest countries and COVID-related loans to middle-income countries, as well as the inclusion of natural disaster and pandemic clauses in debts to allow developing countries to spend for disaster relief in the event of a disaster. Second, the initiative called for the expansion of MDB lending by $1 trillion by using remaining headroom, increased risk appetite, new guarantees, and the holding of SDRs in a way to prioritise achieving the SDGs and building climate resilience. Third, it suggested the establishment of a global grant-making mechanism for any country's reconstruction needs after a climate disaster, and the issuance of additional $650 billion equivalent of SDRs or other low-interest, long-term financing to catalyse private investment in low carbon transition.

The Bridgetown Initiative was reshaped late in 2022 with five proposals, focusing on financing for climate mitigation, adaptation, and loss and damage.[19] The first proposal of the updated initiative clarified the idea behind the last part of the original one-pager. It suggested the establishment of a Climate Mitigation Trust which would borrow up to $5 trillion of private finance in the international capital markets supported by SDRs worth $500 billion, donor guarantees, or similar and invest borrowed funds in mitigation projects. The second proposal suggested the widening of access for climate-vulnerable countries to concessional loans, at lower interest rates and longer repayment schedules, to finance adaptation activities. The third proposal called for a $1 trillion increase in MDB lending for climate and SDGs, including both non-concessional and concessional finance, again suggesting donor guarantees and SDRs to back this funding. The fourth proposal put forward the idea of a tax on fossil fuels or an international carbon border tax to fund a $200 billion per year grant mechanism for loss and damage. The fifth proposal repeated the original disaster clause for lending, including MDB lending instruments. When an independently verified disaster hits, these clauses lead to an immediate and unconditional suspension of debt service for two years and an extension of the loan maturity by two years.

UN proposed reform to the GFA

UN Secretary General Antonio Guterres has been vocal in pressing for major reforms to the GFA.[20] He has called for major reforms that would scale up financing for economic development and tackling the impact of climate change, strengthen the representation of developing countries (through increases in voting powers and board members) at the IMF and the World Bank, help countries restructure debts, and revamp the use of IMF funds. The UN lays out a global SDG Stimulus Plan of at least $500 billion annually, to scale up long-term financing for countries through GFA reforms (UN 2023a). The Plan identifies three areas for immediate action: tackling the high cost of debt and rising risks of debt distress through conversion of short-term high interest debt into long-term debt at lower interest rates; scaling up long-term financing for development, especially through MDB capital increases, improved terms of their lending, and alignment of financing flows with the SDGs; and expanding contingency financing to countries in need through the integration of disaster and pandemic clauses into all sovereign lending and more automatic issuance of SDRs in times of crisis.

Based on these views, the UN proposes reforms to the GFA in five areas (UN 2023b): global economic governance; the global financial safety net; development banking; sovereign borrowing and debt sustainability; and financial system rules and regulations. These reform proposals are comprehensive and many of them are reasonable, although the developed countries in the Global North may hesitate in adopting some. In addition, more details would have to be provided for development banking, which is one of the focal points of the current debate on GFA reform.

Table 1: The UN's proposed reforms to the global financial architecture

Global economic governance	**Transform international financial institution governance** • Adopt double majority decision-making rules • Reform IMF quotas and voting rights to reflect the changing global landscape • Delink access to resources and allocation of SDRs from quotas (with access determined by income and vulnerabilities) • Improve transparency and leadership selection **Create a representative apex body for economic coordination** • Ensure coherence of all rules and frameworks with the SDGs
Global financial safety net	**Strengthen liquidity provision and widen the financial safety net** • Issue SDRs automatically in response to shocks (with allocations based on need) • Expand the overall size of IMF and make IMF lending more flexible, with fewer conditionalities and access limits and the removal of surcharges • Set up a multilateral currency swap facility • Strengthen regional financing arrangements

	Lower capital account volatility • Strengthen international macroeconomic policy coordination to reduce capital flow volatility (with developing countries using the full range of policy tools to soften the impacts of capital flows and with source countries actively reducing volatility)
Development banking	**Massively scale up multilateral development banks** • Increase the volume of development lending and improve terms of lending • Align MDB operations with SDGs • Ensure allocations be based on need and vulnerability **Scale up climate finance with additionality** **Leverage private finance more effectively** **Increase concessional finance to support the poorest for poverty eradication and sustainability**
Sovereign borrowing and debt sustainability	**Reduce debt risks and enhance sovereign debt markets to support SDGs** • Update principles of responsible borrowing and lending to incorporate SDGs • Improve debt management through enhanced capacity development and transparency • Improve debt sustainability analysis by incorporating climate risks and the impacts of investment in climate and SDGs • Improve debt contracts by including state-contingent clauses • Promote the greater use of debt swaps for SDGs and climate **Enhance the debt crisis resolution architecture** • Set up a debt workout mechanism to support the Common Framework (by expanding its eligibility to debt-vulnerable middle-income countries and set up a mechanism to accelerate its progress) • Establish a sovereign debt authority in the medium term
Financial system rules and regulations	**Strengthen financial regulation and supervision to promote stability with sustainability** • Improve regulation and supervision of banks and non-bank financial institutions, according to the principle of "same activity, same risk, same rules," to better manage risks and rein in excessive leverage • Address short-termism in markets through tax policies, long-term performance-based compensation, and the development of long-term indices and credit ratings **Make businesses more sustainable and reduce greenwashing** • Mandate company sustainability reporting and disclosure • Design policy and regulatory frameworks to align with SDGs and climate action

Note: The UN also proposes reform of international tax norms, but this is omitted in the table.
Source: Compiled by author from United Nations, "Reforms to the International Financial Architecture."[21]

Discussions at the G20 on GFA reform

The G20 member countries share the view that the IMF should continue to have an important role in crisis prevention and maintain a strong capacity to respond to financial crises for the sustained development of the global economy. The G20 statements repeatedly claim that there is a need to "maintain a strong and effective global financial safety net with a strong quota-based and adequately resourced IMF at its center." The G20 members are also "committed to revisiting the adequacy of quotas and continuing IMF governance reform under the 16th General Review of Quotas, including a new quota formula as a guide, by 15 December 2023."[22]

After the IMF's new general allocation of SDR, equivalent to $650 billion in 2021, the G20 statements have urged members with strong external positions to channel part of the allocated SDRs voluntarily to help vulnerable countries to significantly magnify the impact of the new allocation and set the global objective of mobilising voluntary contributions of $100 billion. The IMF also began the operationalisation of the Resilience and Sustainability Trust (RST) in October 2022. The G20 members also welcome voluntary contributions to the RST and call for additional pledges and timely contributions to the PRGT.

They also share the view that the MDBs have a critically important mission in promoting long-term development and SDGs in developing countries and should secure more resources to support these efforts in the poorest countries. The G20 countries urge MDBs to explore options for implementing the recommendations of the G20 Independent Review of MDBs' Capital Adequacy Frameworks, such as balance sheet optimisation measures and other avenues, so that they can maximise developmental impact.[23] They also emphasise the importance of safeguarding the MDBs' long-term financial sustainability, robust credit rating, and preferred creditor status. The G20 also commissioned an independent experts group to explore ways to strengthen MDBs. (see Box 1).

Box 1: G20 Independent Experts Group, "Strengthening MDBs: The Triple Agenda"

Volume I of the Report by the Independent Experts Group[24] (2023) for the G20 process provides the vision of the" triple agenda" and urges development institutions, particularly the MDBs, to identify the best ways to significantly boost non-concessional commitments and concessional contributions by 2030. The "triple agenda" refers to: (i) adopting a triple mandate of eliminating extreme poverty, boosting shared prosperity, and contributing to GPGs;[25] (ii) tripling sustainable lending levels by 2030; and (iii) creating a third funding mechanism to deploy concessional lending for global challenges.

The Report assumes that developing countries excluding China which have sufficient domestic resources to finance its transition, would need to spend an additional $3 trillion annually by 2030, to meet the SDGs and climate goals, of which $1.8 trillion represents additional investments in climate action (adaptation, resilience and mitigation), mostly in sustainable infrastructure, and $1.2 trillion in additional spending to attain other SDGs.[26] To finance the additional annual $3 trillion, developing countries need to secure $2 trillion domestically through additional domestic finance and $1 trillion externally through official and private channels. A half of external financing of the $1 trillion may come from official external financing and another half from private financing for sustainable development. Of the $500 billion additional official external financing, $320 billion would be in the form of non-concessional official lending and $180 billion in the form of concessional, non-debt-creating financing. The MDBs should provide an additional total of $260 billion, i.e., $200 billion in non-concessional lending and $60 billion in concessional financing.[27] Of the $500 billion incremental private financing,[28] $240 billion should be directly and indirectly mobilised by the MDBs and $260b should be partly catalysed by MDB supported policy reforms.

The Report thus emphasises the important role of the MDBs in both boosting its own additional financing capacity and mobilising and catalysing additional private financing and offers suggestions for doing so. To increase non-concessional lending, the report suggests: the improved efficiency of use of existing capital or optimising balance sheets, such as better accounting for callable capital, preferred creditor treatment, and shifting in the direction of an originate-and-distribute model of banking (as recommended by the G20 Capital Adequacy Framework report), which may expand lending by $40 billion per year by 2030; augmenting capital through non-traditional mechanisms, such as hybrid capital, including capital backed by recycled SDRs, and much greater use of portfolio and capital guarantees, which can boost lending by an additional $40 billion; initiating a process for a significant general capital increase across all MDBs; and establishing a new "Global Challenges Funding" mechanism, which can add lending capacity by $20 billion by

The Report also argues that the MDBs should strengthen their capacity to mobilise private capital from the current $0.6 for each dollar they lend on their own account to at least $1.2 and ideally to $1.5-2. It suggests that the MDBs should change their approach to active private capital mobilisation in three ways: placing the mobilisation and catalysation of private capital at the center of their sustainable development strategies; prioritising support for developing country governments to reduce policy and regulatory risk that impedes private investment; and aligning financial product offerings to private capital market gaps.

Source: Author's compilation from Independent Experts Group (2023).

The G20 members also underline the importance of sustainable finance and strengthen the alignment of all sources of financing with SDGs and a pathway towards low GHG emissions and climate-resilient development. They are committed to scaling up adaptation finance, while achieving a balance with the provision of finance for mitigation. They reaffirm the developed countries' goal of mobilising jointly $100 billion per year through 2025 to address the needs of developing countries in the context of climate mitigation action. The G20 members support the Financial Stability Board's work for addressing climate-related financial risks, on achieving globally consistent, comparable and reliable climate-related financial disclosures, and supervisory and regulatory approaches to climate-related risks.

V

Conclusion

In earlier years, GFA reform focused largely on financial crisis management—such as measures for crisis prevention, response, and resolution, including external debt resolution – and was led by the G7 countries in the Global North as the body managing global economy and finance. The current debate on reform in the GFA is led by the G20 countries, with significant inputs from the Global South (as observed in the case of the Bridgetown Initiative) and the UN system, focusing on how to mobilise a substantial amount of financing for developing countries to enable them to respond to the rise in poverty and inequality, achieve food and energy security, prepare for the risk of new pandemics and natural disasters, and address the crises of climate change and biodiversity loss. Essentially, GFA reform is needed to help developing countries achieve the SDGs and contribute to GPGs.

GFA reform today revolves around ways to improve the functions of the IMF and the MDBs, even though they successfully channeled a large share of the international resources to the COVID-19 crisis. As their ability to continue providing exceptional levels of financing is constrained by their current funding and operating models, they need to evolve to help address a growing list of development and global challenges, including the provision of GPGs. A review of the various reform proposals conducted in the previous section leads to the following set of recommendations for GFA reform:

- Develop a holistic vision for the multilateral development system to ensure it can meet new global development challenges;

- Enable the MDBs, particularly the World Bank, at the centre of this system, to play a critical role in scaling up non-concessional and concessional financing for investments in SDGs and GPGs through general capital increases, balance sheet optimisation, and re-channeling of SDRs and in mobilising private finance more effectively;
- Expand the financial resources of the IMF through quota increases and further voluntary contributions by members, particularly for the PRGT and the RST, make IMF lending more flexible, with the reduction of surcharges for LDCs, and consider new SDR allocations in the event of large shocks;
- Provide sufficient, sustainable, and predictable funding to the MDBs and the IMF and support the implementation of innovative approaches to expand their financial capacity;
- Improve coordination across the IFIs, other multilateral institutions, bilateral donors, and private investors to improve the coherence and complementarity of multilateral efforts;
- Transform the governance of the IFIs to make them more representative, equitable and inclusive in a way to safeguard their long-term financial sustainability.

It is natural that India's G20 Presidency emphasised on strengthening multilateral institutions and international cooperation and mobilising public and private financing to tackle the SDGs and global challenges. Agendas include advancing the MDBs' evolution to boost their non-concessional and concessional financing; mobilising private investment in quality, sustainable, and resilient infrastructure; and improving the sovereign debt restructuring process. India is positioned well to pursue GFA reform as the Global South continue to preside the G20 meetings between 2022 and 2025 (Indonesia in 2022, India in 2023, Brazil in 2024, and South Africa in 2025).

Developed countries in the Global North have the incentives to support developing countries in the Global South. First, they are willing to assist developing countries in financing GPG-promoting activities, such as climate mitigation, which also benefit them. After all, developing countries in the Global South not only suffer the most from the climate crisis but have also contributed the least to it. Second, given the geopolitical competition among the major powers, the Global North is willing to work with the Global South. The Global North benefits from the rules-based multilateral order and requires a large number of partners to maintain it. Cooperating with the Global South on GFA reform provides an excellent opportunity for the governments of the Global North to expand the space of like-minded partners willing to work with a rules-based multilateral order.

NOTES

1 United Nations. 2023, *United Nations Secretary-General's SDG Stimulus to Deliver Agenda 2030*. February 2023. https://www.un.org/sustainabledevelopment/wp-content/uploads/2023/02/SDG-Stimulus-to-Deliver-Agenda-2030.pdf

2 The "Washington Consensus" was put forward by three Washington, D.C.-based institutions, namely, the U.S. Department of Treasury, the IMF, and the World Bank and later embraced a broader set of policies underpinned by a strong belief in the role of unfettered markets and a reduced role for government. See J Williamson *Latin American Adjustment: How Much Has Happened?* Washington: Institute for International Economics, 1990, Also see J Williamson, "The Strange History of the Washington Consensus", *Journal of Post Keynesian Economics*, 27(2) (Winter, 2004-2005), pp. 195-206

3 The IMF created the Enhanced Structural Adjustment Facility (ESAF) to provide low-interest loans for developing countries in 1987.

4 United Nations. *World Economic and Social Survey 2017: Reflecting on Seventy Years of Development Policy Analysis*. Department of Economic and Social Affairs, E/2017/50/Rev.1 (2017), ST/ESA/365, United Nations Secretariat, New York. https://www.un.org/development/desa/dpad/wp-content/uploads/sites/45/publication/WESS_2017-FullReport.pdf

5 The IMF replaced the ESAF with the Poverty Reduction and Growth Trust (PRGT) in 1999 to provide concessional loans to low-income countries.

6 Kawai, Masahiro. "Reform of the International Financial Architecture: An Asian Perspective." *Singapore Economic Review*, 55(1) (March 2010), pp. 207-242.

7 The G20 was designated the "premier forum for international economic cooperation" in 2009.

8 The Asian Development Bank and the African Development Bank saw a 200% capital increase each in 2009 and 2010, respectively. The Inter-American Development Bank, the European Bank for Reconstruction and Development, and the International Bank for Reconstruction and Development saw 100, 69, and 31 per cent capital increases, respectively, in 2010.

9 The Precautionary Liquidity Line (PLL) later replaced the Precautionary Credit Line (PCL).

10 In 2022, the G20 countries commenced work on the restructuring (including debt reduction) of the vulnerable countries' public external debts under the Common Framework. Chad, Ethiopia, Ghana, and Zambia have participated in debt restructuring negotiations with bilateral and commercial creditors under the framework, with varying degrees of progress. Sri Lanka, which is not a DSSI-eligible country, also launched debt restructuring talks with bilateral creditors (led by France, India, and Japan), although China, the largest bilateral creditor country, has not joined talks as a full member.

11 The 17 goals are: no poverty; zero hunger; good health and well-being; quality education; gender equality; clean water and sanitation; affordable and clean energy; decent work and economic growth; industry, innovation and infrastructure; reduced in equalities; sustainable cities and communities; responsible consumption and production; climate action; life below

water; life on land; peace, justice and strong institutions; and partnerships for the goals. There are also 169 targets to be achieved.

12 As the $100 billion commitment will expire in 2015, negotiations on the New Collective Quantified Goal for climate finance are under way between developed and developing countries.

13 GPGs include climate change mitigation and adaptation, the preservation of biodiversity and the global water cycle, and pandemic preparedness and response. Investing in these GPGs goes together with addressing closely related transboundary challenges such as conflict and fragility, food security, cyber security, and energy security.

14 Dana Vorisek and Shu Yu. "Understanding the Cost of Achieving the Sustainable Development Goals." Policy Research Working Paper 9146 (February 2022), World Bank Group.

15 "More investment needed to get global goals back on track, says UNCTAD chief", 19 January 2023, https://unctad.org/news/more-investment-needed-get-global-goals-back-track-says-unctad-chief-0 (Accessed 15 January 2023).

16 World Bank data cover 123 developing countries in its *International Debt Statistics 2022*, leaving out data for 12 developing member countries of the Bank (such as Iraq, Libya, and Malaysia). Providers of external debt include both developed and developing countries (i.e., emerging donors such as India, China, and Russia) and recipients include China.

17 OECD. *Multilateral Development Finance 2022*, OECD Publishing, Paris. https://www.oecd.org/development/multilateral-development-finance-2022-9fea4cf2-en.htm

18 Barbados, Government of. 2022. *Bridgetown Initiative*. September. https://pmo.gov.bb/wp-content/uploads/2022/10/The-2022-Bridgetown-Initiative.pdf

19 Avinash Persaud. The Bridgetown Initiative, Explained, 15 November 2022. https://unclimatesummit.org/opinion-the-bridgetown-initiative/

20 He describes the response by the IMF and the World Bank to the COVID-19 pandemic as a "glaring failure" that left dozens of countries deeply indebted, and claims that the two institutions should correct the "bias and injustice built into the current international financial architecture." When the IMF allocated $650 billion of SDRs during the pandemic, the wealthy G7 countries, with a population of 772 million, received the equivalent of $280 billion while the LDCs, with a population of 1.1 billion, were allocated just over $8 billion. Guterres says this was done according to the rules, which were "morally wrong.", Edith M. Lederer, "UN steps up criticism of IMF and World Bank, the other pillars of the post-World War II global order", AP, 17 June 2023, https://apnews.com/article/un-imf-world-bank-covid-15baf3a9e4d939dd2e085ff0aa18087a

21 United Nations, "Reforms to the International Financial Architecture." *Our Common Agenda, Policy Brief* No. 6, May 2023. https://www.un.org/sites/un2.un.org/files/our-common-agenda-policy-brief-international-finance-architecture-en.pdf

22 See *G20 Rome Leaders' Declaration*, 30-31 October 2021 as well as the *G20 Bali Leaders' Declaration*, Bali, Indonesia, 15-16 November 2022. Developments that are more recent can be seen in the Third G20 Finance Ministers and Central Bank Governors Meeting, *G20 Outcome Document and Chair's Summary*, Gandhinagar/Gujarat, 17-18 July 2023

23 In 2021, the G20 commissioned an independent review of MDBs' capital adequacy frameworks. The main objective of the review was to enable shareholders to consider how MDBs can make the most effective and efficient use of their capital as they face the challenging combination of the pandemic and longer-term development needs. Given that MDBs may not flexibly provide counter-cyclical and large-scale financing at the time of global crisis due

to their cautious approaches to capital adequacy, the independent review suggested to: (i) redefine the approach to risk appetite for MDB capital adequacy frameworks; (ii) incorporate uplift from callable capital into MDB capital adequacy frameworks; (iii) implement innovations to strengthen MDB capital adequacy and lending headroom; (iv) work with credit rating agencies to improve their assessment of MDB financial strength; and (v) improve the enabling environment for capital adequacy governance. If implemented, such measures could substantially expand MDB lending Boosting MDBs' Investing Capacity. *2022. An Independent Review of Multilateral Development Banks' Capital Adequacy Frameworks.* https://www.dt.mef.gov.it/export/sites/sitodt/modules/documenti_it/news/news/CAF-Review-Report.pdf

24 Independent Experts Group. *Strengthening Multilateral Development Banks: The Triple Agenda.* Report of the G20 Independent Experts Group (July 2023). https://www.cgdev.org/sites/default/files/The_Triple_Agenda_G20-IEG_Report_Volume1_2023.pdf

25 The WBG adopted the twin mandates of ending extreme poverty and boosting shared prosperity in 2013 and is now urged to adopt the provision of GPGs as its third mandate.

26 These figures are expressed in constant 2019 US$ equivalents, and "additional" is defined as a comparison with pre-COVID-19 (or 2019) levels.

27 The MDBs need to triple non-concessional lending from $100 billion (in 2019) to $300 billion and concessional grants and loans from $30 billion (in 2019) to $90 billion by 2030.

28 Private financing should rise from $240 billion (in 2019) to $740 billion (in 2030).

CHAPTER 6

Crisis of Bretton Woods 2 and Global Financial Institutions

Stanislav L. Tkachenko

Introduction

In 2023, the military conflict in Ukraine reached the highest point in modern world politics as was the case with the confrontation between the two nuclear superpowers (Russia and the US). Nowadays, it threatens to lead to a catastrophe of a much larger dimension. It began in its current stage in the spring of 2014, when the first weapons thundered in eastern Ukraine. According to Moscow, this conflict is a proxy war waged against Russia by the United States and its allies.[1] At the same time, the trend towards the deterioration of US-Russia relations, which are at the centre of this conflict, first manifested itself in the fall of 2004. Then the Administration of President George W. Bush supported a peaceful coup-d'etat in Ukraine via funds and diplomatic support for the colour revolution in that country.

For the Russian Federation, the current war in Ukraine is an existential threat. Its sustenance requires the use of practically all material, financial and human resources available to the government. In a conflict of this kind, which the famous Marxist historian of the last century Eric Hobsbawm called a 'total war',[2] the goal of the warring parties is to defeat the enemy, or at least undermine his power for a sufficiently long period. Inheriting the perception of Russia as a threat from the Cold War period, Washington has now returned to contain Moscow on the international stage, both through interference in its internal affairs and the use of military force along the borders of Russia.

The key elements of US State power are:

(a) An advanced national economy based on a highly developed technological platform, which is sufficient to create and use the latest weapons;

(b) Nuclear weapons' arsenals and the largest navy at present, allowing Washington to project its power to any region of the world more effectively than any other competitor in the international arena;

(c) The US dollar as the key global currency, cementing the world economy and allowing Washington to spend funds on a scale exceeding the capabilities of its GDP for the purposes of its foreign and defence policy.

The Russian Federation is deprived of the opportunity to seriously undermine the security of the United States. At the current stage of the conflict, its goal is more modest – to limit Washington's opportunity to use human and industrial resources of other States for its own interests by 'purchasing' their loyalty through US financial resources of its federal budget. The Kremlin seeks to turn the conflict into a confrontation in a theatre far from the coast of the United States, where Moscow has every advantage to project its military power and ensure security by preventing hostile NATO member states from establishing military bases on its borders.

The existential nature of the conflict between Russia and the West requires Moscow's careful handling of all these elements of State power of the US and its allies. Russia today is facing the need to confront indirect US aggression in the form of a proxy war in Ukraine. The first two elements of US and NATO power – the latest technologies and a powerful US Navy – are used in the framework of the ongoing military conflict in Ukraine. As for the 'dollar weapon', the United States has been actively using it against Russia. Washington seeks to destroy the Russian economy, cause a social upheaval and achieve a change of political power in the country to a regime loyal to the West.

This study is devoted to the monetary and financial aspect of the conflict between Russia and the West. Among expert in the NATO countries, the opinion that Russia is extremely weak in the monetary and financial sphere has been firmly established. Therefore, Washington can afford to be firm against the Russian economy and society, since it is not troubled by Moscow's response to its economic aggression. The turbulent events of 2022-2023 demonstrated that the monetary balance of power between Moscow and Washington has altered to such an extent that the US' ability to use the dollar has decreased and no longer poses a fundamental threat to the Russian economy. On the contrary, the Kremlin's efforts to protect national industry, agriculture and financial markets, together with its efforts to de-dollarize the global monetary system, have already brought Russia and the world, the first positive results.

Current attempts of the United States and other powers to use 'dollar weapons' against Russia are irrational. They do not lead to immediate tangible results for a military operation in Ukraine and do not guarantee their achievement in the future. Instead of relying on negotiations and the interests of other States, the United States has relied on indirect military confrontation with Russia, and in its course, Washington is trying to isolate Russia financially and economically from its most valuable international partners. This foreign policy course originated from the notion that US strategy is based on universal values, and not on egoistic national interests. Therefore, in addition to bipartisan support at the US Congress, Washington seeks to enlist the help of a wide range of States, including from countries of the Global South. Its main goal is to stop the erosion of the unipolar world, using the example of containing Russia to show all the States what price they will have to pay for leaving the US-centred system of the global political economy.

Emerging Economic Crisis of the West: Russia's Perspective

The financial and economic warfare, being waged by the US against Russia, is unique due to three crises threatening the world economy at once.

(a) *The banking crisis,* which has already affected large banks of the US and Switzerland, such as the Silicon Valley Bank, First Republic Bank, Signature Bank, Silvergate Bank and Credit Suisse. Crises of this type develop rapidly, within a few days, destroying banking and financial institutions, which are the supporting elements of the world's largest economies. Within just five days in March 2023, three major US banks went bankrupt at once, prompting a sharp decline in global bank share prices and a swift response from US regulators to bail out those banks.

(b) *Economic and debt crisis.* This crisis has actually been ongoing for several years. It originated from a sharp and large-scale economic decline in the States of all regions caused by the COVID-19 pandemic (spring 2020) and the subsequent energy crisis (2021-2022). This type of economic turmoil does not occur overnight, it is the result of both "external shocks" (COVID-19) and erroneous decisions of the US and EU monetary authorities to ease monetary policy, and then turn around their course via a rapid increase in key interest rates of central banks since spring 2022.

(c) *The crisis of the multilateral model of organisation and management of the global political and economic system,* which the experts of the Russian

Valdai Club, characterise with the metaphor of 'crumbling world'.[3] This model, built by the United States after the end of the Second World War, reached fruition in the 1990s. In response to the recognition of its hegemony, Washington provided client States in Western Europe and elsewhere with several public goods: the dollar as a key currency, the provision of emergency assistance in case of economic crises, a liberal trading system, and the ability to save budgetary funds on military spending after getting American security guarantees. The behaviour of the United States after 11 September 2001 and the global financial crisis of 2008 showed that Washington has ceased to be an 'honest broker', it provides common goods on a smaller scale, and pursues a policy that is unilaterally beneficial to US national interests.

Each of these crises, considered separately, do not pose an immediate fatal threat to the modern world economy and its actors – sovereign States. In earlier periods of world history, States in different regions have already faced banking panic, economic crises and solved problems of adapting management systems at the national or international level, due to changing external environment. Therefore, the international community, including States and private business institutions, have experience in countering certain types of crises. But, in the event that all three crises develop simultaneously, they can become a "perfect storm", which may cause a cumulative effect that is destructive.

During the previous global economic crisis in 2008-09, the G20 played a key role in mitigating its negative consequences, primarily through cooperation between the US, the EU, India, China and Russia. Nowadays, such cooperation seems almost impossible, primarily due to aggressive US foreign policy. In 15 years since the previous crisis of 2008, Washington has sought to extract unilateral economic benefits on account of its hegemony. Now, the threat of a global financial and economic crisis has reappeared, which will engulf the key players of the global economy – the United States and Europe. There is every reason to doubt that again, as in autumn 2008, the leaders of the 20 largest economies met and agreed on joint action. This means that the response to the crisis will be worked out taking into account the realities of deglobalisation. Possibly, the international community's response will be less effective than it was in 2008-2009.

As a possible scenario of an approaching global crisis, little that is familiar to us since the end of the 20th century will remain of the global economy. It will break up into regional blocs, connected not by the intergovernmental agreements formalised within the framework of the IMF, WTO and a number of integration unions in Europe, Eurasia, Middle East and Africa, but by informal trade, economic and investment ties between private businesses with the tacit consent and implicit support of government structures. The Russian authorities consider this scenario as the most likely, and in practice in the international arena, they are trying to protect the national economies from threats, associated with collapse of intergovernmental agreements.

Why Bretton Woods-3? Political Economy of International Monetary Affairs in Transition

The international monetary system led by the US dollar has a history of almost eight decades. The US economy transformed into the largest in the world in the 1870s.[4] However, the dollar received the status of the dominant international currency only after the Second World War, because of the establishment of the Bretton Woods system and the implementation of the Marshall Plan to restore the destroyed economies of Western and Southern Europe.

The Bretton Woods system arose at the final stage of the Second World War (1944) as a result of negotiations between 44 States, led by the United States and Britain. Its purpose was to prevent future fatal mistakes in the management of international trade and finance, like those made by the US and Western Europe in the 1930s, which paved the way for the Great Depression and the most destructive war in human history. The two key Bretton Woods institutions were the International Monetary Fund (mission – currency stability and convertibility) and the World Bank (assistance in the reconstruction of war-torn States, as well as assistance to countries embarking on the path of decolonisation).

The history of the Bretton Woods System can be split into two stages. The first period (Bretton Woods-1, 1945 – early 1970s) was characterised by a rigid fixing of the price of gold in US dollars and fixed (but open to change in an emergency) US dollar exchange rates for other currencies. This period also coincides with the most acute phase of the Cold War and a period of unprecedented rates of economic growth throughout the world.

The second period (from the beginning of the 1970s to the present), which is known as 'Bretton Woods-2', characterised by the US refusal to convert dollars for gold at the official rate and the introduction of a free float regime, in which the exchange rates of all national currencies were determined by the market. In 1973, through the efforts of then US Secretary of State Henry Kissinger,

Washington concluded a secret deal with Saudi Arabia, according to which, oil was priced and traded only in dollars, which governments and private companies had to buy from the United States in order to pay to OPEC countries. In response, Washington agreed to the placement of these 'petrodollars' in American banks in unlimited volumes and their free investment in the US economy. Washington provided its security guarantees to the oil-producing States of the Persian Gulf (deployment of large military bases in the region). Thus, oil replaced gold as a key assurance to emission of US dollars; it guaranteed a stable and ever increasing demand for US currency as the world economy grew.

Bretton Woods-1 lasted a quarter of a century, and Bretton Woods-2 – twice as long. The stability of the petrodollars system and a regime of free floating of currencies was ensured by the success of Ronald Reagan's reforms in the 1980s and financial globalisation of the 1990s. The latter increased the demand for US dollars even further. It played a remarkable role in the triumphant end of the Cold War for the United States. This led to the 'unipolar moment', for a short period when all Washington's opponents in the international arena disappeared. However, the decline in the competitiveness of the US economy, the rapid growth of the Asian States, the difficulties in the war on international terrorism, as well as the growing confrontation with China and Russia, made the inevitable dismantling of Bretton Woods-2 extremely popular.[5]

This issue has been discussed intensively during periods of turmoil in world markets. Thus, in October 2008, in the midst of the previous global financial crisis, French President Nicolas Sarkozy called for the dissolution of the Bretton Woods-2 institutions and the creation of something new and more effective instead. However, after the crisis was over, that call, like many others, was forgotten. Today, we are witnessing another wave of interest in reforming Bretton Woods-2, and perhaps this time it will be possible to move from words to deeds.

Three approaches that dominate the modern discussion about reforming Bretton Woods 2 are detailed below.

Technocratic approach

The supporters of the technocratic approach, representing the UN and its international financial institutions (IFIs), believe in the preservation of the current system. They argue for correcting only the form and activities of IFIs and adapting their system of management to modern realities. They recognise the situation as abnormal when the US and China, which are nearly equal in their economic prowess, have different rights when making decisions in IMF: 16 per cent for the

US versus 6 per cent for China. Technocrats also call for an increase of the role of developing economies in the structures of Bretton Woods-2.

Liberal approach

During the period when Christine Lagarde held the post of Managing Director of the IMF (2011-2019), an attempt was made to introduce a liberal agenda into the activities of the Bretton Woods institutions. During that period, gender equality, sustainable development, the fight against climate change and socio-economic inequality were recognised as new priorities in the IMF's and World Bank's agenda. It is believed that the Liberal approach is replacing the Washington Consensus policy, which has caused sharp criticism,[6] with the even more liberal policy of the Wall Street Consensus,[7] which implies an increased role of private finance and the market instruments they use in providing assistance to developing countries.

Neo-Marxist approach

Supporters of this approach sharply criticise original and modernised versions of the Bretton Woods System for their adherence to the ultra-liberal 'Washington Consensus' and the practice of 'conditionality', i.e., putting forward political conditions when providing financial resources to the countries of the Global South. They call on the IMF and the World Bank to return to Keynesian economics on a global scale; to redistribute the incomes of the countries of the North in favour of working people and the poorest citizens of developing countries. Among the proposed practical recommendations, the following are highlighted: 1) transformation of the IMF into a full-fledged World Central Bank, that issues a global currency and ensures its stable exchange rate against national currencies; 2) revamping of the World Bank into a fund that will withdraw excess profits from the richest countries (the US, Japan, Germany, the Persian Gulf countries) and redistribute them among the countries of the Global South to achieve development goals; 3) establishment of a fundamentally new International Trade Organisation to replace the WTO, which will not follow the lead of developed countries, helping them protect their domestic markets with non-protectionist policies, and in practice achieve the opening of the markets of the Global North States to goods from the poorest countries.

How Bretton Woods-3 may look like?

Over time, Russia and other BRICS member-states as an international forum with claims to certain functions of an intergovernmental organisation are increasingly inclined towards establishing an international monetary regime, Bretton Woods-3. For more than a decade, the BRICS community have been growing in number (from four to five States) and in key socio-economic indicators. Their leaders have expressed willingness to accept in future the largest economies of Latin America, the Middle East, Southeast Asia and the CIS into their ranks. The BRICS is interested not in the destruction of the current US-led system, but in the construction in parallel with it, a system of institutions with new functions. The system should be BRICS-centred; it has to be closed for United States and its allies from among the G7/NATO member countries. To date, an analogue of the IMF (the Pool of Conditional Foreign Exchange Reserves) has already been established. BRICS members have formed an extensive network of development assistance financial institutions (the New Development Bank, the Asian Infrastructure Investment Bank, and the Eurasian Development Bank) as well.

Our 'crumbling world' is in dire need of a minimum degree of stability in this transitional period of its history. Therefore, the reproduction by the BRICS countries, as a new pole of the political and economic architecture of the planet, of individual elements of the Bretton Woods System, which proved to be quite good during the Cold War, is both a reasonable step and long overdue.

We should note that it is always easier to create a new system from scratch than to repair an existing one. The Bretton Woods system is almost 80 years old, and has enjoyed a glorious period of its history. That is why there are a few politicians in the world who can take the initiative to destroy the contemporary Bretton Woods institutions and build a new one atop its ruins. We also know from the history of the 20th century that it is easier to create a system that unites only allies rather than a global system, in which it is necessary to find a balance of interests among all parties. Therefore, the idea of uniting the United States, China and Russia within the framework of an innovative Bretton Woods-3 global financial and development management system looks to be a utopian idea for Washington, but not for Moscow.

In 1944, the Bretton Woods System was created by two States (the United States and Britain), who at that time had the authority and resources to impose their will on four dozen States that were guided by them during the Second World War. Today, there is no State or group of States capable of imposing its will on the entire world community. A new or radically reformed Bretton Woods, of course, should take into account the opinion of all States, regardless of their size. The solution of such a problem through negotiations will last for many years, while the likelihood of success will be minimal.

Turn-of-the-century globalisation has undermined the economic and political power of national governments, without simultaneously creating effective structures of international cooperation and supranational management. Any group of States (developed and developing) must be able to withstand turmoil in the commodity and financial markets, as well as the threats of irregular migration, international crime, drug trafficking, illegal trade of weapons and counterfeit goods. The main task of the new Bretton Woods-3 is to solve the developmental problems faced by the States of the Global South.[8] If a global format for its solution within the framework of the UN and the current IFIs institutions is not sufficient, space will open up for more local, more egalitarian structures formed by the BRICS and other centres of the emerging multipolar system.

From the Russian perspective, the destruction of Bretton Woods-2 and the construction of Bretton Woods-3 should undermine US economic power and ease the pressure that Washington is putting on Moscow to change its domestic and foreign policies. The main driver of the Russian elite's interest in destroying the current global financial order and creating a new one is purely political. Due to the relatively small size of its national economy, Moscow is not able to create financial chaos or upheaval for the US and its allies. The Kremlin also understands that none of the BRICS member states will accept the collapse of the US dollar as the goal of their cooperation in the monetary and financial spheres. Even if it is clear for New Delhi, Beijing and other capitals that the days of American unipolarity are numbered, it does not follow by agreement that the US dollar crisis needs to be provoked or accelerated.

To advance its desired goal, which is 'de-dollarisation', Russia relies on those sectors of its national economy, in which its global position appears to be particularly strong: energy, agriculture, ferrous and non-ferrous metals. The decision to export these goods only for Russian Rubles or for currencies of 'friendly' States has two dimensions that complement each other:

(a) Increase the demand for Russian Rubles in the world economy, strengthen its status as a regional currency for States that emerged after the disintegration of the USSR;
(b) Mitigate the negative impact on Russia of Western monetary sanctions,

which resulted in the impossibility of using key world currencies in the interest of the Russian budget and by national businesses operating in the international arena.

US Treasury bills are the major source of US economic power internationally. In Russia, there is a strong belief that monopolistic control of the key global currency gives the United States an instrument of influence that is inaccessible to any other country. We are talking about Washington's ability 'to buy' individual political figures and entire States that, in exchange for US dollars, carry out specific missions on instructions from Washington or are involved in the implementation of strategic goals dictated by the Administration of the US President. Also in Russia, the politicisation of the IMF as the key Bretton Woods-2 institution is being watched keenly. Conditionality was always ingrained in its loans to developing States, and it especially intensified as the Washington Consensus prevailed in the 1990s. Today, the United States and its allies use IMF's monetary power for financing the military economy of Ukraine, as well as for reinforcing Russia's financial blockade. Created to ensure monetary stability and international cooperation, the IMF has now been turned by Washington into an instrument for preservation of American hegemony in international affairs.

According to Alexei Miller, the CEO of the largest Russian energy company Gazprom: '...the demand for raw materials is increasingly replacing foreign exchange reserves, this is a serious tectonic shift ... the paradigm is changing, the dominance of the dollar is leaving, settlements in national currencies are appearing'.[9] Bretton Woods-3, in his opinion, is intended to become the foundation of a new global monetary order based on commodity-backed currencies. Under the Bretton Woods-2 system, the dominance of the dollar was based on the close connection of the US currency with the oil market. In the context of the 'energy transition strategy' and the extension of energy sources from natural gas, coal and nuclear energy to renewables, the emerging international energy order should be based on variety of national currencies instead of only on the US dollar. Demand for energy sources guaranteed in contemporary world economy, increases due to ongoing urbanisation, population growth and improvement in the quality of life at the Global South.

From Moscow's perspective, the US dollar should not continue to keep its current function of the only proxy between energy-rich States and consumers all around the world. Russia, which possesses almost all types of mineral resources and provides energy to dozens of countries, is confident that the new monetary order will be more in line with its national interests than the existing one. Kremlin believes that confidence in the Ruble should be based on mineral resources and a sovereign technological platform, on the volume of goods produced, on the capacity of the domestic market and the transport infrastructure. The accelerated development of these components of State power is an important element for strengthening Russia's national security.

Eclipse of the US Dollar: not whether but when?

Experts note that the share of the US dollar in international trade and investments is steadily declining. This process is far from complete and the American currency is still the most demanded in the world. A distinctive feature of the dollar's behavior nowadays is that in previous periods it felt great in times of crisis. 'Flight to the dollar' was the most popular scenario for policy of central banks and private investors in times of cyclical crises and military conflicts. Russia notes that current crisis, which started with the onset of COVID-19 and continued though the energy turmoil is developing according to a completely different scenario. As Ruchir Sharma from Rockefeller Capital Management noted: 'Right now, for the first time in my memory, we have an international financial crisis in which the dollar has been weakening rather than strengthening'.[10]

In the era of the dominance of the US dollar (1940-2010s), a typical reaction of the world economy to the rise of the Federal Reserve's interest rate was on expected lines: the influx of capital from all over the world into the US market, the fall in exchange rates of other currencies against the US dollar, lower prices for key commodities – primarily oil – and a sharp increase in demand for US treasuries. Almost nothing like that happened in 2022-2023. Despite all the Federal Reserve's efforts, inflation in the US remains high (9.1 per cent in June 2022). There has been no significant influx of foreign investments into the US market, and the American economy is teetering on the brink of an economic recession. These signs of the 'dollar disease' are well seen in Russia, which is actively promoting within the framework of BRICS, the SCO and the EAEU, a discussion on de-dollarisation and refuses to use the US dollar for its foreign trade. The unprecedented freeze of Russian foreign exchange reserves, denominated in US dollars in February 2022, by Washington, also undermines confidence in this currency as a reliable store of value, and Russia constantly reminds its partners of this in the international arena.

The States of the Global South, which in Russia are now called 'the World Majority', are deprived of stable access to the dollar reserves of international financial institutions or donor States. The need for constant dollar borrowing makes them dependent on decisions made in the US, the EU and major economies of Europe and Asia. The intensification of Washington's use of economic sanctions coincided with the end of the Cold War and caused a sharply negative attitude among developing countries. The use of the dollar weapons against Russia has shown that the US will utilise this instrument more actively and destructively for its opponents. Russia, with its huge domestic market and wide network of partnerships in the world, is able to withstand such pressure, but most States of the Global South do not have this capacity. If nothing changes in the rules of international politics in the near future, then the prospect of spreading a new form of neo-colonial policy towards the Global Majority becomes inevitable.

US' anti-Russian sanctions policy has affected the status of the US dollar in two main ways:

(a) *As a global reserve currency*: international markets reacted by transfer of their forex reserves into gold and the Chinese yuan.

(b) *As a currency for international transactions*: although it is still profitable to use the dollar for international payments, it is politically more attractive for Russia and other States dissatisfied with American unilateralism, to pay for goods and services through national currency or through currencies of partner-States.

Recent US sanctions against Russian forex reserves held abroad, combined with increasingly confrontational relations of Washington and Beijing have created conditions for monetary cooperation between Russia and China. Its essence is the rejection of the dollar as a monopolistic currency for reserves and cross-border settlements in the long-term. Russia would like it to happen sooner, believing that US sanctions are harmful for its national economy. But Moscow understands that it is in China's interest to take a more gradual strategic approach to dismantling the global dominance of the US dollar. Beijing believes that in the near future, the Chinese currency Renminbi will become an equal global competitor to the dollar. However, since conditions for the rise of the Renminbi to the status of a global currency are yet to be created, there is no reason for Beijing to accelerate this process.

Moscow is watching with great interest India's efforts to switch its foreign trade to the use of the Rupee and to abandon the US dollar in bilateral trade with Russia and the UAE. Kremlin was especially positive towards Saudi Arabia's decision to accept the Chinese Renminbi as payment for oil delivered to China as well as efforts of the Brazilian President Luiz Inácio Lula da Silva to reduce the usage of the US dollar in the foreign trade of the largest economy in Latin America. Overall, central banks today experience a significant shortage of foreign currencies in managing their reserve assets. In this regard, the emergence of additional reserve currencies besides the dollar will serve to diversify reserve assets and reduce vulnerabilities associated with dependence on the US dollar.

In conclusion, we should note that the deep crisis of the half-a-century old Bretton Woods-2 system is beyond doubt today. Therefore, the question of how the new system, which in Russia is known as Bretton Woods-3, will look like, remains one of the most discussed in political and expert circles. The structure of a new system will be determined by fully sovereign States, whose number is significantly less than the number of UN member states. Russian diplomacy believes that the five BRICS member states, as well as a small number of other States (Iran, Saudi Arabia, Indonesia, Turkey, and Egypt) are among the fully sovereign States capable of formulating and defending national interests despite pressure from Washington. The BRICS+ format is highly likely to become the forum where discussions about the new architecture of international finance will take place and key decisions will be taken.

There are several assumptions about the direction in which Russia intends to transform the modern structure of Bretton Woods-2, how it sees the Bretton Woods-3, and what goals it pursues.

First, Russia seeks to create a truly multipolar monetary system. Under this system, the US dollar will have its own 'currency area', but it will cover only part of the world economy, and not the whole, as it does today. To achieve this goal, Russia uses the formats of integration associations in which it is a full member: the Union State of Belarus and Russia, the EAEU, the SCO, as well as the BRICS.

Secondly, Russia converts payments for exported goods into Rubles, as well as into currencies that it considers reliable and not subject to US sanctions. The decision of the Russian monetary authorities to use the Ruble and the currencies of friendly States in international settlements, could be explained by the willingness to protect the national economy and undermine US attempts to use the dollar as an instrument of coercion.

Thirdly, the Russian monetary authorities have not yet been able to solve the two main problems of the Russian Ruble: the high volatility of the exchange rate, as well as the high 'normal' level of inflation. Along with the Turkish Lira and the Brazilian Real, the Russian Ruble has a dubious reputation of being the most volatile currency in the G20. Through the implementation of measures to provide raw material support to the Russian Ruble, the Central Bank plans to solve both problems simultaneously: reduce inflation and limit the corridor of exchange rate fluctuations.

Fourth, by focusing on predominantly market-based tools for managing the national economy and by switching to 'the expensive Ruble policy', Russia proceeds from the assumption that the Russian Ruble will become neutral in the long term with respect to political influences within the country and will be able to absorb the impact of external shocks.

Turn-of-the-century globalisation has undermined the economic power and political influence of national governments, without simultaneously creating effective structures of international cooperation and supranational governance. They must be able to withstand the turmoil of the international commodity and financial markets. Political and economic globalisation of the 1990s will only partially survive an upcoming crisis. Its rules will be completely rewritten, and instead of strict obligations within the framework of the IMF or the WTO, a network of forums will emerge following the example of the G20 and BRICS, where the leading national economies will regulate their relations on an ongoing basis and in "manual mode", to prevent possible conflicts. We believe that this model will be known as Bretton Woods-3.

NOTES

1 F. Lukyanov, "Why the West Has Failed to Get the Rest of the World on Board to Support Its Confrontation With Russia," at https://eng.globalaffairs.ru/articles/why-the-west-failed (Accessed 11 July 2023).

2 Eric Hobsbawm, *The Age of Extremes: The Short Twentieth Century (1914-1991)*, Abacus, London, 1994, p. 21.

3 O. Barabanov, T.Bordachev, Y. Lissovolik F.Lukyanov, A. Sushentsov, I. Timofeev, "Living in a Crumbling World. Valdai Club Annual Report," at https://valdaiclub.com/a/reports/living-in-a-crumbling-world (Accessed 22 July 2023).

4 Dorothy S. Brady (ed.), *Output, Employment, and Productivity in the United States after 1800*, NBER, Boston, MA, 1966.

5 Stanislav Tkachenko, "BRICS and Development Alternatives: Russia and China", in Stefano Bianchini and Antonio Fiori (eds.), *Rekindling the Strong State in Russia and China: Domestic Dynamics and Foreign Policy Projections*, Brill, Leiden, Boston, 2020, pp. 271-297.

6 Rodrik, Dani, "Goodbye Washington Consensus, Hello Washington Confusion?" *Journal of Economic Literature*, 44 (4), 2006, pp. 973-987.

7 Yannis Dafermos, Daniela Gabor and Jo Michell, "The Wall Street Consensus in Pandemic Times: What Does it Mean for Climate-aligned Development," *Canadian Journal of Development Studies / Revue canadienne d'études du développement*, 42 (1-2), 2021, pp. 238-251.

8 Stanislav Tkachenko, "The Political Economy of Global Development", in Andrey Baykov and Tatiana Shakleina (eds.), *Polycentric World Order in the Making*, Palgrave MacMillan, Singapore, 2023, pp. 155-180.

9 Alexey Miller, "Presentation at Panel Discussion on 'Global Market of Oil and Gas Today and Tomorrow'" at https://tomsk-tr.gazprom.ru/press/news/2022/06/146893/ (Accessed 22 July 2023).

10 Fareed Zakaria, "The Dollar is Our Superpower, and Russia and China are Threatening It" at www.washingtonpost.com/opinions/2023/03/24/us-dollar-strength-russia-china/ (Accessed 11 July 2023).

CHAPTER 7

Awakening Sea Monster: Shifting Tides in the Indian Ocean in the Emergent and Emerging World

Manisha Dookhony

Introduction

Geopolitical changes within the Indian Ocean have led to evolving economic trends. Increasingly, large crude and cargo carriers find it easier to pass through the region, enhancing the role of maritime routes. Port control, development, or management systems are attracting investment. Potentially, there has been a rise in the source of critical raw materials, seabed exploration for nodules.

Security and securitisation of trade became a key concern with the insurgency in Mozambique launched by Somali pirates and Shabaab. Record drug seizures have attracted much attention. Australia recently purchased nuclear submarines from the US. Within the region, China and Japan have been quite interested in countries such as Mauritius and Madagascar.

For Mauritius, India has been at the centre of its foreign policy. India has funded and provided loans for major infrastructure development. The security advisor of Mauritius is from India. The SAGAR[1] initiative has made India a "net security provider", which marked a turning point in the relationship between Mauritius and India and was perhaps linked to the activities of Indian entities on the island of Agalega. The range of bilateral agreements signed included Comprehensive Economic Cooperation and Partnership Agreement (CECPA) and the Double Tax Avoidance Agreement (DTAA) Agreement of 1983 which was revised on 7 March 2024 with signing of Protocol amending double-tax treaty.

However, there is a significant increase in competition between China and India in their bilateral relationship with Mauritius. In May 2017, India and Mauritius signed an agreement on maritime security which came only two weeks after a Chinese summit on the Belt and Road Initiative. Similarly, the Comprehensive Economic Cooperation and Partnership Agreement (CECPA) between Mauritius and India was signed after 16 years of negotiations, and shortly after the FTA with China came into force.

Emerging dynamics in the Indian Ocean

Over the past decade we have witnessed a number of key changes that have contributed to the shifting of tides within the Indian Ocean. It has emerged as a busy maritime route. Very Large and ultra large vessels- Cargo and Crude Carriers, means the preferred route for such vessels is now the Indian Ocean. Increasing traffic in the Suez Canal has meant that vessels face delays. Hence the Indian Ocean Maritime route is becoming increasingly important.[2]

Maritime Route is subjected to threat from non-state actors. The attack on Cabo Del Gado in Northern Mozambique[3] that peaked in 2020 was an eye-opener that the Southern Western Indian Ocean Zone is no more a sleepy zone. The threat of terrorism is real. And it is next door. Northern Mozambique is right across the channel to Northern Madagascar, and thereby also very close to one of the busiest maritime routes.

Oil Spill is another challenge. The running aground of the Japanese bulk carrier MV Wakashio in July 2020 on the reefs of South East Mauritius at Pointe d'Esny, a rare wildlife sanctuary, and the fuel leak that followed, together with the vessel split in Mid August 2020.[4]

The UN court ruling of January 2021 confirmed the sovereignty of Mauritius over the Chagos Archipelago. In a David against Goliath case, Mauritius won its case against the United Kingdom. The fact that a very small state, has prospered and that is now asserting its own sovereignty so strongly is further testimony of changes happening. It also comes with its load of responsibility. The role of Mauritius in securing the seas has expanded.[5]

The acquisition of Nuclear powered submarines by Australia as part of AUKUS from the US, is a testimony of this shifting tide. This purchase tends to enhance the assertiveness of Australia, a middle-sized power which is also an US ally. It also seems that the deal between the US and Australia (to the detriment of France) also incorporates collaborations in cyber, artificial intelligence, quantum, unmanned underwater vehicles, and different technologies.[6]

As such, it would seem that there are now new actors that are both capable and willing to make sure that they step up to provide stability for the region.

All these are strewn in a backdrop of an economic game of monopoly being played across the Indian Ocean, where real estate is the land and sea, its resources, and its enabling capacity for allowing safe movement and passage with the Belt and Road Initiative (BRI) of China, the policy of SAGAR of India (and its launch in Mauritius in 2015), the trade war between China and the US and, the trade war between China and Australia. In this geopolitical competition the role of Mauritius has grown exponentially.

Mauritius, India, and China have shared a long-standing relationship based on historical, cultural, and economic ties. While India and Mauritius have been close allies for many years, the relationship between China and Mauritius has grown significantly in recent years. The presence of the growing competition in the Indian Ocean cannot be ignored. While India is positioning itself more strongly on the seas, China is seeking a bolder presence compared to the traditional colonial allies like France and the United Kingdom. Some countries such as South Africa and Australia are more subtle in their relationship. This chapter follows the New Players in the Indian Ocean- a win-win for Mauritius[7] a report prepared by R. Kasenally and Manisha Dookhony. This chapter will explore the shifting tides and ties in the relationships between Mauritius, India, and Mauritius and China.

Mauritius-India Economic Relationship

The relations between Mauritius and India date back to the 1830s when more than 500,000 Indians landed in Mauritius as indentured labourers over a 90-year period. About 70% of the island's population today is of Indian ancestry. When Mauritius gained independence from the UK in 1968, the newly formed administration, under the direction of Sir Seewoosagur Ramgoolam, the island's first Prime Minister, chose to place India at the center of the nation's foreign policy.

DTAA was signed initially in 1983 to ensure that Indian consultants who were coming to support Mauritius were not subject to double taxation. The DTAA was not used for the first ten years since foreign firms were not permitted to operate in Indian stock markets, but this situation changed in 1992. Following the opening of the Indian economy in the early 1990s, the advantages of the treaty started to come to fruition. At the same time, in 1992, the offshore industry debuted, ushering in a new era for Mauritius and starting a new pillar for economic development. The DTAA has been a high point of the strong bilateral ties between India and Mauritius. By virtue of the provision stating that capital gains realised by investors residing in Mauritius on the sale of shares in Indian firms would be subject to taxation only in Mauritius and not in India, this treaty has been the cornerstone of the development of the offshore sector in the 1990s.

The quantity and variety of bilateral agreements inked between Mauritius and India, which are founded on ancestry and shared cultural heritage, also attest to the strength of the two countries' relations- Marine security, biotechnology, the environment, infrastructure, energy, ICT, the Blue economy and more recently, with the GIFT city. Over the years, India has offered Mauritius lines of credit and funding for development at a relatively low-interest rates. These have proven to be very useful, especially during Mauritius' difficult developmental phase.

With SAGAR, India aims to "intensify economic and security cooperation with its maritime neighbors and support the development of their maritime security capabilities". Additionally, it gives India the ability to "protect its national interests and to make sure that the Indian Ocean region becomes inclusive, collaborative, and respects international law." By transforming India's role into a "net security provider," SAGAR also shapes India's marine strategy. This appears to have signalled a turning point in Mauritius and India's relationship.

Finally, in 2016, India succeeded in negotiating a revision of the treaty. The treaty revision led to a major reduction in the Global Business transactions between Mauritius and India. With effect from the financial year 2017–18, the new Protocol, which was signed on May 10, 2016, has granted India the authority to impose capital gains tax on the sale of shares in Indian corporations. The capital gains tax was one of the most important to 'curb revenue loss, prevent double non-taxation, streamline the flow of investment and stimulate the flow of exchange of information between India and Mauritius' Previously, capital gains from the sale of shares in Indian corporations by Mauritian residents' were exempted from tax in India. However, under the updated treaty, India taxes capital gains from the sale of shares purchased on or after April 1, 2017. For a period of two years following the date the new treaty went into operation, these gains are taxed at a lower rate of 50% of the domestic tax rate. As a result, the capital gains tax exemption was gradually phased out. Moreover, to avoid treaty abuse and ensure that only legitimate Mauritius citizens can take advantage of the treaty benefits, the new treaty added a Limitation of Benefits (LOB) clause. To be eligible for the treaty benefits, a business must meet the requirements outlined in the LOB clause. Furthermore, subject to a few limitations, the amended treaty permits India to source tax interest and royalties. As a result, citizens of Mauritius who receive interest or royalties from India might be subject to withholding tax in that country.

The amendments to the India/Mauritius treaty, particularly the changes in capital gains taxation and the introduction of the LOB clause, have had an impact on Global Business License Category 1 (GBL 1) and Global Business License Category 2 (GBL 2) companies in Mauritius, as well as the volume of funds transferred between the two countries. GBL 1 and GBL 2 enterprises have been impacted by the phase-out of the capital gains tax exemption on the sale of shares bought on or after April 1, 2017. As a result, when selling shares of Indian corporations, these entities are now subject to capital gains tax in India.[8] Due to this modification, there is no longer a tax benefit for utilising Mauritius as an entry point for investments in India. Introduction of this LOB clause attempts to prevent treaty misuse and ensure that only legitimate Mauritius citizens can take advantage of the treaty benefits. The LOB clause's precise requirements and criteria must be satisfied by GBL 1 and GBL 2 companies in order to be eligible for the treaty benefits. This may have affected these organisations' eligibility for treaty benefits and increased their scrutiny and compliance obligations for them.

The amendments to the India/Mauritius treaty have had an impact on the volume of funds transferred between the two countries. Historically, Mauritius has been a popular destination for routing funds into India due to the tax advantages provided by the treaty. However, with the revision of the treaty, some investors may have reconsidered their investment strategies and potentially diverted funds to alternative jurisdictions or restructured their investments to optimise tax efficiency. The exact impact on the volume of funds transfer would depend on various factors such as investor sentiment, the attractiveness of alternative investment destinations, and the overall business environment. It is important to note that investment flows are influenced by a multitude of factors beyond tax considerations, including market opportunities, regulatory frameworks and geopolitical factors.

Projects for Economic Development by India

In return for the review of the DTAA and as compensation, India provided Mauritius a 'gift' of MUR 12.7 billion (353 million dollar grant) for the development of different projects. These initiatives have been important in forging Mauritius' contemporary identity, and cover a range of economic sectors, including public transportation, education, healthcare, social housing, and the judicial system. The Metro Express project is planned to get $ 275m, with the remaining funds being distributed among the other projects. For Metro Express Phase III, an extra grant of $ 10m and $ 190m were offered.

Table 1: Funding Instruments

Key Projects Funded	*Amount in $ (in Million)*	*Financial Instrument*
Metro Express Phase-I (Port Louis-Rose Hill)		**Special Economic Package**
Metro Express Phase-II-A (Rose Hill – Quatre Bornes)	$ 260m	Line of Credit
Metro Express Phase-II-B (Quatre Bornes – Phoenix)	$ 267m	Grant
Metro Express Phase-II-C (Phoenix to Curepipe)		
Metro Express Phase-III (Rose Hill to Reduit)	$ 80m $ 10m	Line of Credit Grant
Metro Express Phase-IV Reduit to Cote d'Or[9]	$ 300m $ 25m	Line of Credit Grant
8 MW Solar PV Farm at Henrietta	$ 7.52m	Line of Credit
New ENT Hospital	$ 23m[10]	Grant

Total LOC = $ 647.52 Million
Total Grant = $ 302 million

In 2017, the EXIM Bank of India established a second source of funding by providing Mauritius with a 500 million dollar line of credit at 1.8 per cent interest. This took the form of SBM (Mauritius) Infrastructure Development Company Ltd., a special purpose company in the form of a guarantee fund instrument.[11]

The Mauritius Metro Express project has received the bulk of funds and credit lines from the Indian government on an ongoing basis. Initially, a 26-kilometre-long Metro project was built in two phases, the project has now completed three phases and a fourth phase is currently in preparation that will go up to Cote d'Or. On 3 October 2019, both the Prime Ministers Narendra Modi and Pravind Kumar Jugnauth e-inaugurated Phase I, which connects Port Louis and Rose Hill. Regarding Phase II, which connects Rose Hill and Curepipe the completion initially planned for the end of 2022[12] happened in October 2022.[13] Construction for Phase III, which will connect Reduit and Rose Hill was inaugurated on 22 January 2023.[14] The Indian government released funds for a further expansion of Cote d'Or, the planned new metropolis in the island's center, in August 2022. In March 2025, Prime Modi visited Mauritius to attend the National Day celebrations and he was conferred with The Grand Commander of the Order of the Star and Key of the Indian Ocean, highest civilian honour of the country. He said "Mauritius is also a bridge connecting India to the wider Global South".

India is a development partner of Mauritius. Below are the details of the Special Economic Package, which the Government of India extended to the Government of Mauritius in 2016 to realise five projects (Table 2). Table 3 summarises further projects that were financed between 2015 and 2022.

Table 2: Special Economic Package from India (2016)

Project	*Value ($)*
Metro Express Project	275 million
Supreme Court Building	30 million
New ENT Hospital	14 million
Social Housing Project	20 million
Supply of Digital tablets to primary schools	14 million

Source: High Commission of India Website

Table 3: Other Projects Financed by India (2015 – 2022)

Project	*Value ($) million*
Civil Service College	4.74
8 MW Solar PV Farm.	Not Available
Extension of a Line of Credit (LoC) to Mauritius to finance social and infrastructure projects	500
Extension of Line of Credit financing procurement of defence equipment from India	100
Phase III Metro	190
Additional Grant for Phase III Metro	10
Phase IV Metro Express	300

Source: High Commission of India Website[15]

The numerous initiatives started since the DTAA was revised in 2016 show an expansion of the economic cooperation between Mauritius and India. In contrast to earlier Lines of Credit, which were provided to governments directly, current ones have been made through the EXIM Bank of India and the SBMIDCL (Exim Bank of India Website).

Besides economic support, India has consistently assisted Mauritius over the past twenty years in defence technology. It should be noted that Mauritius received funding for the procurement of defence equipment, including helicopters and airplanes for surveillance, in 2005, 2012, and 2021 totaling $450million. India supplied 64 per cent of Mauritian defence purchases between 1990 and 2020. To highlight the importance of the relationship, the defence advisor of Mauritius has always been from India. In addition, the National Coast Guard is headed by a naval officer from India. This becomes more important as securing of the maritime route is a priority for countries in the region. In addition to the CECPA Agreement, Mauritius also signed a Line of Credit of $100 million for defence purposes. This LoC is towards the facilitation of the procurement of Indian defence equipment.[16]

The island nation offers Indian investors and enterprises a secure platform to carry out their Africa-focused activities through the MIFC, due to Mauritius' geostrategic position as a centre for channelling cross-border investments between Asia and Africa. Being a multilingual nation, Mauritius has the ability to facilitate Indian businesses, particularly with the Francophone nations, creating a wealth of opportunities.

Indian Investments in Mauritius

Prior to the DTAA's modification in 2016 (Reserve Bank of India Data), Mauritius accounted for the largest proportion of foreign investment flows into India. Mauritius lost the top position by 2019. Prior to the modifications, Mauritius received the majority of its investment from India for more than three decades. The provisions in the new DTAA permitted grandfathering advantages until April 2017, after which the Indian government would start imposing capital gains tax. However, it seems that Mauritius is now making a comeback and reaching top position again.

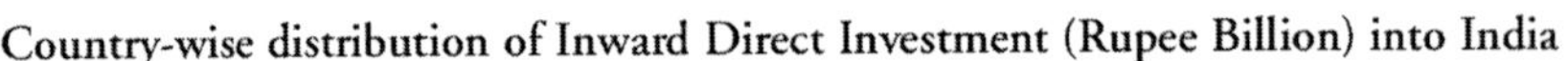

Country-wise distribution of Inward Direct Investment (Rupee Billion) into India

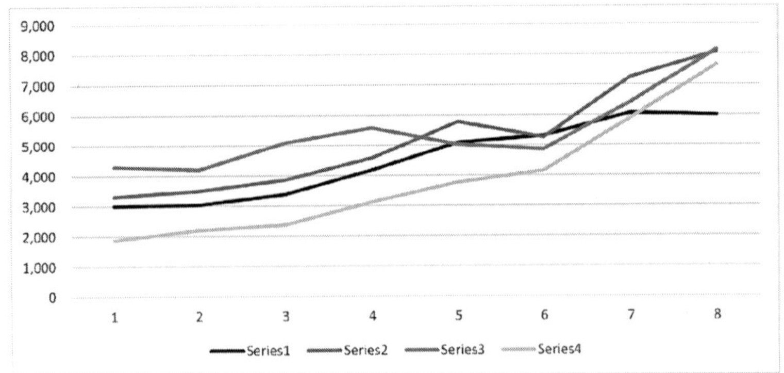

Source: Census on Foreign Liabilities and Assets of Indian Direct Investment Entities, 2015-2022[17]

From April 2000 to March 2021, cumulative FDI equity inflows from Mauritius to India totalled $ 148.35 billion,[18] or 28 per cent of all FDI inflows during this time. With FDI equity inflows of $ 5.63 billion for the financial years 2020–21, Mauritius ranked third among FDI sources for India (Reserve Bank of India Data). Indian Public and Private Sector Enterprises that have invested in Mauritius (not financial intermediation-offshore type of investment) include Bank of Baroda, Life Insurance Corporation, New India Assurance Corporation, Indian Oil (Mauritius) Limited, Mahanagar Telephone (Mauritius) Ltd, State Bank of India (Mauritius) Limited, Amity University, Infosys, Agarwal's Eye Hospital, Oberoi Hospitality, Metropolis Pathology.

With respect to trade, India was the second-largest source of imports to Mauritius in 2021, accounting for 16 per cent of all imports (Trading Economics, 2021).[19] India exported goods worth $1,027 million to Mauritius in 2018, $776 million in 2019, and $405 million in 2020 (the low amount may have been a result of the pandemic) $808 million in 2021 and USD 632 million in 2022 and USD 646 million in 2023.[20] Rice, pharmaceuticals, and petroleum products are among the main imports from India. It is also a significant provider of raw materials for the regional economy, providing yarn and fabrics to the textile and apparel sectors.

In 2019, 2020 and 2021 respectively, Mauritius exported a total of $24 million and $32 million and $44.41 million to India. The top exports in 2020 will be fish meal, scrap copper, medical devices, and scrap metal. Medical devices are growing in importance in the basket of goods exported by Mauritius to India. Other significant Mauritian exports to India in 2020 were waste aluminium, vanilla beans, scrap paper, machinery parts, and clothing.

Mauritius-China Economic Relationship

Mauritius has a community of Chinese origin that has thrived through the expansion of business and trade despite being relatively small. Mauritius and China have a growing trade relationship, with China being one of Mauritius' major trading partners. China is Mauritius' largest source of imports. As per 2021 data, China exported $1.01 billion to Mauritius. It is also worth noting that in 1995, exports of China to Mauritius were to the tune of $61.7 million. This means that there has been an annualised rate of growth of trade of 11.4 per cent.[21] In 2021, Mauritius exported $34.1 million to China, and similarly high, the annualised rate of increase was 18.8per cent from 1995.[22]

In 2022, the total trade volume between Mauritius and China was Rs 3.53 billion, with Mauritius exporting Rs 250.1 million worth of goods (representing 2.7 million kilograms worth of goods) to China and importing Rs 3.28 billion worth of goods from China (representing 2.92 million kilograms worth of goods)[23]. The main exports from Mauritius to China include sugar, beverages, textiles and clothing, and chemicals. machinery, electronics, manufactured goods, and construction materials were amongst the top imports of Mauritius from China.

China has also invested significantly in Mauritius, particularly in infrastructure development, such as the construction of the new airport terminal or the construction of a smart city near the port areas. Chinese companies have invested in other sectors, such as telecommunications, energy, and real estate.

The Economic Partnership Agreement between Mauritius and China went into effect in January 2021. This Agreement is quite interesting and further consolidates the relationship. It is on the other hand quite interesting to examine as to why would a large country like China be even interested in concluding such an agreement with a relatively smaller country like Mauritius? It is worth looking at some aspects of the Agreement in further detail.

China and Mauritius started a feasibility study for a free trade agreement (FTA) in 2016, and the results revealed that the agreement "was in line with both China's and Mauritius' interests and will help further deepen the existing bilateral trade and economic relations between China and Mauritius." It was the first time China had ever conducted a cooperative feasibility study with an African nation. Vice Minister of Commerce Wang Shouwen and Ambassador Dhalladoo of Mauritius signed the Memorandum of Understanding on launching China-Mauritius FTA Negotiations between the Ministry of Commerce of the People's Republic of China and the Ministry of Foreign Affairs, Regional Integration, and International Trade of the Republic of Mauritius.[24] This signalled the beginning of formal FTA talks between China and Mauritius, a first in Africa.[25]

FTA between Mauritius and China was signed in October 2019 and became effective after being ratified by both nations. Discussions took two years. The Agreement, although termed as an FTA, is in fact an economic cooperation agreement that covers trade in products, trade in services, investment, and economic cooperation as four main pillars of the FTA. In addition, other chapters cover dispute resolution, electronic commerce, competition law, intellectual property rights, technical trade barriers, and phytosanitary and sanitary regulations.

The FTA includes a specific section seeking to develop a Renminbi clearing and settlement facility in Mauritius. While trade and services aspects of the Agreement dominate the headlines, perhaps it would be useful for us to understand the relationships under the lens of the financial transaction between Mauritius and China and the facilitation thereof.

Comparing Economic Relationship: Mauritius-China-India and their focus on CECPA[26] and FTA[27]

The analysis that follows compares the CECPA between India and Mauritius and the FTA between China and Mauritius on a few important fronts:

- Timing
- Trade in Goods
- Rules of Origin
- Financial Facilitation
- Trade in Services

Timing

As stated above, China and Mauritius started a feasibility study for a FTA in 2016 following which negotiations were launched. These negotiations lasted for two years and were signed in October 2019 and were ratified by both nations and entered into force on 01January 2021.

CECPA negotiation with India started in 2004. Negotiations were stalled for many years because India sought renegotiations of the DTAA. It was finally signed between Mauritius and India on 22 February 2021, and came into force on 1 April 2021 (DTAA was revised in 2016). As such, while it took around four years for the FTA with China to come into force, for the CECPA, it took 17 years.

Trade in goods Chapters CECPA versus FTA

Under CECPA Mauritius receives trade privileges from India on 615 products in three main categories: duty free, Reduced Duty and Tariff Rate Quotas.

White sugar, vodka, polishes, creams from tariff line 34052000, envelopes, letters, and cards are some examples of products that do not benefit from preferential access.

In contrast, Mauritius grants India preferential access to 310 products with TRQs on 88 of them, including tea, spices, wooden furniture, plastic items, and parts for motor vehicles, among other things.

Table 4: CECPA and FTA Privileges

	Number of Items provided privileges access by India under CECPA	*Number of Items provided privileged access by Mauritius under CECPA*	*Number of Items provided privileges access by China under FTA*	*Number of Items provided privileged access by Mauritius under FTA*
Duty-free access	376			
Reduced Duty	127			
Tariff Rate Quotas (TRQs)	112			
Number of Tariff Lines	615	394	8,547	6,120[28]

These TRQs include for example,

- 40,000 tons of Special Sugars may be exported to India at 10 per cent duty instead of 100per cent tariff;
- Alcoholic Beer for 2000 litres at 10 per cent duty instead of 15 per cent;
- 2 million litres of beer may be exported to India at 25 per cent duty instead of a tariff of 150 per cent;
- 50 tons of polishes and creams of HS code 34022090 @50 per cent mop over five years;
- 200,000 litres of canned beverages of HS code 22030011 at 10 per cent duty over five years;
- 1.5 million litres of Rum of HS codes (22084011, 22084012, 22084091, 22084092) at 50 per cent duty instead of a tariff of 150 per cent;
- 5000 litres of fruit wine at 50 per centduty instead of a tariff of 150 per cent;
- Duty-free on garments on 7.5 million pieces at zero duty with the sourcing of 5 millon yarn/ fabric from India, and 2.5 million yarn/fabric from any other country covering a range of tariff lines of chapters;
- 7000 tons of duty-free access to canned tuna.

Mauritius benefits from duty-free access on 8,547 products in the FTA. This is quite sizeable as it represents in effect 96 per cent of Chinese tariff lines. Eighty-eight per cent of these products benefit from immediate duty-free access, while for the remaining 12 per cent, the tariff is eliminated over a period of five to seven years. The FTA covers key export items for Mauritius such as rum, frozen fish, noodles and pasta, wafers and biscuits, fresh fruits, juices, mineral water, linen, garments, watches, and leather articles. However, given its very broad coverage, it in effect, therefore, provides Mauritius with market access to products that are not currently produced locally. In addition to duty-free access, Mauritius benefits from a Tariff Rate Quota of 50,000 tons of market access for special sugar with an in-quota rate of 15 per cent.

Rules of Origin

Another significant aspect of both agreements is the Rules of Origin. Rules of Origin under the CECPA stipulates that a product is eligible for preferential tariffs if it has been wholly sourced or manufactured in either India or Mauritius. Products that are wholly bought or produced in Mauritius and qualify for preferential tariffs include plants, animals, fish, and other products that are cultivated and collected there. They are regarded as originating if their combined value does not exceed 12.5 per cent of FOBt, which is also covered by the Product Specific Rule. Under HS chapters 50–63, less than 7 per cent of the total weight of materials used to create export products, must be non-originating materials in textiles and garments.

	CECPA	*FTA*
Wholly obtained	wholly sourced or manufactured in either India or Mauritius	wholly sourced or manufactured in either China or Mauritius
Wholly Produced		
non-originating materials	their total value does not exceed 12.5% of FOB price	
Regional Value Content		Products may benefit from Regional Value Content rule of e" 40% regional value addition
Product Specific Rule		Depending on change in chapter, change in Tariff Heading and Change in Tariff Subheading
Rule for Textiles (HS Chapters 50-63)	non-originating material < 7% of total weight of materials used in export product.	
DE minimis rule	deemed as originating if: (a) their total value does not exceed 12.5% of FOB price of export product.	value of all non-originating materials <10% of FOB value of product

Under the FTA with China, products can benefit from Rules of Origin in many ways. Changes in tariff chapter/heading/subheading are considered often to be an easy way to determine origin. Regional Value Content is also quite interesting. In other similar FTAs, it also ties in to other parties to an agreement – thus benefiting an FTA partner country or countries. We could therefore consider that FTA between Mauritius and China could in the long run be extended to other partner countries or that there could be collaboration at the regional level. This could make sense in particular in the context of the he African Continental Free Trade Area (AfCFTA) coming into force. This bears testimony to the longer-term approach of the FTA. It is conceivable that in future, more goods may be produced in Mauritius and can make use of the FTA's advantages within the AfCFTA's larger framework by producing imported Chinese goods and exporting them to Africa. Mauritius, for instance, may assemble imported Chinese electronics or vehicle parts into finished goods for export to Africa. Many nations on the continent are striving to take advantage of the enormous potential that the development of the biopharmaceutical sector t in Africa affords.

By utilising the FTA, Mauritius might relay the delivery of inputs for that sector, given that China is the second-largest country in the biopharma sector.

Trade in Services

Trade in services (TIS) is likely to be quite beneficial for India. As per the commitments, Indian service providers have access to around 115 sub-sectors from 11 broad service sectors. These cover professional services, computer-related services, R&D, and other business services. Mauritius benefits from access in 94 sub-sectors from 11 broad services sectors, including professional services, R&D, other business services, telecommunication, environmental, health, financial services and commercial services.[29]

Additionally, the Agreement contains clauses for the negotiation of mutual recognition for degrees and credentials in the fields of engineering, medicine, dentistry, architecture, accounting and auditing, nursing, veterinary medicine, and corporate secretariat. Since Mauritius is bilingual and has a highly qualified labour population, there is a lot of room for Indian service companies to set up shop in Mauritius and use it as a base to target both Anglophone and Francophone nations. In this area, there are already Indian firms, in the financial services sector, that are looking to set up base in Mauritius, in particular, to cater for their French-speaking businesses in Africa. There is a likelihood that as the Mauritian and Indian economy consolidate their services sector, the TIS benefits may even outweigh trade-related components (limited in current form).

Financial Facilitation

(a) Renminbi Clearing Centre

Under Articles in the FTA related to financial services, there are a few interesting and specific sub-clauses seeking to modernise and diversify the financial services industry in the respective countries' economies, to enhance collaboration by: (a) sharing of expertise in Fintech to promote innovation in financial services; (b) strengthening capacity building, including facilitating exchanges of professionals and experts; (c) reinforcing regulatory cooperation with the signature of Memoranda of Understanding between the regulators of Mauritius and China; (d) exploring further the possibility of cooperation in the implementation of best international standards in anti-money laundering practicesand (e) promoting the development of a Renminbi clearing and settlement facility in Mauritius.

On the latter, the Mauritius Renminbi Clearing Centre (MRCC) was established in 2022. The Centre serves as a gateway for African countries to access the Chinese market through the RMB. With ever-increasing transactions between China and African countries, there is a likelihood of financial transactions expanding in the near future, as de-dollarisation (and internationalisation of the RMB by China) is now formally on the Agenda of the BRICS countries. China is the main business partner of African countries, whether it is imports of products to be sold in Africa or export of raw materials.

The MRCC helps in the clearing and settling of RMB-denominated transactions. It provides clearing and settlement services for RMB-denominated transactions, including cross-border trade settlements and investments, issuance of offshore RMB bonds, and other financial transactions. The Centre aims to promote the use of RMB in cross-border trade and investment, facilitate trade and investment between China and Mauritius, and enhance the internationalisation of the RMB. The Bank of Mauritius (BoM) launched the clearing centre for Renminbi payments on 16 December 2022 as a means to implement the clauses of the FTA.[30] This is the third such clearing centre in Africa after South Africa and Zambia. The advantage of such a centre is that Mauritian importers may now be invoiced directly in RMB. Hence, the Mauritian exporter does not need to getdollars for purchases from China. This can help attenuate the exchange pressure on the US dollar in Mauritius. It also supports trade by reducing exchange rate costs. Mauritian banks can then use the local RMB centre for international settlements.

It is worth noting that in September 2015, there was another agreement preceding the FTA, which also serves as a basis for the MRCC. An agreement was signed then between the People's Bank of China (PBOC) and the Bank of Mauritius (BOM) to establish a clearing centre for RMB transactions in Mauritius. The Bank of China opened its first subsidiary in Mauritius in 2016.[31]

The MRCC ties into the linkages made under the COMESA REPSS (Regional Payment and Settlement System) and the SADC RTGS (regional cross border real-time gross settlement) as well as the PAPSS (Pan African Payment and Settlement System), which are important regional payment systems. Moreover, Mauritius has in place agreements to avoid double taxation with 16 African countries or regional country groupings, and a well regarded legal and regulatory framework.

In the agreement with India, apart from the elements in the Trade in Services

Schedule for financial services, no such explicit clauses exist for the facilitation of financial transactions. As a result, a few, more privately led initiatives have been set up by banks that have a bank account held by a local bank in India on behalf of a foreign bank which accepts payment through different payment systems namely, Instant Payment System (IPS) , Unified Payments Interface (UPI), Vostro and Rupay.

(b) Instant Payment System

The Mauritius Instant Payment System (IPS)[32] is a real-time payment system that enables people and companies to instantly transfer payments between Mauritian banks. The Bank of Mauritius runs the system, which was introduced in 2018.[33] The Unified Payments Interface (UPI) is the Instant Payment System used in India. The National Payments Corporation of India (NPCI) introduced the UPI real-time payment system in 2016. It enables people and companies to transfer money immediately across Indian bank accounts by using a virtual payment address (VPA) or mobile phones.[34] With over 1.3 billion transactions processed in March 2021 alone, UPI has experienced considerable growth in popularity in India. Additionally, the system has been enhanced to include features like biometric authentication and transactions using QR codes.[35]

UPI[36] has played a crucial role in encouraging digital payments in India and in lowering the use of cash there. It has also helped with financial inclusion by making it simple for people to open bank accounts and use mobile devices to access financial services.[37] In general, the Instant Payment Systems in India and Mauritius serve as illustrations of how technology can be used to advance financial inclusion, curtail the use of cash, and stimulate economic growth.

The IPS and UPS are currently pilot projects, which are being tested in the Bank of Baroda and CIM finance in Mauritius and India. Upon finalisation of this project, it will allow Indians to debit their account directly for a payment made in Mauritius by simply scanning the QR code. The same facility will be applicable for Mauritians who would be able to debit their local accounts directly for purchases made in India.

(c) RuPay Card

The RuPay card has been growing in popularity. In Mauritius, the State Bank of Mauritius (SBM) launched the RuPay card in 2018 in collaboration with NPCI.[38] The introduction of the RuPay card in Mauritius aimed to provide a cost-effective and convenient payment option to customers in the country. It can allow customers to make purchases using their RuPay cards at POS terminals, internet retailers, and ATMs and for purchases online. The RuPay card is currently in a pilot phase, with the Bank of Baroda and State Bank of India (SBI) issuing these RuPay cards.

The RuPay card has gained significant popularity in Mauritius since its launch, with over 150,000 RuPay cards issued in the country as of 2021.[39] The card's acceptance has also increased in Mauritius, with several banks and merchants now accepting RuPay card payments. The card has brought significant benefits to customers in Mauritius, including lower transaction fees, better security features, and access to various discounts and offers.

The capacity of the RuPay card to encourage financial inclusion in Mauritius is one of its key benefits. People in remote locations can now use the card to access banking services and conduct cashless transactions. This has aided in encouraging digital payments throughout the nation and reducing the use of cash. Customers can use their RuPay card at international merchant outlets, thanks to the interoperability that the RuPay card enables with various payment networks. RuPay allows customers in India and Mauritius to have affordable and practical payment alternatives.

(d) Vostro Account

The Vostro account allows payments to be made in local currency[40] and as the Renminbi Clearing House, it also allows cross-border payments to be made without having to go through a third currency.

These mechanisms with respect to exchange with China and India are all aimed at reducing the dependence on the US dollar for international trade and exchange. India maintains Vostro accounts with a handful of countries, and Mauritius is one of them.

Chagos Islands

The discussion about the shifting tides would not be complete without a short analysis of the Chagos factor. Amid growing competition, the question of Chagos is the key in Mauritius' relationship with a range of players. After the outcomes from the UN General Assembly and the International Court of Justice's (ICJ) ruling in Mauritius' favour over the sovereignty over the Chagos, the maritime law tribunal of the United Nations further ruled that Britain has no sovereignty over the Chagos Islands.[41] These together with the recent definition of the maritime zone around the Chagos archipelago have served to consolidate the sovereignty of Mauritius over the Islands. However, the Chagos also includes a US military base. However it is worth highlighting that with the Chagos, Mauritius will dominate the Indian Ocean from around 4 degrees (Chagos) to 20 degrees (Mauritius Island) South latitudes and from 56 East (Agalega) to 121(Rodrigues) degrees East in longitude. Mauritius has an Exclusive Economic Zone (EEZ) of 2.3 million square kilometres including the Chagos region and a continental shelf of 396,000 square kilometres co-managed with the Republic of Seychelles.[42] These place Mauritius at the heart of geo-economic challenges to protect maritime channels in the Indian Ocean. Hence, several nations (traditional and non-traditional) are players in the archipelagic nation of Mauritius.

Conclusion

Strategically speaking, Mauritius now controls an area equivalent to the size of India. As a sea-faring nation, it also controls the safe passage of vessels in this region, as with the recent decisions at the global level. Since the International Court of Justice ruled that the British occupation of the Islands was unlawful. The geo-economics of the discussions to hand over the Chagos, begun under the leadership of UK Prime Minister Truss, are now setting in motion other moves on the chessboard as Diego Garcia where US has a base has now come into strategic play. It has also heightened China's interest, which could also be looking to secure its long-range routes through the Indian Ocean – to the Middle East. They may be interested in positioning their navy, as they have done in the South China Sea, to protect the trade route in the Mid to Southern Indian Ocean region. Similarly, India as amounting emerging economic power and with its expansion of global trade, is also interested in securing the trade routes.

As tides shift, different currents could lead to an expansion of diplomatic tensions, where China, India, the US and perhaps other countries, could or are already courting Mauritius for a foothold on some of its islands including the Chagos, St Brandon, or Agalega. All this leads to new geo-economic parameters.

NOTES

1 Ankita Singh Gujjar, "Sagar Policy: Analyzing India's Vision for Maritime Diplomacy", Center For Land Warfare Studies (CLAWS): at https://www.claws.in/ Sagar Policy: Analyzing India's Vision for Maritime Diplomacy

2 "Maritime competition in the Indian Ocean", CEIP at https://carnegieendowment.org/2022/05/12/maritime-competition-in-indian-ocean-pub-87093 (Accessed 03 June 2023).

3 "The Mozambique Channel – Troubled Waters?" International Institute for Strategic Studies

at https://www.iiss.org/online-analysis//military-balance/2021/05/mozambique-channel-maritime-security (Accessed 04 June 2023).

4 "Mauritius oil spill: Wrecked *MV Wakashio* Breaks up", 2020 BBC News at https://www.bbc.com/news/world-africa-53797009 (Accessed: 04 June 2023).

5 "UN court rejects UK claim to Chagos Islands in favour of Mauritous(pl. correct) *The Guardian*, 2021 at https://www.theguardian.com/world/2021/jan/28/un-court-rejects-uk-claim-to-chagos-islands-in-favour-of-mauritius (Accessed 04 June 2023).

6 "Australia to purchase nuclear-power submarines from the US as part of Aukus Alliance", Le Monde with AP and AFP, Le Monde.fr 2023 athttps://www.lemonde.fr/en/international/article/2023/03/13/aukus-australia-to-purchase-nuclear-power-submarines-from-us_6019209_4.html (Accessed 04 June 2023).

7 M. Dookhony, and R. Kasenally, "New Players in the Indian Ocean- A win-win situation for Mauritius", *Mauritius Society Renewal*, June 2022.

8 "Amendments to the India/Mauritius treaty", Simmons & Simmons at https://www.simmons-simmons.com/en/publications/ck0a2lz1ucg4a0b593n6r2zx3/13-amendments-to-the-india-mauritius-treaty (Accessed 15 May 2023).

9 "Application Document", Exim Bank at https://www.eximbankindia.in/Assets/Dynamic/PDF/LOCTenders/1728LOCTenders.pdf (Accessed 04 June 2023).

10 "Mauritius - Medical Equipment" at https://www.trade.gov/country-commercial-guides/mauritius-medical-equipment (Accessed 07 June 2023).

11 Iqbal Ahmed Khan, 'Dossier: comment les prêts de l'Inde à Maurice ont évolué' l'express 27 April 2022.

12 "Metro Express Phase 2 Works" at https://mauritiusmetroexpress.mu/phase-2/?lang=en (Accessed 07 June 2023).

13 https://defimedia.info/en-images-metro-express-lancement-de-la-ligne-curepipe-phoenix (Accessed 07 June 2023).

14 https://hcimauritius.gov.in/statement?id=dBgJe (Accessed 07 June 2023).

15 High Commission of India, Port Louis, Mauritius at https://hcimauritius.gov.in/pages?id=9avme&subid=yb8md&nextid=RdG7d

16 "India signs trade deal, $100 million defence agreement with Mauritius", *India Today*, 23 February 2021.

17 Census on Foreign Liabilities and Assets of Indian Direct Investment Entities,– Data Release from 2015-2021 - v (Accessed 04 June 2023).

18 Quarterly Fact Sheet Fact Sheet On Foreign Direct Investment (FFDI) From April, 2000 to December, 2021- Department of Industry and International Trade at https://dpiit.gov.in/sites/default/files/FDI%20Factsheet%20December%2C%202021.pdf (Accessed 07 June 2023).

19 Mauritius Imports By Country at tradingeconomics.com (Accessed 07 June 2023).

20 High Commission of India, "India and Mauritius Economic Relations" https://hcimauritius.gov.in/pages?id=9avme&subid=Pe9xd&nextid=1aKRe (Accessed 07 June 2023).

21 Mauritius (MUS) and China (CHN) Trade | OEC - The Observatory of Economic Complexity.

22 Mauritius Imports from China - 2023 Data 2024 Forecast 1997-2021 Historical at trading economics.com (Accessed 07 June 2023).

23 https://statsmauritius.govmu.org/Pages/Statistics/By_Subject/External_Trade/Detailed_Trade_Data.aspx (Accessed 07 June 2023).

24 China Mauritius, A strengthening Economic Partnership Futures Directions.org at https://www.futuredirections.org.au/publication/china-mauritius-a-strengthening-economic-partnership/ (Accessed 07 June 2023).

25 China FTA Network mofcom.gov.cn at http://fta.mofcom.gov.cn/enarticle/enrelease/201712/36682_1.html (Accessed 07 June 2023).

26 CECPA Text at https://www.mcci.org/media/286492/cecpa-text-final-1-april-2021.pdf (Accessed 27 April 2023).

27 China Mauritius FTA at https://www.mcci.org/media/278863/doc-1-mauritius-china-fta-text.pdf (Accessed 27 April 2023).

28 "Mauritius: New Free Trade Agreement positions the country as a middleman between Asia and Africa", Bowmans at bowmanslaw.com (Accessed 27 April 2023).

29 https://www.allbrightlaw.com/EN/10531/e5969b8c6c9c43c5.aspx (Accessed 27 April 2023)

30 http://fta.mofcom.gov.cn/mauritius/annex/mlqs_12_en.pdf (Accessed 27 April 2023).

31 Interview of Governor Rameswurlall Basant Roi, G.C.S.K. *China Daily* https://www.bom.mu/media/media-releases/interview-governor-rameswurlall-basant-roi-gcsk-china-daily (Accessed 27 April 2023).

32 "Bank of Mauritius Launches Instant Payment System," Bank of Mauritius, 7 May 2018 at https://www.bom.mu/media/news/bank-mauritius-launches-instant-payment-system-ips

33 "Mauritius Instant Payment System," *World Bank*, https://www.worldbank.org/en/topic/paymentsystems/brief/mauritius-instant-payment-system (Accessed 27 April 2023).

34 https://www.npci.org.in/product-overview/upi-product-overview (Accessed 07 June 2023).

35 https://economictimes.indiatimes.com/industry/banking/finance/banking/upi-transactions-cross-1-3-billion-in-march/articleshow/81967602.cms (Accessed 07 June 2023).

36 "UPI is a revolution in digital payments," *Financial Express*, 11 November 2020 at https://www.financialexpress.com/money/upi-is-a-revolution-in-digital-payments/2126214/ Ministry of External Affairs, Government of India2021, India-Mauritius (Accessed 07 June 2023).

37 https://www.financialexpress.com/money/upi-is-a-revolution-in-digital-payments/2126214/ (Accessed 07 June 2023).

38 "Mauritius and India launch RuPay and Unified Payments Interface Linkage Bank of Mauritius", 12 February 2024, https://www.bom.mu/media/media-releases/media-release-mauritius-and-india-launch-rupay-and-unified-payments-interface-linkage (Accessed 07 June 2023).

39 Ministry of Foreign Affairs and External Trade, "Virtual launch of the second phase of the RuPay Card by H.E. Shri Narendra Modi, Prime Minister of India, and H.E. Dr. Lotay Tshering, Prime Minister of Bhutan", https://www.mfa.gov.bt/press-release-484/ (Accessed 07 June 2023).

40 "India, Mauritius Review Vostro Account Mechanism, Implementation Of CECPA" https://www.bqprime.com/politics/india-mauritius-review-vostro-account-mechanism-implementation-of-cecpa (Accessed 07 June 2023).

41 "UN court rules UK has no sovereignty over Chagos Islands" https://www.bbc.com/news/world-africa-55848126 (Accessed 04 June 2023).

42 Marine Resources https://blueconomy.govmu.org/Pages/Marine-Resources.aspx#:~:text=Mauritius%20has%20an%20Exclusive%20Ec onomic%20Zone%20%28EEZ%29%20of,developed %20as%20a%20major%20pillar%20for%20economic%20development.

CHAPTER 8

Geo-economics and the Reform of Multilateral Financial Institutions

Vova A Chikanda

The fundamental tension and dynamic interaction of actors in the international system has now reached unparalleled levels than ever before since the Second World War. COVID-19 tested the resolve of international society, it shook the world economy, which is now in recession and slowly recovering with the head on collision of politics and economics sharpened and the battle lines were drawn between economies, States and markets. The Russia-Ukraine War has not only deepened the scar and crack in the world economy, but even threatened the existence and essence of humanity. Are we on the brink of a third world war? How can we connect and differentiate national interest from individual self-interest?

We need a breath of humanity for a sustainable end to this War at the end of the War there will be no victors. Diplomacy as an effective tool of statecraft must find the way as Mahatma Gandhi, one of the fathers of diplomacy and peace said, "I have nothing new to teach the world; Truth and Non-violence are as old as the hills"

The end of the World Wars paved the way for the rise of multilateralism, having realised its importance to new world order. Multilateralism has played a significant role in addressing challenges affecting world governance, such as peace and security, effects of climate change, cybersecurity only to mention a few. The role of multilateral institutions to curb these challenges cannot be overstated. Nevertheless, some reforms need to be implemented in a bid to address new challenges. The Indo-Pacific region should be applauded for coming up with Resolutions to counter grievances. This great initiative enlightens the other regions especially Africa, one of the regions with a huge population of 1.5 billion. However, a globalised world facing globalised challenges requires an open, rules-based international order to ensure that the system works in the service of all nations and peoples. The right balance needs to be struck between the true multilateralism, defined as the universal rules of the game, and the large number of plurilateral agreements that permit greater flexibility to move an agenda forward when universal consensus cannot, or need not, be achieved.

Asia has been one of the continents that has been maintaining its cordial relationship with Africa, given the shared struggle against colonialism, the Non-Aligned Movement and socio-economic and demographic challenges. Geopolitically, India's desire for a more equitable world order resonates with many African sovereign nations that have become disillusioned with the liberal hegemonic Western order. India has been forthright in its desire for greater representation in multilateral bodies as a leading member of the BRICS bloc. This extends to the United Nations (UN) Security Council, where India has been an influential voice and has pushed for a permanent seat while expressing support for Africa's Ezulwini Consensus. There are similarities in approach towards climate issues as well – where India and the African nations refuse to be the West's sacrificial lambs. This positioning has championed the interests of developing countries in a way that is largely congruent with African interests.[1]

The Security Council has maintained the five permanent seats since its inception. African and Latin American countries have been airing their concerns to multilateral institutions for many years without desired results. The inequalities within the Security Council should be dealt with since Asia has only a single representative compared to Europe, which has three. This damages the legitimacy of the Security Council if it is seen as a forum dominated by the West and the Great Powers, where the Global South and smaller States are under-represented. Although the majority of UN peacekeeping operations occur in the Global South, the most affected nations wield little influence over them. In order to maintain its legitimacy, the Security Council should incorporate a geographically diverse slate of new permanent members.

The substantial significance of both the Indo-Pacific region and Africa to global economic multilateralism is a paramount acknowledgement in the African perspective. Preliminary to contemporary geo-economics is the critical reformation of Global Financial Institutions. The prevalence of geo-economic unilateralism in Global Financial Institutions has disenfranchised Africa's place in the global economy.[2] The emergence and existence of 'black swan' problems such as the COVID-19 pandemic and contemporary geopolitical tensions is the reason why reforming multilateral institutions is important. Furthermore, multipolarity is gaining traction in the Indo-Pacific region, prior to the emergence of geopolitical power houses in the Indo-Pacific region.

Asia in the era of the Indo-Pacific balances global power in the contemporary transition. Meanwhile, India is a giant of the future in this evolving paradigm. The country is expected to become the fastest-growing economy in the region; growing 169 per cent between 2016 and 2030. In terms of demographics, one of its key strengths. India will add 169 million people to its working-age population by 2030, bringing demographic dividends according to the IMF. In conjunction with the economic growth that India is projected to attain; India is a seed in the soils of global power transition. Developed countries like Japan, Singapore and rapidly developing China and Indonesia, all resemble Asia's geo-economic positioning in the global power transition. The IMF states that Asia accounts for more than 35 per cent of the world's GDP. These "shares" in the global economy are a result of economic dynamism. India's noticeable contribution to the global economy makes its role valuable to the geo-economic framework of the globe.

The Asian powers India and Japan, two of the trilateral members of the initiative, have displayed commendable responses through the evolutionary geo-economic Supply Chain Resilience Initiative (SCRI)[3]. The Pacific Forum mentions, "The Quadrilateral Security Dialogue (SCRI) seeks to ensure global supply chains remain resilient to future 'black swan' events, such as pandemics and geopolitical tensions." An important factor is the fact that several States prioritised supply chain risk diversification, particularly the establishment of the Indo-Pacific Economic Security Dialogue. A further contribution of rapid reform of the global financial institutions is counter-hegemony by the Indo-Pacific SCRI. Counter-hegemony is an urgent need among the delimitation complications of China's assimilation in the South China Sea, which is traced to the highly profitable geo-economic advantages to China's trading capacity. The inclusion of other Indo-Pacific States into the SCRI could evoke multilateral reformation of global financial institutions, particularly diversified inclusivity for the WTO – to African and Indo-Pacific States in these trying times. The United Nations Conference on Trade and Development, stated, "An estimated $3.37 trillion worth, or 21% of all global trade, transited through the South China Sea."[4] The geo-economic tensions are indicated through the statistics, deciphering China's hegemonic initiatives in the Indo-Pacific region. Therefore, responsive reformation of multilateral institutions, including the WTO could further the goals of shared multilateralism in the region.

It is of paramount importance to note that amongst all multilateral institutions the World Health Organization needs serious attention. A healthy globalised village is the rationale behind the achievement of the United Nations agenda. A handful of challenges affecting WHO include – but are not limited to the fact that there is no single document which comprehensively describes its responsibilities, obligations and powers with respect to infectious diseases. The Organization's responsibilities during a pandemic include surveillance, monitoring and evaluation, developing guidance for member states that lack the ability to direct an international response to a life-threatening epidemic. WHO's annual operating budget is lesser than that of many university hospitals. It had delayed the declaration of COVID-19 as a Public Health Emergency, which sparked widespread international concern and showed WHO's lack of preparedness for the global pandemic

The level of policy coordination required within the complex of global institutions is extremely high. The security threat of the COVID-19 pandemic showcased the possibility for policy coordination through responsive global vaccination through the World Health Organization, however, further substantial reform is necessary to respond to such threats in the future. The World Health Organization's active involvement in assisting vaccination in States has successfully led to more than 5.55 billion people worldwide having received a COVID-19 vaccine, equal to about 72.3 percent of the world population according to Our World in Data. Despite the success rate, reform is significant for WHO's adaptability for medicinal research and production to involve itself in the geo-economic constructs of the globe.

A familiar component to the infusion of geo-economics in globalisation is the World Trade Organisation, which requires substantial reform to support the inclusion of African and Indo-Pacific States. The lack of Western interest in African industrialisation for example, is a truth that prompts the propagation of future multilateral integration in South-South cooperation.

The WTO has been less effective in addressing trade protectionism, which raised questions over its credibility. The WTO has played a very limited role in helping address other global issues related to trade, such as food security, climate change and global trade imbalances.

The 'malignant illicit trade'[5], is extensively paralytic to domestic and international trade flows, prompting resolute responses in governance. The Indo-Pacific's potential exponential benefits in multilateral trade with Africa are unquestionably hindered by selfish capitalisation by individuals and entities. This prompts an even greater response in favour of WTO reform. Illicit financial trade as defined by the Second UNCTAD Illicit Trade Forum in 2022[6], creates a triple threat to the financing of development: crowding out legitimate economic activity, depriving Governments of revenues for investment in vital public services and increasing the costs of achieving the Sustainable Development Goals (SDGs).

The UN Conference on Trade and Development (UNCTAD) statistically represents comparisons to the notions in a 2020 Report, stating, 'Africa loses about US$ 88.6 billion in illicit capital flight every year – equivalent to 3.7 per cent of the continent's gross domestic product. The depreciation of the global supply chains inherently begins domestically, with an epidemic bearing on geo-economic multilateralism. The maintenance of geo-economic cooperation is a responsibility that resonates to the WTO. COVID-19 pandemic and Russo-Ukraine war's bearing on the Indo-Pacific supply chains require further responses of consideration from the WTO.

The International Labour Organisation (ILO) requires substantial reform, as for one hundred years, in a world of complex supply chains, insecure jobs, increasing global deregulation of the labour market and millions of people stuck in forced labour in factories, farms and fishing boats, is the ILO still relevant? Without policy coordination, the complexity of resolve is heightened in the ILO's failure to respond to its global responsibilities. Despite a vast coverage of member states, the ILO needs reform as it inadequately advocates for regulations of labour markets, causing concern. The irregularities in labour markets crosshairs the geo-economic disparities that are creating a lack of availability of public goods.

The Bretton Woods global financial institutions require reform in favour of diversified cooperation, to adapt to the inevitable rise of Asia. The alternative sources of finance, in the form of digital currency and State-to-State foreign investment, has created a bridge of financial infrastructure and connectivity excluding Bretton Woods institutions. Multilateralism is therefore the next viable option.

The decentralisation of MDBs to facilitate fair financial assistance for struggling developing States, is a key subject requiring reformation. The World Bank states that, "The lending program in Zimbabwe is inactive due to arrears and the role is now limited to technical assistance and analytical work through Trust Funds."[7] This reveals a geo-economic disparity that excludes in-depth cooperation between MDBs. However, 'the government has prepared an Arrears

Clearance, Debt Relief and Restructuring Strategy and resumed token payments to IFIs and Paris Club creditors.' Global Financial Institutions or Multilateral Development Banks (MDB) for example, The World Bank, Asian Development Bank (ADB) and African Development Bank (AfDB) are essential multilateral constructs in geo-economics They however questioned the incentives of these institutions, rationalised geopolitical divisions prior to mainstream cooperation within State macroeconomics. The lack of assistance from Bretton Woods institutions proliferates ineffective macroeconomic sustainability hindering adaptability, therefore Zimbabwe's multilateral economic cooperation with the Indo-Pacific region provides an opportunity for enhanced multilateral industrialisation in the fourth Industrial Revolution.[8] The call for African governments to awaken from slumber forms a critical prerequisite for modernisation.

India's cooperation with Zimbabwe is desirable, as India is at the forefront of aerospace engineering, AI and technological developmental projections. Indo-Pacific and African geo-economic multilateralism for technological proficiency is urgent, as a PwC study revealed' "AI could contribute up to $15.7 trillion to the global economy in 2030, primarily by increasing labour productivity through automation and product enhancement across various sectors."

The fourth Industrial Revolution, comprising technological evolution, bridges the digital divide globally. The Indo-Pacific region's technological infrastructure makes technology affordable and accessible as shown by the Internet Society, which mentions, "region accounts for a little over half of the world's internet users, and these users are primarily young and mobile: over 90 per cent access the internet using their phones".

The Digital Indo-Pacific concept shows the region is "home to the largest, most rapidly growing internet user bases in the world."

However, despite the resilient digital resolve in the region, discrepancies are observed in financial digitisation and geo-economics within the global cyber threat to finance. Digital currency, as an alternative source of finance, is susceptible to cyberattacks. Maurer and Nelson, (2021) through the International Monetary Fund (IMF) noted, "February 2016, hackers targeted the Central Bank of Bangladesh and exploited vulnerabilities in SWIFT, the global financial system's main electronic payment messaging system, trying to steal $1 billion. While most transactions were blocked, $101 million still disappeared."[9] The heist was a wake-up call for the finance world that systemic cyber risks in the financial system had been severely underestimated. Furthermore, North Korea has stolen some $2 billion from at least 38 countries in the past five years. The risks to global cyber financial systems, shows the urgency of reformation in multilateral financial institutions such as the IMF to counter cyber-attacks. Therefore, multilateral cooperation between Indo-Pacific regional banks and African banks in technological cyber security, propels the reform of these institutions, with security being a priority.

The recent economic initiative, The Indo-Pacific Economic Framework for Prosperity (IPEF) launched by the former US President Joe Biden in May 2022, resembles growing global economic multilateralism in the Indo-Pacific region. This agreement includes India, Indonesia, Japan, Republic of Korea, Malaysia, New Zealand, the Philippines, Singapore, Thailand, Australia, Brunei, and Vietnam.[10] Together, all the countries included represent 40 per cent of the world GDP. The concept and implementation measures of the IPEF are significant for Africa's adoption, concurring with the notion that the Indo-Pacific region is on the right track of multilateralism and 'Africa desires to learn and implement'.

Within the IPE , four pillars – improved committed mechanisms for anticipation and prevention of supply chains, advancements in clean energy, decarbonisation, and green infrastructure and corruption, effective tax implementation, anti-money laundering, and anti-bribery regimes crack downs – postulate economic integration through data localisation.[11] These exemplary proponents of economic integration are features of geo-economic security in the region that require consistent implementation for refined results.

Reforming multilateralism in the Indo-Pacific region and Africa assumes real significance now. The aforementioned geo-economic challenges and the minimalist response from multilateral global financial institutions discussed in the chapter, require exigency through implementation. The following Resolutions are proposed for multilateral reform through the Conference.

Recommendations

1. Expansion of the Security Council to allow fair and equal representation of all the continents.
2. Reaffirming regional engagement with the Indo-Pacific Economic Framework for Prosperity (IPEF) and Supply Chain Resilience Initiative (SCRI).
3. The election of India as a permanent member of the United Nations Security Council (UNSC)

4. The veto powers granted to the permanent members should be clearly analysed.
5. There is a need to strengthen the Economic and Social Council's role in policy guidance, oversight and coordination.
6. There is a need to preserve a balanced approach and a rational division of labour between the different principal organs, missions, agencies and funds, based on the UN Charter and on specific mandates.
7. There is a need for an efficient and accountable UN Secretariat to strengthen accountability and oversight, improve its management performance and transparency, represent and reinforce ethical conduct.
8. There is a need to ensure that extra budgetary or voluntary contributions are earmarked to ensure that the WHO has necessary flexibility for its usage in areas where they are most required.
9. There is an urgent need for effective involvement of member states in discussions on budget implementation and spending.
10. Establishing strong and robust financial accountability frameworks will enable maintenance of integrity in financial flows.
11. There is a need to create a monitoring mechanism and support for member states on international health regulations, preparedness of infrastructure, human resources and relevant health system capacities, such as testing and surveillance
12. A reaffirmed commitment to the rules-based liberal order with a developmental dimension must be the foundational starting point.
13. A reformed WTO will have to be constructed on the foundation of liberal multilateralism, resting on open, non-discriminatory plurilateral pillars, an improved Appellate Body, explicit accommodation of regional trade agreements, and appropriate safety valves for rules-based sovereign action.
14. The emerging new economic powers, particularly India and China, and some other African, Asian and Latin American countries should be given due place and role.
15. There is a need for reflection on the purpose, the substantive role it should play in the future, the need to strengthen inclusive multilateralism, and the action needed to bolster the position of emerging economies and developing countries.
16. Governance reform in the recruitment processes of the World Bank by ensuring selection through an open and merit-based process.
17. IMF loan conditions should be paired with other reforms; for instance,

trade reform in developed nations, debt cancellation, and increased financial assistance for investments in basic infrastructure.

18. There is a need to make the IMF responsive to human rights, environmental sustainability and labour rights.

Conclusion

There is a need for the establishment of a Working Group on the Future of Multilateralism to develop a set of principles that can help lay the foundations of a new pact on multilateralism with an eye towards accepting institutional diversity, while ensuring the provision of global public goods and managing the Global Commons. Multilateralism needs to address its discontent and evolve to be fit for purpose in an era of renewed great power competition, political-economic tensions, politicisation of issues, and a decoupling of economic prosperity from social prosperity. Globalisation and multilateralism are means to an end (i.e., social and economic prosperity), rather than ends in themselves. Multilateralism ought to be used as an instrument to promote strong, sustainable, balanced, and inclusive growth within all nation-states.

NOTES

1 Africa could gain $89 billion annually by curbing illicit financial flows, 28 September 2020, https://unctad.org/news/africa-could-gain-89-billion-annually-curbing-illicit-financial-flows (Accessed 21 March 2023).

2 *Africa Renewal*, January 2023, United Nations Department of Economic and Social Affairs (DESA) at www.un.org (Accessed 21 March 2023).

3 "PacNet #31 – The Structural Limits of the Supply Chain Resilience Initiative" at www.pacforum.org (Accessed 21 March 2023).

4 "How Much Trade Transits the South China Sea?" *China Power Project* at www.csis.org (Accessed 21 March 2023).

5 "Tackling illicit trade in medical products: Better international cooperation for better health" at https://www.wto.org/english/res_e/booksp_e/tackling-illicit-trade e.pdf (Accessed 20 March 2023).

6 "Case Study: Mapping the impact of illicit trade on the UN Sustainable Development Goals: SDG 8 Decent Work and Economic Growth", Second UNCTAD Illicit Trade Forum, 6-7 September 2022, Palais des Nations, Geneva at DITC2022_Contribution_ ITF_TRACIT_en.pdf (unctad.org) (Accessed March 2023).

7 "The World Bank in Zimbabwe", Zimbabwe Overview: Development News, Research, Data, *The World Bank Group* at https://www.worldbank.org/en/country/zimbabwe (Accessed 21 March 2023).

8 Hannes Ebert, "India and the Fourth Industrial Revolution: Promises, Perils, and Policy Responses", 2018, at www. gmfus.org (Accessed 21 March 2023)

9 T. Maurer & A. Nelson, "The Global Cyber Threat" International Monetary Fund, Finance & Development, Spring 2021, at https://www.imf.org/external/pubs/ft/fandd/2021/03/global-cyber-threat-to-financial-systems-maurer.htm (Accessed 21 March 2023).

10 ASEAN-Outlook-on-the-Indo-Pacific_FINAL_22062019.pdf (Accessed 22 March 2023).

11 "Mobile Internet Usage Trends in Asia-Pacific", Internet Society, February 2016 at https://www.internetsociety.org/wp-content/uploads/2017/08/Mobile20Internet20Usage20Trends20in20Asia-Pacific.pdf. (Accessed 22 March 2023).

CHAPTER 9

The Evolution of Multilateral Development Banks' Missions and Operations

Samir Elsadek Mahmoudi

Connectivity, Trade, Investment and Resilient Supply Chain

A larger-than-ever development finance gap incentivises the international community to consider options to enhance Multilateral Development Banks' (MDBs) financial firepower. Important factors impacting the development finance landscape make the evolution of MDBs imperative. First, estimates of the financial flows needed to fulfil the international community's Sustainable Development Goals (SDGs) are in trillions, far beyond the collective capacity of major MDBs In fact, in response to a growing external financing gap, developing countries recognised the value of establishing new development finance institutions including the Asian Infrastructure Investment Bank (AIIB) and the New Development Bank (NDB). More recently, the international community agreed on the establishment of a funding arrangement to respond to loss and damage emanating from increasingly frequent climate-related events. Second, the current tightening of global credit conditions raises the cost of developing countries' access to capital markets and emphasises the relevance of MDBs in times of crises.

This chapter describes the challenges facing the expansion of the financial footprint of MDBs, especially the limitations on their risk-capacity. It also discusses the points of strength that make MDBs efficient intermediaries between capital markets on the one hand and developing countries on the other. It also describes the current evolution process of MDBs that the international community launched in response to these challenges. To support the expansion, the International Bank for Reconstruction and Development (IBRD) is used as an example throughout the chapter, given its status as the oldest and largest MDB.

The Strength of Multilateral Cooperation in Development Finance and MDBs Financial Model

Maximising the developmental impact of MDBs is in the best interest of both donor and recipient countries. A plethora of factors make the case for the relevance of these institutions as efficient vehicles of delivering financial support to developing countries. Given their shareholders' support and prudent Capital Adequacy Frameworks (CAF), MDBs are able to translate their relatively limited paid-in capital into a much larger volume of developmental lending. This is particularly pronounced in the case of IBRD, the institution in charge of providing financial and advisory services to middle-income countries and creditworthy low-income countries within the World Bank Group.[1] IBRD's governance has usually been subject to criticism regarding its representativeness of developing countries' interests. Voting powers within IBRD's Executive Board are allocated to each shareholder nation based on its subscription to the Bank's capital. The largest shareholder countries include the United States, IBRD's largest shareholder country, holding 16.64 per cent of total capital subscriptions followed by Japan (7.59 per cent), China (5.88 per cent), Germany (4.50 per cent), France and the United Kingdom (4.12 per cent each).

Since their establishment, MDBs' efficiency in intermediating between capital markets and developing countries has proven to be particularly critical in alleviating developing countries' cost of access to capital, but also to maximise the financial impact of a relatively limited capital base subscribed by shareholders. Being able to maintain low Equity-to-Loans ratios (E/L), MDBs maximise the developmental impact of limited shareholders' capital. For instance, having an E/L ratio of 22 per cent, IBRD translates each dollar of equity into approximately $5 of lending. Put simply, a mere 22 per cent of IBRD's lending is financed using shareholders' equity while IBRD's borrowing enables it to maintain a total lending portfolio of $229.25 billion. To sustain this size of lending, MDBs leverage their screening expertise in developing countries to achieve superior asset quality while maintaining MDBs' superior credit rating, as well as low cost of capital to MDBs. MDBs generally have little non-performing loans. For instance, IBRD has a Non-Performing Loan (NPL) ratio of 0.2 per cent.[2]

However, currently, MDBs, with their relatively limited capital, are unable to fill the growing development finance gap. Their strength emanates from their efficiency in intermediating between capital market investors and borrowers in developing countries. To overcome the high cost of accessing capital markets, developing countries rely on this financial intermediation function of MDBs. In recognition of their superior credit rating, MDBs issue long-term bonds at low yields in capital markets to re-channel these funds to developing countries. MDBs' superior creditworthiness is critical for them to keep the cost of fulfilling this intermediation function in check, but also to strike the balance between a low equity to lending ratio on the one hand and maintaining a superior credit profile on the other. IBRD is no exception as it maintains a triple-A credit rating by the three rating agencies S&P, Fitch and Moody's. Relative to the larger aspirations of developing countries, by the end of June 2022, IBRD had a mere $229.25 billion of total loans outstanding. This size of lending is supported by approximately $50.48 billion of usable equity, including $19.35 billion of usable paid-in capital and $32.05 billion of general reserves.[3] In addition to its equity, IBRD finances its lending portfolio through its low-cost access to capital markets. By the end of June 2022, the borrowing portfolio of IBRD reached approximately $256.9 billion. IBRD earns interest income on the loans extended to developing countries in addition to return on its equity investments.[4] IBRD also transfers part of its income to the International Development Association (IDA).

Table I

IBRD's Equity		IBRD's Total Loan Exposure and Capital Adequacy Indicators
Usable Paid-in Capital	19,352	229,250
General reserve	32,053	**Equity to Loans** ≈ 22%.
IBRD's Usable Equity Usable Paid-in Capital General Reserves Special Reserves and Adjustments	H" 50,481	
Callable Capital	286,636	Statutory Lending Limit (SLL) = Total Subscribed Capital + Reserves ≈ 339,000
Total Subscribed Capital IBRD's Paid-in Capital IBRD's Callable Capital	307,135	

Note: Usable Paid-in Capital is the amount of capital available to support IBRD's risk-bearing capacity. General Reserves include earnings from prior fiscal years approved for retention by the Board. IBRD's Article of Agreement (Article III, Section 3) determines the Statutory Lending Limit. Special Reserves and Adjustments include amount held in liquid forms to meet IBRD's obligations on its borrowing and guarantees, in addition to other adjustments (negligible amounts relative to paid-in capital and general reserves). *Source:* IBRD's Management's Discussion and Analysis and Financial Statements, June 30, 2022. Figures are in US $ millions.

Importantly, shareholders' support is a main factor that strengthens MBDs' risk profile to enable these institutions to maintain this level of borrowing. MDBs' capital base is structured to signal shareholders' commitment to protect MDBs' bondholders against potential default events. For instance, while IBRD's usable paid-in capital amounts to $19.35 billion, this amount of capital is dwarfed by IBRD's callable capital amounting to $286.64 billion. Callable capital may not be used to finance IBRD's operations, but to support MDBs in the event of a default. In the event of a call for capital, shareholders commit to respond with their shares of callable capital to help IBRD meet its debt obligations.[5] However, MDBs capital adequacy frameworks aim to minimise the likelihood of a call for capital. In fact, to date, IBRD has never resorted to its callable capital.

Equally important, the Preferred Creditor Status (PCS) enjoyed by MDBs is another signal of support of the international community to the developmental mission of these institutions. PCS has significant positive repercussions on MDBs creditworthiness by mitigating credit risk. Being preferred creditors, they are expected to be repaid in full in the event of a default of a sovereign borrower on its obligations toward bilateral or private creditors. Unlike other creditors, MDBs do not offer debt restructuring and continue to seek full repayment in the event of a sovereign default.[6]

MDBs' Capital Adequacy Frameworks and the Limitations on MDBs' Risk Taking

While the international community calls for an enhanced role of MDBs, a variety of factors complicate the expansion of MDBs' financial footprint beyond their current lending size. Unlike commercial financial institutions, MDBs are not subject to the regulation of a specific regulatory body. Being constrained by a limited capital base and reliant on market-based funding, MDBs rely on their own Capital Adequacy Frameworks, in addition to market factors including the cost of capital and credit rating agencies' assessment of their creditworthiness. To achieve their explicit goal of maintaining a triple-A credit rating, MDBs' Capital Adequacy Frameworks set standards governing the minimum capital to be held to cover for unexpected losses, including through statutory rules on maximum lending and leverage. IBRD is no exception.[7] IBRD's Articles of Agreement puts limitations on the total lending it can issue, so the total amount outstanding of loans, participations in loans, and callable guarantees may not exceed the sum of subscribed capital (including callable capital), reserves and surplus. This cap on lending is referred to as the 'Statutory Lending Limit' (SLL).[8] To quantify the extent to which subscribed capital supports IBRD's developmental lending, the Gearing Ratio (GR) is defined as the ratio of loans outstanding and callable guarantees to total subscribed capital (including callable capital), reserves and surplus. Based on IBRD's Articles of Agreement, the Gearing Ratio cannot exceed one. Currently, IBRD's total subscribed capital amounts to $307 billion, including $20.5 billion of paid-in capital with the remainder of $286.5 billion being in callable capital. Accordingly, IBRD's lending does not reach its full statutory lending as its loans outstanding and callable guarantees stand at approximately 69.5 per cent of its (SLL) by June 2022.[9]

In relation, IBRD puts a cap on its leverage and risk-bearing capacity using a policy minimum E/L ratio, currently set to a policy minimum of 20 per dent. By setting a policy minimum for the E/L ratio, IBRD seeks to strike the balance between extending the maximum amount of lending supported by available equity on one hand and preserving IBRD's triple-A credit rating on the other. In practice, through continuous balance sheet optimisation, IBRD's E/L ratio declined over time from approximately 38 per cent in 2008 to 22 per cent in 2022 to allow for a more aggressive use of shareholders' capital and increased lending. Currently, the World Bank's Executive Board is considering lowering the policy minimum to 19 per cent, relative to the current minimum of 20 per cent. While being costly, increasing IBRD's usable equity in support of more risk bearing, through a capital increase, is a straightforward way to boost its financial footprint. In 2018, shareholders approved an IBRD capital increase package of $7.5 billion of paid-in capital, in addition to $52.6 billion of callable capital.

Equally important, MDBs' loan portfolios are inherently concentrated within a limited number of sovereigns. Relative to commercial banks, which extend their services to a much larger number of private borrowers, concentration risk is more pronounced in the case of MDBs. For instance, IBRD, the largest MDB, has only 85 IBRD-eligible sovereign borrowers (including 15 Blend countries). In addition to the limited number of client countries, IBRD's lending is disproportionately concentrated among larger Middle-Income Countries (MICs) whose absorptive capacity allow them to make greater use of MDBs' lending. To manage exposure risk, IBRD limits its lending to each individual sovereign to the minimum of two benchmarks, the 'Equitable Access Limit' (EAL) and the 'Single Borrower Limit' (SBL). The former metric states that IBRD must not extend more than 10 per cent of its maximum lending, the SLL, to a single sovereign. As of June 2022, IBRD's EAL stands at $34 billion. On the other hand, SBL puts a cap on the exposure of IBRD to its most creditworthy borrowing nations to either $24.9 billion for countries below the Graduation Discussion Income (GDI) and $21.2 BN for countries above the GDI.[10] To further limit loan portfolio concentration, IBRD sets an SBL surcharge of 50 basis points to be applied on the incremental exposure of a country beyond the SBL surcharge limit that is $2.5 billion below the respective SBL.

Proposals to Expand MDBs' Lending Capacity

Meeting the financial needs for the fulfillment of the SDGs, including climate finance, would likely require more risk bearing capacity than what MDBs' equity could support. Kharas and Bhattacharya (2023) argue that a fresh capital increase is key to supporting IBRD's expansion of lending, as it provides an explicit signal to credit rating agencies about the credibility of shareholders' commitment to supporting IBRD. A fresh capital increase directly expands the capital base against which IBRD borrows in capital markets to finance its operations. In the absence of a boost to equity and relying solely on balance sheet optimisation, reaching a lending portfolio of a trillion dollars would require an unrealistic decline in E/L ratio. However, a capital increase implies a fiscal cost to shareholders and is also subject to political considerations among shareholder nations. In fact, due to the fiscal cost to taxpayers and required legislative approvals, limiting the likelihood of future capital increases is particularly important for some shareholder nations.[11] Accordingly, shareholders are generally more supportive of a more aggressive usage of MDBs' existing equity, by lowering E/L ratio, rather than a capital increase. Since contributions to capital are proportional to the allocation of voting powers within the institution, a capital increase needs to preserve MDBs' existing voting structure, as any deviation from such structure, leading to the increase in the voting power of some shareholder nations at the expense of others, would require political consensus among MDBs' shareholders. In practice, since its establishment, IBRD has had both General Capital Increases (CGIs) and Selective Capital Increases (SCI). GCIs aim solely at increasing IBRD's capital base and lending capacity in accordance with its existing distribution of capital shares and voting structures. On the other hand, SCIs increase IBRD capital base, but also rebalance IBRD's shareholding structure based on political compromises within the institution. For instance, the 2018's IBRD capital increase package included both a GCI and a SCI.[12]

Consequently, policy discussions within the Group of Twenty (G20) and MDBs, consider a wider set of balance sheet optimisation options in addition to innovative ways to expand MDBs' capital base. Importantly, in 2021, G20 launched an independent review of MDBs' Capital Adequacy Frameworks with a view to provide a better understanding of these frameworks to shareholders and to credit rating agencies. The review discussed ways to expand MDBs' financial firepower while preserving their triple-A credit rating and financial sustainability.[13] This includes ways to bring additional public and private capital to MDBs balance sheets, in addition to creating more headroom for MDB lending by transferring risk to investors.[14]

The independent review explored ways to make more influential incorporation of callable capital into MDBs' capital adequacy frameworks. While most of MDBs' capital is in the form of callable capital rather than paid-in equity, such form of capital cannot be used for operational purposes.[15] In fact, MDBs adopt prudent capital adequacy frameworks with a view to limit the likelihood of resorting to callable capital. However, since callable capital is intended to be a guarantee against MDBs' insolvency scenarios, the independent review called for MDBs to incorporate a prudent uplift from callable capital into their capital adequacy frameworks. Accounting for callable capital can support MDBs' creditworthiness and reflect shareholders' support.[16] However, to date, callable capital has never been employed by MDBs. This lack of precedent for the usage of callable capital implies significant uncertainties about its potential deployment in the event of MDBs' insolvency. These uncertainties make callable capital of questionable value as a guarantee. Accordingly, proposals about a greater reliance on callable capital in MDBs capital adequacy frameworks are tightly linked to suggestions on ways to clarify the procedures for its potential operationalisation and the procedures that would be followed by MDBs to trigger a call for capital. Lankes et al. (2022) argue that the credibility of callable capital requires MDBs to define the scenarios in which MDBs' financial situations would deteriorate to the extent that the deployment of callable capital could be triggered and the likelihood of occurrence of these scenarios.

Equally important, introducing forms of non-voting shares can circumvent shareholders' aversion to the dilution of their relative weights within MDBs' capital structure. Non-voting shares can expand MDBs' capital base and also provide safe interest-bearing asset class to public and private investors. For instance, IBRD's management explored ways to issue hybrid capital instruments to be made available to shareholders and to capital market investors with no voting rights associated with the investment [Development Committee, 2023]. Other MDBs, including the African Development Bank, are considering hybrid capital as well. Hybrid capital has the features of both debt and equity instruments. It provides fixed income to investors and, similar to debt instruments, does not dilute MDBs' capital or entail voting rights, but have a perpetual maturity making them appear like permanent investments in MDBs.[17] By raising hybrid capital, MDBs could aim to leverage hybrid capital's equity characteristics to expand MDBs borrowing capacity and, in turn, their lending portfolio. However, a main concern about hybrid capital is its expected higher cost of capital relative to IBRD borrowing rates and, in turn, its potential impact on IBRD loan pricing [Development Committee, 2023].

In principle, MDBs' screening expertise in developing countries could be leveraged to attract private capital through risk transfer schemes. MDBs could leverage their risk assessment expertise in developing countries to originate loans with a view to shift risks to investors through securitisation. First, due to their extensive expertise in developing nations, they could lessen information asymmetry concerns preventing investment flows to developing countries. Second, transferring risks to investors can free lending headroom that can be recycled to originate more loans. However, concerns have been raised about the viability of securitisation programmes. Due to the very developmental nature of MDBs, their loans are priced below market rates making them less attractive to investors [Humphrey, 2017]. Moreover, while loans maintained on MDBs' balance sheets receive Preferred Creditor Status treatment in the event of a sovereign debt restructuring, there are uncertainties about whether loans originated by MDBs, but transferred off their balance sheets, would still be granted Preferred Creditor Status treatment by the Paris Club.[18]

However, other types of risk transfer schemes have been put into implementation by MDBs including shareholder guarantee programmes. Recently, the World Bank announced a $5 billion shareholder guarantee programme with a view to $30 billion of lending over 10 years.[19] Through these programmes, shareholders of superior credit ratings agree to be guarantors and commit to step in and repay MDBs in the event of borrowing nations default to MDBs. Having these guarantees in place de-risk MDBs' lending and allows MDBs' equity to support more lending.

In the same vein, MDBs' are penalised by credit rating agencies for having portfolios that are inherently concentrated among a limited number of borrowing nations.[20] While MDBs' exposure limits are a first line of defence against concentration risks, innovative techniques such as Exposure Exchange Agreements (EEAs) also allow MDBs to alleviate concentration risks. EEAs allow MDBs to rebalance their portfolios by swapping their exposures between each other to reduce their exposure to countries at which they are highly concentrated and in turn, increase their exposure to countries at which they have little presence. Through an EEA, an MDB agrees to assume the risk on a portfolio of loans owed by some borrowing countries and held by another MDB and vice-versa. However, while MDBs exchange their exposure to risk on their portfolios, loans remain on their respective balance sheets and each MDB remains the lender of record for the loans it originated. Reducing risks emanating from excessive exposure to individual borrowers enhances MDBs' capital adequacy and can create room for additional lending.[21] For instance, very recently in July 2023, the African Development Bank and the Asian Development Bank agreed on an EEA of a billion dollars. The Asian Development Bank and the Inter-American Development Bank entered into a similar agreement in 2020.

In addition to its approach to expand its capital base and to mitigate risks, since 2017, the World Bank has adopted a 'cascade' approach that prioritises the involvement of private capital involvement in development finance and deploy public funds only after the failure of private alternatives. The cascade approach addresses potential upstream policy reforms that could potentially be deployed to unlock investments on a commercial basis. In the event of persisting market failures preventing private investment flows, MDBs could intervene by providing credit enhancement products supporting the viability of the project paving the way for private sector participation. Only in the event de-risking could still fail to unlock private investment flows, scarce public resources could be deployed. For instance, MDBs' efforts to support electricity market reforms, design efficient fed-in tariffs and provide political risk insurance leading to wide scale private sector participation are referred to as examples for the implementation of the cascade approach.

Conclusion

MDBs' capital and risk-bearing capacity are limited in relation to estimates of financial flows needed to fulfill the SDGs. While a capital increase is the most straightforward way to boost MDBs' borrowing and lending capacity, a challenging political process and global economic circumstances might hinder its progress. To maximise the usage of their available equity, MDBs have traditionally resorted to balance sheet optimisation measures including by progressively lowering their equity to loans ratio. Relying solely on further declines in these ratios is unlikely to enable MDBs to respond the current development finance gap, particularly given their need to maintain their triple-A credit rating. The current international efforts to overcome these constraints have been focusing on strengthening MDBs' Capital Adequacy Frameworks and designing alternative ways to raise capital or diversify and mitigate risk with a view to free up additional lending headroom. While the impact of these strategies remains limited compared to the demands of developing countries, significant efforts are being made to optimise the usage of MDBs' existing capital, to further emphasise shareholders' support to these institutions and to mitigate concentration risks. Moreover, the crowding-in other sources of capital, including those from private investors, is still an under-explored avenue for MDBs' evolution.

***I thank Ragui El-Etreby for his inspirational mentorship throughout my appointment at the Department of Economic Affairs at Egypt's Foreign Ministry, a period during which I followed G20's discussions on the evolution of Multilateral Development Banks. I am also grateful to Maged Refaat for having accepted to proofread a draft of this chapter. All errors and omissions are my own.*

NOTES

1 The world's poorest countries and those of lower creditworthiness are eligible for the support of another institution within the World Bank Group, the International Development Association IDA that is the soft lending window of the World Bank. However, some IDA-eligible are still creditworthy enough to be considered for some IBRD lending. These are referred to as "*Blend countries*". Moreover, IBRD also transfers part of its income to IDA. For a more detailed discussion of the World Bank's operational lending categories.

2 As of June 2022, only 0.2 per cent of IBRD loans were in non-accrual status and are all related to Zimbabwe. However, recently, IBRD placed Belarus on non-performing status raising IBRD's non-accrual ratio to 0.6 per cent.

3 General Reserves consist of IBRD's earnings from prior fiscal years that the Executive Board approves for retention as part of IBRD's equity.

4 While usable paid-in capital is $19.35 billion, accumulation of general reserves throughout time led IBRD's usable equity to its current value of $50.48 billion. Since general reserves accumulation originates from the bank's profits from its lending in developing countries, this argument has been used in favour of a more democratic governance of IBRD [Griffith-Jones, "New Financial Architecture as a Global Public Good", Paper Prepared for UNDP, 2002].

5 IBRD's Articles of Agreement: Article II, Section 5. However, not all MDBs are supported by callable capital. The International Finance Corporation (IFC) and the Inter-American Development Bank Invest (IDB Invest) do not have callable capital.

6 A body of literature argues this senior treatment of International Financial Institutions' loans, including MDBs and the International Monetary Fund, is a de-facto market practice rather than an implication of international law [Tito Cordella and Andrew Powell, "Preferred and Non-Preferred Creditors", *Journal of International Economics*, Vol. 132, 2021.] On the other hand, debt treatment for obligations owed to non-multilateral creditors is subject to the comparability of treatment principle.

7 The World Bank earned its triple-A in 1959 and was followed by regional MDBs including the Asian Development Bank, the InterAmerican Development Bank, the European Bank for Reconstruction and Development.

8 IBRD's Articles of Agreement: Article III, Section 3.

9 By June 2022, the Gearing Ratio is given by the ratio of outstanding loans, participation in loans and callable guarantees, $235.7 billion, to the sum of subscribed capital, $307 billion, and General Reserves, $32 billion leading to a Statutory Lending Limit of $339 billion and a Gearing Ratio of 69.5 per cent. Accordingly, while callable capital is not directly used to finance IBRD's operations, it does set limitations on the maximum lending of IBRD, Statutory Lending Limit, even though it is currently not binding.

10 The Graduation Discussion Income is the level of Gross National Income (GNI) per capita that triggers graduation discussion. As of July 2021, the GDI stands at $7,155. Exceeding the GDI does not automatically imply ineligibility for IBRD's lending.

11 For instance, in its justification of support to its international programmes, the US Treasury argued that IBRD's financial discipline limits the likelihood of future capital increases [U S Department of the Treasury, 2023].

12 The 2018's Capital Increase Package included a $7.5 billion out of which $5.6 billions correspond to a GCI and $1.9 billion correspond to a SCI. A particularly important outcome of the SCI is the strengthening of China's shareholding and voting power within IBRD.

13 The independent review was launched by the G20, during the Italian Presidency of G20 in 2021, to provide an evaluation of the factors influencing MDBs' Capital Adequacy Frameworks and ways to enhance their lending capacity without putting at risk their credit rating and financial sustainability.

14 "Boosting MDBs' investing capacity." An Independent Review of Multilateral Development Banks' Capital Adequacy Frameworks, https://www.gihub.org/resources/publications/boosting-mdbs-investing-capacity-an-independent-review-of-multilateral-development-banks-capital-adequacy-frameworks/ https://doi.org/10.1002/9781119300762.WSTS0012 echnological

15 While it is not used for lending purposes, callable capital is part of MDBs' total subscribed capital. Together with reserves and surplus, it puts a ceiling on the maximum lending size of MDBs, the Statutory Lending Limit, although is currently non-binding (in the case of IBRD).

16 Credit rating agencies follow a two-steps approach to assess MDBs creditworthiness. First, MDBs are rated based on their own financial strength including measures of their capital adequacy (including equity, lending size and asset quality) and their liquidity. Second, MDBs' stand-alone rating is further augmented by uplifts reflecting shareholders' support to MDBs [C Humphery, "Challenges and Opportunities for the Multilateral Development Banks in the 21st Century Infrastructure Finance" Global Green Growth Institute and G24 Special Paper Series on Infrastructure Finance and Development, Seoul]. While callable capital is pledged to be deployed by shareholders in the event of an insolvency, the fact that callable capital has bever been put to the test puts ambiguity around its value as a guarantee. Moreover, MDBs themselves do not incorporate callable capital in their capital adequacy frameworks.

17 Hybrid capital is intended to have both debt and equity characteristics. Its equity characteristics are useful as it is intended to be leveraged to enhance MDBs borrowing capacity. On the other hand, it does not dilute MDBs capital. A main criterion for the success of hybrid capital is how credit rating agencies perceive its equity component.

18 Securitisation of non-sovereign assets is more straightforward and is already practiced by

several MDBs, including IFC, AFDB and the European Bank for Reconstruction and Development. In these cases, securitisation is synthetic. Although loans are sold to investors, MDBs remain the lender of record and remain responsible for project oversight and implementation.

19 World Bank's Factsheet: https://www.worldbank.org/en/news/factsheet/2023/07/17/world-bank-announces-new-steps-to-add-billions-in-financial-capacity (Accessed 19 October 2023).

20 To assess MDBs' capital adequacy Credit rating agencies, compare shareholders' equity to MDBs' Risk-Weighted Assets (RWA). MDBs' capital adequacy is further adjusted to reflect loan portfolio concentration. In essence, a loan portfolio of higher concentration requires a more equity to support it.

21 For a detailed synthesis of EEAs, see Belhaj et al. (2017).

Connectivity and Trade: Investment and Resilient Supply Chain

CHAPTER 10

Connectivity and Emerging Initiatives in Asia: A Conceptual Framework

Dareskedar Taye

Introduction

Studies in International Relations in the 21st century are now considering connectivity as an emerging theme. Most knowledge about connectivity is found in policy documents and political papers. But there is far less attention being given to connectivity in the world of academic literature. In this chapter, an attempt is made to provide conceptual clarity to the subject under study. It is followed by the discussion on the political aspect of connectivity and its role in shaping related decision making. This is further strengthened by the available facts that show the way recent developments, i.e. the COVID-19 pandemic and the Russia-Ukraine War, changed the course of connectivity. Lastly, the connectivity initiatives by China and Japan are uncovered to give practical examples for the discussion.

Conceptual and Theoretical Understanding of Connectivity

From time immemorial, people met one another, exchanged their commodities and moved, either to militarily raid or in search of new places for settlement. The social nature of human beings requires people to live together, to communicate with one another, and to share what they have, either through trade or barter. Archaeological excavations show that the ancient human society as well as modern ones built roads to enable them to move from one place to another. Connectivity had been the lifeblood of ancient civilisations and it is the same today. The established fact then and now is that no one community is self-sufficient on its own. The transition from the traditional, agrarian/primitive and autonomous society towards a relatively urbanised or modern way of life places society in a position of interdependence. The survival of one is affected by, and is dependent on, the other. Goods and services produced somewhere have to be available to the community that is in need which can only be achieved when there is a means of transport.

At the time that we are living today, as States are modern, sovereign, they are also increasingly interdependent to one another. The uneven distribution of wealth across the world – be it in industrial products, energy sources, labour, innovation, natural resource and capital – is driving States towards exchange through trade. The availability of connectivity networks thus shape the nature of exchange among States. The transaction process from the area of surplus to the area of scarcity is the first function of the market but it also demands connectivity networks if it has to be efficient.

Though the practice is as old as the early traces of human civilisation, it is now emerging as an area of study with new terminology called 'connectivity'. According to Gary Hawke and Anita Prakash, connectivity was first used to refer to the connections achieved because of the developing Information and Communications Technology (ICT). The publications from the Association of Southeast Asian Nations (ASEAN) further helped in the development of the concept as a separate area of study.[1]

Since 1996, the Asia Europe Meeting (ASEM) was trying to integrate diverse economic and security issues by calling in leaders and policy makers every two years. It was shaping to be a cooperative mechanism in the Eurasian landmass. In 2016, ASEM discussed connectivity and adopted a Resolution that emphasised infrastructure development in the Eurasian landmass, if integration and cooperation were to be realised.

When ASEM came up with the vision of creating an ASEAN community in 2011, connectivity was considered as the instrument towards achieving that end. It therefore defined connectivity as "the physical, institutional, and people-to-people linkages that comprise the foundational support and facilitative means to achieve the economic, political-security and socio-cultural pillars towards realising the vision of an integrated ASEAN community."[2] It also identified different areas of connectivity, which include, physical connectivity composed of infrastructure development on land, on the sea ports and on air transport that would help connect people and their products through transport facilities. The physical aspect also includes the development of ICT and energy infrastructure like underground optical cable facilities, electric power grids and natural gas pipelines. The second area of connectivity refers to the institutional aspect, which encompasses legal adjustments towards easy flow of trade and investment as well as customs arrangements and capacity building of law enforcement agencies. The third is people-to-people connectivity in education and tourism. When ASEAN came up with a new Connectivity Master Plan for 2025 in 2017, the three areas of focus morphed into five strategic areas. Though there is no substantive change in the definition of connectivity, the five strategic areas are identified as sustainable infrastructure, digital innovation, seamless logistics, regulatory excellence and people's mobility.

Two years after the Belt and Road Initiative (BRI) was launched, the Chinese government disclosed a vision document and stated the objective of "connecting the vibrant East Asia economic circle at one end and developed European economic circle at the other, and encompassing countries with huge potential for economic development"[3] in order to go through with the BRI. Even though it does not directly define the concept of connectivity, it is framed as a set of networks on land and at sea to connect people and their products. It involves identifying economic corridors and planning to connect major cities and ports either through roads, railway lines or sea ports.

W. Pascha tried to equate the study of connectivity with that of international trade and foreign direct investment in the international relations policy study areas since connectivity and infrastructure matters in the world we live today. By sharing the perspective of OECD[4], Pascha emphasised the role of transport infrastructure in understanding connectivity. This is attributed to different factors like the importance of transport for international trade, economic growth and regional integration. The second factor is related to the changing nature of global supply chains, which is requiring better and lower priced transport now than ever before. Third, following the financial crisis of 2006-08, there is a widening gap between the demand for financing infrastructure development and the available funds. At the time, investment on infrastructure was considered an essential instrument for economic growth, resilient against the impact of the crisis.

Connectivity is therefore the process of facilitating the connection of States by building alternative infrastructure facilities. The facilities can be built on land or on the sea shores to ease land, air and maritime transport. As human civilisation is progressing, energy and information are becoming essential necessities, which therefore requires connecting people through infrastructure like energy pipelines, grids and optical cables. The instrument of connectivity may vary across time and place based on the need of the community.

Tod Sandler identified two essential forces, i.e., globalisation and new regionalism, as drivers for the widespread practice of connectivity. The author emphasised connectivity infrastructure as essential public goods at global, regional or domestic level. Such public goods can be divided into global, trans-regional, regional and domestic, depending on the source of finance for the building of infrastructure and sharing the benefits once it is in use. Whatever their scope, connectivity helps to achieve sustainable development by facilitating market integration and social welfare.[5] Globalisation aspires to create a world that is free from trade barriers and stretches towards an integrated world. New regionalism is a recent revival towards developing one's own region. Regional integration schemes through regional governance and infrastructure development are pursued in different parts of the world. As globalisation is a force for creating a global market and society, regionalism focusses on regional identity and regional integration. In both cases, connectivity is at the centre of advancing the respective goal.

Economic and Political Debate Behind the Decision making to Connectivity

That the primary benefit of connectivity is economic is well understood. By reducing trade costs and time, it helps facilitate economic growth and market efficiency. The contribution for the improvement of the tourism sector is also immense by providing better transport facilities. When people move, they share experiences and get the chance to spend their money somewhere else. The connection of cities with other cities, growth corridors and sea ports means there is an impetus for further urban development.

However, economic calculations are not the only variables to be considered as far as decision making on connectivity is concerned. Geopolitical considerations sometimes outweigh economic efficiency. Initiatives like the BRI by China, the Quality Infrastructure by Japan, the International North-South Transport Corridor (INSTC) that stretches from Moscow to India through Iran and Azerbaijan, and the Global Gateway by the European Union, have geopolitical ramifications. Decades of economic growth in China has a global scale, which requires global reach. However, its investment in Pakistan compared to that in India – a State with huge economic potential– or in Indonesia – strategically located at the centre of the Indo-Pacific water body– make an impression that China gives priority for geopolitical interests while trying to advance economic goals. Japan's move towards ASEAN using Quality Infrastructure Initiative has its own geopolitical calculation given the divergent positions Japan and China have over the status quo of the

Indo-Pacific region. As there is intensified tension between both nations on revising the status quo or maintaining it, Japan is trying to use the Quality Infrastructure Initiative within ASEAN, which may cultivate cordiality and a common purpose against China. The North-South Corridor, which was initiated in 2000 has now got renewed attention after many years of relatively scant attention and policy intervention for the accomplishment of the project. The Russia-Ukraine War and the resultant sanctions against Russia prevented the full exploitation of the previously constructed transport corridors connecting Russia with the rest of Europe. Russia has to look for alternative routes to trade with countries that need Russian products. States like India, a growing economy and a population of more than 1.3 billion, are trying to satisfy their energy needs from different countries including Russia. As Iran is also a sanction-affected country, it is logical for the two nations to agree on matters of infrastructure development and to facilitate their own trade.

The intervention of politics over the decision-making process concerning whom to connect with has also to be seen from the perspective of established International Relations (IR) theories. In the beginning of the 21st century, traditional IR theories of Realism and Liberalism are still dominant in interpreting the politics of the world. Both theories have their own perspective for the changing nature of global power distribution and the associated behaviour of the State. To begin with, the Realist tradition, Mearshimer began his argument by downplaying the post-Cold War notion of no more great power war because of the end of history. For him, as long as there is change in the global power distribution mainly due to the rise of the material capability of any given State, rivalry, or war among the great powers, is inevitable, between the existing hegemon and the emerging one. He used standards like population, the size of the economy, and the strength of the military to scrutinise countries with the potential to be a great power. In 2001, he could foretell the rise of China to the extent of challenging the US.[6] When the economy of the West experienced the financial crisis of 2006-08, Fareed Zakaria published a book titled *The Post-American World*[7] and argued that America promoted globalisation and helped spread liberal democracy. The America-led world system enabled others to grow and become competitors as well. Such a State-centric perspective is common in the Realist tradition and believes that the change in the material capability of the State will definitely lead to change in the distribution of power at the global level. Any change in the system means, it is open for competition among the States. Since the advent of China's growth in early the 1980s, the Asian nations have experienced an increase in the size of their economy, population and military as well, which allowed them to have a strengthened material capability and the chance to independently launch connectivity initiatives, some with regional scope and others with global reach.

Contrary to the previous assumption, some writers from the liberal tradition try to see the change in the 21st century with a different lens other than the State-centric view. It is different from the previous century mainly in terms of the redundancy of material capability as the sole determinant of State behaviour. "The emerging networked world of the twenty-first century, however, exists above the [S]tate, below the [S]tate, and through the [S]tate. In this world, the [S]tate with the most connections will be the central player, able to set the global agenda and unlock innovation and sustainable growth."[8] In the liberal tradition, it is common to expect suggestions related with the necessity of supranational institutions in shaping the behaviour of States. The emergence of connectivity in the academic discourse may be added into one potential area of interdependence with the capacity to shape the nature of the State and its foreign policy orientation. For long, the integration of States through infrastructure has been discussed under the umbrella of functionalism and neo-functionalism, still extensions of the Liberal School.[9] States promote the formation of supranational institutions and willingly obey the constitutive element of the institutions. The same is true for connectivity in diverse areas. States once agreed to construct infrastructure and avoid legal differences, for example, in the areas of customs and international trade, will definitely be influenced by the rules of the game.

The theoretical debate is replicated at the policy level as well. As it has been discussed before, globalisation is one of the driving forces towards greater connectivity. Recent policy developments from the US side pointed out: "we recognise that globalisation has delivered immense benefits for the United States and the world, but an adjustment is now required to cope with dramatic global changes."[10] This is an effort to thwart the rise of China, both at the global level and in the Indo-Pacific region. China, on the other hand, is still pushing the agenda of globalisation forward, in order for the world to be more opento the free flow of goods and services. Such policy differences have their own implications for connectivity initiatives by different States.

Connectivity in the Era of COVID-19 and Russia-Ukraine War

The COVID-19 pandemic contradicts with the promises and practices of connectivity. People around the world like to move from place to place to the extent possible with the help of the available infrastructure. Connectivity also helps the global division of labour to function properly by providing easy flow of goods and services from the place of production to the available market posts. To the contrary, COVD-19 pushed States to restrict the movement of their people and to close their borders against any entry or exit from the nation. Once interdependent economies were shattered, some countries experienced new forms of economic nationalism. COVID-19 occurred at a time when China emerged as the leading manufacturing hub of the world. The closing of borders and the clampdown of manufacturing cities in China contributed for the disruption of the global supply chain. Market failures and the swift increase in the price of commodities contributed to the emergence of new voices that questioned the relevance of the advancing interdependent world through alternative mechanisms of connectivity.

On the other side, COVID-19 has contributed to a new emphasis for digital connectivity. Countries with established digital infrastructure managed to fill the contact and communication gap caused by the pandemic. The available digital technology facilitated the delivery business to boom and the relocation of workplaces from offices into homes. Countries with inadequate ICT infrastructure, could not exploit the potential of the technology; at the time, it was hardly necessary. The world soon realised that digital infrastructure should be given appropriate emphasis like that for transport infrastructure. The issue of addressing the digital gap, or the lack of access to expanding ICT technology in the global South, is also a critical concern.[11]

The Russia-Ukraine War is ongoing at a time when the world is recovering from the pandemic. The War has had its own repercussions on the global connectivity initiatives in general and within the Eurasian landmass in particular. The warring parties are major producers of food items, soil fertilisers and energy in the world. Therefore, it is natural for the prices of food and energy worldwide to escalate. The already functional transport and energy infrastructure like roads, railway lines and pipelines must be kept intact if the products in both countries have to be distributed as it was before the start of the War. However, it is impossible to protect the established infrastructure from the dangers of the War. Sometimes, the infrastructure itself is the target of attack, which aligns with the thinking that destroying them means destroying the backbone of the warring nation. Those ports that were used as loading and unloading centres of food and fertilisers converted into war zones, which by default meant that special negotiations were required by parties concerned to allow the transporting of those items. This is one factor for the rise of food commodities around the world since the beginning of the War. Though United Nations and Turkiye tried to negotiate and open the port and the water body for safe transport, they were never able to make it as safe as it was before the start of the War. The other manifestation of the impact of the War is observed in the Northern Corridor. It is a railway line stretched from Eastern China to Western Europe through Kazakhstan and Russia. The Corridor was essential for easing the trade link between China and Europe. Once the War began, because of the multiple sanctions imposed on Russia and the risk of the use of the Corridor in the War, it became dysfunctional. There are also energy pipelines from Russia to Europe – both through the sea and through Ukraine, which were at risk. These energy infrastructures were either targets of attack as had happened against the Nord Stream, or were operationally crippled.

Apart from its destructive impact on established infrastructure, the protracted war is creating new corridors and opportunities for connectivity. First, the transport corridor that crosses China, Kazakhstan, Azerbaijan and Turkey on its way to Europe – also called the Middle Corridor – has the chance to catch the attention of policy-makers. Baku, the capital of Azerbaijan, is now becoming the centre of the new corridor that connects Eastern Europe with Central Asia and China. This shows that, (1) the connectivity infrastructure is vulnerable to political differences and violence; (2) disruption in connectivity infrastructure easily leads to trade disruptions and market failures which in turn affect the day-to-day life of the people; and (3) as interdependency is good and inevitable, avoiding dependency on a single State, especially for strategic needs of a nation, is beneficial.

Connectivity Initiatives by China and Japan

A few years before China launched the BRI in 2013, its regional and global posture was changing. Since Deng Xiaoping initiated economic liberalisation, support from the US and Japan was easily available, to prepare the economy for 'take off'. For the US, an economically advanced China was thought to be peaceful and friendly. The intention of the US during the Cold War was to create a strong counter-balancing State against Soviet Russia. The dominant thinking in the immediate aftermath of the Cold War was that the US had emerged as the unrivaled great power, and globalisation would easily help to integrate any growing economy, including that of China, to the US-led system. Japan's policy of Japan towards engaging China was driven by the expectation that a growing China would easily conform into the regional status quo. Japan was expecting China to be a peaceful rising economy without any intention or action that might challenge the regional order established since the end of the Second World War.[12] As an island State with a developed economy, any change in the Indo-Pacific region is considered to be an economic and security threat to Japan.

Rising China, on the other hand, was emerging with a new vision of regional and global order. In the years between 2010 and 2013, China outpaced both Germany and Japan to become the second largest economy next to the US. It was also entering into a boundary dispute with Japan in the East China Sea, and with other littoral States in the South China Sea. These developments antagonised Japan and other States. The Shinzo Abe government was actually critical of the rise of China and its consequential behaviour in the surrounding region. He was trying to organise States that shared the threat of China, with the agenda of Free and Open Indo-Pacific (FOIP). China's foreign relations in the east were deeply troubled because of its territorial claims. 'Thus, implementing the BRI was part of a strategic "China Goes West" proposal to de-escalate head-on conflicts in Maritime Asia by intensifying connectivity on Eurasia.'[13]

The global economic environment was also changing, though the reality in China was different from what was happening in the rest of the world. Following the 2006-08 financial crisis mainly in the West, the world had passed through additional economic crisis until 2010. Some major economies were introducing protective national economic policies disregarding the notion of globalisation. Even though the global dynamics had a reverse effect in comparison with the economic miracle of China, it remained in a better position. The question for Chinese policy makers was how to navigate through the changing global fortunes and disturbed foreign relations with its eastern and southern neighbours, without compromising its economic principles. The "industrial overcapacity and weakened momentum for high-speed economic growth [was] necessitating a broader international cooperation for larger overseas markets."[14]

China launched the Silk Road Economic Belt from Kazakhstan and the 21st Century Maritime Silk Road from Indonesia in 2013. The absence of official documents about the initiative at the time of its launch prevented concerned researchers from properly understanding the details of the initiative. In 2015, however, China brought out a vision document. It made it clear that China had launched the BRI just to cope with the profound changes across the world due to the financial crisis, the slow pace of economic recovery and the change in the international trade and investment environment. It clarified that "China's economy is connected with the world economy. China will stay committed to the basic policy of opening-up, build a new pattern of all-round opening-up, and integrate itself deeper into the world economic system."[15]

The BRI on land followed three directions. The first refers to the transport network to connect China with Europe through Central Asia and Russia. The second crosses Central and West Asia to connect China with the Persian Gulf and the Mediterranean Sea. The third direction starts from China and goes to Southeast Asia, South Asia and the Indian Ocean. Corresponding to the focus areas of connectivity, three development corridors on land were identified: (1) China-Mongolia-Russia, (2) China-Central Asia-West Asia, and (3) China-Indochina. The Maritime Silk Road stretches towards Europe and the Southern Pacific by crossing water bodies like the Pacific Ocean, the Indian Ocean, the South China Sea, the Red Sea and the Mediterranean Sea. The corresponding growth corridors for the Maritime Silk Road are the China-Pakistan economic corridors and the Bangladesh-China-India-Myanmar economic corridor.

The BRI has even gone beyond the Eurasian landmass in 10 years. The Second Belt and Road Forum in 2019, saw the participation of leaders from Africa and Latin America. The Annexure to the Communique of the Forum highlighted many projects other than those that were initially anticipated. New economic corridors in Africa and Latin America and in Eurasia and the Indo-Pacific are added to the list.[16] What was new in the Forum was that the issue of quality garnered renewed attention. The Communique indicated that future BRI projects will consider environmental concerns, quality issues and transparent governance. The government seems committed to the issue of quality even in recent years.[17]

The momentum of the BRI however, has slackened when compared to its early years. It is limited by various factors. The COVID-19 pandemic and China's response to it was challenging for the success of the BRI. The zero-COVID policy thwarted the decades of economic growth and diverted the attention of the State to be more introverted. Before it fully recovered from the consequences of the pandemic, it had to face the challenge associated with the Russia-Ukraine War. In those years, some of the BRI projects could not be accomplished as planned. The high-speed railway line in Indonesia is a case in point, where the project took many years and could only be completed by 2023.

The Chinese approach to connectivity was taken up by Japan as well. Japan and China had enjoyed a bilateral relationship based on mutual partnership between 1972 and 2010. Japan as the second largest global economy was supporting China to develop its economy and created strong economic foundations in the form of investment and trade. However, when China emerged as a stronger economy than Japan, the relations between the two nations turned into a rivalry.

Japan tried to come up with its own connectivity initiative, the Quality Infrastructure Investment (QII) in 2016, aiming to invest especially in the ASEAN region and partly in Africa. The initiative by Japan is also influenced by its political worldview as it is witness to efforts of integrating QII with G7 and G20 standards and norms. At the same time, the connectivity initiative is the continuation of its vision for a Free and Open Indo-Pacific (FOIP), largely a reflection of resistance against the rising influence of China in the region. Japan also views India, China's rival, as its strategic partner to achieve FOIP aspirations.[18]

Conclusion

The discussion so far shows that political developments are essential factors both in advancing and in restricting connectivity initiatives. This led one to think of the relevance of the nature of inter-State relations even in the 21st century. When States forge peaceful relations and work towards globalisation and regionalism, it becomes a fertile ground for launching connectivity initiatives. But there are times when inter-State relations are disturbed by boundary disputes and hegemonic rivalries. Unexpected economic shocks and pandemics also affect the prospect of any State to go through connectivity initiatives. So, any effort towards connectivity needs to consider the nature of power distribution at the global and regional level. Possible economic shocks and project management gaps have to be part of the equation while planning to pursue new connectivity networks. In fact, it may be difficult to avoid unintended consequences that may arise once the initiative is put in place.

NOTES

1 Gary Hawke and Anita Prakash, "Conceptualizing Asia-Europe Connectivity: Imperatives, current status, and potential for ASEM", in Anita Prakash (Ed.), *Asia-Europe connectivity vision 2025: Challenges and opportunities,* an ERIA-Government of Mongolia document, Economic and Research Institute for ASEAN and East Asia, 2016,pp. 3-10.

2 "Masterplan on ASEAN Connectivity", ASEAN Secretariat Jakarta, January 2011 at https://asean.org/wp-content/uploads/2018/01/47.-December-2017-MPAC2025-2nd-Reprint-.pdf (Accessed 14 April 2023).

3 Vision and Actions on Jointly Building Belt and Road, Issued by the National Development and Reform Commission, Ministry of Foreign Affairs and Ministry of Commerce of the People's Republic of China, with State Council authorisation, March 2015.

4 "Enhancing Connectivity through Transport Infrastructure: The Role of Official Development Finance and Private Investment", *The Development Dimension,* OECD Publishing, Paris, 2018.

5 Todd Sandler, "Public Goods and Regional Cooperation for Development: A New Look", *Integration and Trade Journal,* 36 (17), January-June 2013, Inter-American Development Bank, INTAL, pp.13-24.

6 John Mearsheimer, *The Tragedy of Great Power Politics*, W. W. Norton & Company, Cambridge, 2001.

7 Fareed Zakaria, *The Post-American World*, W.W. Norton & Company, New York, 2008.

8 Anne-Marie Slaughter, "America's Edge: Power in the Networked Century", *Foreign Affairs*, January/February 2009 at https://scholar.princeton.edu/sites/default/files/slaughter/files/americasedgefa.pdf (Accessed 10 January 2023).

9 This was a dominant debate in Europe after the Second World War. There were some functionalists who were advocating for the full realization of the Federation of Europe by political intervention. This was opposed by a neo-functionalist scholar, Ernst B. Haas, who proposed integration of technical matters to be achieved first then proceed to political integration.

10 *National Security Strategy*, The White House, Washington DC, December 2022.

11 Vanessa Ratten, "The Ukraine/Russia Conflict: Geopolitical and International Business Strategies, *Thunderbird International Business Review*, 2023, 65, pp. 265–271. Makhtar Diop, "COVID-19 Reinforces the Need for Connectivity", *World Bank Blogs*, 2020 at https://blogs.worldbank.org/voices/covid-19-reinforces-need-connectivity (Accessed 1 May 2023); Alexsandro Silva Solon and Marcos Paulo Leite Silveira, "The Impacts of the COVID-19 Pandemic in Supply Chain Operations", 2022 at https://www.intechopen.com/chapters/1084333 (Accessed 1 May 2023).

12 Stephen Nagy, "Accommodation versus Alliances: Japan's Grand Strategy in the Sino-US Competition", *The Asan Forum*, 27 August 2020 at https://theasanforum.org/accommodation-versus-alliance-japans-prospective-grand-strategy-in-the-sino-us-competition/

13 Min Ye, "Ten Years of the Belt and Road: Reflections and Recent Trends, Global Development Policy Center, 2022 at https://www.bu.edu/gdp/2022/09/06/ten-years-of-the-belt-and-road-reflections-and-recent-trends/ (Accessed 9 May 2023).

14 Zhexin Zhang, "The Belt and Road Initiative: China's New Geopolitical Strategy?", *SWP Working Paper*, Session No. 2, German Institute for International and Security Affairs, October 2018.

15 Vision and Actions on Jointly Building Belt and Road, no. 3.

16 Joint Communique of the Leaders' Roundtable of the 2nd Belt and Road Forum for International Cooperation, 27 April 2019, Beijing, China.

17 Xi Jinping, *The Governance of China*, First Edition, Foreign Language Press Co. Ltd., Beijing, 2022, pp. 571-577.

18 A. Prakash and F.P. van der Putten "Connectivity Plans for Asia and Europe: Public Goods and Collective Growth", in A. Prakash. (Ed.), *13th Asia-Europe Meeting (ASEM) Summit: Multilateral Cooperation for a Resilient, Sustainable and Rules-Based Future for ASEM*, ERIA Jakarta, ERIA, ASEM 13 Phnom Penh, and The Royal Government of Cambodia, 2021, pp. 20-42.

CHAPTER 11

Policy Considerations to Advance the Strategic Partnership Between India and the Republic of Korea Based on the Framework of G20

Beeho Chun[1]

Introduction

On 1 December 2022, India assumed the Presidency of the G20, which continued until 30 November 2023. Prime Minister Modi unveiled India's G20 Presidency theme – "*Vasudhaiva Kutumbakam*" – "One Earth. One Family. One Future". The G20 member countries together make up 85 per cent of the global GDP, over 75 per cent of the global trade, and two-thirds of the world population.

Holding the G20 Presidency with more than 200 events in the run up to the 2023 Summit all over the country, India had a mission to bring about a shared global agenda to promote a rules-based order, peace and just growth for all.[2]

India's thematic priorities for G20 New Delhi Summit were as follows:

- Green Development, Climate Finance & Life
- Accelerated, Inclusive & Resilient Growth
- Accelerating progress on SDGs
- Technological Transformation & Digital Public Infrastructure
- Multilateral Institutions for the 21st century
- Women-led development

Prime Minister Modi reiterated that India advocated the interests of the countries of Global South under its G20 Presidency.

Geopolitical and geo-economic changes in the Indo-Pacific

The world is confronting unprecedented challenges. Russia's invasion of Ukraine, US-China strategic competition, North Korea's nuclear development and its convergence to Russia, greater US global dominance through the Inflation Reduction Act as well as Chips and Science Act, and a disrupted global supply chain are throwing new challenges to the international community.[3]

Under these new global environments, Asia – particularly with China and India emerging – is being repositioned as a dominant player in global politics. Economy and Security are becoming closely interrelated. Global pivot States such as India and South Korea in the Indo-Pacific are required to enhance their engagement in securing global peace and security.

The Indo-Pacific accounts for 62 per cent of the world's GDP, 46 per cent of international trade, and half of global maritime transport. It is a dynamic region where key trading partners of strategic industries such as semiconductors, electric vehicles and biomedicines are located.

How are Asian powers responding to the New Supply Chain Resilience (SCR)? What will be the impact of SCR on the evolving geo-economics of Asia? This issue is the task that the major countries in the Indo-Pacific region must settle together.

India-Republic of Korea bilateral relations

On 22 November 2025, Prime Minister Narendra Modi and South Korea's President Lee Jae-myung met on the sidelines of the Johannesburg G20 Summit, reaffirming both leaders' willingness to intensify the India–South Korea Special Strategic Partnership and expand cooperation across trade, investment and advanced technologies. The two leaders also met in June 2025 on the sidelines of the G7 Summit in Kananaskis, Canada. They agreed to seek cooperation in sectors including commerce, investment, technology, green hydrogen and shipbuilding.

On 20 May 2023, on the sidelines of the G7 Hiroshima Summit in Japan, Indian Prime Minister Shri Narendra Modi and ROK former President Yoon held a bilateral meeting. The two leaders reviewed the progress of India and South Korea Special Strategic Partnership and discussed ways to strengthen bilateral cooperation, particularly in areas of trade & investment, high technology, IT hardware manufacturing, defence, semiconductors and culture.[4]

Both sides noted that both countries are celebrating 50th anniversary of establishment of diplomatic relations this year, and agreed to enhance the bilateral cooperation further. President Yoon appreciated Prime Minister Modi's leadership of the G-20 and confirmed full support. By extending invitation to the G20 Summit, Prime Minister Modi welcomed Korea's "Indo-Pacific strategy" and its policy consideration to India.

India and South Korea are essential strategic partners and like-minded countries, respecting the principle of liberal democracy, rule of law and market economy. However, there is a gap between the potential for strategic partnership and the actual status now. Therefore, there is still a lot of room for cooperation. Semiconductors, automobiles and defence industry are good areas for further strategic cooperation.

The bilateral trade volume between India and South Korea registered US$ 27.8 billion in 2022. Both countries underlined that the target of trade volume in 2030 would be of US$ 50 billion. Korean companies' FDI in India was worth US$ 300 million in 2022, which is contributing to the Make in India initiative of the Indian government.

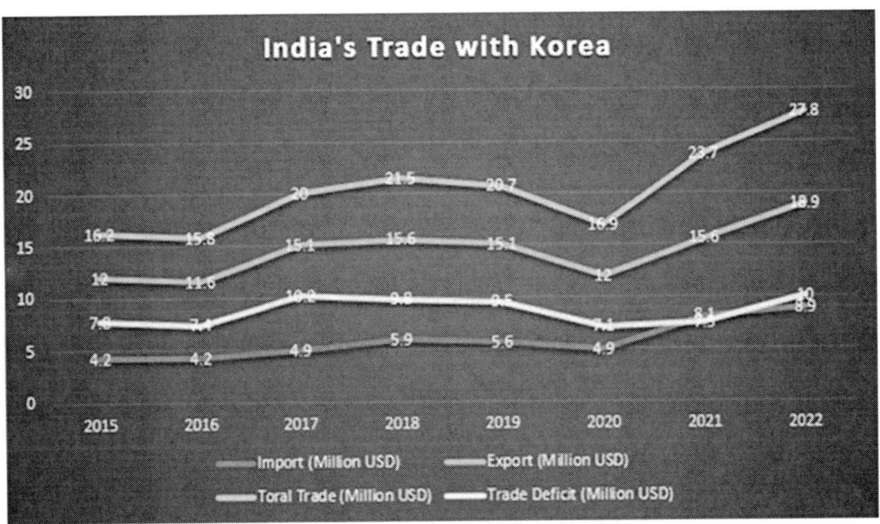

Source: Ministry of Foreign Affairs, ROK, Choonje Cho[5]

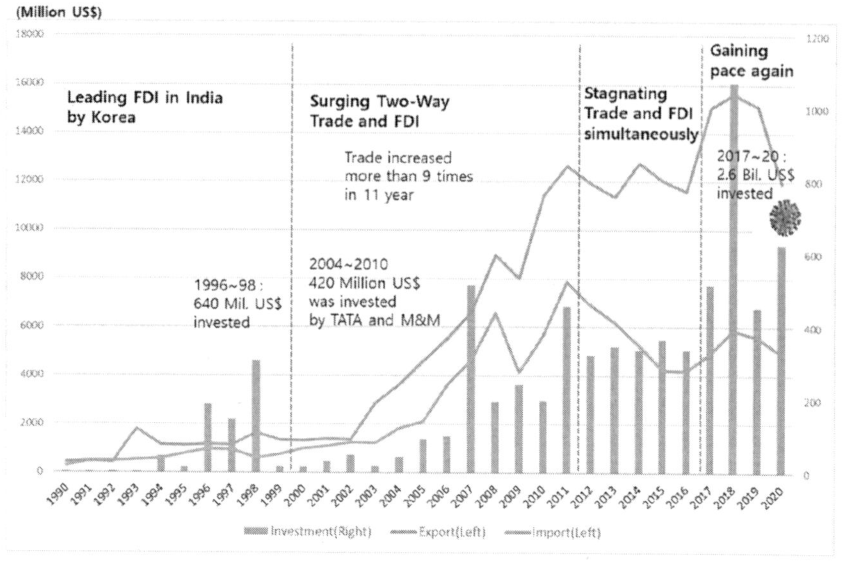

Source: Choonje Cho[5]

For Korea, India is the 11th trading partner, and 23rd destination for FDI. Successful cases of Korean companies' investments in India are as follows:

Korean Companies Investment in India

The potentials for strategic partnership between India and South Kore should combine South Korea's dynamic industrial capacities with India's industrialisation capabilities. Already many South Korea's key enterprises such as Samsung, Hyundai Motors, LG, SK, Hanhwa and POSCO are expanding their investments in India. The key areas for intensified industrial cooperation would as follow:

Automobile sector

The Indian automobile market has emerged as the world's third largest market after China and the United States; 4.76 million new vehicles were sold in 2022. The country is becoming an important centre for electric vehicle (EV) production and sales. The Indian government is pursuing a strong electrification policy, with the aim of increasing EV sales up to 30 per cent of total vehicle sales by 2030.

Hyundai Motor India Limited is now firmly standing as the second largest automaker in the Indian market. Following last year's record-breaking sales of 807,067 units in 2022, in 2023 sales target was 873,000 units, 8.2 per cent more than last year.

On 7 August 2023, Executive Chairman of Hyundai Motor Group, Euisun Chung visited Hyundai Motor India Engineering (HMIE), the R&D hub in at Hyderabad and the plants in Chennai. He discussed with his staff on the mid-to-long-term growth strategy by reviewing the Indian market's growth potential and electrification. HMIE plays an important role in increasing sales in the Indian market and works closely with the Hyundai-Kia Namyang R&D centre centre in Korea to develop vehicles that are tailored suited for the Indian market.

Hyundai Motor India would invest Rs 200 billion rupees ($2.45 billion) in the state of Tamil Nadu over the next one decade to produce electric vehicles. Hyundai Motor India signed a memorandum of understanding (MOU) with the Government ofTamil Nadu, and Hyundai agreed to set up a battery pack assembly unit with an annual capacity to assemble 178,000 batteries.

Hyundai Motor India Limited (HMIL), on August 16, 2023, signed an Asset Purchase Agreement (APA) on 16 August 2023, with General Motors India (GMI) for the acquisition and assignment of identified assets related to General Motors India (GMI)'s Talegaon Plant in Maharashtra. Manufacturing operations at the plant are planned to commence in 2025. With the Sriperumbudur (Chennai) and Talegaon plants, Hyundai Motor India aims to achieve a production capacity of 1 million units a year.

In 2024, Hyundai Motor India made an initial public offering (IPO) that raised 3.3 billion US dollars. Building on this, the company has a plan to invest around $3.6 billion in India during the next decade to establish a new plant in Pune, and expand facilities in Chennai. With the annual production capacity of more than 1 million automobiles in India, Hyundai Motors has a strategy to penetrate the Indian market and even to export to other countries. The Hyundai Motors CEO José Muñoz highlighted that these developments were part of the company's global manufacturing plan to increase its production capacity by 1.2 million units by 2030. This includes 500,000 additional units from HMGMA in US, 250,000 units from the Pune multi-model export hub in India, and 200,000 units from the dedicated EV plant in Ulsan in South Korea.

Kia produces small EVs optimised for the local market from 2025, and will then gradually offer various EV models and Purpose Built Vehicles (PBVs). The company will also develop EV charging infrastructure.

Through its 'Kia 2.0 Strategy,' the company aims to increase its market share in India from 6.7 per cent in the first half of 2025 to 10 per cent in the coming years. Kia plans to expand its vehicle ranges. Kia Motors sells its EV6 model of electric vehicles, exported from Korea, making use of the India's customs tariff policy. The Indian government imposes high customs tariffs of 60 to 100 per cent on imported finished cars and 15 per cent on completely knocked down (CKD) vehicles.

Electronics and digital technologies

The South Korean technology giants are shifting their production lines away from China to India, a consequence of the damage and uncertainties resulting from the US-China rivalry and decreasing Chinese demand and increased competition in the Chinese domestic market.

Indian Council of World Affairs (ICWA) analysed that the US-China Chip war, triggered by Biden Administration's restrictions on Chinese access to semiconductor technology since 2019, has disrupted global supply chains of semiconductors which are widely used in critical sectors such as AI, 5G, and defence. With the intensifying US–China technological war, particularly in the semiconductor industry, India and South Korea are pursuing new collaboration in semiconductor industrial strategies.

Samsung Electronics and SK Hynix are key players in the global semiconductor supply chain – producing over 70% of DRAM and more than half of NAND flash memory, The US-China technology war in chips prompted South Korea to reconsider its strategy, to secure and diversify safe semiconductor production sites.

Samsung Electronics employs nearly to 70,000 employees in India, a considerable part of its global employment of 266,000, spread across 74 countries. In Asia, Samsung is manufacturing mobile phones in South Korea, China, Vietnam and Indonesia. Currently, the Noida factory is Samsung's second-largest manufacturing facility in the world, The Company is operating a major R&D centre in Bengaluru. Samsung Electronics is going to invest around 260 billion won ($205.7 million) into a new factory to manufacture major parts such as refrigerator compressors, in addition to its Chennai plant that produces home appliances and televisions. The factory's annual production capacity is projected at around 8 million units.

In this context, India is seeking an opportunity to position itself as a competing alternative production centre of semiconductors in the global value chain. The $10 billion Semicon programme of India could provide strong policy support to the national industry. India's proactive semiconductor policies, particularly Gujarat's semiconductor strategy launched in August 2022, attracted serious international interest. Vedanta signed MoUs in April 2023 with 20 Korean display glass firms for the development of an electronic manufacturing hub.

Institutional momentum was further strengthened in September 2023 by a Memorandum of Understanding (MoU) between the India Electronics and Semiconductor Association (IESA) and the Korea Display Industry Association (KDIA). This agreement focused on four pillars: joint R&D, display technologies, workforce development, and technical exchange.

LG electronics has begun work on 5000 crore plant city, Andhra Pradesh, in May 2025, to produce consumer electronics, supported by Korean component suppliers. SK Hynix was also reportedly evaluating India's semiconductor incentive schemes, particularly in packaging and testing. Korean firms are showing interest in Gujarat for semiconductor parts and R&D. This reflects the growing interest in deepening strategic and economic ties between India and South Korea in the semiconductor sector.

Defence Industry

At the G-20 summit in New Delhi, India and South Korea agreed to boost their defence cooperation. Seoul is "totally committed" to expanding defence cooperation with India. It is recognising India as a crucial player and partner of regional stability in the Indo-Pacific.

In the field of defence cooperation, defence ministers of India and South Korea have met regularly since 2015. They have held regular meetings on defence industry and logistics cooperation. In September 2019, the two countries agreed on a Roadmap for Defence Industry Cooperation. Naval and Coast Guard ships from both sides now make regular port visits and conduct joint exercises To further solidify their strategic partnership, both countries established a "2+2" ministerial dialogue in 2019. This high-level framework brings together the foreign and defence ministers from both nations to coordinate on regional security, maritime safety, and diplomatic synergy.

The Stockholm International Peace Research Institute (SIPRI) analysed that, over 5-years, from 2018 to 2022, South Korea was the fifth largest arms exporter to India with 2.8% of India's total arms imports, following Russia (45.1%), France (28.6%), Israel (7.7%), UK (2%) and Germany (1.4%).

Hanwha Aerospace developed the K-9 Thunder self-propelled howitzer. Larsen and Toubro assembles it in India in the name of the K-9 Vajra. Early in 2025, a second order of 100 units was agreed upon, following completion of the first order in 2020. Shipbuilding is another area of defence collaboration. In 2019, both sides finalised a logistics agreement and set out a roadmap for defence industrial cooperation in 2020.

Shipbuilding Industry

India has ambitious plans to expand its shipbuilding capabilities. In this regard, it wants to leverage South Korea's expertise in this area as a global powerhouse. with industry leaders such as HD Hyundai, Samsung Heavy Industries, and Hanwha Ocean. In July 2025, HD Korea Shipbuilding & Offshore Engineering Co. Ltd. (KSOE) signed a MOU cooperation agreement with India's Cochin Shipyard Limited (CSL).

CSL is India's largest state-owned shipbuilder and KSOE is one of global leaders in shipbuilding and marine engineering. Both sides agreed to launch long-term cooperation for joint exploration of newbuilding opportunities in India and abroad, sharing of technical expertise, identification of initiatives to enhance productivity, joint efforts to upskill and strengthen workforce, and exploration of potential collaboration in other shipbuilding-related projects.

India as global hub state in the Indo-Pacific

The Indo-Pacific is emerging as a new geographic space – bringing together India and the Pacific Ocean – to represent the new strategic gravity of the twenty-first century. India's role in the Indo-Pacific is recognised to be crucial by Australia, Japan, the United States and South Korea.[6]

For India, the Indo-Pacific is an opportunity to expand its influence across the region. Extending its partnerships lies at the core of India's Indo-Pacific interests, where it is a key player. India is approaching the Indo-Pacific under a new strategic environment, coinciding with the rise of China, particularly in the Indian Ocean region and South Asia.

India's *Chandrayaan-3* spacecraft has landed on the moon. India became the fourth nation to accomplish such a feat, to be a global superpower in space. In the past, only the United States, China and the former Soviet Union have completed soft landings on the lunar surface. Unlike any other spacecraft in history, *Chandrayaan-3* landed at a site closer to the moon's South Pole. The South Pole region is an area of significant scientific and strategic interest for spacefaring nations. Scientists believe that the region is home to water ice deposits.

India's Economic Potential

India celebrated its 75th anniversary of independence in 2022. The Indian government has set a goal of becoming a "developed" economy by 2047, the centenary of Indian independence.[7] India has attained critical mass as the fifth-largest economy in the world, realised primarily because of its policies of market-oriented economic liberalisation and a greater role for private capital and in the process enhanced its global competitiveness.[8] India's progress over the past decade has been quite remarkable. The economy's position has gone from the tenth-largest ten years ago to the fifth-largest today. By overtaking Germany and Japan, India will be the third-largest economy after China and the US by 2030. In 25 years, at a size of US$26 trillion, per capita GDP would be over US$15,000, six times its current level. Currently many global companies are rushing into India since India is emerging as the destination for FD beyond China.

As the World Bank has pointed out, certain challenges remain. Employment indicators have improved since 2020, but concerns remain about the quality of jobs created and the real growth in wages, as well as around the low participation of women in the labour force. The inflow of FDI would contribute to qualified job creation and 'Make in India'.

India's Strategic Partnership in the Indo-Pacific

(a) The US-India Comprehensive Global and Strategic Partnership

In 2025, US President Trump's announcement to double tariffs on imports from India to as much as 50% seriously damaged ties between two powerful strategic partners. In addition to 25% tariff on many imports from India, Trump Administration imposed an additional retaliatory 25% tariff, due to India's purchases of Russian oil. It takes total duties to 50% which is the highest imposed by the US and roughly at par with tariff on Brazil and China. Indian government is seeking a diversification in its foreign policy, putting priority on the Global South, BRICS and oil import from Russia, while President Trump is trying to enhance strategic competition with China and sanctions on Russia. In the meanwhile, US and India have finalised a trade deal under which the US tariff has been lowered to 18% while India has agreed to stop buying oil from Russia.

In the past, in June 2023 Prime Minister Narendra Modi and US president Joseph R. Biden, Jr. adopted a joint statement on 2 June 2023.[9] The two leaders affirmed a partnership of democracies looking into the 21st century. The US-

India Comprehensive Global and Strategic Partnership is reflecting a new level of trust and mutual understanding between the two nations.

The two leaders agreed to make joint efforts to implement a Comprehensive Global and Strategic Partnership in the following key areas:

- Charting a Technology Partnership for the Future
- Powering a Next Generation Defence Partnership
- Catalysing the Clean Energy Transition
- Deepening Strategic Convergence
- Propelling Global Growth
- Empowering Future Generations and Protecting the Health of both Peoples

The summit meeting resulted in substantial agreements across various issues. Out of these, three developments could positively affect bilateral trade and further India's trade imperatives:[10]

- On the multilateral front, the meeting resulted in the termination of six trade disputes at the WTO.
- India will join the Minerals Security Partnership (MSP) – a "partnership aimed at securing the supply of critical minerals.
- Investments in India by US memory chipmaker Micron Technology and by semiconductor toolmaker Applied Materials, will further integrate India into the value chain of chip manufacturing.

While Applied Electronics will establish a new engineering centre in India to support more than US $2 billion of planned investments and create 500 new advanced engineering jobs, Micron will set up an assembly, testing and packaging plant in India for assembly and test manufacturing of both DRAM and NAND products. The investment by Micron will put India on the map of global semiconductor supply chain. In addition to integration into the semiconductor supply chain, the new plant by Micron will create a positive spill over effect in the Indian electronics industry by localising component manufacturing.

(b) Japan-India Free and Open Indo-Pacific Initiative

During his visit to India in March 2023, Japanese Prime Minister Fumio Kishida outlined the Japanese new plan to establish a "Free and Open Indo-Pacific (FOIP)". India and Japan, as the hosts of the G20 and G7 respectively, agreed to establish the Indo-Pacific as the geo-economic and geopolitical centre of the world and as the engine for prosperity for the Global South.[11]

The idea of a FOIP has found growing convergence between Japan and India. Japanese Prime Minister Kishida and Indian Prime Minister Modi have called for a forceful joint defence system and derided the use of force to undermine sovereign territories. At its core, a FOIP respects sovereignty, accountable governance and the rules-based order. India and Japan emphasise FOIP's inherent attributes, encompassing inclusivity, diversity, resilience and openness. At a time when Japan is advancing its geopolitical significance and positioning, the Quad is more important for Japan than the G-20.

The two nations would lead the effort to establish a FOIP Infrastructure Fund worth US$100 billion per year, to leverage private capital with the United States, Australia, South Korea, Europe and others.

Japan concluded the Comprehensive and Progressive Agreement for Trans-Pacific Partnership (CPTPP) with 10 countries after former US President Donald Trump, refused to ratify the original TPP. Supporting a congruence between the CPTPP and the Indo-Pacific Economic Framework is in both countries' interests. Bearing in mind that Australia and India concluded the "comprehensive economic partnership", the Japanese government wishes to provide a mechanism to support relocation of Japanese companies to India under Japan's "China plus one" initiative.

(c) ASEAN-India Comprehensive Strategic Partnership

The year 2022 marked 30 years of ASEAN-India relations. ASEAN and India reaffirmed their commitment to strengthen their comprehensive strategic partnership at the 25th ASEAN-India Senior Officials' Meeting (AISOM).[12] They also reiterated their commitment to intensify their longstanding relations at the 23rd ASEAN-India Joint Cooperation Committee (AIJCC) meeting, held at the ASEAN Secretariat. The move is in pursuit of the establishment of the Comprehensive Strategic Partnership at the 19th ASEAN-India Summit in 2021.[13]

They looked forward to the steady progress in the implementation of the ASEAN-India Plan of Action (POA) (2021-2025) and to the finalisation of the Annexure to the ASEAN-India POA (2021-2025), to ensure that their partnership becomes substantive and mutually beneficial in the future.

ASEAN recalled that India continued support for ASEAN Centrality through peace and stability in the region and various ASEAN-led mechanisms. Both sides underlined the need to exert efforts to implement the ASEAN-India Joint Statement on the India-Pacific for peace, stability, and prosperity in the region.

BRICS and India

As of 2025, BRICS is a group consisting of eleven emerging economies, representing 49.5 % of the global population, 40 % of the global GDP and 26% of global trade. India took presidency for BRICS Summit in 2021. The Priorities for India's Presidency in 2021 were 1) Reform of the Multilateral System 2) Counter Terrorism Cooperation 3) Digital and Technological Tools for Achieving SDGs 4) Enhancing People to People Exchanges.

In August 2023 in Johannesburg, leaders of the BRICS – Brazil, Russia, India, China and South Africa – committed in principle, to expand the group. Six new countries – Saudi Arabia, Iran, UAE, Egypt, Ethiopia and Argentina have become part of BRICS with effect from 1 January 2024.

Prime Minister Modi, in a tweet, said, "On the occasion of the 15th anniversary of BRICS, we have taken the decision to expand this forum. India has always fully supported this expansion. Such an expansion will make BRICS stronger and more effective. In that spirit, India welcomes Argentina, Egypt, Ethiopia, Iran, Saudi Arabia and UAE into the BRICS family."

On the sidelines of the BRICS summit, Prime Minister Modi spoke to President Xi and highlighted India's concern on border issues along the Line of Actual Control. The Line of Actual Control has been disputed since the 1950s. The two countries went to war over it in 1962.

South Korea's strategic partnership in the Indo-Pacific

South Korea's next leap forward depends on a peaceful and stable Indo-Pacific. The growth of the Korean economy relies heavily on exports, as foreign trade accounted for approximately 85 per cent of South Korea's GDP in 2021. The Indo-Pacific represents approximately 78 per cent and 67 per cent of South Korea's total exports and total imports, respectively. It is noteworthy that Korea's top 20 trading partners are in the Indo-Pacific region and that 66 per cent of Korean FDI is in Indo-Pacific.

South Korea's Indo-Pacific Strategy

The former Government of South Korea made public Indo-Pacific Strategy, called "Strategy for a Free, Peaceful and Prosperous Indo-Pacific Region" in December 2022.[14] Korea's Indo-Pacific strategy called India a special strategic partner. India is one of the "like-minded" partners in the region. This new policy direction is signifying a major break from traditional foreign relations that concentrated on the United States, China, Japan, and Russia, which are key players in the politics of the Korean Peninsula and North East Asia.

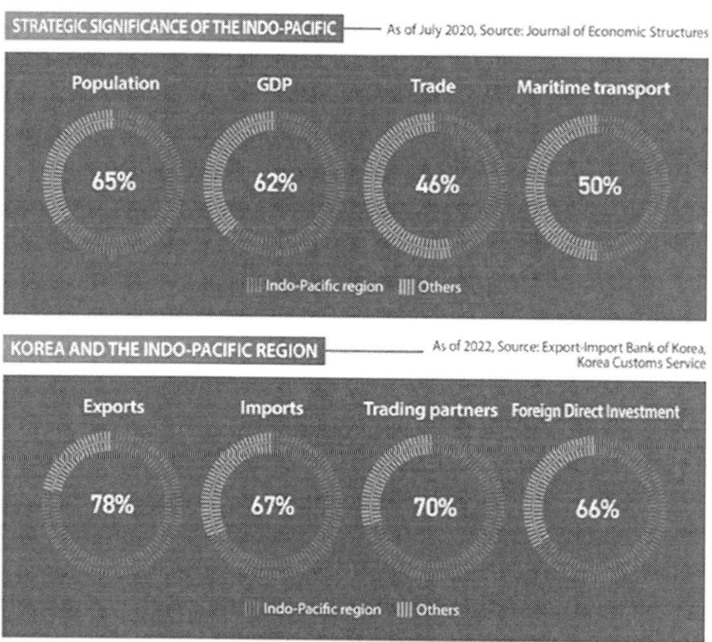

Given its increasing influence in the Indo-Pacific region, India will be a strategic priority for Seoul. Considering the complementary interests, India and South Korea are likely to formulate a comprehensive strategic partnership as early as possible.

South Korea-India Cooperation in G20

India's G20 Presidency at the New Delhi summit provided an opportunity for Seoul to find a key regional partner beyond its immediate ambit of US, Japan, Russia, and China.

With uncertainties such as disrupted global supply chain due to US-China rivalry, and Chinese pressure on South Korea to try and balance foreign relations with the US, South Korea is trying to find a new global partner at the bilateral, regional and global level, even in the G7 plus and G20. India is a natural choice for the ROK for further coordination in the Indo-Pacific.[15]

India's presidency of the G 20 New Delhi provided an opportunity for greater coordination between India and South Korea, particularly implementing the interests of the Global South. On economic security, India-South Korea cooperation could create synergy effects through the upgraded CEPA, QUAD plus and the Indo-Pacific Economic Framework.[16] On maritime issues, South Korea's participation as partner country in the Indian Ocean Rim Association (IORA) will contribute positively in the region. South Korea's new Indo-Pacific Strategy reflects the importance of the Indian Ocean Region, where India has a stronghold.

Source: Trade Ministry, South Korea

South Korea concluded a series of FTAs with its major trading partners India, the US, China, ASEAN, Australia, New Zealand, European Union, EFTA, Canada, Peru, Columbia and Chile. South Korea also joined the Regional Comprehensive Economic Partnership (RECEP). The RECEP encompasses the three Northeast Asian countries with Pacific States Australia and New Zealand plus ASEAN economies. It covers 30 per cent of the global population and 29 per cent of the global trade volume at $5.4 billion.

The Korean government plans to be a member of another multilateral FTA, the Comprehensive and Progressive Trans-Pacific Partnership (CPTPP). The extensive network of FTAs of South Korea is a vital instrument for increasing trade and investments with its trading partners.

South Korea's Technological Transformation & Digital Public Infrastructure

Korea ranks first among 29 OECD countries in the 2019 OECD Digital Government Index. In June 2021, the Korean government announced its digital strategy for 2021-2025, a roadmap to implement intelligent service design and delivery, data-driven public administration, and robust and inclusive digital infrastructure, strengthening weaknesses identified by the DGI. The government will seek to continue building an inclusive digital ecosystem for public data and public services.

E-Government Developement Index (2022)		Online Participation Index (2022)	
1	Denmark	1	Japan
3rd	S.Korea	3	Estonia
7	Australia	6	New Zealand
10	USA	6	UK
11	UK	9th	S.Korea
12	Singapore	10	USA
13	UAE	11	Brazil
14	Japan	13	China
22	Germany	14	Canada
32	Canada	25	Spain
43	China	61	India

Source: Invest Korea https://www.investkorea.org/ik-en/index.do

Korea's Strategic Partnership with Major Countries in the Indo-Pacific

(a) Korea-US Strategic Partnership

South Korea is United States' key strategic and economic partner in Asia. The economic relationship is institutionalised with the US-South Korea Free Trade Agreement (KORUS FTA), which came into force in 2012. In 2022, South Korea was the United States' seventh-largest trading partner with goods and services trade combined, and the United States was South Korea's second-largest trading partner, following China.[17]

In 2024, South Korea was the seventh-largest trading partner of the US while the latter was the former's second-largest trading partner, followed by China. The US-South Korea Free Trade Agreement (KORUS FTA) was the United States' second-largest trade agreement by value. Over the past decade, American interests in US-ROK relations has focused on cooperation on North Korea, China and Indo-Pacific policies, the US-ROK alliance, US-ROK-Japan relations, and bilateral trade and investment.

In the summit meeting with Donald Trump in August 2025, South Korean President Lee Jae Myung has identified US-ROK relations, as well as ROK-US-Japan cooperation, as "core pillars" of the foreign policy of ROK. In August 2025, he had the first summit meeting with President Donald Trump. The two leaders underlined the strength and importance of the US-ROK relationship

Notwithstanding the positive atmospherics of the first Trump-Lee summit, the bilateral relations between South Korea and the US has certain level of tension, since Trump Administration demanded huge amount of FDI from Korean side in return for lowering the tariffs from 25 per cent to 15 per cent.. Both parties have discussed to settle the issue and the Korean side tried to settle it before the APEC Summit, which was held at the end of October 2025.

(b) Korea-China Strategic Partnership

China has been South Korea's largest trading partner and second-largest destination for foreign direct investment from Korean companies. In 2014, a free trade agreement between China and South Korea was signed.[18] However, with the tensions due to the rivalry between the US and China, the latter's actions are disrupting relations between South Korea and the US. Chinese media outlets have repeatedly warned countries including Japan and Taiwan, against South Korea's efforts to join US-led initiatives such as the Indo-Pacific Economic

Framework and the "Chip 4" Dialogue among semiconductor manufacturers, since South Korean former President Yoon has assumed office in May 2022.[19]

The sensitive response by China was intensified in March 2023, when South Korea made efforts for a rapprochement with Japan. In April 2023, the Chinese government responded sharply when former President Yoon characterised a possible cross–Taiwan Strait conflict as an international security issue. The Chinese government reacted with formal diplomatic protests warning South Korea not to abandon its One China policy.[20] China's intention lies in achieving regional dominance and reducing the power and engagement of the US-Japan, US-ROK and the US-Japan-ROK alliance.

On the side-line of the 2025 Gyeongju APEC Summit, South Korean President Lee Jae-myung held a summit meeting with Chinese president Xi Jinping on 1 November 2025. It was the first bilateral summit meeting between the two leaders since President Lee assumed the presidency in June 2025. The two leaders agreed to move forward together on the path to peace. President Xi underlined that China and South Korea are friendly neighbours and strategic cooperative partners. The two leaders agreed to institutionalise high-level communication channels and expand people-to-people and regional exchanges as well as deepen and develop friendly relations. Chinese President Xi Jinping mentioned that in the face of rapidly changing international and regional circumstances, China and South Korea should continue the tradition of friendship and draw upon eastern wisdom by respecting and trusting each other, cooperating and achieving mutual benefit and maintaining a good neighbour relationship.

(c) Korea-Japan Strategic Partnership

ROK-Japan relations are characterised by controversial historical legacy issues from Japan's colonisation of the Korean Peninsula for 35 years from 1910 to 1945. In 2018 and 2019, both governments took a series of actions and retaliatory countermeasures in trade, security, and history-related controversies.

The year of 2025 marks the 60th anniversary of normalised Korea-Japan diplomatic relations since the year of 1965. South Korean President Lee Jae Myung and Japanese Prime Minister Takaichi Sanae held talks in Takaichi's hometown of Nara on January 13, 2026. The two leaders agreed to continue "shuttle diplomacy" as well as to strengthen security ties against regional threats and to cooperate in economic security. Both countries are committed to enhancing "future-oriented" partnership under the slogan "Joining Hands for a Better Future".

The summit meeting was held following President Lee's proposal during the October 2025 Gyeongju APEC summit to convene in Nara, the hometown of Prime Minister Takaichi. The meeting is characterised by institutionalising shuttle diplomacy, a new modality for addressing historical issues, expanding citizen-focused cooperation, and managing cooperation and conflict in parallel.

(d) Korea-ASEAN Strategic Partnership

In 2005, the ASEAN-ROK Plan of Action was adopted to implement the goals set out in the Joint Declaration on Comprehensive Cooperation Partnership and to promote political, economic, social, and cultural cooperation. It also laid out ways to support ASEAN to build a fully integrated ASEAN community by 2020.

In 2019, ASEAN and the ROK celebrated the 30th anniversary of ASEAN-ROK dialogue relations with a commemorative Summit on 25-26 November in Busan. Leaders adopted the ASEAN-ROK Joint Vision Statement to provide a strategic framework for solidifying the ASEAN-ROK partnership in the years ahead. In 2020, ASEAN and the ROK adopted a Plan of Action to implement the Joint Vision Statement, and in 2021 adopted the Joint Statement on Advancing ASEAN-ROK Cooperation for People-centered Community of Peace and Prosperity.[21]

The ROK and ASEAN are invaluable trading partners to one another. In 2021, the trade volume between ASEAN and the ROK recorded a turnover of US$ 176.5 billion. ASEAN is ROK's second largest trading partner. Furthermore, ASEAN is the ROK's second largest investment destination, with foreign direct investment inflow from the ROK reaching US$ 9.77 billion in 2020, and US$ 6.15 billion in 2021 respectively.

The ASEAN-ROK Free Trade Agreement (AKFTA) came into effect on 1 January 2010. The Third Protocol to Amend the ASEAN-ROK Trade in Goods Agreement was signed in November 2015.

Policy Considerations for South Korea-India Comprehensive Strategic Partnership

India-ROK Summit in the Framework of G20

In 2023, South Korea and India celebrated the 50th anniversary of diplomatic relations. India and South Korea should work together to elevate bilateral, regional and global cooperation. The G20 is an excellent mechanism by which both countries could work together with a global perspective. In view of the active foreign policy and global competitiveness of both countries, it is recommended that India and South Korea establish a new Comprehensive and Strategic Partnership by upgrading the current "Special Strategic Partnership". India's "Act East Policy" and South Korea's new "Indo-Pacific Strategy" should be good platforms for advancing the bilateral and regional partnership and connectivity between the two countries.[22]

In order to strengthen the bilateral relations to the level of relations with major powers including US, Japan, and China, South Korea has to design device another version of the New Southern Policy for Great South. In the meanwhile, India recognise South Korea as a special strategic partner with specific action plans.

In addition, as partners of G7 Plus, India, South Korea and Australia should proceed together with an in-depth dialogue with G7 members to formulate a G10 mechanism. The current G7 plus mechanism would be a stepping-stone. Japan, as the host of the G7 in 2023, provided a platform for the Indo-Pacific economies to share the values of the G7 countries. The Indo-Pacific region's strategic importance in global security and prosperity should be reflected in regional institutions. As leading free and open Indo-Pacific economies, India, South Korea and Australia should work together with their Atlantic counterparts in the G7, forming G10 in the future. A new G10 would better represent liberal market economies and rule of law to ensure a free and open rules-based international economic order.

Initiatives for Comprehensive Strategic Partnership

In order to upgrade the current Special Strategic Partnership into a Comprehensive Strategic partnership, both sides need to expand the bilateral cooperation in a variety of sectoral areas together with the substantial upgrade of the CEPA.

The reference model for a comprehensive strategic partnership would be of India-the US, India-Japan and India-ASEAN models. Both sides could refer to some key elements available for the strategic partnership between India and South Korea.[23]

Advancing the India-South Korea Comprehensive Economic Partnership (CEPA)

The India-South Korea Comprehensive Economic Partnership (CEPA) came into effect on 1 January 2010. At the ninth round of negotiations to upgrade the

CEPA in November 2022 at Seoul, both sides discussed trade in goods, services, rules of origin, investment, and SPS/TBT issues. In order to increase bilateral trade and investment, a more comprehensive, advanced CEPA is required. To attain the goal of $50 billion in trade volume by 2030, both sides should upgrade CEPA immediately.

The key points for advancing the CEPA include trade balancing and improving market access, advancement of investment environments, tariff reduction to import of automobiles in India, protection of IPR, promotion of e-commerce, further liberalisation of services in IT and telecommunications, opening of pharmaceuticals market, etc. India raised concerns on the growing trade deficit. However, as long as more investments by Korean companies are realised, it would be inevitable that the trade deficit might have increased due to the import of Korean parts and components for manufacturing products in India.

Action plans for India-Korea Technology and Industry Cooperation

In order to upgrade the current strategic partnership, both sides need to implement action plans in various sectors such as Innovation Ecosystems, Defence Innovation and Technology Cooperation, Resilient Semiconductor Supply Chains, Industry-academia cooperation, and Next-Generation Telecommunications.

Strengthening Bilateral Innovation Ecosystems

- Facilitating the Korea-India Joint Programme of Cooperation in Science and Technology through bilateral cooperation between scientists and researchers from the two countries with joint R&D projects and technical missions.[24]
- Designating India's Department of Science and Technology (DST), Ministry of Electronics and Information Technology (MEIT) and Korea's Ministry of Science and ICT (MSICT) as a channel to implement the cooperation programme in India and South Korea.
- Exploring potential areas of cooperation in the areas of Green Mobility, Robotics & Manufacturing, Renewable Energy including Green Hydrogen, Information & Communication Technology and Material Science & Technology with special focus on Semiconductor and Display, and inviting Indian and Korean scientists/researchers to submit proposals for joint research projects.

- Signing a new Implementation Arrangement for a Research Agency Partnership between Korea's National Research Foundation (NRF)/the Korea Science and Engineering Foundation (KSEF) and Indian Science and Technology Foundation (ISTF) to expand international collaboration in a range of areas – including artificial intelligence, quantum technologies, and advanced wireless telecommunication – to build a robust innovation ecosystem between the two countries.[25]
- Establishing a joint Indo-Korea Quantum Coordination Mechanism with participation from industry, academia, and government to facilitate research and industry collaboration.
- Making global efforts to develop international standards and benchmarks for trustworthy AI through coordinating on the development of consensus, multi-stakeholder standards, ensuring that these standards and benchmarks are aligned with democratic values.

Defence Innovation and Technology Cooperation

- Advancing the bilateral Defence Industrial Cooperation Roadmap to accelerate technological cooperation for joint development and production of defence munition, with an initial focus on exploring projects related to defence munition-related technologies, and other systems.
- Launching a Korea-India Defence Acceleration Ecosystem by mobilising a network of universities, start-ups, industry and think tanks to facilitate joint defence technology innovation, and co-production of advanced defence technology equipment.
- Enhancing long-term research and development cooperation, focusing on identifying maritime security and intelligence surveillance reconnaissance (ISR) operational use cases.

Resilient Semiconductor Supply Chains

- Enhancing bilateral collaboration on resilient semiconductor supply chains; supporting the development of a semiconductor design, manufacturing, and fabrication of an ecosystem; and leveraging complementary strengths, promoting the development of a skilled workforce that will support global semiconductor supply chains, and encouraging the development of joint ventures and technology partnerships in mature technology nodes and packaging.

- Establishing partnership between the Korea Semiconductor Industry Association (KSIA) and the India Electronics Semiconductor Association (IESA) with the engagement from the Government of India Semiconductor Mission, to develop a "readiness assessment", to identify near-term industry opportunities and facilitate longer-term strategic development of complementary semiconductor ecosystems.
- Signing of an MoU on Semiconductor Supply Chains and Innovation Partnership and providing opportunities to Indian technicians to be trained in Korean R&D centres

Industry-academia Cooperation

- Exploring joint research and dual academic degree programme by the Association of Korean universities and leading Indian educational institutions, including Indian Institutes of Technology, which will make recommendations for research and university partnerships.

Next Generation Telecommunications

- Launching a public-private dialogue on telecommunications and regulations.
- Advancing cooperation on 5G and 6G R&D, facilitating deployment and adoption of Open RAN in India and ROK, and fostering economies of scale within the sector.

Korean Financial Investment in Indian Financial Market

Recently inflow of Korean funds into the Indian stock market has increased. The Indian exchange traded funds (ETF) market are expected to expand faster over time. During February and April 2023, Indian funds set up in Korea attracted 250.1 billion won (US$188.8 million). India is evaluated as the next investment destination as beyond China.[26] In order to compensate the trade deficit, Indian financial institutions will have to attract more Korean financial investment in the stock and security market.

Other Global and Regional Cooperation

South Korea-India Defence and Security Cooperation

Defence Industries Cooperation is one of the key elements of Comprehensive Strategic Cooperation between the two countries. A Roadmap for Defence Industries Cooperation was signed between the two countries in September 2019.

Both sides are should actively implement multiple agreements extending from logistic support to information exchanges pertaining to operational matters which were signed during Prime Minister Modi's visit to Seoul in February 2019.

In May 2022, the Ministry of Defence (MoD) has approved plans to procure Future Ready Combat Vehicles (FRCVs) and engines to upgrade in-service T-90 main battle tanks (MBTs). The two projects were granted 'Approval in Principle' (AIP) by the MoD. The programmes will proceed under the government-funded 'Make in India' initiative. The FRCV project will see the acquisition of 590 vehicles in the first phase to replace the Indian Army's old license-built Russian T-72 MBTs.[27]

Prior to the approval of procurement, in June 2021, the Indian Army issued a FRCV request for information (RFI) to procure a total US $5 billion for 1,770 vehicles, maintenance and training requirements, as well as performance based logistics and engineering support packages over several phases. The Ministry of Defence (MoD) will evaluate South Korea's *Hyundai Rotem K2* since it is competitive and preferred model by Indian Army, while the American *M1 Abrams* and the German *Leopard,* due to high price and heavy weight, may not fit the specifications priority mentioned in the RFI.[28]

On the other hand, the Indian Army is operating 100 in-service K9 *Vajra-T* self-propelled howitzers (SPHs), which are the Indian-manufactured variant of the Korea's *K9 Thunder*, with 50 per cent of their components being manufactured in India that applied for a technology transfer from South Korea's Hanwha Defence, based on a contract signed in May 2017. The Indian Army ordered additional one hundred 155 mm/52-caliber SPHs known as *K9 Vajra-T* designed and developed by South Korea's Hanwha Aerospace.[29]

Increased cooperation in the defence industry by both countries is certain to create a synergy effect by combining Korean technology and Indian political will for capacity building and resources. The South Korean defence industry will be an optimal selection by the Indian Army, taking into account its competitiveness in technology, distinct cost effectiveness advantage and capacity for capital investment.

South Korea- India cooperation in QUAD Plus

South Korea and Quad countries could closely collaborate in eight areas that correspond with Quad working groups and activities: critical and emerging technologies, infrastructure, public health, climate change and sustainable development, education and people-to-people exchange, maritime safety and security, cybersecurity, and outer space.[30]

South Korea, India and other QUAD countries could:

- Work together for facilitating the Indo-Pacific's digital integration through 5G and 6G network architectures;
- Apply the South Korea-Australia 2021 Memorandum of Understanding on Cooperation in Critical Mineral Supply Chains, to a bilateral agreement with India;
- Expand the South Korea-US Semiconductor Partnership Dialogue to India;
- Cooperate in establishing a shared set of rules and norms for digital governance in the interconnections between technology and national security
- Establish a Clean-Hydrogen Partnership between India and South Korea

South Korea's partnership of the Indian Ocean Rim Association (IORA)

The Indian Ocean Rim Association (IORA) was established in 1999 to cooperate on Maritime Safety and Security (MSS) in the Indian Ocean Region (IOR). The IOR is the place of 2.7 billion people, more than a third of the world's population. Its vast coastline includes the world's important shipping routes – from the Strait of Hormuz to the Malacca Strait. Eighty per cent of the world's maritime oil shipments pass Indian Ocean waters.

In August 2021, as the President of the UNSC by rotation as a non-permanent member, Prime Minister Narendra Modi chaired the first UNSC meeting on maritime security. Prime Minister Modi proposed five principles to ensure global maritime security: removing barriers from legitimate maritime trade; encouraging responsible maritime connectivity; settling maritime disputes through peaceful means and based on international law; jointly facing natural disasters and maritime threats created by non-State actors and preserving the maritime environment and resources.[31]

Such cooperation between India and the ROK should be extended within the framework of the IORA, since both countries are keen on maintaining maritime safety and security in the Indian Ocean Region (IOR).

NOTES

1 Amb. Beeho Chun, Ph.D. is a Visiting Professor of Sungkyunkwan University by giving lectures and making researches on global business strategy and a Vice President of Korean Council on Foreign Relations. He served as Former Korean Ambassador to Mexico and Bulgaria respectively. He was awarded a Ph.D. in Political Science and Sociology from the Complutense University of Madrid, Spain together with and doctor honoris causa in linguistics

science by Sofia University "St. Kliment Ohridski, and doctor honoris causa of Bulgaria Academy of Science, Bulgaria.

2 G20 Summit, New Delhi at https://www.g20.org/en/g20-india-2023/new-delhi-summit/ (Accessed 14 April 2024).

3 Russia's invasion of Ukraine has caused world economy recession. However, the global economic impact of China-US rivalry, and a sluggish Chinese Economy, China-induced challenge in the East or South China Seas might have surpassed that of the Russian-Ukraine war.

4 "Prime Minister's meeting with the President of the Republic of Korea", Prime Minister's Office, Government of India, 20 May 2023 at https://pib.gov.in/PressReleaseIframePage.aspx?PRID=1925767 (Accessed 14 May 2024).
"South Korea's Yoon, India's Modi agree to step up cooperation on defence", Reuters, 20, May 2023 at https://www.reuters.com/world/asia-pacific/skoreas-yoon-indias-modi-agree-step-up-cooperation-defence-bio-health-sectors-2023-05-20/ (Accessed 24 April 2024).

5 Choongje Cho, "Economic Cooperation between Korea and India in the midst of Covid-19: Opportunities and Challenges," 2nd Online Academic Workshop on 'Facets of India-ROK Partnership,' Seoul, Indian Embassy in Korea, 2 September 2021.

6 Darshana M. Baruah, "India in the Indo-Pacific: New Delhi's Theater of Opportunity", Carnegie Endowment for International Peace, 30 June 2020 at https://carnegieendowment.org/files/Baruah_UnderstandingIndia_final1.pdf (Accessed 03 May 2024).

7 Observer Research Foundation at https://www.orfonline.org/research/india-at-75-the-emerging-global-role-of-india-81072/

8 N. Chandrasekaran, Executive Chairman, Tata Sons, "Realizing the potential of a US$26 trillion economy", India@100, Ernst Young, https://www.ey.com/en_in/india-at-100 (Accessed 14 April 2024).

9 "Joint Statement from the United States and India", The US White House, 22 June2023 at https://www.whitehouse.gov/briefing-room/statements-releases/2023/06/22/joint-statement-from-the-united-states-and-india/ (Accessed 04 May 2024).

10 Urvi Tembey, "The India-US Summit: Going beyond bilateral trade gains", Observer Research Foundation, 13 July 2023 at https://www.orfonline.org/expert-speak/the-india-us-summit-going-beyond-bilateral-trade-gains/ (Accessed 14 April 2024).

11 SDINE: "India-Japan Sustainable Development Initiative for the North Eastern Region of India", Act East Forum at https://www.in.emb-japan.go.jp/files/100319132.pdf (Accessed 20 April 2024).

12 "ASEAN, India strengthen comprehensive strategic partnership", ASEAN Secretariat News, 7 March 2023.

13 "ASEAN, India intensify comprehensive strategic partnership", ASEAN Secretariat News, 29 March 2023.

14 "Strategy for a Free, Peaceful and Prosperous Indo-Pacific Region," Press Releases, Ministry of Foreign Affairs, Republic of Korea at https://www.mofa.go.kr/eng/brd/m_5676/view.do?seq=322133 (Accessed 14 April 2024).

15 Pratnashree Basu, "Why Seoul and New Delhi should leverage the G20 momentum for advancing collaboration in the Indo-Pacific", Observer Research Foundation, 9 March 2023 at https://www.orfonline.org/expert-speak/why-seoul-and-new-delhi-should-leverage-the-g20/

16 Jagannath Panda and Choong Yong Ahn, "Where is India in South Korea's New Indo-Pacific Strategy?" *The Diplomat*, 27 January 2023.

17 Council on Foreign Relations at https://www.cfr.org/backgrounder/us-south-korea-relations (Accessed 24 April 2024).

18 "Free Trade Agreement between the Government of the People's Republic of China and the Government of the Republic of Korea", MOFCOM China.

19 Scott A. Snyder, "What's Causing the Rise in China-South Korea Tensions?", US Council on Foreign Relations, 30 June 2023, at https://www.cfr.org/in-brief/whats-causing-rise-china-south-korea-tensions (Accessed 13 June 2024).

20 Ibid.

21 Ministry of Foreign Affairs of ROK, "Overview of ASEAN-ROK relations."

22 Observer Research Foundation, at https://www.orfonline.org/research/india-south-korea-relations-need-for-a-comprehensive-strategic-partnership-81074/ accessed on 15 July 2024

23 "Joint Statement from the United States and India", The White House, 22 JUNE 2023, at https://www.whitehouse.gov/briefing-room/statements-releases/2023/06/22/joint-statement-from-the-united-states-and-india/ (Accessed 13 June 2024).

24 "2023 Korea- India Joint Program of Cooperation in Science & Technology, Call for Joint Project Proposals", Korea-India JRP call 2023, at https://dst.gov.in/sites/default/files/Korea-India%20JRP%20call%202023.pdf (Accessed 03 June 2024).

25 United States and India Elevate Strategic Partnership with the initiative on Critical and Emerging Technology (iCET)", The White House, "Fact Sheet 31 January 2023, at https://www.whitehouse.gov/briefing-room/statements-releases/2023/01/31/fact-sheet-united-states-and-india-elevate-strategic-partnership-with-the-initiative-on-critical-and-emerging-technology-icet/ (Accessed 15 June 2024).

"U.S.-India Defence Relationship", US-India Fact Sheet, at https://dod.defense.gov/Portals/1/Documents/pubs/US-IND-Fact-Sheet.pdf (Accessed 27 June 2024).

"India-US Brief on India-U.S. Relations", Embassy of India, Washington DC.

26 "Indian Stock Market Draws US$250 Billion in Korean Funds in 3 Months", Business Korea, 8 May 2023, at https://www.businesskorea.co.kr/news/articleView.html?idxno=114277 (Accessed 23 June 2024).

27 "Future Ready Combat Vehicle (FRCV) Brief of Project", The Ministry of Defence, Government of India, 31 May 2023 at https://www.makeinindiadefence.gov.in/admin/writereaddata/upload/project/project_file/FRCV_ (2).pdf (Accessed 13 June 2024).

28 Kapil Kajal, "India approves plans to procure Future Ready Combat Vehicles", *Janes*, 13 June 2023 at https://www.janes.com/defence-news/news-detail/india-approves-plans-to-procure-future-ready-combat-vehicles (Accessed 13 June 2024).

29 Kapil Kajal, "Indian Army orders 100 additional K9 howitzers", 20 February 2023 at https://www.janes.com/defence-news/news-detail/indian-army-orders-100-additional-k9-howitzers (Accessed 15 June 2024).

30 Kristi Govella, Garima Mohan, and Bonnie Glaser, "Expanding Engagement among South Korea and the Quad Countries in the Indo-Pacific", GMF Policy Paper, June 2022 at https://www.gmfus.org/news/expanding-engagement-among-south-korea-and-quad-countries-indo-pacific (Accessed 17 July 2024).

31 "English translation of Prime Minister's remarks at the UNSC High-Level Open Debate on "Enhancing Maritime Security: A Case for International Cooperation", Ministry of External Affairs, Government of India, 9 August 2021 at https://www.mea.gov.in/Speeches-Statements.htm?dtl/34151/English_translation_of_Prime_Ministers_remarks_at_the_UNSC_ HighLevel_Open_Debate_on_Enhancing_Maritime_Security_A_Case_For_International_Cooperation_A (Accessed 17 June 2024).

CHAPTER 12

Deepening Bangladesh-India Connectivity: Realising the Emerging Opportunities

Mustafizur Rahman

Context and Importance of the Discussion

Regrettably, South Asia has continued to remain one of the most disconnected regions in the world. However, it is encouraging to note that in recent years several initiatives have been set in motion to reverse this situation. In this context, the initiatives to deepen multimodal connectivity between Bangladesh and India merit special mention since these have a far-reaching impact and importance for the two countries as well as for the region. For Bangladesh, these developments are of crucial significance from the perspective of realising its developmental aspirations in the twenty first century.

That *geography matters in development* is by now a proven statement. It is widely recognised that Bangladesh has a natural advantage to potentially emerge as a regional transport hub thanks to its strategic location as a gateway to the Bay of Bengal (with a large hinterland going back to southern China), as a transit route between western part of Bangladesh and Northeastern states of India and as a major link in the SASEC (South Asia Subregional Economic Cooperation) transport network that connects Western Asia with the ASEAN and East ASEAN regions. Indeed, realisation of the opportunities that could originate from this unique geo-economic and geo-strategic location should be seen by Bangladesh as a major driver of its socio-economic development going forward in the twenty-first century. This should also be seen by Bangladesh as an important source of revenue in the form of export of transport and connectivity services, involving India and other neighbouring countries.

As may be recalled, in FY2022-23, India imported about US$ 714.0 billion worth of goods, while Bangladesh's export to India was about US$ 2.1 billion (less than one-third of 1.0 per cent of India's total global import). On the other hand, Bangladesh's import from India, of US$ 15.2 billion, was about 17.0 per cent of the country's global import (in FY2021-22). So the question to ask, and actions to take, concern identifying concrete steps which would enable Bangladesh to take advantage of the growing import market of India. Not that Bangladesh is not making some headway in the right direction: it took Bangladesh 47 years to cross the milestone of US$ 1.0 billion export to India, in 2017; in contrast, it took only five years to cross the landmark of US$ 2.0 billion in 2022. There is a growing understanding in Bangladesh that the challenge at hand is to identify and implement appropriate strategies to tap into the expanding import market of India, through enhancement of supply-side capacities, attracting Foreign Direct Investment (FDI), stimulating product diversification, reducing lead-time and raising price competitiveness.

Closer multimodal transport connectivity could play a critically important role in view of the above. The cost that the traders, producers and consumers are paying on account of lack of good connectivity, and the resultant high cost of transport, is evidenced by a recent World Bank Report which estimates that exporting from Bangladesh to Nepal (by land, via India) was 1.5 times costlier than exporting from Bangladesh to Sao Paulo in Brazil. In view of this, an efficient bilateral multimodal connectivity with India could not only help reduce transport costs and raise trade competitiveness, but also play a critically important role in the wider and broader scenario of bilateral cooperation. The major challenge here lies in identifying appropriate modalities to realise the attendant possibilities in a manner that delivers *win-win outcomes* for both the participating countries.

In view of the above, Section I traces the evolution of the discussion on Indo-Bangladesh connectivity by highlighting the shift in the discourse in recent period. Section II presents a review of some of the ongoing measures to deepen multimodal transport connectivity between the two countries. Section III identifies the opportunities to take the bilateral transport initiatives forward towards win-win outcomes. The discussion is rounded up with some concluding remarks.

Shift in the Discourse on Connectivity

There was a time when establishing closer transport connectivity with India was taboo in Bangladesh and was met with strong opposition from powerful quarters, driven by a number of concerns and reasons. These were related to political considerations, security apprehensions and doubts as to whether Bangladesh would benefit at all from connectivity arrangements with India. The realities on the ground, however, have since changed. Over the recent past, the mainstream discourse in Bangladesh has shifted from 'whether to provide connectivity' to 'how best to negotiate any such deal, and how to address the attendant concerns of Bangladesh and safeguard its interests and how this could be done in a way that assures win-win outcomes for both the countries'.

There are several reasons for this change in the perspective and the mindset. These call for a closer look.

The economic advantages of closer bilateral cooperation, through transport connectivity, investment connectivity and trade connectivity have become increasingly evident in recent years. The experience of regional cooperation and integration involving countries of the neighbourhood regions has revealed the benefits of harnessing deeper integration among geographically contiguous regions and helped to change the perspectives (the ASEAN-wide cooperation; Mekong Delta cooperation; SIJORI growth triangle that include Singapore, Johor State of Malaysia and Rio state of Indonesia; and others).

Experience on the ground and research and analysis bear out that developing value chains with India will not only benefit the two countries, but also strengthen global integration of the Bangladesh economy from a position of strength. This is visible most prominently in the case of Bangladesh's export-oriented readymade garments (RMG) industry. For example, the large bilateral trade deficit with India is in part because of the significant import of cotton, yarn, fabrics, accessories and related machineries from India. These imports helped Bangladesh maintain a large (about US$ 9.0 billion) trade surplus with the US where more than 90.0 per cent exports from Bangladesh constituted RMG products.

The argument that transport facilitation with India is mainly import facilitation also proved to be without merit. It needs to be emphasised that it is not the Government of Bangladesh that imports from India; it is the country's private sector that does most of the imports. And they do so because the business people find it cost-effective and profitable to source from India. Imports from India allow the consumers in Bangladesh to get agricultural commodities and inputs and other goods at competitive prices, which helps maintain food security and reduce price volatility in the country. These imports allow the Bangladeshi entrepreneurs and producers to get intermediate products and inputs at competitive prices and with a short lead-time; a large number of export-oriented industries in Bangladesh import intermediate goods and raw materials from India at competitive prices, as was noted above. RMG backward linkages through imports from India help Bangladesh to remain competitive in the global market (RMG accounts for 84 per cent of Bangladesh's total exports; Bangladesh is the second largest exporter of apparels in the world with 6.0 per cent of the global market). The bottom line is the profit motive that induces the private sector of Bangladesh to source increasingly from India instead of from other countries. With India's economic and technological development over the recent years, its labour and capital productivity has been on the rise. This, and supply-side capacity and production diversification, have allowed Indian goods to gain competitive strength against those coming from many of Bangladesh's traditional import sourcing countries. Hence the import diversion is in India's favour.

A concern which used to be voiced rather often, related to the loss of the so-called *captive market of Northeast India*. The argument is that Bangladesh will lose the Northeast market if it provides transport connectivity to India, through its territory, for movement of goods between the western and eastern parts of India. It is well known that the Northeastern region, which includes the seven sister states of India, remains a relatively underdeveloped economic zone of India. The purchasing power in the Northeast states has been significantly lower than the rest of India, as also that of Bangladesh. As is well known, historically Bangladesh's exports to the Northeastern states has been very low when compared to not only her global exports, but also in terms of exports to India. A major reason driving this is the low purchasing power of the Northeastern states. India is at present investing heavily in these states. Connectivity through Bangladesh could be a significant win-win for both the countries in this context. This will facilitate the ongoing development work in the Northeastern region and significantly reduce the cost of transporting goods to carry out India's ambitious development plans for the region. An economically prosperous Northeast would have greater capacity to import from Bangladesh than at present. So the argument about losing the captive market was untenable.

It is a fact that Bangladesh has a large and growing bilateral trade deficit with India. But this should not be overplayed – in a globalised world it is not bilateral deficit but global trade deficit that should be the reason for concern.

However, this is not to say that Bangladesh should not place greater emphasis on increasing its exports to India, but to draw attention to the fact that bilateral trade deficit with India, as was noted earlier, allows Bangladesh to maintain a trade surplus with many countries such as the US the UK and the countries in the

EU which are key destinations for Bangladesh's export of apparels. All these help Bangladesh reduce the global trade deficit. Apparels constitute about 47.0 per cent of Bangladesh's exports to India; a significant part of these exports use imported inputs from India. The important and pertinent question to ask is, why have Bangladesh's export earnings from India remained so low, and how these could be increased by taking advantage of the expanding import market of India.

One recalls the time when Bangladesh allowed India to transport heavy machinery and equipment for the Palatana Power Plant in Tripura (by riverine transport from Kolkata to Ashuganj, and then via road from Ashuganj to Agartala). Bangladesh is now importing 100 MW worth of electricity from the plant. The price of electricity is Tk6.43 per unit or kilowatt-hour and with the transmission cost added the import price will stand at Tk6.71 per unit.[1] These infrastructures are contributing to the economic development, higher standard of living and the consequent higher purchasing power of people in the Northeast. The argument here is that when such development-induced purchasing power of these states rises, it is bound to be reflected in higher imports from Bangladesh.

Ongoing Initiatives to Deepen Bilateral Multimodal Connectivity

Bangladesh has signed a number of bilateral agreements and Protocols with India in recent years in areas of multi-modal connectivity. As may be recalled in this connection, some transport connectivity between the two countries existed historically, preceding the emergence of an independent Bangladesh. However, these connectivity were was ruptured following the India-Pakistan war in 1965. Some of these, such as the Akhaura-Agartala rail link, are being revived only now. The bilateral Protocol on Inland Waterways Transit and Trade was signed in 1972 (with eight Protocol routes). The Coastal Shipping Protocol was signed more recently, in 2015. India has offered Bangladesh free transit for exports to Nepal and Bhutan. These two countries already have land transit deals with New Delhi which allows Nepalese and Bhutanese vehicles carrying export-import goods to come to the Bangladesh border points. Bangladesh has allowed India the use of Ashuganj river port for multimodal transport of cargo (through riverine and road routes) to Agartala. Regular transit between Bangladesh and Northeast of India by using the Chattogram and the Mongla ports was granted in April 2023. The cargo from these two ports can be transported using 16 transit routes as agreed by the two countries.[2]

Currently, Bangladesh is investing a considerable amount of resources in building its transport infrastructure. Medium to long-term viability of some of these – including the Padma bridge and the rail link over the bridge – will be ensured if these play a role in harnessing sub-regional economic cooperation (Bangladesh, Nepal, Bhutan and the Eastern states of India). Expected economic and financial returns from these infrastructures will rise significantly if the benefits of the sub-regional cooperation could be reaped.

Several roads are being built at present, which, besides meeting Bangladesh's domestic transport needs, will also facilitate road connectivity between Bangladesh's western and Northeast India, by taking advantage of the transit agreement. As per the coastal shipping Protocol, Indian vessels will now be able to use Bangladesh's ports (Mongla and Chattogram), and goods can then be transhipped to trucks for onward journey to the Northeastern states by road. Standard Operating Procedures (SOPs) have been agreed upon for transhipment of goods from Chattogram and Mongla ports through road, rail and water routes: to Agartala via Akhaura, Dawki (Meghalaya) via Tamabil, Sutarkandi (Assam) via Sheola and Srimantapur (Tripura) via Bibir Bazar. Some roads in Bangladesh are being upgraded keeping the emerging needs in mind. Several roads and transport-related infrastructures are being built as part of the three lines of credit which India provided to Bangladesh over the past years (in 2010, 2015 and 2017, worth about US$ 8.0 billion).

One could add a number of other connectivity-related initiatives which are ongoing. The recently commissioned friendship pipeline supplying high-speed diesel from Numaligarh Refinery Limited in Assam to 16 districts in northern Bangladesh is yet another example. The pipeline will help reduce transport costs for Bangladesh by about 40 per cent. Also, the BBIN Motor Vehicle Agreement, signed in 2015, could provide an important opportunity to facilitate vehicular movement between India, Bangladesh and Nepal (Bhutan has decided to remain an observer for the time being). The MVA could prove to be an important step towards seamless multimodal connectivity in the Eastern part of South Asian region.

The Search for Win-Win Outcomes

The important issue for Bangladesh, and also for India for that matter, is to take advantage of the aforesaid Agreements and Protocols, investment, infrastructures and other bilateral initiatives in a way that best serves the interests of both countries, by generating win-win outcomes. In all negotiations – be it bilateral, trilateral and multilateral– there are concerns and national interests which each party needs to take cognisance of while searching for ways to arrive at consensus-driven resolutions and solutions. There are questions of offensive and defensive interests, issues of offers and requests, and there may as well be non-negotiable elements. This is a common feature in any negotiation. In case of Bangladesh and India, it is through bilateral discussions that attendant concerns will need to be addressed and resolved.

For Bangladesh, for connectivity, the involved issues concern both those *of principle* (modalities of sharing benefits and costs through fixation of fees, charges, tolls etc.) and *of operationalisation* (putting in place the necessary connectivity-related infrastructure and measures).

In view of the above, issues of cost-sharing and benefit sharing are important considerations for Bangladesh from the perspective of establishing seamless multimodal connectivity with India. In addition to the fees and charges, cost-sharing needs to address issues of sharing the various expenditures related to the construction, use and maintenance of the multimodal connectivity infrastructures: for example, costs involved in keeping the rivers navigable; maintenance and depreciation cost; payment of road use tolls; costs associated with incremental air pollution, environmental degradation and congestion; sharing of costs to build new transport corridors, geared mainly to provide transit facilities to India, to name a few. The principle of proportionality should guide the fixation – in case of existing roads, marginal costs involved in the use of multimodal connectivity may be considered, while in case of new corridors to be built primarily for purposes of transit, both countries could share the cost, by keeping in view the asymmetries in the of use of the particular link (cost-sharing ratios could, however, vary over time and will need be fixed through regular bilateral discussions).

Some of the corridors will have asymmetric use, to mainly benefit the Indian economy and to serve the interests of Indian transport operators and businesses. It will be in India's interest to share the associated costs (in accordance with proportional use of the infrastructure). An enlightened and strategic perspective on the part of India will be of advantage to both the countries. It may be noted in this connection that the aforementioned principle is in accordance with the relevant GATT Article with regards to providing Transit facilities by one country to another.

One recalls that when the bridge on the *Padma* was being built, India converted US$ 200 million from the first line of credit into a grant and contributed the amount towards construction of the bridge. If the *Padma* bridge is to be elevated from a mere *transport corridor* to *an economic corridor* (which will be required if the expected internal, financial and economic rates of returns are to be realised), the *Padma* bridge will need to serve not only as link between southern Bangladesh and rest of the country, but also as a sub-regional transport nodal point that services the needs of the adjoining regions of India as also Nepal and Bhutan. The bridge has the potential to emerge as a major connectivity link to Mongla and other ports in Bangladesh and as a key infrastructure for cross-country vehicular movement. One is persuaded to believe that this broader perspective has informed India's decision to make the aforementioned grant. Keeping the riverine routes navigable is also in India's interest if the water connectivity and coastal shipping Protocols are to be operationalised. Hence, the issue of cost sharing is not merely a theoretical concept but has practical significance. For example: to improve navigability along the Sirajganj–Daikhowa and Ashuganj–Zakiganj stretches of the Indo–Bangladesh route, India is investing nearly Rs 245 crore and Bangladesh 60 crores (out of Rs 305.84 crore) for improving navigability on a 80:20 cost sharing basis.[3]

On the other hand, the benefit sharing principle considers that the gains accrued should be shared by the two countries. The benefits through savings arising from the difference between the costs of using the traditional routes and the new opportunities of connectivity should be shared by both parties (this would arise from savings in the form of shorter distance, reduced fuel costs, lower time and other cost cutting elements arising from use of connectivity through Bangladesh by the Indian users). Bangladesh will need to be cognisant of the fact that the fees, charges, tolls, construction cost sharing, etc. to be borne by Indian operators should be fixed in a way that makes the new routes commercially attractive to the Indian users. Otherwise, there will be no incentive for the transport operators to use the new connectivity. Transit-related payments to be fixed by Bangladesh for each route and corridor ought to take these factors into consideration. Also, it may be noted that it will be Bangladeshi transporters, freight-forwarders and others who will benefit the most from the transhipment business within Bangladesh. Indo-Bangladesh joint venture companies may also be set up as business entities to handle cross-border trade.

On the other hand, Bangladesh will need to ensure that the facilities, support and infrastructure to service the transit, are put in place in a timely manner. The road rail, riverine connectivity and transport corridors will have to be fit for the purpose if Indian businessmen and transporters are to be encouraged and incentivised to use the connectivity. Both sides have an interest in establishing the facilities to operationalise the Agreements. There could also lead to business opportunities in the form of joint venture with participation of transport operators from both the countries.

The above argument is not merely a theoretical conjecture but draws on experience and has practical significance. For example, it was envisaged by many at the beginning that connectivity between Kolkata-Ashuganj-Agartala would be a major transit route once the Transit-Connectivity Agreement is operational. The Ashuganj river port was planned to be elevated to an international river port, and the cargo, transported by the riverine route by ship from Kolkata, was to be transhipped on trucks for the onward journey to Agartala. The route, it was thought, would be a key link for transportation between eastern and western India, since it was expected to significantly bring down transport costs as distance and time would be reduced (compared to transporting through the tortuous 1200-1600 km *chicken neck* in the Himalayas). The route would also allow the Indian government to save on subsidies that were being given to transporters using the traditional route. However, while the Agreement was signed several years ago, the necessary infrastructure were not ready; transhipment services, logistics, customs clearance and other trade facilitation measures were not put in place on time. The road from Ashuganj and Agartala was also not developed. Consequently, the initial enthusiasm of Indian transport operators and businesses soon evaporated. In an investigative report, published in July 2020, it was stated that in five years since the first shipment was made in June 2016, only 17 Indian shipments passed through the port (till July 2022). A negligible US$ 40 thousand (35 lakh taka) worth of fees and charges was collected by Bangladesh's concerned authorities. No cargo was transported from Agartala via Ashuganj to Kolkata. More frequent use of the multimodal connectivity and transhipment facilities would have created business opportunities for Bangladesh's truckers and transporters and through the various other transhipment activities, in addition to the government's income in the form of fees and charges. This was not to be because of lack of readiness.

This particular experience reveals that the two countries will need to make the needed investment in infrastructure, logistics, roads and trade facilitation measures with due urgency. If not, transport operators will not be able to take advantage of the connectivity. The same holds true of fixation of fees, charges and tolls. Transport operators will have to find it economically viable to use any particular route. One needs to keep in mind that governments sign Agreements and Protocols, but it is primarily the private sector and businesses, driven by the profit motive, who will choose to take (or not take) advantage of any specific connectivity option.

From the perspective of operationalising bilateral connectivity, as also the BBIN (BIN)-MVA, putting in place the required infrastructure at the borders on both sides, is also critically important. The borders should be crossing points, rather than control and choking points. For this to happen, integrated customs stations (ICS) with harmonisation and standardisation of procedures and protocols, paperless trade, interoperability of systems and closer customs cooperation will be required. Political will and a sense of urgency are needed to make the BBIN-MVA functional (the MVA covers cargo-carrying vehicular movement, bus service and private transport). To recall, the Agreement was signed in 2015 (the SOPs have also been negotiated); however, it could not be operationalised in seven years.

There needs to be single-window facility at the Integrated Customs Stations (as in the case of ASEAN) for border crossing and customs clearance. Mutual Recognition Agreements (MRAs) involving quality standards (e.g., in case of food items), certification, accreditation and lab testing, among others, would need to be negotiated to reduce hassle at customs points. Collaboration between the Bangladesh Standards and Testing Institution (BSTI) and the Indian Bureau of Indian Standards (BIS) is already put in place,[4] and cooperation between Bangladesh Food Safety Authority and the Food Safety and Standards Authorities of India (FSSAI) will be required to enhance trade in perishable food items. BSTI's capacity will need to be significantly strengthened to service the needs of the MRAs. Through negotiations, non-tariff measures and barriers that impede Bangladesh's export to India will need to be addressed. For example, a moratorium on anti-dumping duties (ADDs) may be put in place by India vis-a-vis Bangladeshi exporters to the country (India, to recall, has imposed ADDs on a number of jute exporters from Bangladesh). A change in the visa regime (such as visa on arrival, as with Sri Lanka), would facilitate movement of people between the two countries, which would strengthen other connectivities.

As is known, India has been offered two dedicated Special Economic Zones (SEZs) by Bangladesh (in Mirsharai Bangabandhu Sheikh Mujib Economic Zone in Chattogram and in Bagerhat in Mongla). While the SEZs will provide the investors access to unencumbered land, it is important that investors from India (and other countries, as also Bangladeshi investors interested in investing in SEZs) are able to get the other necessary services (services that are to be provided as per Bangladesh's One Stop Service Act of 2018 may be recalled here). A few private SEZs have already started functioning. Their experience could provide important guidance and insights to encourage Indian investment in the SEZs.

Attracting Indian investment to Bangladesh, targeting the Indian market, taking advantage of duty-free, quota-free preferential market access (to India and other countries), could potentially be a game changer for Bangladesh's economic interests. In this backdrop, extending the DF-QF market access to Bangladesh, for a time-bound period beyond Bangladesh's LDC graduation in 2026, merits serious consideration on the part of Indian policymakers.

Conclusion

In recent times, a number of positive measures have been put in motion towards deeper Indo-Bangladesh bilateral multimodal connectivity. Work has been initiated to build a functional International River Port in Ashuganj; the four-lane Ashuganj-Agartala road is under construction. Some of this infrastructure is being put in place with support of the Indian LOCs. Some transport connectivity is being built with Bangladesh's own resources, some with borrowed money. While serving Bangladesh's domestic needs, these could also serve bilateral and sub-regional trade-investment needs.

As is known, Bangladesh is currently in the process of negotiating a Comprehensive Economic Partnership Agreement (CEPA) with India. Deepening transport, investment, logistics and people-to-people connectivity and efficient trade facilitation measures (at the border and behind the border) will play a crucial role if the CEPA is to be operationalised and be successful. Indian investment in SEZs and connectivity initiatives should be seen as complementary to transport, investment and trade, which will help realise the potential benefits of the proposed CEPA with India. An enlightened and strategic view will be required on the part of both countries in order to realise the potential of opportunities originating from deeper bilateral cooperation in a win-win manner.

Bangladesh is at present gearing up to face the challenges of LDC graduation and middle-income graduation. In this backdrop, taking advantage of economic partnership with India ought to be seen by Bangladesh as a key strategy to address the emergent challenges in view of the dual graduation.

NOTES

1 Aminur Rahman Rasel, "BD to start importing 100MW from Tripura", *Dhaka Tribune*, 22 March 2016, https://www.dhakatribune.com/bangladesh/bangladesh-others/123793/bd-to-start-importing-100mw-from-tripura (Accessed 04 October 2023).

2 Reazul H Lashkar, Bangladesh okays India's use of 2 ports to transport goods to the northeast",

The Hindustan Times, 26 April 2023, https://www.hindustantimes.com/india-news/bangladesh-clears-use-of-chattogram-and-mongla-ports-by-india-for-transit-and-trans-shipment-of-cargo-cutting-time-and-cost-of-transport-to-northeastern-states-101682509293677.html (Accessed 05 October 2023).

3 Abhishek Law, "Dredging contracts with Bangladesh underway, more waterways to be operational to reduce cargo movement time: Sonowal", *Hindu Business line*, 16 October 2023, https://www.thehindubusinessline.com/economy/logistics/dredging-contracts-with-bangladesh-underway-more-waterways-to-be-operational-to-reduce-cargo-movement-time-sonowal/article67426725.ece (Accessed 10 November 2023).

4 MEA, "Agreement Between Bureau Of Indian Standards And Bangladesh Standards And Testing Institution on Cooperation in the Field of Standardization and Conformity Assessment", https://www.mea.gov.in/Portal/LegalTreatiesDoc/BG15B2967.pdf (Accessed 07 October 2023).

CHAPTER 13

Connectivity and Trade, Boosting Investment, Incubating Resilient Supply Chains: Towards Interdependent independence

Herrick Mpuku

Introduction

In recent years, the world has been rocked by a succession of crises, which have altered the direction of global public policy. Not since the Second World War have we witnessed circumstances, which have questioned the nature of international relations on the current scale.

Following the collapse of the old order of the post-Cold War era, viz. the fall of Soviet communism, the disintegration of the Warsaw Pact as well as the Soviet Union on the one hand, and subsequently the political liberalisation in Africa, the era of political and economic liberalism emerged. It was apparent that a new world order, a liberal order, founded on more openness at the national and international level, and indeed greater multilateralism, had emerged.

As we "beat our guns into ploughshares", a new dawn had indeed arrived, and the people all over the world could look with hope and confidence towards an era of peace, harmony and prosperity among peoples and nations.

Yet, the events of recent times have perhaps, suggested that visions of post-1989/91 were but a chimera, an illusion or indeed a rapturous dream from which we were rudely awakened. International Relations and in-country political processes have started to degenerate back into Cold War mode. Extremism is on the rise and conflicts characterise regions, coups d'états are back with impunity and the threat of nuclear war hangs in the air.

The needle of extremism is turning fast on the heels of the major public health crisis of the century, the COVID-19 pandemic, which has struck the world since 2019 and brought about widespread economic disruption through the sudden and unprecedented disruption of global supply chains.

As economies ground to a screeching halt, it was clear that the globalisation agenda and its liberal philosophy was coming apart at the seams. As the world gradually and tentatively moved towards recovery from this crisis, the Russia-Ukraine War broke out, bringing the Russian Federation into conflict with the North Atlantic Treaty Organization (NATO). The invasion of Ukraine, and its destruction coupled with the countervailing NATO sanctions, led to a disruption of the global supply of oil, fertilisers, rice and wheat across the world with the concomitant effect on prices.

Once again, the world was moving back into economic depression, global tension and uncertainty. This spectre necessitated a review of existing alliances and their realignment, as each party sought to swing international public opinion and resources in their favour.

This tenuous situation forced – and continues to force– developing countries, and developed ones as well, to rethink their political and economic status and alliances, and revisit their strategies with respect to their international relations, to guarantee their existence and the welfare of their peoples.

It is such a situation that forces nations to explore the options available to the South-South countries of varying sizes. In this regard, the relationship between African countries and their Indo-Pacific counterparts is pertinent. The focus of this chapter is the relationship between India and the African continent and in particular, Zambia.

It will be apparent from the author's perspective that a new world paradigm will need to evolve, driven by the South-South cooperation principles, to achieve a more equitable global dispensation which guarantees mutual respect amongst nations and a fairer sharing of global resources among their peoples.

Background

Africa as a continent has a population of approximately 1.3 billion distributed across 54 African States, with a combined gross domestic product of US$ 3 trillion. By this fact, Africa represents a great market potential for goods and services, but also has the resources to produce a wide range of goods and services for export. By comparison, India, by itself, has a GDP of US$ 2.651 trillion, ranked fifth in size after the United States. To contextualise that, India's GDP is larger than that of the United Kingdom, France or Brazil. With a population of 1.3 billion, it is apparent that India offers a considerable market opportunity for any potential exporter to the country.

Trade

According to the Observatory of Economic Complexity (OEC)[1], in 2023, India was ranked the 12 economy In terms of its total exports and ranked 8th in terms of its total imports[2]. Table 1 below shows India's top five exports and the top five export destinations, as well as the top imports and sources.[3]

Table 1: Top Exports and Export Destinations of India

Exports		*Imports*	
Commodity	(USD, Billion)	**Commodity**	(USD, Billion)
1. Refined petroleum products	25.3	1. Crude petroleum	59.0
2. Packaged medicaments	17.8	2. Gold	21.9
3. Diamonds	16.0	3. Coal briquettes	20.9
4. Rice	8.2	4. Petroleum gas	13.8
5. Jewelry	7.6		
Destinations		**Sources**	
1. United States	49.7	1. China	64.2
2. China	18.5	2. United States	26.6
3. United Arb Emirates	18.1	3. United Arab Emirates	22.1
4. Hong Kong	9.2	4. Saudi Arabia	16.8
5. Germany	8.8	5. Iraq	14.4

India's trade with Africa in its totality is significantly lower. As at 2020, India's total exports to Africa amounted to US$ 27.2 billion, while India's imports from Africa amounted to US$ 27.3billion. India exports primarily refined oil products and pharmaceuticals to Africa, while importing crude oil, gold, coal and other minerals.

Clearly, Africa does not feature significantly in India's export/import trade. The colonial vestiges and subsequent orientation of trade towards the metropoles may have limited the prospect of trade between the two regions. The scenario is even more acute in the case of Zambia where the trade, while existing, is very insignificant in India's overall trade portfolio. Indeed, Zambia has a negative trade balance with India.

Between 2008 and 2012[4] exports from Zambia to India included copper, pearls, precious stones, cotton, among others. The total value of these exports fluctuated over the period starting from US$ 32.6 million in 2008, falling to US$ 19.0 million in 2010 and rising again to US$ 70.6 million in 2012. During the same period, Zambia's main imports from India included pharmaceutical products, photo and medical apparatus, machinery, electronics and plastics. The total value of these exports rose from US $206.7 million in 2008 to US$ 310.2 million in 2012, but buffeted by headwinds in the period in between.[5]

In general, bilateral trade between these countries has been growing steadily, though it remains below its potential, and biased in favour of India, as indicated below. Trade volumes peaked at 2019/20 at a value of US$ 1,090.96 million, before plummeting to US$ 395.37 million at 2020/21.[6]

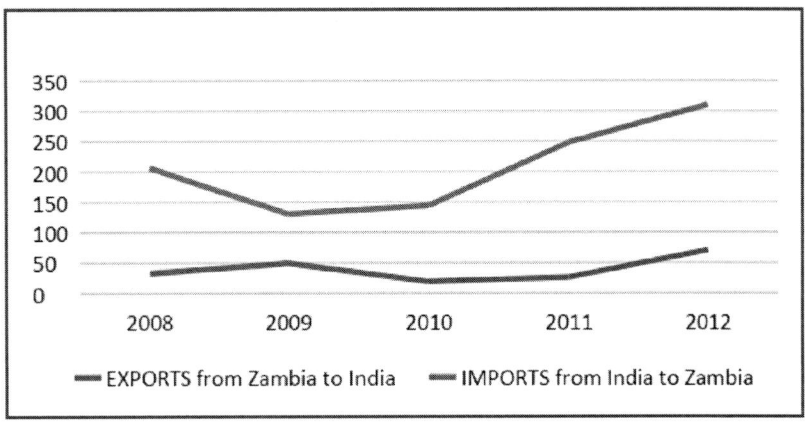

Figure 1: Export & Import Trend between Zambia & India (US$ million)

Source: Author's Construction from OEC database

Investment Relations

According to the International Institute for Sustainable Development (2022), India is now one of the top five investors in Africa with about USD74 billion in investments in such areas as agribusiness, pharmaceuticals, information and communications technology, and energy. According to the Exim Bank of India (2018), the substantial stock of investment can be attributed to strong economic growth, a favourable business environment and investment regulations, high rates of return and a rising consumer market in India.[7]

According to the Observer Research Foundation (2017), of India's total outward investment, 21 per cent (US$ 52.6 billion) went to Africa. Of this 90 per cent (US$ 49.7 billion) went to Mauritius, with the rest (10 per cent) being distributed across the rest of Africa. The main areas of investment have been oil and gas, hotels, pharmaceuticals, ICT and manufacturing, among others. Increasingly, oil and gas exploration in Mozambique have expanded.

Zambia: An African Case

Zambia is a landlocked country in the heart of Africa with a Gross Domestic Product (GDP) of $30 billion and a population of just under 20 million people (as per the 2021 National Census). Zambia, as a developing country, is struggling with economic and social problems. Among these are substantial infrastructure deficiencies, crippling and rising debt and serious socio-economic problems. Zambia is currently on a three-year IMF Extended Credit Facility and presently trying to resolve its debt issues with private and official creditors.

The predominant sectors contributing to Zambia's GDP and employment are mining, industry and agriculture. Exports are dominated by mineral products, which contribute upwards of 70-80 per cent of export earnings. With this mining commodity concentration of exports, the country sits on a knife-edge, and has often fallen off.

The foregoing discussion of Indo-Africa economic relations demonstrates that the African continent has a minimal relationship with the Indian sub-continent. The role that India can play, and has played in the past, has not been very significant for historical and geographical reasons. However, the changing global scenario and the unprecedented challenges that the world and the nation states confront, require a reappraisal of these relationships going forward. The world going forward must recognise that the solutions to any nations' problems do not consist of only looking in one direction. The contemporary challenges require versatility and flexibility.

Crisis

COVID-19 Pandemic

The COVID-19 pandemic, which struck in 2019-20 was one of the worst public health disasters in shared memory. The debilitating, pervasive and malignant effects of this disease across the world, without respect to borders evoked global soul-searching and collaborative health research across the world.

As countries raced to catch up and contain the disease, they put in place tighter measures such as public gathering restrictions. The breakdown in movements of goods and services result in a slump in global production and threatened human survival. Flows of essential goods, foods, medicines, machinery and spares dried up. Human travel became practically impossible. The world was on the edge of a global catastrophe. Mankind was at a tipping edge.

Nevertheless, unprecedented human solidarity, ingenuity and determination, and by God's grace, the looming catastrophe was averted.

However, the carnage that this disaster left in its wake was palpable. Millions of lives lost. Once thriving businesses eliminated, never to see the light of day. Jobs were lost, and food stocks were wasted. Hopes and dreams shattered.

Russo-Ukraine War

As the spectre of COVID-19 receded, and a glimmer of hope arose over the global horizon, Russia invaded Ukraine in February 2022, and precipitated another political, economic and logistical crisis. The military conflict and the sanctions imposed by the Western powers disturbed global food supply and agricultural supplies, such as fertiliser, as well as oil and gas. Once again, the global economy teetered into recession and a slump in global output. African countries were particularly hard hit as they struggled under the severe shortage of food and materials, which are supplied by the belligerents.

Other Disasters

In recent time, a meteorological disaster has been brewing over the Pacific Ocean which has impacted the Southern African region. Mozambique and Malawi, in particular, have been hard hit by the Hurricane Freddy, which brought death and destruction in its wake on some of the poorest countries in Africa. Agricultural crops and livestock were irreversibly destroyed. Bilateral and multilateral efforts were mobilised to assist these countries mitigate these crises.

With rising incidents of climate change in the world, it is likely that we shall continue witnessing such incidents more often. Countries must prepare themselves for the cycles of floods, droughts, wildfires as well as animal-human conflict.

The Challenge of the Times: Globalisation or Multilateralism

As the world moves ever forward towards globalisation with the unification of markets, diffusion of technology, low costs of production and higher standards of living across the globe, we must be cautious of the adverse effects and risks which come with it.[8] The opening of markets makes for easier spread of recessions, risk of contagion, labour exploitation, and the marginalisation of small and local businesses. Inevitably, it also leads to unequal economic growth and the concentration of economic and political power among the national elites and powerful countries. This has a tendency to undermine the international democratic system, as powerful nations disregard or dictate the agenda of international institutions.

In the face of globalisation, and its pressures, the extant economic and trade structure, recurrent crises, it is obvious that mankind must act in unison to establish a fairer and balanced trading and financial system, as well as a social system which is responsive and sensitive to the global challenges and the interests of all nation states.

The design of a multilateral system where institutions respond to the needs and requirements of all nation states as equal partners and stakeholders in global affairs is therefore imperative.

Resilience

The lop-sided global and national economic and trading structures and the recurrent political economic and natural crises have exposed the structural weakness within the economies around the world and their vulnerability and exposure to shocks.

Many developing countries tend to rely on a single or few sectors for their economic fortunes. Thus, when that one sector is affected then their complete socio-economic system grinds to a halt. Similarly, countries whose markets are concentrated in a few global destinations run the risk of serious setbacks in the event of adverse changes in their partners' fortunes.

While countries may receive aid and assistance from bilateral and multilateral sources, in the event of a disaster, the key is for countries to have a strong base on which to build a sustainable long-term recovery.

A more comprehensive approach to diversification is called for in terms of suppliers and markets across the whole value chain, with strong local values added.

Future Strategy - Options

India

There are significant trading opportunities that are available to India in Zambia and vice-versa, which have been underexploited so far. Bilateral engagements will be necessary to explore opportunities for preferential access to markets.[9] These opportunities lie in manufacturing, agro-processing, fertilisers, chemicals, pharmaceuticals, ICTs, textiles, medicine, etc. In the light of the risks to global supply chains during various crises, it is imperative that Indian businesses consider large-scale investment in the Zambian economy to entrench itself in the Zambian market and provide on-shore solutions, and avail themselves of the opportunities arising from Zambia's membership of SADC, COMESA and ACFTA.[10]

Zambia has considerable mineral and natural resources, which have not been fully exploited. Presently, at an output of about 700,000 tons of copper per year, Zambia intends to increase production to 3 million tons in a decade. In addition, about 50 per cent of the country is unexplored for mineralisation. There are clear indications that other mineral resources exist, including gold, manganese, uranium, sugellite, emeralds and others.

The paucity of infrastructure, while a challenge, also provides opportunities for investment in economic infrastructure, such as roads, bridges, rail, dams, electricity generation, etc. Such investments could be undertaken as business ventures in partnership with government, using the Public-Private Partnerships (PPP) model.

The Indian government could supplement this by rendering economic support to develop critical infrastructure, which in turn support these investments. The Belt and Road Initiative is instructive as a model to develop critical sectors of possible under the framework of regional economic groupings such as SADC, COMESA and AFCTA, that already have their regional infrastructure programmes.

Zambia

The gross vulnerability of the Zambian economy to the vagaries of the international environment and natural disasters makes it imperative to seek to diversify the economy across the mining sector and beyond, and to diversify its markets beyond Europe and China.

It must also prioritise its infrastructure development, particularly economic infrastructure, which can draw in private capital and be self-financed (through PPPs). Such an approach can have a catalytic effect on the development of a wide range of infrastructure.

The country should also continue on the path of prudent economic management and good governance, to inspire confidence among foreign investors, as well as governments.

Conclusion

The emerging theme from the foregoing discussion is that the African countries are caught in the horns of a paradox. While globalisation opens up considerable opportunities for economic growth through international specialisation and globally integrated production systems and markets, it is fraught with risks through the transmission of crises on account of overdependence on external suppliers.

This raises the conundrum of interdependence, whereby countries seeking to capitalise on the efficiency of production by specialising, however need to have their own independent facilities to attenuate the risk of disruption. It is inevitable that countries will integrate increasingly in the global world and will specialise and become the go-to for supplies of some goods. But there must be a mechanism that protects countries from grinding to a halt because of failures in their supply chains.

This conundrum should command our attention. But it seems that intensified cross-border investment and trade against a backdrop of aggressive diversification, will be the cornerstone of our resolution of this incipient crisis. It thus requires concerted partnership efforts between all partner governments (bilateral), multilateral institutions and the private sector, to achieve the desired results.

NOTES

1 Observatory of Economic Complexity, https//www.oec.world/en/profile/country/ind (Accessed 24 October 2023).

2 The Observatory of Economic Complexity 2023, https://oec.world/en/profile/country/ind

3 The worlds largest economies by GDP, https://www.worlddata.info/largest-economies, (Accessed 04 February 2024).

4 C. Malancha, C. "Indian Investments in Africa: Scale, Trends, and Policy Recommendations", *ORF Working Paper*, May 2017.

5 "Zambia exports, imports and trade partners" at https://oec.world/en/profile/country/zmb, Also see "Zambia Imports & Exports" at https://trendeconomy.com/data/h2/Zambia/TOTAL (Accessed 05 February 2024).

6 C. Malancha, no. 4.

7 A. Tago, "Multilateralism, Bilateralism, and Unilateralism in Foreign Policy", *Oxford Research Encyclopedia of Politics*, 2017.

8 *Deepening South-South Collaboration: An Analysis of Africa and India's Trade and Investment*, Afrexim Bank and Exim India, Cairo 2018. Also see, "Indian investment into Zambia exceeds US$3 billion", Africa Review, 14 June 2012, http://www.africanreview.com/financial/economy/indias-fdi-to-zambia-tops-us3 billion (Accessed 12 February 2023).

9 Chimuka Singuwa and Gospel Singuwa, "Zambia¼s Overlapping Membership in SADC and COMESA International Organisations", *International Organisations Research Journal*, 18(3) (Accessed 21 February 2023).

Multilateral Approach to Climate Adaptation and Mitigation

CHAPTER 14

Nontraditional Security Challenges and True Multilateralism

Huang Yunsong and Li Linjie

Introduction

Non-traditional security has rapidly expanded the connotation and extension of security and is a paradigm and even vision update for studying security in the international political arena. This note starts with the definition of non-traditional security, highlighting human security at the center of its agenda of value concern and sorting out the overall security architecture from the perspective of non-traditional security. Secondly, the analysis of the non-traditional security community and the issue of multilateralism constitutes the main grip to reach the non-traditional security agenda and the climate change agenda falsifies the path dependence of the Western-style multilateralism paradigm. The second half of the article focuses on the empirical and normative shortcomings of the Western paradigm of multilateralism, which is categorised as "old multilateralism." It then uses China's "True Multilateralism" approach as a practical and conceptual alternative to the former, focusing on the climate change agenda as a pivot point. This note concludes with a proposal for cooperation between India and China on non-traditional security agendas, hoping that the two countries will join hands on the path toward a "new multilateralism."

Nontraditional Security and Human Security: A Broad Security Architecture

The psychologist Maslow, in his book *Hierarchy of Needs,* regarded security as the first need of humans after satisfying survival needs and the primary necessities to maintain survival; international political scientists defined security as the most basic need of a country for survival and development and as the core factor in the development of international relations.

According to Terry Terriff's elaboration in the book *Security Studies Today*, among scholars researching on security, the definition of security can broadly be divided into three categories. The first category of scholars believes that security is indefinable, that the concept of security is fundamentally controversial and difficult to unify, or that security is a given condition, precisely like health and identity, and does not have an exact meaning; it can even be said that security is without any specific purpose rather represent vague symbols. Another group of scholars believes that security is too complex and has too many levels, and its essence is different at different levels. Thus, a uniform discussion is difficult and it can only be defined according to different levels or scopes. The third group of scholars believes that security can be appropriately defined, emphasising that the connotation of security, though seemingly vague, can be understood and described in minimalist terms. Arnold Wolfers for example, in his book *Discord and Collaboration: Essays on International Politics* summarises security as "the absence of threat when value is acquired."

The definition of security is ambiguous because the does not only exist as an objective situation and involves a subjective perception, which involves not only an objective but also a psychological state, the so-called sense of security. From this point of view, security includes two aspects: the objective aspect refers to the current state of the outside world, while the subjective aspect refers to the state of people.[1]

This means, security is an objective state, while the sense of security is subjective. The sense of security is a reaction to the objective state of security; this reaction may be correct, or incorrect, and sometimes even if there is no threat from the viewpoint, subjective fear may arise, which is insecurity. Also, even if there is an objective threat, subjectively there may be no fear. The first is a subjective psychological understanding of the concept of security, which is undefinable. The third reduces security to an objective non-threatening situation and defines security based on the definition of threat, as "freedom from war destruction or value damage". The second is a combination of the subjective and objective aspects of security, based on the different subjective and objective aspects of the reference of the subject and the resulting security. This leads to a variety of levels of the concept of security that are not reducible, and the attempts to examine security confined to a single level or domain, will lead to serious misinterpretations.

Introducing the analysis of the concept of "security" into academic discussions, American columnist Walter Lippmann first introduced the concept of "national security" in 1947, and the American academic community defined national security as the threat to use and control of military force. Since the late 20th century, the concept of security centred on military security has been referred to as traditional security, military threats as traditional security threats, and non-military security threats as non-traditional security threats. Following the third conceptual definition above, non-traditional security refers to "freedom from existential threats posed by non-military force." In all security theories, the two fundamental questions are: who is the subject security serves and what are the dominant values that constitute the distinction between traditional and non-traditional security theories, whose security and how does security determine the answer to the question of what threats are to be addressed and by whom and in what way is security to be achieved. If the object of security is defined as the State, the dominant value emphasises military and political security. The doctrine must be particularly concerned with external military incursions, as the threat often endangers territorial integrity and the regime's existence, which is included within traditional security.

The focus of non-traditional security theories on security threats other than the military, is a testament to the fact that they have moved their focus away from the State level and have become more focused especially on human security, and in terms of preferred values, on economic security, environmental security, social security, human liberation, and women's security, thus taking a different path from traditional security paradigms. Above all, there is a view that non-traditional security is an expansion of traditional security that incorporates human security as the centre of attention in its vision, reducing it to the "freedom from fear and want" of the human subject.[2] The State is the primary provider of security for its citizens; it is an instrument of security, not an end in itself; and threats to the security of the individual are beyond the scope of the State to deal with, so non-governmental actors are introduced as relevant and responsible parties to the non-traditional security agenda. As the focus of security gradually shifts from traditional to non-traditional security, the scope of what constitutes security issues has expanded to include economic, environmental, climate, energy, social, health, cultural, and transnational crimes.

The traditional security agenda concerns with military threats, i.e., military and political security concerns, often the focus of attention is territorial integrity and presence of regime. There is a tendency to set aside seemingly less pressing or imminent issues and focus on geopolitical issues such as war and peace, grand strategy, and foreign policy. Suspending the nontraditional security agenda to draw on the military-political considerations of traditional security has become the norm for most observers. However, around the topic of traditional and nontraditional security, it is necessary to distinguish between the concepts of "real imaginary" and "imaginary real," the former corresponding to traditional security and the latter to nontraditional security. The "real imaginary" refers to the macro-narrative of traditional security of war and peace, although rarely or even never directly experienced it exists objectively and is realistically and concretely involve people's lives and even in their lives; even if such topics are a fiction in people's minds, they are at least a fiction that exists objectively in the minds of the vast majority of people, and the vast majority of the world's population lives in this kind of inner reality. A vast majority of people in the world live in this inner fiction, and the real-life perceptions and relationships are shaped by this inner fiction, which is a characteristic of human beings. "Imaginary reality" refers to the non-traditional security agenda based on human security, which has been removed from the State level and reduced from the abstract to the concrete as the life of each individual, and which may seem to be "imaginary", that does not concern itself with ordinary psychological thinking, but which is directly related to the life situations of individuals. However, the agenda is directly related to the "reality" of individual life situations, such as climate change and the disasters it causes, which indeed cause serious damage and casualties, and these are the "realities" that ordinary people can directly perceive. The "real imagination" is certainly exciting, but the "imaginary reality" should be removed and restored to a "reality" by removing the "mask" put on it. The important agenda of "imaginary reality" is to act.

Human security, a key pillar of non-traditional security, encompasses "freedom from fear" and "freedom from want." The latter emphasises the urgency of issues beyond violence, liberating people from threats and even mere bondage to achieve a quality of life. At the same time, the former believes that an overly broad agenda is meaningless for policymakers and analysts, focusing on life maintenance rather than the quality of life itself, liberating people from the threat of death caused by violence.[3] Nevertheless, the history of international security and the increasing prominence of non-traditional security issues today shows that the dilemma facing humanity in terms of theoretical discussion is not only a matter of military and political security or territorial sovereignty, but also a matter of economic, social, cultural, and ecological security for the preservation of the quality of life or the quality of human rights within a sovereign territory. Therefore, "freedom from want" has taken precedence over "freedom from fear" in the dominant narrative, and new security issues such as environmental security, human rights security, information security, health security, social security, and cultural security, in addition to traditional territorial security and sovereignty, have now become part of the larger human security debate. Security is now part of human development. In this new situation, security strategies should be considered at the bottom of the security gradient (freedom from fear) and at the top (freedom from want) which deals with the quality of life.[4]

Therefore, non-traditional security, especially human security, is essentially a natural derivation of an overall security architecture based on different variables. A security model with four intersecting dimensions can be constructed.[5] The first dimension is the variables characterising the state of security – survival of the superior, survival of the weak, survival of the inferior, and survival of the critical, representing respectively: no threat, indirect threat, direct threat, and existential threat. The Second dimension is the dimensional variables characterising the level of security: individual, society, State, and global; the third dimension are the variables that characterise the content of security: political, economic, cultural, and ecological; the fourth dimension characterises the time of security: past, present, and future, and the processes that characterise the intertwined nature. They constitute hundreds of essential relationships that shape the spatiotemporal architecture of security in a broad sense. The definition and assessment of non-traditional security faced by several States can be placed in this architecture to locate their coordinates, examine the sustainability of the security situation, improve its consistency in the system, or review its coherence in the orientation for its improvement.

Non-traditional security theory adopts a broad research agenda that focuses on the linkages between different security domains, naturally deriving an overall security architecture and thus all-encompassing. As the possible security values expand, the analysis of threat sources must also expand, making non-traditional security researchers adopt a broader research agenda. Moreover, the linkage between different security values or threats prevents non-traditional security theory from focusing on security issues in a single area. More importantly, the discussion of the non-traditional security agenda has been far ahead of the practice of its process, and the richness of the theoretical results of the dimension of "freedom from want" has obscured our perception of "freedom from fear." The danger and destruction of life from non-traditional security threats cannot be underestimated: the terrorist attacks of 11 September 2001, claimed nearly 3,000 lives, more than the number of US fatalities at Pearl Harbour in 1941, and according to some estimates more than 2,900 people were killed and 8,200 injured in large-scale terrorist incidents worldwide in 2004 alone. According to a study, in the 30 years from 1974 to 2003, major natural disasters caused at least 2 million deaths and displaced 180 million people around the world, while the Indian Ocean tsunami in December 2004 killed nearly 300,000 people and caused economic losses of $1.3 billion to $1.5 billion in Sri Lanka alone, corresponding to 6.5 per cent of its economy. Although many non-traditional security threats may not appear as potent as a world war, they are sometimes no less harmful than war and have become a severe threat to world development and human survival.[6] After judging that a world war is unlikely in the medium to long term under the nuclear deterrence posture, non-traditional security has become a daily security issue for all countries worldwide.

From "non-traditional security community" to "multilateralism": An Essential Grip for Addressing Non-traditional Security Challenges

In addressing all security challenges, both traditional and non-traditional security agendas, it is crucial to understand the relative nature of the concept of security itself, i.e., as mentioned above, security involves both an objective and a psychological state. In the pursuit of security, the State and society are sometimes aligned and sometimes not; the bottom line however is survival. It also encompasses a concern for the citizens and their well-being. Barry Buzan's argument reveals that the determination of security is not objective and is not a response to a change in material power, but rather a large part of the State's determination is subjective.

Therefore, in the pursuit of security, the State, as a subject, often operates keeping its security concerns in mind through the subjective determination of challenges posed by other States. Under the consideration of relative share and relative benefit, it stimulates its power balance mechanism, creating an insecure end of the subject's security efforts, which is the "security dilemma" under the relativity of security. The Americans first introduced the concept of security dilemma.

John H. Herz suggests, "In international relations, each individual is always in fear of being violated, dominated, or even eliminated by the other, and is thus bound to pursue more and more the balance of strength and power in order to obtain national security, which in turn causes the other to feel insecure and thus also strive for the balance of strength and power, with the result that it further exacerbates the original security concerns." Later, Robert Jervis further developed this concept by arguing that, "the security dilemma is the key to understanding why states with the same goals in an anarchic international system still end up in competition and war, and that the security dilemma exists when the various ways in which a state seeks to enhance its security necessarily constitute a security threat to other states."[7] In sum, the lack of genuine inter-subjective mutual trust among States derives from the inconsistency of subjective determinations of security among them, and the security efforts and inconsistency of subjective determinations of one State inevitably brings about a deteriorating end of security under the action of balancing mechanisms in other States.

The existence of a security dilemma makes the construction of a "security community" a viable means of achieving security goals, referring to a "collection of actions" or a "unit of responsibility" of a coalition which is established based on the responses to traditional security threats. The "security community" has become a viable means of achieving security goals. Throughout history, international cooperation on non-traditional security issues has become increasingly possible. Only the "security community" can effectively overcome the security dilemma and bring about an authentic security posture of actors, which makes the relative security of the country possible through "shared security, shared risk, and shared responsibility". The relative nature of security can be overcome by the collective safeguards of the "collective of actions," "organic organisations" or "units of responsibility", that are combined in a specific way. The collective organisation is used as the trust and guarantee unit of mutual trust between subjects to overcome the dilemma of trust deficit between subjects. It was first seen in the Liberal School's collective security theory, which calls for the international community to protect each country's national security through collective power to deter or stop possible aggressors and acts of aggression within it. From constructing the "security community," the emergence of a so-called traditional security community, that was primarily concerned with devising a response to military threats to a non-traditional security community, which is committed to frame a response to non-military threats. The former is a community approach to the "arms-based security dilemma" in response to military threats, while the latter is a community approach to the "resource-based security dilemma" in response to non-military threats.[8]

To a certain extent, establishing a traditional security community has eliminated the negative impact of the arms-based security dilemma of a single State. However, the establishment of the security community dealing with traditional military threats may create an inter-subjective trust deficit between a larger "subject" and a more comprehensive "other," which brings about a more far-reaching "arms-based security dilemma" The expansion of the traditional security community often leads to the expansion of the universality of security threats. During the Cold War, the two superpowers had their largest traditional security community. However, the result was a "nuclear fear" never before seen by the humankind is based on "mutual destruction. It is clear that the traditional threat security community while deconstructing the traditional security dilemma, has constructed a broader and deeper "arms-based" security dilemma outside the alliance. The nontraditional security community, on the other hand, mainly deals with the "resource-based" security dilemma, in which the increase in resource use and protection in one country leads to the shortage of resources in another country, thus creating the need for joint solutions. Even for nontraditional security threats at the global level, such as climate warming, their deeper impact on countries is ultimately characterised by the depletion of resources and whether they can be shared. There is also a "resource-based" security dilemma pertaining to resource allocation. Since the resource categories included in the non-traditional security agenda are public, which brings about the shareability and externality of the resource categories, the construction of a non-traditional security community will not create the opposition between the "we" and the "other" as in the case of the traditional security community. Since the resources of the centre of gravity are public, they can be shared and can benefit equally, but there is a problem with decision-making, and the major bottleneck is to make the willing parties cooperate.

From the perspective of decision-making, how and when to compete and cooperate on an issue involves several considerations for decision-makers, including cost, benefit, and risk.[9] Concerning cost, decision-makers must consider whether the issue can be completed independently. Concerning benefit, decision-makers must consider whether the benefit structure of the issue is a zero-sum game or a win-win situation. Concerning risk, decision-makers must consider the risk of cooperation. The decision maker is more willing to take the risk of cooperation when there is a risk of loss of benefit and is less willing to do so, when there is a possibility of enjoying the benefit alone. When costs can be met independently, and the benefits are zero-sum or high-risk, policymakers would not want to take the risk of cooperation, but are willing to take advantage of competition or even confrontation. When costs cannot be achieved independently, and the benefits are non-zero-sum or low-risk, policymakers are willing to risk cooperation.

The non-traditional security agenda, especially the construction of a non-traditional security community, having a win-win situation benefits because of the public nature of the State's resource that needs to be deployed in meeting the security challenges. Every country must solve the non-traditional security challenges after assessing the cost of non-cooperation. In contrast, in terms of risk, the externalities of cooperation and the public nature of its resource raises concerns about "free-riding" on resources of other actors involved in security cooperation. The fear of negative "spillover" after the formation of a security community, cannot be ignored. Rationally speaking, policymakers are in the middle of cooperation and competition to meet non-traditional security challenges. States require a cooperative mechanism that catalyses the will to cooperate among States and overcomes the State's oscillation between cooperation and competition, for which multilateralism constitutes the natural cooperation model.

Multilateralism is the international governance model under which the majority of the countries participate. They aim at defining some principles, especially against discriminatory international agendas, and reach solutions to competing international agendas through consensus building, norm formation, and enforcement, in which each country as a participating subject, also treats the other countries as equal so that the participants are in mutually beneficial relations and together, they catalyse the cooperation agenda. The essence of multilateralism, namely sovereign equality, the indivisibility of political rights and responsibilities, and diffuse reciprocity also means that once an agreement is reached, no player in the multilateralism framework can expect that it would benefit specific members who will draw specific benefits from the cooperation, but not control the process of benefits. As long as the cooperation operates according to the rules of business, the benefits generated are sustainable, which helps to overcome the problem of the non-traditional security dilemma. This makes the extraction and distribution of resources acceptable through consensual decision making and avoids the "negative externality" of distribution of benefits and addresses challenges of posed by "free-riders". Therefore, constructing a non-traditional security community, multilateralism has become essential to overcome the resource-based security dilemma and addressing non-traditional security challenges.

From "old multilateralism" to "True Multilateralism": The Falsification of the Western Paradigm of Multilateralism by the Climate Change Agenda

In 2020, the Biden administration had raised the banner of so-called "multilateralism" and made "multilateralism" the most distinctive feature of its diplomatic strategy, and set off a global wave of "multilateralism". From the standpoint of the US' national interests, this was a major adjustment and correction of the Trump administration's behaviour of pursuing the US national interests in a unilateral manner. On the other hand, it was also a new strategic attempt by the US administration to monopolise the definition of "multilateralism" by giving full play to the comparative advantages of the US and the West in the global discursive arena, and to compare itself to "multilateralism," while labeling their identified strategic opponents as "non-multilateralists", thereby regaining the moral high ground in the increasingly heated strategic game of great powers.[10] Multilateralism, as an essential tool to deal with nontraditional security challenges, has the core connotation of multiple countries as the main body to carry out various activities in a communicative and consultative manner. However, multilateralism has become an iconic term that attracts the attention of all parties, and there is not only fierce competition at the level of discourse but also a deep-rooted game at the level of building a narrative on what is genuine multilateralism, how to practice it, and what kind of positive impact it can bring.

Objectively speaking, the definition of "multilateralism" has long been in the hands of the United States and the West, and the interpretation of the guiding principles and even the practice of "multilateralism" has been in the hands of the United States and the West. Since its inception in the early nineteenth century, it is rooted in the experiences of international interactions with specific regions and countries, where the practice of multilateralism originated and was practiced by the European powers from the 19th century. After the two World Wars or orderly achievements led by the US hegemonic designs after the end of World War II, Western experience has objectively monopolised the definition and interpretation of "multilateralism." In terms of conceptual orientation, multilateralism, as a problem-solving institutional arrangement, is a tool serving the international agenda, as John Roggie explains, "what is distinctive about multilateralism is not merely that it coordinates national policies in groups of three or more states, which is something that other organisational forms also do, but that it does so on the basis of certain principles of ordering relations among those states."[11] As a methodological and instrumental social arrangement, the value measurement or assessment of effectiveness of various versions of multilateralism is based on the utilitarian perspective – whether it can effectively address various international agendas it is supposed to address. The Western paradigm of multilateralism can also be judged by the resolution of various non-traditional security agendas; however, an assessment would indicate that it is yet to serve the intended purpose.

The climate change agenda has always been a high point of politically correct attention in the US and the West, and climate policy constitutes one of the dominant discourses in the US and the West. Climate crises such as global warming have been called the most challenging non-traditional security issues for human beings, so the importance of the climate change agenda can serve as a litmus test for the value and usefulness of the Western paradigm of multilateralism. But the outcome is always unsatisfactory.

Climate disasters are rising despite the international community's concerted efforts to adapt, mitigate, and finance climate policies under the Paris Agreement. Climate change-related losses and casualties have increased dramatically in recent years, and some climate disasters are happening in places that had not witnessed such disasters before. Typhoons, for example, used to be concentrated in the lower latitudes of southern China. Nevertheless, last year, for the first time in history, a typhoon landed in the high latitudes of northeastern China. This highly unusual situation suggests that some significant changes are occurring or have occurred in the climate system and that the current international agenda for climate change needs to be equipped to meet such challenges. In all seriousness, climate disasters are sometimes like a game of dominoes, where a single disaster can trigger additional non-traditional security challenges in areas such as food, water, recreation, and infrastructure security, which are interconnected, and the situation would be exacerbated if we do not take them seriously. For example, we have traditionally thought that urban areas are much safer from climate disasters than rural areas because they have robust infrastructure, better planning, and a steady supply of services, but we have been proven wrong. The heavy rainfall in Henan, China, which killed many people and drowned them in tunnels, cars, and underpasses, is disheartening and unimaginable and challenges our common sense and foresight about climate change disasters. In the past two years, the world has seen extraordinary weather conditions, such as extreme droughts during the rainy season. In 2022, many people worldwide experienced the hottest summer in 60 years, the heaviest rainfall in 100 years, and the deadliest drought in 60 years, and if this trend continues for much longer, humanity will face even more deadly climate disasters. There is little difference between the developed North and the developing South with regard to climate disasters, and humanity is in the same boat to deal with such challenges, while we may need to change ourselves more to avoid such humanitarian disasters. According to the Paris Agreement, we need to reduce global greenhouse gas emissions by 30 per cent by 2030 compared to 2010 if we are to limit average temperature increases to well below the target of 2 degrees Celsius. However, a United Nations Environment Programme Report suggests we could achieve less than a 1 per cent reduction by then. In this sense, multilateralism, or climate multilateralism, has yet to catch up, because in this multilateral framework, the common and long-term interests of humanity cannot prevail over the specific or even special interests of individual countries, which are witnesses to its limitations, i.e., the imagination of the agenda of the moment is lagging behind the reality of the problem's solution.

Nevertheless, in addressing non-traditional security challenges such as climate change, we no longer have an alternative to multilateralism, and need effective multilateralism more than ever to meet the challenges of national and non-traditional security challenges. However, the role of Western-style multilateralism in building global consensus, resources, and collective action has fallen to its lowest level in history. An examination of the limitations of past multilateralism programmes leads us to an exploration of the need for so-called "true multilateralism" programmes.

The reasons why the Western-style multilateralism paradigm has not served its intended purpose are manifold and are specifically divided into three dimensions: benefits, costs, and risks, as discussed earlier. Many developed countries, especially in recent years, have escaped extreme weather with their excellent infrastructure and resources. Hence, the benefits of the non-traditional security agenda are not as substantial as those perceived by countries that experience climate change disasters. Second, in terms of cost, the reduction targets set by the Paris Agreement may be too high to be achieved, so perhaps before setting a more feasible target, we need to re-examine the reality and parameters so that the costs of the non-traditional security agenda are broadly acceptable and can indeed be implemented. Third, in terms of risk, the lack of accountability of some Western developed countries is one of the reasons why they have yet to fulfill their commitments to address climate change by reducing greenhouse gas emissions without incurring accountability from multilateral mechanisms, which minimises the risk of non-compliance. At the same time, the proliferation of populism and electoral democracy have kept populist forces as potential opponents or even veto players on non-traditional security agendas such as climate change. That also poses a policy risk that some countries will essentially lack the capacity to implement or even propose a range of potentially costly non-traditional security policy agendas, or that they will propose new goals which lack immediate action or the capacity to act. Therefore, it is important to systematically evaluate past commitments and provide explanations and solutions for unfulfilled promises. In addition, the strategic games between the major powers have undermined the multilateralism agenda. For example, with the growing tensions between China and the United States, their divergent climate policies, the intertwining of non-traditional security agendas with traditional security considerations, has complicated the process of working on this agenda itself, making it more difficult and costly to implement. The non-traditional security agenda itself has been instrumentalised by some countries. The agenda has lost its relevance and degenerated into a blunt instrument serving the geopolitical needs of traditional security: a blunt instrument because it also hurts the long-term interests and common interests of all countries.

Further examination of the Western paradigm of multilateralism at the doctrinal level reveals that it is an "old multilateralism" rather than a "new multilateralism." In the context of deep globalisation, dealing with numerous transnational non-traditional security threats requires replacing the unilateral activities of the past with bilateral or multilateral cooperation. However, even for bilateral and multilateral cooperation, there are problems of collective action: of who leads, moves, makes decisions. There are also a series of representational and equity problems: whose interests are represented by the multilateral mechanism, whose interests are served, and what kind of interests are covered. In this regard, there is the problem of "mono dimension" and "multi-dimension."[12] If "lateral" refers to the number of countries, and bilateral and multilateral refers to two or more countries, then, "dimension" refers to the nature of representation and governance. The "mono dimension" refers to the uni-dimensional nature, as is the case with "monarchy", which presupposes a cooperative approach to decision-making but represents the narrow interests of a homogeneous combination of small circles is dominated by a single country – like governance in multilateral forums. "Multi-dimension" refers to the multidimensional nature of "shared governance," which truly covers a plurality of interests in terms of representation and democratises the nature of governance in terms of the majority or even through unanimous decisions. In this way, international cooperation in non-traditional security governance can be divided into four basic types according to different combinations of "lateral" and "dimension": multi-dimensional multilateral cooperation, mono-dimensional multilateral cooperation, multi-dimensional bilateral cooperation, and mono-dimensional bilateral cooperation. Multilateral cooperation represents the special interests and homogeneous identities of a small circle is "modular multilateral cooperation," which presents "multiple countries, modular interests," or multilateral cooperation in which a hegemonic power essentially holds the "veto" is "modular multilateral cooperation," which presents "multiple countries, hegemony world," which is hegemonic multilateralism. Only a democratised form of multilateralism that truly covers multiple interests and is representative of the majority or even through unanimous decisions regarding the nature of governance, is "new multilateralism" and constitutes "multi-dimensional multilateral cooperation with multiple countries.

When examining the Western paradigm of multilateralism, both the European and US experiences of multilateralism can be categorised as "mono-dimensional multilateral cooperation," with the former's experience of multilateralism being homogeneous in identity and "mono-dimension" in nature of representation and the latter's experience of multilateralism being hierarchical in operation and "mono-dimension" in the nature of governance. The former is homogeneous in its identity and is a "mono-dimension" in representation, while the latter's multilateralist experience is hierarchical in its operation and is a "mono-dimension" like governance.[13]

Identity homogeneity is an indispensable condition for Europe's ability to build a supranational governance model out of the unprecedented division of inter-State relations caused by two World Wars. By identity homogeneity, we mean that the parties involved in multilateralism have a high degree of consistency in their perception of "self and other." Since 2008, irreconcilable intra-regional developmental disparities (e.g., Western vs. Eastern Europe) and value rifts (e.g., Southern vs. Northern Europe) repeatedly challenged the identity homogeneity essential for maintaining integration. Once this basis of consensus is lost, the European experience of multilateralism will also become dysfunctional. The second dimension is the operational hierarchy of the US experience of multilateralism. Suppose the European experience of multilateralism still insists on achieving equality among European member states – in that case, the US experience of multilateralism blurs the functioning hierarchy by creating an international system of symbolic equality with a symbolic representational relationship. Since 2022, the United States has instigated and used the Ukraine crisis to quickly push NATO to adopt a "New Concept for NATO Strategy" that reinforces strategic competition against China and Russia while transforming Western-dominated mechanisms such as the G-7 into tools to serve US strategic needs which are ostensibly a more active manifestation of "multilateralism" advocated by the US government. It is, in essence, a tool for implementing the desire to consolidate its hegemony and absolute superiority. Both are either "mono interests", constitute club multilateralism or "hegemony world", and hegemonic multilateralism. Both are classified as "mono-dimensional multilateral cooperation", as "old multilateralism" rather than "True Multilateralism."

"True Multilateralism": China's Approach to Non-traditional Security Challenges and Sino-Indian Cooperation on Non-traditional Security Issues

Multilateralism is the foundation of global governance and provides various ways to address the world's non-traditional security challenges. Maintaining and practicing multilateralism is also the basic principle for China to promote change to the global governance structure as well as to cope with the unprecedented changes in this century. At the World Economic Forum's Davos Agenda Dialogue, China's leaders clarified that "the world's problems are complicated, and the way out is to uphold and practice multilateralism and promote the building of a community of human destiny." In order to reform and improve the global governance system and solve the major issues of global governance, "such as "who should govern," "how to govern," and "why to govern," we must maintain and practice genuine multilateralism.[14] We must guard against "mono-dimensional multilateralism" in the name of multilateralism, especially against "selective multilateralism." China's advocacy of "genuine multilateralism" differs from the European experience of club multilateralism and the hegemonic multilateralism of the US; rather it is an empirical upgrade and improvement of the "old multilateralism" paradigm in addressing the non-traditional security agenda. It is also a normative replacement of the "old multilateralism" paradigm in terms of the nature of its representation and governance.

Looking at the global response to non-traditional security challenges from an empirical or utilitarian perspective, using the climate change agenda as an example, it is clear that the global response to the climate change agenda has experienced many difficulties in the past few years. The immediate reason for this is that the Western-style "old multilateralism" paradigm has failed to catalyse cooperation in a process committed to the common good and long-term interests due to the misalignment and distortion of the agenda in terms of cost, benefit, and risk. The root cause of this is the conceptual incompatibility of the so-called "old multilateralism" paradigm with the current facts of international politics, resulting in a disconnect between the paradigm and the facts; and notably, the repeated refusal of the United States and other Western powers to fulfill their obligations in the resolution of the agenda. In particular, the first Trump administration has repeatedly withdrawn from the Paris Agreement in favour of putting the United States first, resorting to open unilateralism and creating a huge obstacle to global multilateral cooperation on climate. With the Biden administration's return to the Paris Agreement, there was also concern that the US was attempting to seize a dominant position in climate governance, transforming climate multilateralism into hegemonic multilateralism in the form of "mono-dimension multilateralism". The announcement of new emission reduction targets includes political considerations and geopolitical calculations to put pressure on developing countries to make more concessions. The intertwining of non-traditional security agendas with traditional security considerations complicates the agenda and increases difficulty and cost of collective action.

At the practical level, China advocates a practical path of "true multilateralism" and takes practical multilateral cooperative action to improve the governance effectiveness of non-traditional security agendas such as global climate change. First, China's adherence to the principle of equity is a necessary precondition for reaching a universal global agreement on emission reduction. Second, China's adherence to the principle of common but differentiated responsibilities is an essential condition for global climate governance. Third, China's adherence to the principle of matching capacity is an essential basis for assuming responsibility for addressing climate change. Fourth, China plays a leading role as a responsible power in practice.[15] The principles mentioned above of equity, responsibility, capacity matching, and the leading role, constitute the practical way for China to implement "true multilateralism" in the climate change agenda. First, in the global climate negotiations, China advocates that the agreement on greenhouse gas emission reduction should reflect both inter-generational and intra-generational equity, i.e., developed countries must pay for the historical emissions accumulated since the Industrial Revolution and the current high total emissions. Secondly, developed countries emphasise the "shared responsibility" of each country, deliberately avoid their historical responsibility, ignoring the differences in the capacity of each country, and downplaying the "differentiated responsibility" of each country to deal with climate change. At the same time, China recognises the "shared responsibility" while advocating the "differentiated responsibility." Third, China advocates that while building a global climate governance mechanism, it must fully consider the differences in national capabilities. The Kyoto Protocol failed in the past because the climate governance model needed to consider and reflect the differences in their respective capabilities fully. Fourth, China has solemnly committed to carbon peak and neutrality, to show its sense of responsibility as a significant country, striving to peak CO2 emissions by 2030 and achieve carbon neutrality by 2060.

More importantly, China is seeking to replace the "old multilateralism" paradigm with a normative dimension, especially in the representative and governance nature of the multilateralism model, proposing and continuously improving the concept of "true multilateralism," advocating for the inclusion of the pluralistic interests of emerging countries, and respecting the right to development and survival in the governance structure to democratise the global non-traditional security agenda and system. It proposes and continues to improve the concept of "true multilateralism," which incorporates the pluralistic interests of emerging countries in its representational nature and is mediated by respect for the right to development and the right to survival of all countries in its governance structure, in order to democratise the governance structure and system of the global non-traditional security agenda. On the one hand, China opposes selective multilateralism, i.e., club multilateralism, because it divides the world by ideology and values, practices ideological confrontation, creates a closed and exclusionary "small circle," incites division and confrontation, and hegemonically protects the interests of particular countries or regions. Second, China opposes selective multilateralism, i.e., hegemonic multilateralism, of the US, which promotes rules made by only a few countries and imposes them on others to pursue the interests of individual subjects rather than the common interests of humanity, in order to take advantage of the so-called "position of strength." "The US wants to dictate to the world according to its interests, which is intolerable and unacceptable in climate change and other areas.

Regarding the representative nature of multilateral cooperation, in terms of the evolution of the world landscape, it is now widely believed that the rise of emerging countries will seriously impact the current international order and restructure the global governance landscape. When the UN-centred international governance order framework was built more than seventy years ago, South Asia, Southeast Asia, and Africa were colonies, while today, South Asia and Southeast Asia both have economic aggregates of more than $3 trillion, not to mention populations with apparent advantages. As their comprehensive strength continues to rise, they are bound to raise political demands; perhaps the established old framework will eventually be retained. However, its functions and authority will inevitably degrade and weaken, while the influence of various new regional international organisations will rise. The existing global governance pattern reflects and represents the contrast in power among the major powers. Eighty years ago, this was irrelevant to the current needs of shared global governance and public agenda, which now is China's idea.

In terms of the nature of governance of multilateral institutions, the form of multilateral cooperation in which the "veto" is essentially held by a hegemonic power needs to be urgently changed; the existence of this "veto" not only stems from the material power base of individual countries but also from the country's comparative advantage in the discourse and public opinion, as a conceptual advantage located in "soft power." Genuine multilateralism, however, aims to achieve real and full sovereign equality for most countries and regions and is not just a change in the global governance system but also a change in the global value system. The fundamental conceptual innovation lies in the fact that the "right to development" and "right to life" are dominant values, and each country can choose its development path according to its unique historical, cultural, political, and economic conditions; the focus is on development, cooperation, and economic growth, and the non-traditional security agenda is treated separately from the traditional security agenda. It is also China's idea to uphold the principle of non-interference in each other's internal affairs and to promote the democratisation of the global multilateral governance structure and system.

In this regard, there must be much appreciation and support for India's initiatives on non-traditional security agendas, such as climate adaptation and mitigation. The ultimate goals of China's "true multilateralism" and India's "reformed multilateralism" are the same, and the frameworks are coherent. China and India, as leading representatives of developing countries, have always worked closely on this issue, and it is incumbent on both sides to work together to advance the agenda of the new multilateralism paradigm in terms of representative interest coverage and democratic coherence of governance.

In the face of severe non-traditional security challenges to promote the new multilateralism, China and India have already cooperated in some areas, but the depth and breadth of such cooperation still needs to be increased. Chinese academics and media believe that China-India cooperation in nontraditional security and new multilateralism is still in its infancy and has excellent prospects for development. They are convinced that such cooperation will provide opportunities for the healthy development of China-India relations. However, Indian academia and media are relatively pessimistic, emphasising that although China and India must cooperate, the feasibility is low. It is difficult to achieve a high level of cooperation, and arguing that non-traditional security issues and the new multilateralism agenda only sometimes bring opportunities for cooperation between China and India.[16] Sometimes they may become obstacles to the development of China-India relations. This chapter argues that there is still more room for China and India to cooperate on the agenda, but it remains to be worked together to achieve practical cooperation. Specifically, both sides should:

First, "[keep] the stock unchanged and [explore] the increment": looking at the relationship between China and India, the two geopolitically connected powers, and the bilateral non-traditional security cooperation between China and India has natural reason to drive the relationship. But from the traditional security perspective, the long-standing territorial disputes are the core issues hindering the development of China-India relations. Then the existing stock of issues such as the Tibet issue, the Dalai Lama issue, are other factors that influence the relationship. The two countries should try not to let their bilateral relationship get affected by domestic political opinion on both sides. While the two sides jointly need to further cooperation incrementally, their respective conflicts may get addressed through mutual trust built over the period of time. Second, "separate issues, first easy and then difficult": China-India relations involve complex contacts in multiple areas, so you can select issues for contact in a targeted manner, or even dismantle issues for cooperation, distinguish between economic and security-oriented, traditional and non-traditional security, start first with the easy and then the challenging [issues]. For example, economic security, energy security, national separatism and terrorism, water security, epidemic diseases, maritime security, and ecological security are the priority areas of non-traditional security in which the two sides can achieve cooperation. Thirdly, India-Russia relations have been good since the days of erstwhile Soviet Union, and India's position in the Russia-Ukraine conflict has considered Russian interests, while China-Russia relations are at their best. The Russian factor can play a leveraging role in Sino-Indian contacts and cooperation – whether voluntary or involuntary. Fourth, "talk more about doctrines and less about problems," which is a rational necessity in terms of public opinion, as the public opinion climate in China and India and their respective domestic nationalist sentiments are not conducive to the overall development of China-India relations.

India has always been an ideological and intellectual superpower, while China has long been a practical power. Together with other emerging respective national interests in the Global South, India and China can provide solutions to non-traditional security agendas such as climate change in their pursuance of new multilateralism.

Conclusion

The rise of non-traditional security threats has led to a shift from traditional security issues. This has led to uncertainty due to the source of the threat being asymmetrical. The source of threats and the rapid expansion of both the connotation and extension of security – especially human security–is particularly conspicuous in value-based care. Though many non-traditional security threats may not be as intense as a World War, they are sometimes no less harmful than war, especially climate change, which poses a severe threat to development and human survival. the construction of a non-traditional security community as a multilateral forum which is an essential means to overcome the resource-based security dilemma and address non-traditional security challenges. However, regarding the climate change agenda, there are many reasons why the Western-style multilateral paradigm is yet to serve its intended purpose as a representative example. It is due to the limitations posed by the "old multilateralism" which is plagued with the issues of representation and governance structure. The "true multilateralism" advocated by China challenges the Western paradigm of multilateralism at both the empirical and normative levels, and this is in line with the "reformed multilateralism" proposed by India. The path to a new multilateralism requires the joint efforts of China and India as members of the Southern camp and emerging forces in global geopolitics.

NOTES

1 T. I. Chao and Y. C. K. Chen, "The Focus on the New Era of National Security-development of Non-Traditional Security Trends", *Journal of Crisis Management,* (2), 2009, pp. 101-112.

2 Liu Xuecheng, "The basic properties of non-traditional security and their response", *International Studies,* (01), 2004,pp. 32-35.

3 Barry Buzan. "Non-Traditional Security Studies (NTSS): A Theoretical Framework, *World Economics and Politics.* (01), 2010, pp. 113-133.

4 Li Kaisheng, Xue Li, "Non-traditional Security Theories: Conceptions, Schools and Characteristics" *International Politics Quarterly,* (02), 2012, pp. 93-107.

5 Yu Xiaofeng, "From Dangerous Confrontation to Superior Co-existence: The Broad Security Concept and the Value Orientation of a Non-traditional Security Strategy", *World Economics and Politics,* (02), 2004, pp. 8-13.

6 Patrick Cronin, Abraham Dan, Mark Song Yingying, "Traditional and Non-traditional Security Challenges: Areas of US-China Cooperation, *Contemporary International Relations,* (8), 2010, pp. 45-50.

7 T. I. Chao and Y. C. K. Chen, "The Focus on the New Era of National Security-development of Non-Traditional Security Trends", *Journal of Crisis Management,* (2), 2009, pp. 101-112.

8 YU Xiaofengr and WANG Mengting, "Non-traditional Security Community: A New Exploration of Transnational Security Governance", *Journal of International Security Studies,* (01), 2017, pp. 4-25.

9 Chun-Ju Chen, "Analysis of Competitive Mode between China and India in the 21st Century", *Wenti Yu Yanjiu,* (2), 2018 pp. 59-86.

10 Shen Yi, "Discussing 'True and False' Multilateralism Based on Cognition and Practice", *Frontiers,* (01), 2022, pp. 65-71.

11 John G. Ruggie, "Multilateralism: The Anatomy of an Institution," *International Organization*, 46 (3), Summer 1992, p. 567.

12 Liu Jiangyong. "A Vision of Sustainable Security and Global Security Governance," *Journal of China and International Relations* 7(2), 2019.

13 Li Xiaoyan, "From Multilateralism to New Multilateralism: The Consensus Scarcity Dilemma and its Outlet", *Academics*, (05), 2022, pp. 44-57.

14 Chou Zejing, "Maintain and Practice Multilateralism to Solve the Difficulties of Global Governance", *Red flag manuscript*, (10), 2021, pp. 44-47.

15 Wang Zhidan Zhang dan, "China and the EU Take the Lead in Exploring Global Cooperation on Climate Governance", *World Environment*, (2), 2023, pp. 49-52.

16 Liu Shu. "Sino-India Cooperation on Non-Traditional Security Issues–Water Source Dispute and Cooperation as a Case", *Indian Ocean Economic and Political Review*, (02), 2015, pp. 127-139.

CHAPTER 15

Emerging Green Agendas and Multi-scalar Multilateralism in Asia

Medha Bisht

This chapter analyses the nature of multilateralism in Asia. By taking cognisance of international policy discourses in climate change and water, it examines the impact of such discourses in shaping and influencing green agendas at the regional level. Against this backdrop, the first section of this chapter juxtaposes climate change policies and international water policies which have unfolded at the international level in the last three decades. The primary aim of this section is to examine the unique trajectories that this discussion has followed. The second section examines how these discourses have translated and manifested at the regional level. Cases of South Asia and Southeast Asia become relevant in this regard. Since transboundary rivers are important connectors for regional cooperation, the general patterns associated with regional cooperation and transboundary rivers are discussed. In order to focus the discussion, the case of inland water navigation and hydropower is chosen for analysis, which helps us to also decipher the nature of climate action in both regions. The third section offers some concluding thoughts on the nature of multilateralism in Asia when it comes to handling the emergent water-energy-climate change debate.

International Policies and Discourses

It would not be an exaggeration to say that national developments are influenced, directly or indirectly, by international events, policies, and deliberations. The linkage between these two levels is evident especially in the backdrop of discussions around climate change at the international level, which have increasingly shaped policy ideas in the emergent energy and water sector. In an attempt to examine the role of economic ideas in shaping global climate policy, John Meckling and Bentley A. Allen[1] discuss upfront the nature of shifts that the energy sector has witnessed, particularly in the last three decades. By drawing from the dataset of policy reports of international organisations, which they define as 'central knowledge brokers' in the global economy, they unravel how there has been a shift of perspective from carbon pricing and green growth, and reveal convergence around economic growth and environmental conservation. A key reason for this causal push according to the authors was the diversification of economic thought– which they classify into distinct paradigms such as: (a) limits to growth (b) neoclassical (c) Keynesian (d) Schumpeterian thinking. In order to measure the content of the policy ideas, influenced by these distinct paradigms, three positions that define the relationship between climate mitigation and economic growth, are measured along the lines of conflict, strong complementarity and weak complementarity. Against this backdrop, according to the limit of growth argument, the two (environment preservation and economic growth) are in conflict, and they would be distributive trade-offs between the two. Meanwhile the neo-classical approach sees a weak complementarity between economic growth and environment preservation, as they believe that preserving natural capital is necessary to avoid decline in economic growth. On the contrary, the Keynesians and the Schumpeterians believe that there is indeed strong complementarity between environment preservation and economic growth. While the former believe that by focusing on aggregate demand, economic growth and mitigation can lead to a more balanced environmental policy, the latter argue that technological innovation will act as a key driver for synergising environmental and economic policies. Significantly, what emerges from these is that mitigation has emerged as the best policy option for environmental preservation in global climate policy.

This meta-analysis is significant for many reasons, as it is suggestive of the focus given to climate mitigation rather than climate adaption in global climate policy. It also suggests how the positive relationship between climate mitigation and resilience was emphasised, incentivising States to be the key stakeholders. Interestingly, tracing the trajectory of policy ideas, the authors analytically show that new ideas of green growth have not replaced old ones of environmental protection but have rather diversified policy choices and discourses, and they argue that the concept of sustainable development has been a key bridging framework for reconciling the old policy ideas with the new. Thus, sustainable development in many ways not only helped in breaking the monopoly of neo-classical ideas but also legitimised policy choices for both States and International Organisations (IOs) beyond a market-based climate policy paradigm which was anchored to carbon pricing and emission trading. In other words, while climate action (mitigation) was considered the key criteria for balancing economic growth, it was tempered with green innovation policy options and economic incentives that could further give meaning to green industrial policy, and thus was supported by the larger idea of a low carbon industrial revolution. This is significant, as the focus of international organisations in the 1990s was on environmental protection. After the Kyoto Protocol of 1997, there was a shift to climate change action, particularly through the green economic sector, which later narrowed down to the energy sector in 2005, and investment in green energy technology and energy conservation came to the forefront in terms of policy choices.

These ideas, as the authors argue, got further institutionalised in various forms and forums such as the Green Economy Initiative, Green Growth Strategy, International Renewable Energy Agency, and the Global Green Growth Institute, among others. Thus, for them, the neoclassical ideas merged and evolved along with Keynesian and Schumpeterian ideas. However, for them, the limits of growth idea were relegated to the margins. In their own words, "concepts such as the Anthropocene and planetary boundaries, popular academic reformulations of limits thinking, remain largely absent from the policy reports of IOs. Nonetheless, the discourse on limits to growth appears as the nagging doubt underneath the dominant notion of the complementarity of climate protection and economic growth."[2]

These ideas become an effective starting point to discuss policy discourses around the growth of green agenda because in the last few decades, climate policy ideas have largely shaped the 'green-growth debate'. This is quite evident from the aforementioned analysis where along with the policy ideas of the 1990s, the Asian Financial Crises gave a definite direction to the green debate. Discourse on green transition therefore introduced vocabulary such as green innovation, green industrial policy and climate action. Discussions around climate mitigation, hydropower, and green infrastructure thus became prominent themes at the national level, and energy water and road corridors became popular policy vocabularies at the regional level.

It would be appropriate here to contrast and bring to the fore discussions about the international water policy discourse, to get a more holistic perspective on these discourses. Like climate policy, water policy discourses have also been a prominent feature at the international level. However, it is important to get a perspective on the nature of this discourse and the shifts that it has witnessed in the last few decades.

The roots of the international water discourse go back to the 1960s when a need for a new hydrological initiative was highlighted. The backdrop of this initiative was a Resolution facilitated by the US Department of State to UNESCO to examine a proposition of instituting an international programme on hydrology.[3] UNESCO approved these plans and January 1965 marked the start of the International Hydrological Decade. One of the consequences of this gathering was that a need for a paradigmatic change in the field of hydrology was felt. As a result, in the 1980s, the foundation of modern scientific hydrology through the World Climate Research Programme was laid, which emphasised the linkages and the influence that hydrological variables have on local scales at the global level. It was argued for instance, that "catchments at regional scale are influenced by observable global scale hydro-meteorological fluctuations and may be changing because of the modification of greenhouse gases". Some of these changes, along with technological and information revolutions, as Shuttleworth argues, nudged one to look into issues of hydrological design and water resources management.[4] This was a significant argument, as it also suggested a need for a paradigm shift in water resource management which should go beyond the demand supply dyad, and look at the more dynamic, relational and integrated interlinkages and non-linear relationships between ecological considerations, climate change and water resources. As Saleem Ali and Domenico Grassa appropriately argue, "accessibility of water in international political discourse has always been framed as an engineering challenge rather than as an environmental planning endeavour."[5]

If one observes the evolution of the water discourse at the international level, one can classify different paradigms around water resource development. These are the Rationalists and Neo-Liberals. Varady and Meehan note that, "policy discourses in the first half of the twentieth century were led by rationalists, where state led development projects and centralised institutions were a norm. However, by [the] 1970s there was a radical shift towards neo-liberal governance involving components such as structural adjustment programs and sharp decreases in state spending."[6] They further argue that the late 1980s marked the onset for a new governance paradigm, as the period was characterised by the mushrooming of non-governmental organisations. The themes in the new governance paradigms also broadened to include sustainable development, public participation, transparency, and decentralisation. The new paradigm can also be termed as the constructivist paradigm, as it witnessed the entry of multiple actors who tried to shape norms around water management and governance. Transfer, diffusion and translation of ideas related to water management and governance have been subject to much debate and discussion and need further analysis by water policy scholars.[7] It would be insightful to look at the broad normative shifts which the water discourses have witnessed due to the participation of multiple organisations.

Policy Ideas in the International Water Policy Context

If one briefly examines the shifts of policy ideas at international level, there has been a distinct shift. For instance, in the field of science and engineering, the first international sanitary conference was convened in Paris in 1851, followed by international meteorological conference in 1853. Almost twenty years after the conference, the International Meterological Conference was established in 1873, which later got ratified in 1950. Simultaneously, a significant development was the development of international sanitary codes, for which the World Health Organisation and the United Nations Food and Agriculture Organization (FAO) were established in 1946 and 1945 respectively. Most of these international organisations concerned themselves with various aspects of water.[8] It would be significant to note here that the literature on water governance norms can be broadly categorised into three strands– policy, advocacy and academic. However, for the purpose of this chapter, only the policy and advocacy aspects have been taken up for discussion.

The literature on the policy aspect of water governance has focussed on the nature and diversity of water institutions (formal and informal. One of the most prominent policy platforms in the discourse on water has been the United Nations. The role of the United Nations in terms of linking the issue of water to sustainable development has been significant.[9] The UN Water Conference of 1977, held at Mar de Plata Argentina, made a significant contribution to the water governance debate. The Conference also led to the observance of the International Drinking Water Supply and Sanitation Decade (IDWSSD), in 1981.[10] It also put the cooperation between water-oriented UN bodies and agencies (which had existed since the 1950s) on a firmer pedestal through the UN Intersecretariat Group for Water Resources (ISGWR), and UNESCO and WHO were made responsible for the specific task of promoting activities in water resource assessment. However, by the 1990s, it was clear that the ideas formulated as the Mar De Plata Conference Plan, were being ignored by governments, and no progress was being made in the field of water quality, sanitation and water services. Thus in the 1990s, a number of regional consultations were held. One of them was the New Delhi Statement organised under UNDP auspices. The four guiding principles were (i) protection of the environment and safeguarding health through the integrated management of water resources; (ii) institutional reforms promoting an integrated approach including changes in procedures, attitudes, and behaviour and the full participation of women; (iii) community management of services supported by measures to strengthen local institutions in implementing and sustaining water and sanitation programmes; and (iv) sound financial practices to be achieved through better management of existing assets.[11] It was with this backdrop that the United Nations Conference on Environment and Development (UNCED) was convened. Since this was broadly related to the environmental discourse, and water did not get a special focus, a special conference was conceived in Dublin, and the International Conference on Water and the Environment, was specified to give inputs. Significantly, the Dublin statement contained guiding principles for action at local, national, and international levels, which later gave new meaning to International Water Resource Management (IWRM). A significant difference between the Plata conference and Dublin statement was that it proposed a follow up mechanism for periodic assessment of progress at national and international levels. However, one of the primary criticisms that the Dublin Conference also raised was the lack of global intergovernmental organisation that could take "charge of a comprehensive overview of progress on water-related aspects of Agenda 21[12]" As a response to some of these criticisms, the Commission on Sustainable Development was established in 1994, which, for its first meeting, considered fresh water as a major issue. Meanwhile, the Dublin Conference was criticised because of its advocacy of market-based approaches to address water scarcity challenges and for not taking cognisance of environmental sustainability.[13] As a consequence of these criticisms, there was again an attempt at the UN to focus on the broad themes of water and climate, food quality, human health, environment and conflict, and UNESCO's Inter-Governmental Hydrological Programme (a successor to the International Hydrological Decade), anchored these ideas. Thus, the HELP (Hydrology for Environmental, Life and Policy) initiative, which had a history going back to the 1960s, crystallised its ideas more clearly around 2000, and many of these ideas were taken up by the World Water Forum and other bodies, which had arisen due to powerful donor support.[14] Significantly, at this juncture, one observes the convergence of policy and advocacy approaches. In 1998, another conference on "Water and Sustainable Development" was convened in Paris, France, in March and the Paris Declaration was adopted by the attendees. The Declaration further committed the participants to a number of actions, including the integration of all aspects of development, management, and protection of water resources, progressive recovery of service cost, as well as the creation of an enabling framework through legislative, economic, social, and environmental measures.[15] In 2003, one of the most significant initiatives in the history of global water governance was the establishment of UN Water which is a coordination mechanism that coordinated 27 international agencies with interest in water management. A high-level advisory body was also convened by the UN.[16]

At the level of advocacy around water, apart from the UN, other international bodies such as the World Bank, IUCN, Asian Development Bank, and other donor agencies have also been active. Some of the donor-funded forums that emerged in 1996 were the World Water Council (WWC) and the Global Water Partnership. These institutions primarily focused on the ground water management orientation,[17] with the first World Water Forum being held in 1997 in Marakkesh.[18] WWC was to act as a think tank and was a result of the efforts of the International Water Resource Association, set up in 1972. The Council aimed at an integrative understanding of critical water issues at all levels, having a common vision of integrated water resource management, offering advice to institutions and decision-makers and implementing policies for sustainable water management. The Global Water Partnership was a working partnership amongst all entities – government agencies, public institutions, private companies, professional organisations and multilateral development agencies. The overall mission of the Global Water Partnership was to support countries in the integrated water resources management for the sustainable use of such water resources.[19] The subsequent year also saw the establishment of the World Commission of Water in 1998, which kick-started the process of setting the water discourse around issues on public-private partnerships.

If one was to make an analytical assessment of these developments, the global water governance framework was running on two parallel tracks. The first track was the UN, which anchored its debates to sustainable development. The second was anchoring itself to integrated water resource management. This second track was particularly significant because it was supported by the ADB and the World Bank. The developments post-2000 were important, as once MDGs completed their mandate, one witnessed that by 2015, some of these frameworks had got streamlined, focused, and prioritised by sector. Ali and Grassa note that, "Unlike the MDGs, which relegated water within the 'environment' goal or indirectly linked it to goals for reducing infant mortality or combating infectious diseases, the SDGs have a specific goal focused on water. Water targets for MDGs focused on water, sanitation, and hygiene (WASH), and these were continued in the SDGs with specific targets that were not met during the MDG process. The goal (SDG 6) is focused on water and sanitation and is stated to "ensure availability and sustainable management of water and sanitation for all". They further note, "Water is explicitly mentioned in relation to four additional SDGs, those concerned with health (SDG 3), disasters (SDG 11), pollution (SDG 12), and environment (SDG 15). Furthermore, SDG 14 (related to the oceans) also has a connectivity with broader water and development themes, though is more focused on the ecology and biodiversity conservation. More recently, a planetary boundaries (PBs) approach has been developed that attempts to define a safe operating space for human activity within the context of global life support system sustainability."[20]

What emerges from such an analysis is that while the first strand was dominated by the larger idea of sustainable development, focussing more on making national governments accountable on sustainable goals and targets, the other was an advocacy discourse, which pushed the idea of IWRM, later tethered to the framework of sustainable development. While the former introduced sustainable development as the primary criteria, the latter has taken this concept further by presenting multiple critical and constructive arguments on the desirability and feasibility of the idea, through the concept of IWRM and IRBM. For instance, the World Water Vision, which was presented by the World Commission on Water for the 21st Century in the second Water forum in 2000 needs to be mentioned here, because it talked about holistic and integrated ways to manage water. Three points it particularly emphasised were: decisions on land use effect water; sectoral and fragmented decisions adversely affect the hydrology and ecosystem that we depend on; and decisions the local, national and international levels, are inter-related. While many important ideas and frameworks (for example, WEF nexus, IRBM, waterscapes) have emerged from these discourses, it would be appropriate at this point to examine the translation and manifestation of these discourses at the regional level. Examples from South Asia and South East Asia are taken in this regard.

Patterns of Regionalism: South Asia and Southeast Asia

In order to take some of these ideas forward, this section examines the case of South Asia and Southeast Asia. Both these regions are important, as there has been a recent focus on renewable energy, and ideas of green energy, sustainable energy transition, green cities, etc., have reached policy consensus. Meanwhile, ideas such as IRBM, or sustainable land and water management practices are yet to fructify in a similar manner. In other words, water governance debates have been marginalised to a great extent. It would therefore be apt to ask at this juncture, whether the discussions pertaining to water governance paradigms that have emerged at the international level, should be restricted to academic publications and debate, or would they inform the green policies in holistic ways. It is also important to examine the emergent regional discourses and the value these emerging regional discourses have for green multilateralism. This is particularly true for the Asian rivers as the green agenda, which includes renewable energy and decarbonisation has primarily found expression through hydropower and navigation. Thus, it would be appropriate to examine how these discourses have been translated and embraced at the regional level. In order to address some of these specific questions, two propositions are identified. First, there is a low possibility of water policy discourses influencing sustainable energy transition, as the green infrastructure is heavily supported by economic ideas of climate mitigation and environmental conservation, which often overlook ecological holism. Second, with multi-scalar regionalism there is a high possibility of the normative and analytical water governance framework finding receptivity in policy frameworks, which can further lead to influencing green multilateralism in Asia. In order to answer these propositions, the patterns of regionalism in both South Asia and South East Asia are identified. Both these cases have particularly been seen through the connectivity discourse.

Case Study – South Asia

With regard to South Asia, regionalism can be identified within the frame of an old discourse and a new discourse. While the old discourse on connectivity is ideationally closer to the SAARC (South Asia Association for Regional Cooperation) initiative of the 1980s, the new discourse became more prominent in 1990s. The old discourse was caught up in Cold War politics, distrust amongst South Asian neighbours and domestic political instability. Burdened by the narrative of unequal treaties (in the case of Bhutan and Nepal), and quest for regional primacy which often led to interventions (in the case of Maldives and Sri Lanka), States primarily shaped the regional architecture. In the old discourse, water was a subset of foreign policy, and the focus was on a piecemeal, sectoral approach, when it came to water cooperation.[21]

The new discourse was introduced in the 9th SAARC Summit at Male, when the member countries agreed to focus on specific projects for 'meeting the needs of three or more member states.'[22] The assumption behind this new approach was that it would be pragmatic and collaborative with countries willing to cooperate. Consequently, the new approach was taken forward through collaborative sub-regionalism, expressed through the vision of the South Asia Growth Quadrangle (SAGQ). Though SAGQ did not fructify as some countries believed that subregional cooperation will undermine SAARC. In 2000, the South Asian Sub-Regional Economic Cooperation (SASEC) was launched with assistance from the ADB, which saw the entry of international financial institutions in South Asia. The focus was on priority sectors that included transport, energy and power, tourism, environment, trade, investment and private sector cooperation, and communication and information technology.[23]

Transboundary rivers became significant in this discourse giving importance to connectivity in multiple ways. This is evident in the developments in the past decade, where there had been an evident shift from old to new discourses and the focus had shifted from land to energy and water corridors. With the entry of international financial institutions and multilateral development banks, the process of regional integration has been an extroverted rather than introverted process.

Terms like inland water navigation and sustainable energy transition have also received political traction through a sub-regional vision embodied in groupings like the BBIN, where a case is being made for inland navigation, which requires engagement with transboundary rivers. Further, with India's forays into the renewable energy sector, and with its global vision of going carbon-free, establishing International Solar Alliance, sustainable energy transition has further opened pathways for creating a new discourse around Transboundary Rivers. This vision of connectivity has also created space for non-State actors (international non-governmental organisations, international financial institutions and civil society organisations), which have been salient players in transboundary water cooperation in South Asia since 2000. For instance, the South Asia Sub-regional Economic Cooperation in Regionalism was not only driven by States but by IFIs– with the assistance of ADB.

Earlier in the 1950s, when the wave of the pan-Asian vision was set in through the Asian Relations Conference, South Asian countries like Bhutan and Nepal were passive bystanders. Post-2000, these countries are active participants in the development debate primarily because of the of the new development discourse which focuses on renewable energy. Both these countries are rich in green energy (wind and solar), and have rich potential of hydro-power which also qualifies as renewable energy.

If one looks at the planning and the policy focus which has emerged under the new regionalism, India-Nepal energy cooperation has increased both in terms of transborder transmission lines and export of hydropower from Nepal (Arun IV, West Seti and SetiRiver Hydro project. Narayani and Koshi Rivers have been proposed for inland navigation through waterways that can facilitate seamless trade and commerce at a low cost.

Nepal is already transmitting 40MW of electricity to Bangladesh via Indian territory. On its part, India and Bangladesh have agreed on inland navigation to transport goods through Chittogram and Mongla ports. In fact, some news reports claim that sections of Ganga, Brahmaputra, Meghna and Khowai Rivers have been open for inland navigation under the Protocol on Inland Water, Transit and Trade. Domestically, hydropower and inland navigation have become prominent policy paradigms in Nepal, India and Bangladesh. When it comes to international or extra-regional players, the EU, China and the US are working in different capacities in South Asia and Southeast Asia. Among all these developments, the role of green bonds in South Asia is also a significant development driver.

The Case of Southeast Asia

If one looks at the case of Southeast Asia, ASEAN (Association of South East Asian Nations) has stood out as a regional institution. The Mekong River is often defined as the Danube of the East. Known as an international frontier, the Mekong Basin is also seen as an economic backwater. In fact, the French often saw it as a river road to China. While the wars of the 1950s led to the disbandment of Mekong River Commission (MRC) in 1957,[24] the MRC emerged as an inter-governmental organisation in 1995.

The story of the new discourse on regionalism started with two parallel trends–first, in the 1990s, as China decided to improve the upper Mekong, in 1992 the ADB launched the Greater Mekong Sub-region (GMS) project. The focus of the GMS was on sub-regional infrastructure and power trade. The idea was that Thailand, Vietnam and China could fulfil their growing domestic demand for electricity, and Laos and Myanmar would be able to attract energy investments and export hydropower. Second, the re-negotiations on river relations between the lower Mekong States gave a specific direction to the MRC, which was established in 1995.[25] The agreement extends beyond water allocation to include navigation, irrigation, hydropower, flood control, fisheries, timber floating, and recreation and tourism. No specific water allocations are set, but natural minimal and maximum flows are protected to prevent saltwater intrusion and maintain the flow around the TonleSap Lake, which generally witnesses a bout of floods during the dry season.[26] Thus, unlike the GMS, the focus of the MRC was on sustainable development and environment conservation and balance. Given these developments in the lower and upper stretches of Mekong, there were two emergent patterns to be seen in Mekong: (a) the Upper Mekong Economic Quadrangle (Yunnan, Upper Burma, Northern Laos and Thailand) was established, (b)Transnational geometric economic plans – emphasising growth circles and triangles, where river navigation was seen as the shortest route for economic route between Yunnan and Thailand – was identified, (c) To make the river navigable, smooth flowing water courses were envisioned through the construction of dams.[27]

While all these interventions were taking place under the GMS, the MRC's role to ensure environmental balance has often offered the counter-discourse, thus bringing economic growth and environment conservation at loggerheads with each other. The idea of adaptive governance, which the MRC brought forward, was heavily depended on donor-aided funds. Meanwhile, in 2002, there was an Agreement on Commercial Navigation between China, Laos, Myanmar and Thailand. The Agreement provided for the opening of river ports in each country and freedom of navigation for vessels. While there is much work on the negative externalitiesit was also found that primary driver was good information and data sharing mechanisms at the regional level. However, given the different institutional structures and international debates that have shaped much of the climate and water discourse, there is a growing emphasis on sanitation and clean drinking water in the Mekong Basin. One of the key features of Mekong River is that the financing mechanisms within the MRC are well developed and funding for the initial period is secured for several MRC programmes, including the Climate Change Adaptation Initiative (CCAI), and the Flood Management and Mitigation Programme (FMMP).

However, it has also been found that the linkages among governance levels are often weak and adaptation efforts are insufficient, and improving these links through institutional management mechanisms could contribute to strengthening overall adaptation efforts in the river basin.[28] Sustainable water management and adaptive governance remains a key challenge, in terms of the financial driver being still dependent on donors.

Multilateralism in Asia

At this point, it will be helpful to delve into the nature of multilateral efforts. There is in fact, established scholarship on political and economic multilateralism. There are two meanings of multilateralism which emerge. First, a passive concept–

dependent on and reflective of existing power relations– which primarily means a focus on State actors. Second an active concept– an agential force playing a role in the shaping of regional/world order. What some of these developments also tell us is that power is not just restricted to States; global finance and social forces of policy ideas cut across State boundaries, and makes non-State actors (International Organisations, Multilateral Banks, International Non-governmental Organisations, Non-governmental Organisations) relevant in this process. The discussion on global climate policy and global water initiatives should have made this argument clear.

Thus, it is important to think along the lines of multilayered or multi-scalar multilateralism. Multi-layered multilateralism should work across both horizontal and vertical levels. At the horizontal level four horizontal axis– regional, sub-regional, bilateral and local – should be important. At the vertical level, those issues could be identified which can be relevant across levels. A good way to synergise the vertical and horizontal levels is to think about water governance through the lens of scales. Literature around adaptive water governance could be a significant entry point.

Given that the discussion on South Asia and Southeast Asia also reveals that translation of these concepts has shown a different manifestation in both these regions, understanding regional specificities towards multilateralism is significant, as regional architectures respond and embrace these forces differently. It is also significant to see how the green agenda is affecting regional spaces in Asia differently and how there has been an evident shift in the water sector vis-a-vis the climate sector. As far as the challenges are concerned, both regions witness serious adaptation, and eco-system challenges due to inland navigation and hydel-dams, which can have compound impacts. In fact, the IEA's STEPS estimates that hydropower generation in Southeast Asia will see a remarkable increase, from 164 TWh in 2020 to 347 TWh by 2050, and that hydropower generation in India could increase from 173 TWh to 386 TWh over the same period. The only difference between the two regions is that MRC is an established institution in MRC, whereas South Asia lacks any such regional mechanism. A regional mechanism that takes care of multi-level engagement to improve resilience could be a way forward.

Some of the conclusions that can be drawn are: cross-boundary cooperation in South Asia has increased among civil society groups and donor-funded mechanisms. This means that issues of participation at multiple levels can be considered as appropriate policy interventions where formal and informal institutions can be synergised. Second, while South Asia and Mekong countries need to strengthen coordination and cooperation with non-member riparians for strengthening resilience in the basin, communities of practice also need attention. While it is difficult to arrive at such frameworks at the regional level, existing local practices should be planned and taken into account. Third, the emerging discourse on ecological awareness, social learning through nature-based solutions, structural and non-structural methods for adaptation strategies, are emerging in Asian countries, given the ideational and financial support from the UN and multilateral banks. Fourth, disasters are pathways to diplomacy– however no systematic efforts are being made towards adaptive management. Sixth, the pathway for climate action through green multilateralism is an emerging discourse. How such discourses can be linked to adaptive water governance and management, can be thought through with the regional institutions in South and Southeast Asia. This could channelise interactions between donors from the Global North and Global South, in informing the green discourse.

NOTES

1 Jonas Meckling and B.B. Allan, The evolution of ideas in global climate policy, *Nature Climate. Chang,* 10, 2020, pp. 434–438.

2 Ibid., p. 4.

3 R.G.Varady *et al,* "Global Water Initiatives Redux: A Fresh Look at the World of Water", *Water* 2022, 14(19), 2022, p. 3093 at https://doi.org/10.3390/w14193093 (Accessed 14 July 2023).

4 W.J. Shuttleworth, "New worldwide hydrological initiative needed", *Eos,* 80(9), 1999, pp. 80, 103.

5 Saleem Ali and Domenico Grasso, "Encyclopaedia of Water: Science, Technology, and Society Water and Global Development Goals: The Role of Engineering and Social Science in Meeting International Policy Outcomes" *Human Dimensions: Water, Society, and Law,* https://www.doi.org/10.1002/9781119300762.WSTS0012

6 R.G. Varady, K. Meehan, "A Flood of Institutions? Sustaining Global Water Initiatives", *Water Resource. Impact* 8(6), 2006, pp. 19–22, https://udallcenter.arizona.edu/sites/default/files/2022-01/A%20flood%20of%20institutions.pdf (Accessed 17 July 2023).

7 F. Mukhtarov, "A Review of Water Policies on the Move: Diffusion, Transfer, Translation or Branding? *Water Alternative* 15(2), 2022, pp. 290–306, https://www.water-alternatives.org/index.php/alldoc/articles/vol15/v15issue2/669-a15-2-11/file (Accessed 17 July 2023).

8 J.C. Rodda, "Whither World Water?" *Water Resources Bulletin,* 31, 1995, pp. 1–7.

9 P. Woodhouse and M. Muller, "Water Governance—An Historical Perspective on Current Debates", *World Development,* 92, 2017, pp. 225–241.

10 J.C. Rodda, no. 8; S.M.A. Salman, "From Marrakech through The Hague to Kyoto: Has the Global Debate on Water Reached a Dead End?" Part Two, *Water International,* 28(4), 2003, pp. 11–19. https://www.internationalwaterlaw.org/bibliography/articles/Salman/Marrakesh HagueKyoto1.pdf (Accessed 21 July 2023).

11 S.M.A. Salman, no. 10, 11–19.
12 J.C. Rodda, no. 8, pp. 1–7.
13 P. Woodhouse and M. Muller, no. 9, pp. 225–241.
14 R.G. Varady, A.K. Gerlak, M.O. Wilder, N. Pineda, "New Directions in Hydro-Diplomacy to Meet Global Water Challenges: Learning from the Past, Shaping the Future", *Environment Science Policy*, 124, 2021, pp. 55–63 and p. 14.
15 S.M.A. Salman, no. 10, pp. 11–19 and p. 496.
16 P. Woodhouseand M. Muller, no. 9, pp. 225-241.
17 R.G. Varady, A.K. Gerlak, M.O. Wilder, N. Pineda, no. 14, pp. 55–63.
18 S.M.A. Salman, no. 10, pp. 11–19.
19 Ibid.
20 Saleem Ali and Domenico Grasso, n. 5.
21 Medha Bisht, "Water Diplomacy in South Asia: Towards a Relational Approach," Friedrich Naumann Foundation for Freedom New Delhi, 2023
22 G Padmja, "BBIN Agreement: Building Sub-Regional Corridors of Trust", *South Asia Monitor*, 29 June 2015; Medha Bisht, no. 21.
23 K. Yhome, *Acting East Through India's Sub-Regions*, Issue Brief, Observer Research Foundation, 2017, https://www.orfonline.org/research/-acting-east-through-india-s-subregions (Accessed 21 July 2023).
24 Jessica M. Williams, "Is Three a Crowd? River Basin Institutions and the Governance of the Mekong River", *International Journal of Water Resources Development*, 37 (4), 2021.
25 Ibid.
26 MRC, 1995 cited in Jessica M. Williams Ibid.
27 Ibid.
28 Sussane Schmeier, *Resilience to Climate Change Induced Challenges to Mekong River Basin*, World Bank, Washington DC, 2011.

CHAPTER 16

Climate-Security Nexus at the UN System: Implications for Integration in Eurasia

Anatoly Boyashov

Introduction

While mandated to look at tradition security-related issues and conflicts affecting stability and peace in the world, the UN Security Council has been more concerned with climate change and environment protection. On the one hand, the interrelation between security and non-profile issues (e.g., climate, elections, human rights) can serve as a unifying agenda when there is little room for wide consensus on international security. On the other hand, such an agenda can cause further polarisation since the interrelation between security and borderline matters substitutes conflict resolution with the debate on root causes of conflicts. This chapter takes up the discussion on human rights and underdevelopment, the issues that mostly affect the global south as they struggle to implement development agenda which have implications for the climate-security nexus and get entwined with UN reforms, regional integration, and State sovereignty.

Concerning the UN reforms, the interrelation of security and climate widens scope for reforms of the UN Security Council, but leads to securitisation of human rights at the UN Human Rights Council. As for regional integration, the inability of States to negotiate in New York causes regionalisation of climate-security policies. Finally, such agenda raises the structural debate related to State sovereignty. What are the root causes of conflicts and instability? Is it non-implementation of the right to the environment or rather the right to development?

Bridging security with climate change at the UN Security Council raises the debate on the root causes of conflicts. Why do negative climate change issues have adverse impact on security in the South, while the same negative climate change issues do not multiply risks to the same extent in the North?

Linking Climate to Human Rights: A Western Agenda

Western European and other states from the respective UN grouping answer this question by substituting the developmental side of climate with political human rights language. In July 2022, the UN General Assembly adopted Resolution No. 76/300 "The Human Right to a Clean, Healthy and Sustainable Environment."[1] The North/western media, servants of international organisations, and NGO activists called this Resolution a "historic event": Paragraph 1 of the Resolution "recognizes the right to a clean, healthy and sustainable environment as a human right". According to Inge Andersen, Executive Director of the United Nations Environment Programme, "The resolution will trigger environmental action... It will help people stand up for their right to breathe clean air, to access safe and sufficient water, healthy food, healthy ecosystems, and non-toxic environments to live, work, study, and play."[2] David Boyd, Associate Professor at a Canadian university and Special Rapporteur of the UN Human Rights Council, is of a similar opinion: "These resolutions may seem abstract, but they are a catalyst for action, and they empower ordinary people to hold their governments accountable in a way that is very powerful."[3]

The unilateral use of decisions of international organisations as an instrument, at best, of bringing individuals under external jurisdiction, at worst, of electoral or military intervention, is not new in world politics. The consideration of human rights issues in non-profile structures such as the UN Security Council, the inclusion of human rights issues in trade agreements, financial programmes, decisions of international organisations in the field of humanitarian cooperation, climate change, and development are often used for those purposes. For example, in December 2021, Russia, India, and China did not support the Resolution of Western countries on "Climate and Security" in the UN Security Council. The Resolution proposed to recognise the rise in global temperatures as "the fundamental cause of all conflicts and risk factors for their emergence" and to consider climate change in conflict prevention.[4] While extreme natural events can have devastating consequences, would the Resolution not be used to assert military control over developing countries? Would it not lead to external control over energy production? Not surprising, Russia, India, and China did not join the penholders since there was no consensus on concrete instruments of the climate and security nexus, nor is there agreement on instruments to tackle climate change issues in general.

There is no agreement among the researchers either. In academic literature, "securitisation", "politicisation", or "militarisation" have been used to promote unilateral interests under UN auspices.[5] The discussion on privatisation of information inputs or targeted resources allocation to working instruments or UN experts is less common.[6] Initiatives by Western States have promising human rights implications but create room for politicisation of climate issues. For instance, since 2012 the Western European countries have been actively promoting the concept of a "human right to a safe environment", States from other UN groups have abandoned this concept in favour of a "clean, healthy and sustainable" environment. The word "safe" was removed during the informal consultations phase in 2021, when the so-called right to climate was being drafted at the UN Human Rights Council in Geneva.

If adopted as a universal mechanism at the Security Council, how would the climate-security nexus work in terms of concrete instruments? Would it create "climate-related" peacekeeping operation, allow intrusive civil monitoring, international intervention operations, or sanctions against nuclear energy? If we claim that climate change is a non-traditional threat to security and a risk multiplier, then one automatically admits that climate emergency causes conflict and not underdevelopment. Here, in my view, the developmental language needs to be emphasised rather than securitisation. In this regard, the climate-security nexus should be treated as a sustainable development issue with full respect for the division of labour among the UN agencies: for example: UN Security Council for security issues, UN FCCC for climate change, and UN Human Rights Council and UNGA Third Committee for human rights issues.

The definition of a "clean, healthy and sustainable" environment needs further elaboration. The initiatives on climate and security invariably always contain human rights language. On the one hand, it is very important to ensure coherent implementation of human rights. On the other, all human rights – civil, political, economic, social, and cultural are indivisible. If one digs deeper into the human rights language of the climate-and-security initiatives, it becomes clear that such initiatives are oriented towards civil and political rights; more explicitly, to the freedom of expression and freedom of association. The problem is that such narrow orientation creates room for politicisation and privatisation of international cooperation.

To ensure effective implementation, the socio-economic aspects of climate should be governed by concluding an international treaty that bind the countries and make them adhere to the treaty. It should not be concluded through a UN General Assembly Resolution which is not legally binding. Unlike a declarative and voted Resolution of the UN General Assembly, an international treaty could establish a unilateral mechanism of implementation with a transparent intergovernmental budget. It is for these reasons that General Assembly Resolution No. 76/300 on 'The human right to a clean, healthy and sustainable environment', a non-binding resolution was not adopted by consensus: Eight countries, including three CIS members (Belarus, Kyrgyzstan and Russia) abstained from voting, and 24 States did not participate in the voting at all. Some States such as Turkmenistan, decided to ignore this initiative due to the neutrality foreign policy; the others interpreted the above-mentioned Resolution as a potential precedent for interference into domestic affairs under the pretext of climate.[7] For the same reasons, States cannot come to consensus in the UN Security Councl. At this stage, the climate and security nexus agenda at the UN Security Council causes polarisation among States rather than serving as uniting agenda, which leads to deepening of regional integration in the sphere of climate and ecology. These three processes are related.

First, the climate-security nexus causes a spillover of the securitisation of climate to the UN Human Rights Council. As a result, human rights becomes securitised as well. Second, the inability of States to negotiate the climate-security nexus in New York increases the role of regional organisations in dealing with climate-related risks. Third, the climate-security nexus at the UN Security Council raises the debate on the root causes of conflicts. The question is whether non-implementation of right to environment or rather right to development that constitute a security threat?

The above-mentioned issues have opened a vast space for Eurasian organisations to tackle climate change and deal with environmental protection. It becomes easier for States to find consensus on the root causes of climate insecurity at the regional level, especially on trans-border issues like governance of trans-boundary rivers and water issues. For example, the International Fund for Saving the Aral Sea has fostered regional cooperation in Central Asia.

CIS Countries and Climate Change

The green agenda of the Commonwealth of Independent States (CIS) is on the rise. Besides reduction of carbon emissions, the green agenda of the CIS includes biodiversity, resisting glacier melting, providing wide access to drinking water, and preventing forest fires and threats of land desertification. All CIS countries are parties to the Paris Agreement. Environmental protection is monitored in all CIS member states, specialised agencies are functioning, relevant development concepts have been adopted at the national level, taking into account the development of alternative energy, environmental safety, as well as providing for the strategic nature of environmental protection. The United Nations Climate Change Conference (COP26) held in Glasgow in November 2021, the CIS countries were among the signatories of the Glasgow Declaration on Forests. The CIS countries have examples of best practices on private issues, such as Kyrgyzstan's experience in combating glacier melting, Tajikistan's experience in water resource management, Uzbekistan's initiative of the Multilateral Trust Fund on human security in the Aral Sea Region. On 14 October 2022, the CIS States adopted a joint declaration on ecological and industrial security.

The global inequality of technological development determines the diversity of approaches to environmental protection. At the 26th Conference of Parties in Glasgow, on the initiative of G7 countries, 34 countries and five State financial institutions decided to stop supporting new foreign projects for fossil fuel extraction and electricity generation from fossil fuels without carbon capture directly from the State budget by the end of 2022.[8] However, not everyone was surprised by this decision: according to scholars from the United States, the green agenda of the Western European group has always represented colonialism, which has only changed its form with the change of the technological mode.[9] For example, New Zealand, which has declared a commitment to carbon neutrality by 2050, puts its agriculture outside the brackets of greenhouse emissions because it is a prominent player in the beef market. The United Kingdom, host of the 26th Conference of the Parties in Glasgow, lays claims to world climate leadership but neglects to take into account the greenhouse gas emissions of British shipping and aviation.[10] It seems that the initiatives of individual countries are aimed at reproducing their dominant position in the global economic system by controlling the technological development of other States.

Abandoning hydrocarbon energy in the CIS would mean abandoning socio-economic development. Nevertheless, in recent years, the CIS countries have also developed many technologies to reduce hydrocarbon dependency (wind and photovoltaic stations, small capacity nuclear power plants, digital, remote, space, geotechnical monitoring systems, electric buses, electric charging stations, superfast storage systems, production and use of "green" hydrogen, carbon dioxide capture and utilisation, etc.), but technology development in the CIS region meets indirect resistance in the form of Western sanctions. The unilateral coercive measure against Belarusian firms in the sphere of artificial intelligence aimed at controlling the technological development. In 2022, world manufacturers of IT products (Cisco,

Dell, Schneider Electric, Hewlett-Packard, Microsoft, etc.) began to leave Belarus, disconnected services and stopped supporting the vendors (suppliers of their own IT products), which made it impossible to update software, receive technical support in troubleshooting and other service support.

Within the Shanghai Cooperation Organization, member states recorded a commitment to combat the negative effects of climate change in 2019 (the Bishkek Declaration of the Council of Heads of State); there is regular discussion of coordinated trade, climate and environmental policies to prevent "climate sanctions". In August 2021, the Eurasian Economic Union launched a high-level Working Group to develop proposals for the convergence of the positions of States in the climate agenda, as well as the Climate Technology and Digital Initiatives Bank as an exchange of examples of best practices. The leading outcome of these initiatives has been technology exchange and countering the pressure of sanctions.

The green agenda of the CIS States is determined by the specifics of socio-economic development at a particular historical stage. It is for this reason that CIS States are less involved in the initiatives of a number of Western corporations and States to make a quick transition to a "green economy". According to analysts of audit corporations, although such a transition will not have a significant impact on natural gas, the "green jump" may significantly reduce global demand for oil due to pressure from the transportation industry.[11] Therefore, the CIS oil and gas sector is adapting by improving operational energy efficiency, utilising associated gas, reducing methane emissions, planting forests and cogeneration.

Combating climate change and protecting the environment has become an increasingly topical but also politicised agenda. Discussions among scientists about the level of anthropogenic impact on the climate do not solve the problem of politicisation. The initiatives of individual States to develop "climate sanctions", "climate interventions" and "climate monitoring" pose certain risks. There is absolute dominance of the States of the Western European group in the development of various environmental indices and introduction of assessment methodologies into the methodology of international organisations. This is done gradually through extensive financial programmes, NGO networks, and regional intergovernmental organisations. From this perspective, the CIS has significant potential to build balance of power in climate agenda – to depoliticise the climate and environmental agenda, promote pluralism of approaches to combat adverse climate change, and strengthen regional development cooperation.

At the CIS level, environmental issues are receiving increasing attention. In 2013, an Agreement on cooperation in the field of environmental protection of the CIS member states was adopted in Minsk within the framework of the CIS Interstate Environmental Council. Official representatives of environmental agencies, the Secretariat of the CIS Inter-parliamentary Assembly (CIS IPA), and the CIS IPA Standing Commission on Agrarian Policy, Natural Resources and Environment, the CIS Executive Committee and the Executive Committee of the CIS Electric Power Council take part in the work of this Environmental Council. At its meeting in September 2021, the participants paid special attention to the introduction of green technologies, convergence of approaches and harmonisation of national legislations in the field of environmental protection, greenhouse gas emissions trading system and development of fish farming (aquaculture), phased transition from the use of polymer packaging to environmentally friendly packaging and implementation of the Sustainable Development Goals in the field of environmental protection.

The CIS initiated a platform for multilateral discussion on climate – the Annual Nevsky International Ecological Congress in Saint Petersburg. The Congress has been held annually since 2008 in St. Petersburg and serves as a discussion platform for representatives of public authorities, business circles, educational and research institutions and public organisations on issues of increasing the environmental efficiency of the economies of the CIS member states. As a result of coordination among interested stakeholders, a system of environmental monitoring in the waters of the Northern Sea Route aimed at environmental protection and environmental safety has been established.

Within the framework of the CIS Interparliamentary Assembly, 79 documents on ecology and environmental protection were adopted in the form of "model laws". These documents serve as the basis for unification of regional standards and approaches to climate. The model Forest, Water, Land, Environmental Codes and the Code on Subsoil and Subsoil Use have been adopted to integrate national legislations. The approaches of the CIS countries are united in the model laws "On Environmental Safety", "On Radiation Safety of Population", "On Safe Handling of Pesticides and Agrochemicals", "On Industrial Safety of Hazardous Production Facilities", "On Safety of Activities Related to Genetically Modified Organisms", "On Environmental Disaster Zones", "On Prevention of Major Accidents Associated with Emissions/Discharges of Hazardous Substances and Limitation of Their Possible Consequences". In recent years, model laws "On the assessment of environmental damage", "On ecological tourism", "On agro-insurance", "On the elimination of accumulated environmental damage (harm)", "On the environmental safety of oil products transportation through pipelines", "On state information systems in the field of environmental protection, natural resources management and environmental safety", as well as Recommendations on the formation of environmental policy and Recommendations on the organisation of national centres for environmental protection, have been prepared and adopted.

Further unification of the CIS countries' efforts could serve to depoliticise the climate and environmental agenda. The CIS States have already started to conceptualise frameworks for coordination. According to the CIS Concept for Further Development, an essential component of cooperation is interaction in the field of environmental protection and rational use of natural resources, including those aimed at combating climate change, preventing emergencies, and eliminating the consequences of natural disasters. In accordance with Paragraph 4.4 of this Concept, environmental protection is also included in humanitarian cooperation, which should be actualised in order to adapt the population to climate change effects. For example, the CIS Interstate Statistical Committee is involved in organising the exchange of statistical information on environmental protection issues: timely exchange of information can serve to develop standards, integrate approaches at the domestic level and coordinate positions on international platforms. Additionally, the formation of environmental consciousness among young people is the goal of the international youth cooperation by 2030 (CIS Strategy for International Youth Cooperation for 2021-2030), which creates space for civil society cooperation.

The Economic Development Strategy of the CIS for the period until 2030 specifies conceptual approaches to climate issues in the framework of small hydropower development, use of environmentally friendly motor fuels, non-conventional and renewable energy sources, creation of conditions for the production of "green" equipment at enterprises, innovative energy development and development of advanced energy technologies. The concept of inter-regional and cross-border cooperation for the period up to 2030 approved the effective, rational and safe use of natural resources and the fight against climate change as key objectives of regional development. In the CIS Tourism Development Strategy for 2021-2030, the States identified the development of green tourist routes and agro-ecotourism as priority areas, while other areas of development should minimise the negative impact on the environment and ecology. Technological solutions for ecology, including resource recovery, resource conservation and waste management, are recognised as priority areas of cooperation in the CIS in accordance with the CIS Interstate Programme of Innovation Cooperation until 2030.

A separate result of environmental coordination within the CIS was the CIS Framework Programme on the Peaceful Uses of Nuclear Energy until 2030. The Programme takes into account the growing demand for environmentally friendly electricity, recognises the increasing negative impact of climate change on the functioning of life-supporting infrastructures and consequently, tightens policy in this area. The Programme considers environmental protection from the point of view of nuclear and radiation safety: the development of green nuclear power and the reclamation of nuclear heritage sites: helping nuclear heritage sites comply with modern environmental and sanitary requirements, are priority areas of development.

At the same time, the concept of environmental security has achieved parallel recognition at the conceptual development level, in the CIS. Interaction in the field of biological and environmental security has been approved as a priority area of military cooperation in the CIS (Concept of Military Cooperation until 2025). Changes in the environment are taken into account to ensure border security at external borders (CIS Program of Cooperation in Strengthening Border Security at External Borders for 2021-2025). Environmental security is defined in the 2003 CIS IPA Model Law on Environmental Security, as "a system of political, legal, economic, technological and other measures aimed at guaranteeing the protection of the environment and vital interests of human beings and citizens from possible negative impacts of economic and other activities and threats of natural and man-made emergencies in the present and future". Recognising that the CIS States have advanced far in the field of formation of national environmental interests, this definition seems somewhat outdated and does not take into account the whole range of environmental threats and measures to prevent them in the CIS (water resources management, forest management, development and protection of mountainous areas, green energy, external climate policy, waste management, environmental education, ecotourism development, Arctic ecology, etc.).

The CIS Interstate Programme of Innovation Cooperation until 2030 recognises environmental safety as the main expected outcome of innovation projects. Since climate and food security issues are interrelated, if "climate sanctions" are used against agriculture in the Commonwealth countries, environmental safety can become the basis for retaliatory measures in the form of regulating imports to CIS countries. The CIS concept of agricultural engineering from 2020 has already approved environmental safety as a criterion for assistance to enterprises in the sector.

The concept of environmental security is currently undergoing another stage of discussion: there is a discussion among experts on new editions of model laws "On Environmental Security" and "On Access to Environmental Information" are being prepared within the CIS IPA. Methodologies for assessments, monitoring and indices have already been developed in CIS documents, for example, model laws "On Environmental Expertise", "On Environmental Audit", "On Strategic Environmental Assessment", "On Environmental Impact Assessment", "On Production and Consumption Waste", "On Access to Environmental Information". The latter in light of excessive politicisation of the Aarhus Convention may become a tool to prevent interference in the internal ecosystems of the CIS countries. What the CIS needs, is to ensure consistency, institutional interconnection, and systemic implementation of the existing approaches. Updating the revisions could serve to strengthen the coordination of the CIS countries.

It seems promising to conceptualise a CIS development strategy for environmental protection and combating negative climate change, potentially through the concept of environmental security. Such a strategy would serve the goals of the CIS States voluntarily accepted under the Paris Agreement. Even if there is no consensus on when and how to achieve conditional carbon neutrality, such a strategy could bring together the many solutions and approaches already documented by the CIS, EAEU, and Shanghai Cooperation Organization. Within the SCO, member states have committed to combating negative climate change in 2019 (Bishkek Declaration of the Council of Heads of State), and there is regular discussion of coordinated trade, climate and environmental policies to prevent "climate sanctions".

Why CIS Countries' Approach is Important?

A common CIS strategy in the field of environmental security could serve three main purposes: 1) convergence of legislation, approaches and standards in the field of environmental protection and combating negative climate change; 2) development of environmental monitoring methodology; 3) coordination of foreign policy positions on international platforms in order to prevent external constraints. It is also relevant to develop a CIS climate index that takes into account a wider variety of methods of environmental protection and combating negative climate change. Now, there are networks of organisations assessing carbon dioxide emissions. This is undoubtedly a valuable contribution to the promotion of environmental protection, but such methodology is subject to politicisation, as some States get high positions in the ratings, by moving "harmful" production outside their territories.

The use of standard (development of methodologies, indices, standards, and model legislation), expert and coordination potential of the CIS in the field of greenhouse gas absorption and adaptation of population and economy to climate change and environmental protection, is expected to be particularly promising. The point is that, unlike the Kyoto Protocol of 1997, which is fully focused on reducing greenhouse gas emissions, the Paris Agreement pursues three equivalent objectives: Reduction of greenhouse gas emissions, absorption of greenhouse gases, and adaptation of the population and economy. Western States and financial institutions, based on the needs of industry, emphasise the first task, while the second – absorption – can be solved by forests expansion. Adaptation of population is equally important. At the CIS level, a methodology for estimating the potential of forests to absorb greenhouse gases could be developed, at least in the form of coordination of national cadres and agencies responsible for forest management. Such methodology could be beneficial for the implementation of the Paris Agreement. The methodological potential is enormous; numerous documents have already been adopted, what remains is to unite efforts and give systematisation to the already outlined course on the green agenda of the Commonwealth of Independent States.

NOTES

1 UN, "Resolution 76/300," 28.07.2022 at undocs.org/A/RES/76/300 (Accessed 5 August 2024).

2 "In historic move, UN declares healthy environment a human right," UNEP, 28 July 2022 at https://www.unep.org/news-and-stories/story/historic-move-un-declares-healthy-environment-human-right (Accessed 15 August 2024).

3 Ibid.

4 "Security Council Fails to Adopt Resolution Integrating Climate-Related Security Risk into Conflict-Prevention Strategies," United Nations,13.December 2021 at https://press.un.org/en/2021/sc14732.doc.htm (Accessed 5 July 2024).

5 M. Koch, "World Organizations – (Re-)Conceptualizing International Organizations," *World Political Science*, 11 (1), 2015, pp. 97-131.

6 *The Financing of the UN Experts*, European Centre for Law and Justice, Strasbourg, 2021.

7 United Nations, Seventy-sixth Session, 97th Meeting (AM), https://press.un.org/en/2022/ga12437.doc.htm

8 Intergovernmental Panel on Climate Change, "Carbon Dioxide Storage" at https://www.ipcc.ch/site/assets/uploads/2018/03/srccs_spm_ts_ru-1.pdf (Accessed 03 September 2023).

9 V. Ramachandran, "Rich Countries' Climate Policies Are Colonialism in Green", *Foreign Policy,* 03Novrember2021 at https://foreignpolicy.com/2021/11/03/cop26-climate-colonialism-africa-norway-world-bank-oil-gas/. Дата доступа: 19.08.2022 (Accessed 20 August 2023).

10 "On the growing interest of business in climate issues and priorities for the near future," *LENTA*, 20 April 2021 at https://lenta.ru/articles/2021/04/20/climate/ (Accessed 04 April 2023).

11 "CIS Oil and Gas Industry and the Global Climate Agenda," EY, 09 June 2021 at: https://www.ey.com/ru_kz/oil-gas/cis-oil-gas-industry-and-global-climate-agenda (Accessed 03 June 2023).

CHAPTER 17

Multilateral Approach to Non-Traditional Security Challenges: Climate Adaptation and Mitigation – The Case of Madagascar

Clara Randrianjara

Introduction

The environmental issue was first raised internationally in 1972 by the Stockholm Declaration on Environmental Protection, which led to the adoption of the United Nations Environment Programme (UNEP), the first multilateral entity focused on the environment. Since then, the theme of climate change has taken the issue to a new dimension. This is one of the few areas not contemplated in the Charter of the United Nations in 1945 and which have slowly penetrated the international agenda. Indeed, climate change impacts, such as floods, droughts, damages on coastal property and ecosystems, among others, have been intensifying and affecting to various degrees, a large majority of countries and at some point, threaten their security. Countries, with the means at their disposal, are also trying to adapt to these climate changes as well as to mitigate their effects. However, the task is so vast that many States have expressed their commitments to tackle these new challenges through multilateral cooperation guided by international instruments. In addition, it is indisputable that multilateralism has limitations by way of efficiency due to various reasons. So the question is: Is there a need for a new multilateralism while keeping in mind that effective cooperation is required much more by developing countries to help them cope with the effects of climate change?

This chapter begins with showcasing different impacts of climate change in various sectors in Madagascar. Secondly it analyses the country's climate adaptation and mitigation measures and it dwells further on the main multilateral environmental instruments to which Madagascar is a State Party, along with their different texts and policies adopted at the national level. Thirdly, the chapter focuses on different reasons why multilateralism fails to reach its goals of tackling climate change, and specifically its inefficiency due to the lack of implementation of multilateral instruments. Lastly, it proposes innovative solutions towards a reform of multilateralism and an enhancement of South-South and triangular cooperation in order to handle climate change-related natural disasters. So far, Madagascar has experienced diverse climate change effects in several sectors.

Impacts of Climate Change on Madagascar

Madagascar is located in the Western Indian Ocean, 400 km off the African continent's eastern coast from which it is separated by the Mozambique Channel. Madagascar is the fourth largest island in the world with a total area of 591,896 square kilometers[1] that includes nearly 5,000 km of coastline.

The country is home to 5 per cent of the World's biodiversity within several ecological regions characterised by a variety of terrestrial ecosystems such as forests, agricultural fields and grasslands, as well as aquatic ecosystems including wetlands and inland waters and marine and coastal ecosystems.[2]

Madagascar is proving to be highly exposed and is one of the most vulnerable countries to climate change. In the last ten years, global warming has intensified extreme weather events such as cyclones, droughts, floods or sand winds whose effects were directed at the environment itself and on the population. Between 1961 and 2017, cyclones destroyed 600,000 houses and affected 4 million people while 300,000 persons were victims of floods.[3]

Eighty per cent of the Malagasy population is categorised as rural (20,731,294 people in 2018[4]) and their socio-economic activities are mainly related to agriculture. Thus, climate change has resulted in food insecurity and malnutrition, with the reduction of yield crops due to loss of soil fertility and the dramatic decrease in rainfall. In the south of the country, the "Kere" phenomenon, which is the local name for famine has been described as "the World's first famine due to climate change."[5]

Moreover, the evolution of climatic parameters shows a significant rise in temperatures throughout the country between 1961 and 2017: per year, either minimum or maximum temperatures increased respectively by 0.04 and 0.05 degrees centigrade.[6] In addition, winter and spring precipitations have been noticeably decreasing in most areas. Also, as the sea level was gradually rising at a speed of 1.57 mm per year between 1993 and 2017, the temperature of the sea in the western Indian Ocean was increasing by 0.60 degree centigrade between 1950 and 2009.[7] Eventually, air and subsoil pollution are increasing; the preponderance of the use of fossil energy and wood does affect the environment quality, in particular water resources and soil characteristics.[8]

Natural forests covered 8.9 million hectares in 2014. The whole territory was subject to an expanding annual deforestation rate, amounting to 1.18 per cent per year for the period 2010-2014 (National Environmental Dashboard-TBEN, 2019).[9] The rate of deforestation varies according to regions but on average, forests located at an altitude of less than 800 m are more affected, with a rate of 1 per cent per year. In general, several inter-related social and economic factors cause deforestation, but one overriding factor is the need for wood. The loss of forest area results in the loss of habitat which in turn weakens not only the ecosystems and their ecological functions, but a whole social, economic and cultural environment.

These phenomena are currently resulting in a rural exodus due to the impossibility of cultural and livestock farming, displacement of populations from the south to the centre and north regions, water scarcity, food insecurity and malnutrition, especially in the south and south-east of the country, land degradation, biodiversity loss, coastal erosion, sea-level rise, damage to infrastructure and assets and threats to livelihoods, all of which threaten national security.

It is important to mention that Madagascar is one of the few countries which have enshrined environmental protection in its current Constitution (11 December 2010). The Preamble of the Constitution actually states that Madagascar is "convinced of the exceptional importance of the wealth of fauna, flora and mineral resources with strong specificities that nature has endowed Madagascar and that it is important to preserve for future generations".

It is in this regard that Madagascar has adopted its climate mitigation and adaptation measures in addition to the enhancement of socio-economic development and to the fight against poverty.

Climate Change Mitigation and Adaptation Measures in Madagascar

Climate mitigation and adaptation are two strategies for addressing climate change. On one hand, "Climate Change Mitigation refers to efforts to reduce or prevent emission of greenhouse gases. Mitigation can mean using new technologies and renewable energies, making older equipment more energy efficient, or changing management practices or consumer behavior."[10]

On the other hand, "Adaptation to climate change refers to adjustment in natural or human systems in response to actual or expected climatic stimuli or their effects, which moderates harm or exploits beneficial opportunities (IPCC 2001)."[11]

Climate mitigation derives from the Kyoto Protocol, adopted in 1997[12] which aimed to operationalise the United Nations Framework Convention on Climate Change (UNFCCC) by committing industrialised countries and economies in transition to limit and reduce greenhouse gases (GHG) emissions (5 per cent against 1990 levels over the five-year period of 2008-2012) in accordance with agreed individual targets. The Convention itself only asks countries to adopt policies and measures on mitigation and to report periodically.[13] Madagascar is classified as a carbon sink country which implies that it still has "Reservoirs or locations that sequester or store a greater amount of carbon dioxide than they release. Major carbon sinks include forests and oceans."[14]

The Kyoto Protocol is also designed to assist countries in adapting to the climate impacts of change and facilitates the elaboration and development of techniques that can help increase resilience to the effects of climate change.

Facing the need to adapt to these effects of climate change, the Government of Madagascar adopted the National Policy to Combat Climate Change (PNLCC) in 2011 and revised it in 2019. The Policy aims to manage climate change effectively by reducing greenhouse gas emissions and strengthening carbon sinks through reforestation on a large scale and use of renewable energy resources, among other things, so that its adverse effects on development sectors are minimised. It has also been drafted to enhance action to combat climate change and to serve as a reference for agricultural modernisation, improvements in agricultural yields, restoration and strengthening of ecosystem services, etc. Besides, the Policy provides guidance in the fight against climate change and encourages investors and technical and financial partners (TFPs) to work in the field of climate change.

In 2019, a National Action Plan to Combat Climate Change (PANLCC) was developed to implement the policy (PNLCC). The National Action Plan targets to identify prioritise and promote appropriate national measures taking into account the country's real needs to reduce greenhouse gas emissions and strengthen its capacity to adapt to climate change.[15]

Furthermore, the National Adaptation Plan (PNA) was finalised in 2021 and is targeted at serving as the strategic framework towards medium- and long-term priority actions and for accountability of all stakeholders while identifying appropriate measures adapted to national realities. The National Adaptation Plan isstructured around three main strategic axes defined as follows:

Strategic axis 1: Climate change adaptation governance strengthening and adaptation mainstreaming into planning activities;

Strategic axis 2: Implementing priority sectoral action programmes (agriculture-livestock and fishing, water resources, public health, biodiversity and forestry, coastal areas, infrastructure and spatial planning, risk and disaster management and housing and new cities);

Strategic axis 3: Financing adaptation to climate change.

The PNA also proposes 12 structuring programmes:[16]

- Establishment of a green belt to strengthen the fight against desertification and the resilience to climate change;
- Strengthening the adaptation of the agricultural sector and the resilience of rural populations in the Great South;
- Strengthening the resilience of rural populations through the development and organisation of export chains;
- Strengthening the adaptation of the fishing sector and developing alert systems and associated action plans;
- Improving access to drinking water in urban and rural areas;
- Strengthening early warning systems for the resilience of the health sector to climate change;
- Acceleration of reforestation through the operationalisation of the REDD+ mechanism[17] and the development of ecosystem services;
- Improvement of the conservation of natural forests and the management of protected areas integrating the development of climate refuge zones in the interior and in the peripheries;
- Protection of coastal infrastructure and economic activities (including tourism) against rise in sea-level;
- Improved cyclone early warning systems, as part of a regional effort in the Indian Ocean;
- Development of resilient rice fields that emit less methane;
- Optimisation of the resilience of new cities and sustainable and innovative housing for the modernisation of Madagascar.

Concerning the "Improved cyclone early warning systems", the five island States (Comoros, Madagascar, Mauritius, La Réunion/France and Seychelles), as members of the Indian Ocean Commission (IOC), have developed the HYDROMET project to strengthen the resilience and adaptive capacity of regional and national communities to the impacts of climate change. The French Development Agency (AFD) and the European Union, through the Intra-ACP Clim-SA programme, fund this project. There are three components of the project: 1) strengthening climate, meteorological and hydrological monitoring networks; 2) strengthening climate, weather and hydrological forecasting systems and service delivery; and 3) strengthening national and regional capacities in climate modeling, forecasting and early warning systems.[18]

Regarding the "development of resilient rice fields" programme, the United Nations Environment Programme (UNEP) and other partners were working to build resilience to the effects of climate change in the rice production sector. The project is comprised of three components: 1) strengthening of technical and scientific capacities; 2) implementation of a rice production cycle that is resilient and adapted; and 3) leveraging policy change in the rice sector. The project was implemented in the Alaotra-Mangoro region, the primary rice production area in Madagascar and was funded by the "Adaptation Fund".[19]

As a Least Developed Country (LDC), Madagascar relies on international funds and partners to finance those programmes, which require substantial funding. Financing is a real issue for Madagascar; so far, the European Union is the main funder of the country for climate change issues.

Despite that, Madagascar is still keen on complying with climate change instruments.

Madagascar and the Environmental Multilateral Instruments

Various multilateral environmental instruments have been adopted since the Stockholm Declaration on Environmental Protection in 1972, following international awareness of climate change. The Earth Summit, which took place in Rio de Janeiro on 9 May 1992, adopted the United Nations Framework Convention on Climate Change (UNFCCC). The Convention entered into force on 21 March 1994 and aims to limit human activities on the environment, in order to stabilise greenhouse gas concentrations in the atmosphere. Thereafter, the Kyoto Protocol was adopted on 11 December 1997 to limit greenhouse gas emissions, but the Protocol did not enter into force until 16 February 2005. An essential step was taken in that direction on 12 December 2015, when 196 Parties adopted the Paris Climate Agreement, which is the result of the Paris Conference on Climate Change, known as COP21. It entered into force on 4 November 2016. Its main goal is to hold "the increase in the global average temperature to well below 2°C above pre-industrial levels" and pursue efforts "to limit the temperature increase to 1.5°C above pre-industrial levels."[20]

Even though Madagascar is a low emitter of greenhouse gas, it is one of the first victims of the effects of climate change. Aware of this situation, the country has emphasised its willingness to contribute to the international effort to combat climate change by honouring its commitments to the UNFCCC. Madagascar has ratified the UNFCCC and the subsequent instruments through:

- Law No. 98-020 of 2 December 1998 authorising the ratification of the UNFCCC and its implementing Decree No. 98-168 of 18 December 1998.
- Law No. 2003-009 of 3 September 2003 authorising the ratification of the Kyoto Protocol to the UNFCCC and Decree No. 2003-009 of 3 September 2003, ratifying it.
- Law 2014-022 of 10 December 2014 authorising the ratification of the Doha Amendment to the Kyoto Protocol and Decree No. 2015-701 of 20 April 2015, ratifying it.
- Law No. 2016-019 of 30 June 2016, authorising the ratification of the Paris Agreement of the United Nations Framework Convention on Climate Change.

Consequent to such international commitments to tackle climate change and in order to enable conditions that are conducive to sustainable development, Madagascar adopted different texts and policies at the national level, notably:

- The National Adaptation Plan to Climate Change-PNACC (2021);
- The National Policy to Combat Climate Change-PNLCC (2011);
- The consideration of climate change as part of the risks related to the environment in Law No. 2015-003 of 20 February 2015 on the updated Malagasy Environment Charter;
- The integration of risk and disaster management in climate change adaptation, in Law No. 2015-031 of 22 February 2016 on the National Risk and Disaster Management Policy (PNGRC); and
- The recognition of issues related to climate change on the sustainability of development in Decree No. 2015-1308 of 22 September 2015 setting the National Environment Policy for Sustainable Development (PNEDD).

However, Madagascar is conscious that climate treaties have only been partially implemented by member states. This is the reason why the scope of multilateral instruments in tackling climate change is so limited.

Limits of Multilateralism in Tackling Climate Change

Multilateralism, as opposed to unilateralism or bilateralism, is a "form of cooperation between at least three states"...involving "adherence to a common political project based on the respect of shared system of norms and values".[21] Most of the time, this kind of cooperation is institutionalised through an international organisation. The United Nations has served as the torchbearer of a multilateral system since its founding.

Multilateralism has existed since the 19th century in the Western world. It started with the Concert of Europe, or the 'System of Congresses', notably the 1815 Congress of Vienna, convened to discuss and agree on the new organisation of Europe after the end of the Napoleonic Wars. Many other ad hoc Congresses were convened in order to resolve issues peacefully between European States. This was followed by the creation of international public unions, the first experience of permanent international institutions, which dealt mainly with technical and non-political issues. Their solution required cooperation between States.

After the First World War, the League of Nations was created in an attempt to prevent another war. Unfortunately, the League of Nations failed to prevent the Second World War and the victors of this war replaced it by the United Nations Organisation (UNO) in 1945. From then on, international organisations have developed in different sectors depending on the scope and subject.[22]

So far, the UNEP is the UN body that deals with environment matters. "UNEP's mission is to inspire, inform, and enable nations and peoples to improve their quality of life without compromising that of future generations."[23] According to the Nairobi Declaration on the Role and Mandate of the United Nations Environmental Program, "the role of UNEP was to be the leading global environmental authority that sets the global environmental agenda, promotes the coherent implementation of the Environmental dimension of sustainable development within the UN system, and serves as an authoritative advocate for the global environment."[24]

Unfortunately, there is growing criticism against the UNEP as it has encountered some difficultyin meeting its goals due to its internal limits, principally its designation and its mandate and due to the shortcomings of the UNFCCC and implementation of its subsequent instruments.

The fact that UNEP was created as a programme as opposed to a Specialised Agency has affected its performance given that programmes have the least independence and authority in the UN hierarchy. Consequently, it is challenging for the UNEP to build its authority over other UN entities dealing with the environment or other international organisations. This is the case with the World Trade Organisation (WTO), which has called into question environmental rules deemed incompatible with its own. Moreover, unlike other UN bodies, the UNEP relies on the voluntary contributions of the UN member states, which weakens its financial stability and results in a lack of funding to finance its operations.

Besides, the has limitations on agenda setting, on monitoring, assessment and reporting and on capacity development. On agenda setting, the UNEP has grappled to organise the various environmental activities of other international organisations and to coordinate multilateral environmental agreements. On monitoring, assessment and reporting, the UNEP's, eight divisions are allowed to monitor, assess and report on environmental issues, which generate redundancies. On capacity development, normally, the UNEP's mission is to enable countries to streamline environmental sustainability into development and investment planning through enhancement of technical capacity and strengthening of countries environment institutions. However, since the States expressed their desire to see a less normative role and more concrete action from the UNEP, the latter has shifted from its strengths: "information provision, development of common norms and principles, and institutional capacity development."[25]

Moreover, the UNEP's instruments – precisely the UNFCCC, the Kyoto Protocol and the Paris Agreement – are far from meeting their targets of stabilising greenhouse gas emissions and averting climate change threats because of shortcomings of their implementation. Indeed, high economic and social cost of implementation is one of the sources of the material inability of States to comply with their international obligations. Madagascar is one such country as it struggles to find funds in order to execute its planned activities related to its commitments. Furthermore, some developing countries have a hard time in fulfilling their transparency and accountability duties because of lack of staff capacity to write reports. Additionally, instead of cooperating among themselves, countries tend to turn inward due torise in nationalism or economic downturn, as was the case during the COVID-19 pandemic, making it difficult to secure domestic buy-in, which is necessary for countries to comply with their international duties. With regard to equity, geopolitical and economic changes have widened inequalities between developed and developing countries, with a risk of preventing the international community from achieving its emissions-reduction goals towards limitation of the global rise in temperature. Intensive action and mobilising support for mitigation, adaptation, and loss and damage are challenging and weakening the principle of equity between States.[26]

Meanwhile, who are those left behind due to this lack of implementation and what impact does it have on the multilateral environmental instruments?

Most of the time, Least Developed Countries are the first victims of the lack of implementation of the multilateral environmental instruments, as they are hit the hardest by the impact of climate change. Moreover, without necessarily leading to the rejection of multilateral instruments, this absence of implementation increases the loss of interest in and marginalisation of these multilateral instruments. An important milestone would be reached if the loss and damage fund, started during the last Conference of the Parties (CoP27) in Sharm el-Sheikh (2022) was set up and operationalised.

In this case, will cooperation on non-traditional issues such as climate adaptability strengthen multilateral actions? That is part of some innovative solutions that have been proposed in these last years.

Proposals for Innovative Solutions

Our world today, characterised by complex issues needs better cooperation among States. Interdependence is already a reality that no country could afford to ignore even if the state of current cooperation militates in favour of reformed multilateralism.

Reform of multilateralism

Throughout the UN's history, reform efforts have been made and they were associated with the Secretaries-General. However, calls for reforms in the UN intensified since the late 1990s.

In 2000, after taking office, UN Secretary-General Kofi Annan decided to reform the UN through, among others, a reachout to civil society and the private sector. It was also during his term in office that the Millenium Declaration was made and included measurable targets: the Millenium Development Goals, aiming to combat poverty, hunger, disease and environmental degradation. In September

2003, Annan considered the time to be ripe to assess the UN's situation and appointed a High-Level Panel on threats, Challenges and Change, to address various issues such as collective security, development, climate change, terrorism, establishment of a Human Rights Council and Security Council reform. In March 2006, after convening a High-Level Panel on UN System-Wide Coherence in Areas of Development, Humanitarian Assistance, and Environment, the Secretary-General submitted a new Report: *Investing in the United Nations: For a Stronger Organisation Worldwide*. The Report included 23 proposals on managerial responsibility to address the challenges following the wide expansion of UN activities in the fields of peacekeeping, human rights and development.[27]

Then, on 31 May 2011, UN Secretary-General Ban Ki-moon appointed M. Atul Khare to lead the Change Management Team (CMT) with the mandate of streamlining and improving the efficiency of the UN body. The CMT was tasked to guide the implementation of a reform agenda at the UN that began with devising of a wide-ranging plan to streamline activities, increasing accountability and ensuring the organisation was more effective and efficient in delivering its many mandates and protocols.[28]

In 2005, a cooperation project known as the "Four Nations Initiative (4NI)", named after the 4 initiator-countries (Chile, South Africa, Sweden and Thailand), was created to contribute to the efforts of reforming governance and management systems and structures of the UN Secretariat.

More recently, since the beginning of his term in January 2017, UN Secretary-General Antonio Guterres has proposed reform in the UN in three fields: development, management and peace and security.

Development reform is intended to best position the UN to deliver on sustainable development goals and to better serve the people. Management reform is meant to achieve the decentralisation of decision-making authority, simplification and streamlining of policy and processes, and strengthened accountability and transparency; whereas peace and security reform is designed to make the pillar more coherent, pragmatic, nimble and effective, capable of collaboration with partners across the UN system and outside it, to prevent violent conflict.[29]

Apart from these institutional challenges, multilateral cooperation is also facing an efficiency crisis that must be addressed. Therefore, it is the right time to formulate an agenda for a new multilateralism in line with our era, which will be more effective in coping with the current global challenges, especially the non-traditional ones like climate adaptability. It is in the interest of States to cooperate for better management of the environment. Nature does not make any distinctions between developed and developing countries nor does it bother with the principles of sovereignty, borders, national interests or political alliances. The whole world must mobilise around environmental protection which can federate all the States towards a common goal.

The UNEP, whose foundations were laid at the Human Environment Conference held in Stockholm in 1972, is the leading global authority on the environment. Its headquarters are located in Nairobi, Kenya.

The UNEP's work is focused on helping countries transition to low-carbon and resource-efficient economies, strengthening environmental governance law, safeguarding ecosystems, and providing evidence-based data to inform policy decisions.[30] Given the scope of the UNEP's mandate and following the publication of the *Fourth Assessment Report of the Intergovernmental Panel on Climate Change (IPCC)* in February 2007, a "Paris Call for Action" read out by the French President Jacques Chirac, and supported by 46 countries, called for the replacement of the United Nations Environment Programme (UNEP) by a new and more powerful United Nations Environment Organisation (UNEO), to be modelled on the World Health Organisation (WHO).[31] So far, this call has not received a favourable response even if the creation of a UNEO would enhance the current environmental system. Actually, if the Programme becomes an international organisation and is granted a Specialised Agency Status, it would have budgetary autonomy so that it could determine its own programming. Besides, the core issue related to budget instability would be resolved because member states' contributions into the budget of the new organisation would be assessed thus predictably. Consequently, the Organisation would be able to pursue and achieve its planned activities. Like other Specialised Agencies, it would have an executive organ, an elected Director General, an Executive Board and observers who could be other international organisations or representatives of civil society, whereas its members could be different from those of the UN. In November 2006, the Secretary-General's High-level Panel on UN System-wide Coherence in the Areas of Development, Humanitarian Assistance, and the Environment recommended that 'UNEP should be upgraded and have real authority as the environmental policy pillar of the UN system'.[32]

Moreover, we also need a multilateralism that is more legitimate, not only because of its effectiveness but also because of its inclusiveness and fairness. According to Patricia Espinoza, Executive Secretary of the UNFCCC: "Inclusivity is the only way forward ...with respect to climate change, which is not a regional or continental phenomenon, but is felt globally."[33] At the UN Climate Change Conference "inclusive multilateralism" is being introduced by bringing in more groups such as youth, women, indigenous groups and many others to the table. Madagascar is in favour of a fair and representative multilateralism that includes the voice of all and responds to the needs of all, including the most vulnerable and future generations. This preference has already been realised through the composition of Malagasy delegations attending the last two CoPs (26 in Glasgow and 27 in Sharm-El-Sheikh), when a growing number of representatives of civil society and the private sector were part of the said delegations.

UN reform is a crucial part of a new multilateralism dealing with climate change. With the establishment of a multipolar world, new alliances appear in international negotiations between Emerging and Least Developed Countries (LDCs) which results in strengthening of South-South and triangular cooperation.

Strengthening South-South and triangular cooperation

In parallel with the reform of multilateralism, and to respond effectively to the accumulation of natural disasters due to climate change, we must radically change the way we think and act. If countries act individually, they will be unable to provide appropriate responses to various global issues and challenges. Cooperation is therefore essential.

To enhance equity-based international cooperation on climate change, it is imperative that developed countries help provide means of implementation, including finance, technology transfer and capacity building or development to developing countries in order to back the climate actions, and consequently, eradicate poverty and enable sustainable development in those countries.

We must also promote partnerships between countries of the South as well as triangular cooperation within the framework of platforms such as the ISA (International Solar Alliance) by promoting access to green technology for LDCs, for example. The ISA was conceived as a joint effort by India and France to mobilise efforts against climate change through deployment of solar energy solutions. It was conceptualised on the sidelines of the COP21 to the UNFCCC held in Paris in 2015. The ISA strives to develop and deploy cost-effective and transformational energy solutions powered by the sun to help member countries develop low-carbon growth trajectories, with particular focus on delivering impact in countries categorised as LDCs and the Small Island Developing States (SIDS).[34]

South-South cooperation refers to development cooperation between fellow countries of the Global South[35] with the idea of sharing technological capabilities, experiences and knowhow for their mutual benefit. As an important number of countries in the South have advanced in the fields of technology capabilities and knowhow and learned to exploit the power of science, technology and innovation, a large part of the South is now able and ready to contribute to its own development. Subsequently, innovative, tailor-made, potentially transferable and adaptable solutions have increased considerably to allow the South countries to face their development challenges. This situation has changed the views towards developing countries, which are now seen as sources of technology innovations and knowhow and not only as recipients.

Triangular cooperation, for its part, includes a developed country partner supporting South-South initiatives.[36] Generally, Governments remain the foremost partners in this kind of cooperation. Most of the time, partners share knowledge and implement projects to achieve a common goal: development promotion and poverty reduction.

The Buenos Aires Plan of Action of 1978 (UN, 1978) made the first implicit reference to triangular cooperation in recommending that developed countries "support...technical cooperation among developing countries" and that "all the United Nations organisations should play a prominent role as promoters and catalysts of technical cooperation among developing countries (TCDC)." The term "triangular cooperation" originated in 1980, when the Independent Commission on International Development issues, chaired by former German Chancellor Willy Brandt, suggested the development of triangular cooperation schemes in the context of economic cooperation between developing countries (Chaturvedi, 2012).[37]

In practice, the involvement of three categories of partners is a key to triangular cooperation: one provider of development cooperation or an international organisation who share their development cooperation experience and provide funds, one or more pivotal countries, the providers of South-South cooperation who promote a sharing of knowledge and experience or implement development cooperation projects and one or more beneficiary countries. Thus, triangular cooperation allows the combination of resources, knowhow, skills and expertise from both developed and developing countries. However, ownership, transparency and accountability should govern relations between partners in order to impact their partnership.

South-South and triangular cooperation are increasingly viewed as a complement to North-South cooperation because developing countries while working together can find solutions to common and shared issues. Moreover, South-South and triangular cooperation is included in the UN Sustainable Development Goal 17, which reads, "Strengthen the means of implementation and revitalise the Global Partnership for Sustainable Development", with its 17.9 target which aims to: "Enhance international support for implementing effective and targeted capacity-building in developing countries to support national plans to implement all the sustainable development goals, including through North-South, South-South and triangular cooperation."[38]

In this regard, the UNEP has included South-South and triangular cooperation as a key modality of its medium-term strategy (2010-2013) and established a focal point to oversee implementation. The UNEP regularly promotes triangular cooperation, but it recognises, that, "[in] terms of financial investment and frequency, it is clear that South-South and triangular cooperation are still rather the exception than the rule in the Convention on Biological Diversity. Increasing and enhancing South-South and triangular cooperation is, therefore, a critical element for the success of the Strategic Plan for Biodiversity 2011-2020". The vision of the multi-year plan released in May 2012 is as follows: "By 2020, effective South-South and triangular cooperation will be used in the Convention on Biological Diversity and the Carthagena Protocol on Biosafety, as a complement to North-South cooperation and in support of the Convention's Strategic Plan for Biodiversity 2011-2020 and the Millennium Development Goals, in order to enhance human well-being, promote development and eradicate poverty" (UNEP, 2010).[39]

As an example, Madagascar, along with its eight fellow-Nairobi Convention member states (Kenya, Comoros, France, Mauritius, Mozambique, Seychelles, Tanzania and South Africa), benefited from South-South cooperation through a project entitled "Implementation of the Strategic Action Programme for the protection of the Western Indian Ocean from land-based sources and activities" (WIOSAP). This project intended "to reduce impacts from land-based sources and activities and sustainably manage critical coastal-riverine ecosystems through the implementation of the WIO-SAP priorities with the support of partnerships at national and regional levels."[40] The project was developed under the auspices of UNEP-GEF (Global Environment Facility) and implemented by the Nairobi Convention Secretariat. It started in 2016 and ended in 2021.

Madagascar is convinced that South-South cooperation is the way to achieve its development results. At the same time, it intends to strengthen bilateral cooperation for example with India, particularly on the question of climate change mitigation and adaptation, and other environment-related issues through exchange of knowledge and information and access to Indian expertise and experiences in the field of green technology and energy transition, among other bilateral cooperation mechanisms.

Conclusion

Multilateralism is not doomed to disappear, because it represents an important foundation of international relations at a time when the world is facing multiple challenges and threats that cannot be solved by a single or few States, no matter how powerful they might be. Certainly, multilateralism is in decline. Nevertheless, it is unimaginable to live in a world without a minimum of rules-based institutions. This implies that reforms must be undertaken to fit in the new context of a multipolar world; in particular, new ways of implementing the multilateral instruments must be found and agreed upon. In fact, the decline of multilateralism is the result but not the cause of the international disorder we are experiencing today.

This chapter focused on the multilateral approach to climate adaptation and mitigation through the case of Madagascar. The analysis showcased how climate change has impacted various sectors undermining the country's development and threatening its national security. The chapter discussed climate adaptation and mitigation measures that Madagascar has adopted to comply with the multilateral environment instruments while executing these measures, for their major part, requires outside support to be fulfilled. The possible reasons why multilateralism has limitations in tackling climate change are principally attributed to its implementation. In order to allow multilateral instruments to meet their goals, innovative solutions are proposed like reforms of the multilateral system. The replacement of the UNEP by a UNEO would be helpful to effectively deal with climate change. In this context, it is also crucial to underline that cooperation between countries and key stakeholders is critical, especially through enhancement of the South-South and triangular cooperation. Eventually, the current tasks incumbent on Madagascar with regard to climate change adaptation and mitigation, pertain to raising funds to help it carry out actions to achieve its development targets along with effective implementation of the various national policies, programmes and action plans, including the identification and alleviation of the structural constraints and obstacles to effective implementation of the objectives.

NOTES

1 "Madagascar en chiffres", INSTAT 2023, at INSTAT Madagascar - Institut National de la Statistique (Accessed 27 May 2023) – hereafter 'INSTAT Madagascar'.

2 République de Madagascar-Ministère de l'Environnement et du Développement Durable, "Plan National d'Adaptation au Changement Climatique (PNA) Madagascar", December 2021, p. 8 – hereafter 'PNA – 2021 National Climate Change Adaptation Plan'.

3 République de Madagascar-Ministère de l'Environnement et du Développement Durable, "Politique Nationale de Lutte contre le Changement Climatique Révisée", 9 September 2021, p. 1 – hereafter '2021 Revised National Policy on Combating Climate Change'.

4 INSTAT Madagascar, no. 1.

5 Nations Unies, ONU Info, "Madagascar: une grave sécheresse pourrait provoquer la 1ère famine au monde due au changement climatique", 22 October 2021 at Madagascar: une grave sécheresse pourrait provoquer la 1ère famine au monde due au changement climatique | ONU Info (Accessed 18 March 2023).

6 PNA – 2021 *National Climate Change Adaptation Plan*, no. 2, p. 11.

7 Ibid.

8 Ibid.

9 Ibid.

10 United Nations Environment Program (UNEP), "Mitigation", UNEP at Mitigation, UNEP - UN Environment Programme (Accessed 19 March 2023).

11 United Nations Environment Programme (UNEP), Law and Environment Assistance platform (LEAP), "Climate change adaptation" at Climate Change Adaptation, UNEP Law and Environment Assistance Platform (Accessed 26 May 2023).

12 Adopted on 11 December 1997 and entered into force on 16 February 2005. Madagascar ratified the Protocol on 3 September 2003.

13 United Nations Climate Change, "What is the Kyoto Protocol?" at What is the Kyoto Protocol?, UNFCCC (Accessed 19 March 2023).

14 UN-REDD PROGRAMME, "Carbon sinks", 2023, at https://www.un-redd.org/glossary/carbon-sinks (Accessed 30 May 2023).

15 République de Madagascar-Ministère de l'Environnement et du Développement Durable, "Plan d'Action National de Lutte contre le Changement Climatique (PANLCC) Madagascar", November 2019, p. 3.

16 PNA – 2021 *National Climate Change Adaptation Plan*, pp. 87-88.

17 A mechanism is hereby defined to support the voluntary efforts of developing country Parties to mitigate climate change by reducing emissions from deforestation and forest degradation, promoting conservation and the sustainable management of forests, and to enhancing forest carbon stocks. (UNFCCC, "Article for the REDD+ Mechanism", Papua New Guinea, May 2009 at https://unfccc.int/files/kyoto_protocol/application/pdf/papuanewguinea070509.pdf (Accessed 27 May 2023).

18 Commission de l'Océan Indien, "Projet HYDROMET de la COI", at https://www.commisionoceanindien.org/portfolio-items/hydromet/ (Accessed 26 May2023).

19 "Ecosystem-based Adaptation in Madagascar", at Ecosystem-based Adaptation in Madagascar, UNEP - UN Environment Programme (Accessed 26 May 2023).

20 United Nations Climate Change, "The Paris Agreement" at https://unfccc.int/process-and-meetings/the-paris-agreement (Accessed 30 May 2023).

21 United Nations, "International Day of Multilateralism and Diplomacy for Peace, 24 April" at https://www.un.org/en/observances/multilateralism-for-peace-day (Accessed 30 May 2023).

22 Enclyclopedia.com, "International Organization", 23 May 2018 at https://www.encyclopedia.com/social-sciences-and-law/political-science-and-government/international-organizations/international-organization#:~:text=Its%20emergence%20stems%20partly%20from,public%20administrative%20unions%2C%20established%20for (Accessed 30 May 2023).

23 UNEP, "About the United Nations Environment Programme", at https://www.unep.org/about-us (Accessed 27 May 2023).

24 United Nations, Governing Council of the United Nations Environment Programme, "Nineteenth Session, Nairobi, 27 January 1997-7 February 1997", UNEP/GC.19/34, 17 June1997, p. 55 at https://wedocs.unep.org/bitstream/handle/20.500.11822/17274/97_GC19_proceedings.pdf?sequence=23 (Accessed 31 May 2023).

25 Maria Ivanova, "Assessing UNEP as Anchor Institution for the Global Environment: Lessons for the UNEO Debate", Working Paper No.05/01, Yale University, May 24, 2005at https://www.academia.edu/7835529/Assessing_UNEP_as_Anchor_Institution_for_the_Global_Environment_Lessons_for_the_UNEO_Debate (Accessed 30 May 2023).

26 Yamide Dagnet, Katia Simeonova, Nathan Cogswell, Mima Holt, Tony La Vina, Nate Warszawski, "Toward More Effective Implementation of the Paris Agreement: Learning from 30 Years of Experience", *World Resources Iinstitute*, Washington, DC, October 2021 at https://files.wri.org/d8/s3fs-public/2021-10/toward-more-effective-implementation-of-the-paris-agreement-learning-from-30-years-of-experience.pdf?VersionId=biQB1QIcZBqJx9TnhZqBLQHrsHUTllfq (Accessed 31 May 2023).

27 Jean-pierre Cot, "United Nations, Reform", Oxford Public International Law, *Max Plank Encyclopedias of International Law*, March 2010, Oxford University Press, 2023, p. 9.

28 UNITED Nations, "Secretary-General Appoints Atul Khare of India Leader of His Change Management Team", 31 May 2011at https://press.un.org/en/2011/sga1295.doc.htm#:~:text=The%20 Change%20Management%20Team%20will,the%20delivery%20of%20its%20mandates. (Accessed 27 May 2023).

29 United Nations, "United to Reform" at https://reform.un.org/ (Accessed 22 May 2023).

30 UNEP, no. 23.

31 Alister Doyle, "46 Nations Call for Tougher U.N. Environment Role", *Reuters*, 3 February 2007 at https://www.reuters.com/article/us-globalwarming-appeal-idUSL0335755320070203 (Accessed 30 May 2023).

32 Secretary-General's High-level Panel on UN System-wide Coherence in the Areas of Development, Humanitarian Assistance, and the Environment, "Delivering as one", A/61/583, 20 November 2006 at https://documents-dds-ny.un.org/doc/UNDOC/GEN/N06/621/41/PDF/N0662141.pdf?OpenElement (Accessed 30 May 2023).

33 "Excerpts to the Address of Ms. Patricia Espinoza, Executive Secretary, United Nations Framework Convention on Climate Change" at https://wsds.teriin.org/2022/assets/pdf/plenaries/summary/Multilateralism-final-14062022.pdf (Accessed 22 March 2023).

34 International Solar Alliance (ISA), "About ISA", at https://isolaralliance.org/about/background (Accessed 18 March 2023).

35 World Intellectual Property Organization (WIPO), "Developing Together: South-South and Triangular Cooperation with WIPO", Geneva at https://www.wipo.int/edocs/pubdocs/en/

wipo_southsouth_flyer.pdf (Accessed 18 March 2023).

36 Ibid.

37 The Development Assistance Committee, "Triangular co-operation: What's the literature telling us?", *OECD*, May 2013, pp.13-33 at https://www.oecd.org/dac/dac-global-relations/OECD%20Triangluar%20Co-operation%20Literature%20Review%20June%202013.pdf (Accessed 22 May 2023).

38 United Nations, *Department of Economic and Social Affairs*, "Sustainable Development, Multi-stakeholder Partnerships" at https://sdgs.un.org/topics/capacity-development (Accessed 30 May 2023).

39 Ibid.

40 Nairobi Convention, "WIOSAP Project" at https://www.nairobiconvention.org/nairobi-convention-projects/implementation-of-the-strategic-action-programme-for-the-protection-of-the-western-indian-ocean-from-land-based-sources-and-activities-wiosap/about-wiosap/ (Accessed 27 May 2023).

CHAPTER 18

Devising Multilateral Approach to Non-Traditional Security Challenges: Climate Change, Mitigation and Governance

Felix Wandwe

Introduction

The shifting security paradigm from the end of Cold War era has increasingly accommodated non-military strategies which are commonly labelled as 'non-traditional' – threats to the broader security phenomenon. Non-Traditional Security (NTS) encompasses myriad human security concerns such as climate change, shortage of food and resources such as energy, infectious diseases, natural disasters, transnational crime, mass migration, human and drug trafficking. NTS challenges are defined as challenges to the survival and well-being of people and States that arise primarily out of non-military sources, such as climate change, infectious diseases, natural disasters, irregular migration, food shortages, smuggling of persons, drug trafficking and other forms of transnational crime.

The fact that the threats are transnational in nature with regard to their origins and effects, non-traditional security threats do not stem from competition between States or shifts in the balance of power, but are often defined in political and socio-economic terms. In the course of devising climate change, mitigation and governance strategies for African countries, States need to collaborate for bilateral and multilateral ties[1]. Tanzania, the East African country which borders and connects with more than 20 countries in Africa, is facing the widely reported nion-traditional security threats with strategic implications, like many other countries in the world.

Non-traditional security is generally transnational in scope – neither totally domestic nor purely inter-State – and is transmitted rapidly due to globalisation and the communication revolution. This implies that these non-traditional security threats are much more intimidating than the traditional ones, as they require the national leadership to look not only outwards to cultivate international cooperation, but also inwards, with an open outlook to execute internal socio-economic and political reforms. The fact that national solutions are often inadequate, the non-traditional security threats require regional and multilateral cooperation. Hence countries across the globe are called upon to jointly devise climate change mitigation and governance strategies, including ratifying and adhering to international and regional climate change-related treaties and conventions.

In a majority of African countries, non-traditional security is often perceived as a paradox of various security threats, whose root causes are multi-faceted and multi-dimensional. The view that the region is plagued by instability, conflict and poverty which fuel illicit trade in narcotics and other forms of organised crime, is abundantly visible being widely attributed to climate change-related impacts. With a lot of mixed perspectives, there is no clear consensus in African security literature on the fundamental reasons for instability. This calls for joint initiatives to arrest and curb negative impacts and consequences of climate change- to achieve sustainable livelihoods and a safe planet. This also calls for more academic work to be done to consider and reveal the implications of more effective multilateral approaches towards managing African non-traditional security challenges.

Various changes in international politics have led to alterations in security studies. This includes studies on the end of the Cold War. Modern challenges that are connected to the environment, food, energy, health, development, and other sectors that have usually not been considered as encompassing the security arena, are now at the front-end. They have achieved a greater salience in various discussions aiming to create procedures and processes, some of which are specific to the country and others are bilaterally, regionally and multilaterally agreed upon and implemented among signatory partner countries.

The existing State and regional level engagements to manage NTS challenges in various countries, call for the need to devise more reliable multilateral approaches and strategies to arrest NTS challenges, mainly climate change, mitigation and governance strategies. Besides the case of Tanzania and other East African countries, it has been widely posited that it is high time to embrace both bilateral and multilateral approaches to arrest climate change impacts. In the course of adopting mitigation and governance strategies; a special call is made for ratifying and effectively adhering to international and regional climate change-related treaties and conventions. The subject is part of the very timely debate where climate change issues are costing lives, leading countries into instabilities and turmoil and calling for more effective ways and initiatives to bridge the gap.

Non-Traditional Security Challenges: Recent advances

The evolution of various security dimensions means that security threats are no longer solely defined in military and State terms. This has led to the widening and deepening of the security calculus, such that the terms 'non-traditional security' comes into utmost attention. 'Non-traditional security' encapsulates a variety of issues and critiques of orthodox security approaches and alternative security problematics, and many African countries including Tanzania recognise non-traditional security in their national security strategies to varying degrees. The non-traditional security agenda is currently dominated by issues including climate change, human trafficking, cyber security and terrorism. This given context of security continues to change and become more complex, hence calling for the strengthened regional cooperation and regional engagement.

Non-traditional security – or non-traditional threats to security – is a broad concept that captures various issues, as it stands as a critique of orthodox approaches to security and an alternative security problematic in these modern times. The subject of non-traditional security spans a wide spectrum of threats to include environmental degradation, irregular migrations, infectious diseases, drug trafficking, terrorism and insurgencies, transnational crimes, water and power shortages and natural disasters. Together with many others implicit ones, these threats are dangerously threatening the human security in various areas of Tanzania and East Africa, as a majority of these countries' population suffers from abject poverty. On the other hand, many scholars would argue that categorising an issue as a security threat would indeed bring with it the attention, effort and resources needed to tackle it, including the wide scope of international engagements.[2]

The widely contended dynamics of non-traditional threats that emerge from globalisation such that the globe opens up a threat to one, is a threat to all in the Universe. This transition in non-traditional security is a product of globalisation. Since the non-traditional security threats are non-military in nature, their transnational scope is indeed neither domestic nor purely inter-State, rather they appear without prior warning, cause colossal losses and transmit rapidly due to globalisation and the communication revolution across countries.

Tanzania, like other countries in the world, experiences the non-traditional security threats like natural calamities and the non-State human actions which cannot be restrained within the geopolitical boundaries and hence affect governments, people, societies and institutions alike within or across the geographical boundaries of a State. As globally agreed, these threats are three-dimensional in nature: first; purely related to the natural disasters like hurricanes, floods and droughts, earthquakes, tidal waves, volcanic eruptions and avalanches. Likewise, it also includes outbursts of communicable diseases like; HIV/AIDS, tuberculosis, SARS, swine flu, etc. The second dimension includes the semi-natural threats that affect the essential resources and economic conditions of the States, like water shortages, scarcity of energy resources, poverty and unemployment, etc. The third category however is purely manmade and appears in the form of terrorism, deforestation, transnational crimes, insurgencies, trafficking in illegal drugs, weapons and rural-urban migration, etc. Natural disasters and manmade security crises can potentially lead to mass migrations and displacements. Indeed, the non-traditional security threats have inextricably linked the fates of even those States that are not geographically contiguous to each other. These threats can affect their sovereignty and territorial integrity as well as the safety of their respective societies.[3]

The need for incorporating international engagements in the course of arresting the situation, both local and regional politics are useful instruments in due course. In the prevailing divergences in the world, non-traditional threats affect a portion of a State engulfing the region and ultimately, global security. Since no State can handle the multiple non-traditional threats alone, therefore, in the contemporary world, every nation state requires regional and global cooperation to secure itself. These threats are eventually endangering human security and development in the region. This among other things calls for an in-depth examination of Tanzanian perspectives towards reformed multilateralism in the era of the Indo-Pacific, hence preparing for the platform for devising a multilateral approach to non-traditional security challenges: climate change mitigation and governance.

Scope and Situational Setting Regarding Non-Traditional Security Challenges: Climate Change

The emerging environmental and ecological security paradigm focuses more heavily on the broad array of challenges presented by Nature in various countries across the world. Ecological security grows out of the continually evolving relationships between human societies and an ever-changing physical environment that sustains all forms of life. A central assumption inherent in this new way of thinking about security is that threats are just as likely to come from Nature as they are from other people. The fact that the relationship between climate change and conflict has received copious attention during the past few years, means that climate change related effects are apparently increasing and disturbing the stability of developing and emerging countries.

In a majority of African countries and other developing and emerging countries including Tanzania, climate change impacts are apparent now and are already having negative effects on social and economic development. The two major forms of livelihoods in Tanzania for instance, farmers and livestock herders, are facing the impacts of climate change as their activities are directly hampered by the extended drought and shortage of rainfall. The effects of these changes threaten not only human security in many regions worldwide, but also peace and stability. In this case environmental issues are highly becoming a part of the political trends since it takes the form of a majority of grassroots opposition to environmental degradation and exploitation, inter-ethnic competition for land, water and other resources.

The scope and situational setting of this study is based on Tanzania's reflection regarding the level of preparedness for combating non-traditional threats. The need is for devising a multilateral approach to non-traditional security challenges, mainly climate change mitigation and governance in the country and the region, and its inhabitants now have to pay for its costs: environmental degradation; water shortages and pollution; health problems including high rates of infant mortality, respiratory illnesses. Climate change has already caused a shortage of water resources in various areas in Africa and Tanzania in particular.

Findings and Discussion

Current General Security Situation in Tanzania

Tanzania has abundant natural resources, including minerals, agricultural land, water, natural vegetation and wildlife. The population in both urban and rural areas depends heavily on ecosystem services that provide a clean, regular water supply, fertile soils and trees for fuel, building construction and fencing. In addition, many rural Tanzanians draw on important food sources in the form of wild foods when agricultural produce is unavailable. These vital resources and services have been degraded over the years through various human activities.

Climate change will accelerate the degradation and its impact will be greater. Tanzania's soils, for example, have been increasingly eroded through annual ploughing, burning for land clearing, deforestation and poor grazing management.

Lack of control of water that runs-off on slopes and uncontrolled open-cast mining in some areas have added to the degradation. Deforestation has become a major problem in recent years as forests have been cleared in preparation for agriculture, for fencing and for use as firewood, mainly for tobacco curing and brick-making. Following the rapid population pressure in the country, pressure from human settlements and poaching have decimated natural habitats, wildlife populations, particularly those of endangered species as well as depleting her natural forest cover at a very high rate. This is a serious security concern for Tanzania since the entire economy is based on the natural resources which are plently available in plenty in the natural environmental.

Over the years Tanzania has experienced diverse security threats have been under control of through internal mechanisms as well as because of international engagements. Widely reported security threats include terrorism; organised crime such as fraud, drug trafficking, money laundering, piracy, hostage taking, human trafficking, smuggling, banditry and armed robbery; ethnic, land, political and religious disputes; climate change, global warming and other environmental crisis; cyber crime and cyber security threats; natural and man-made disasters such as accidents, floods, drought; and globalisation among other security threats because of a combination of geographical, regional, historical, political, economic and socio-cultural factors. The security threats in Tanzania are mainly attributed to instabilities in the many neighbouring countries including Congo DRC, Burundi and Mozambique, due to which the spread of security threats becomes easy.

Peace and security, being a national interest and a key objective that Tanzania seeks to advance through foreign policy, justifies the country's pre-occupation with this issue at the expense of other such interests. Insecurity within the country affects the implementation of foreign policy goals in line with the strengthened flow of foreign direct investment from all over the world. The increasing insecurity in the country has affected Tanzania's focus on other foreign policy issues as the government diverts its attention towards efforts to resolve this issue. This means that the country is forced to go for ad hoc policies that are not only short-term in nature, but also have a number of disadvantages in the course of arresting non-traditional security threats including health pandemics and climate change. In addition, the effects of a majority of non-traditional security threats are interconnected with the livelihoods of the country's population including exarcabating food insecurity, poverty and widespread unemployment among the youth, driving a majority of the country's population into a vulnerable situation.

Tanzania has a diverse economy thanks to its amenable climate, abundant resources and moderately educated population. However, the economy is heavily dependent on the availability of water. Her gross domestic product (GDP) has been strongly affected by fluctuating rainfall in the past. During years when rains have been good, the GDP has increased proportionally. During drought years the GDP has fallen. Most agricultural activity is carried out by smallholder farmers, most of whom live in communal farming areas. Mining makes the largest contribution to the economy and is the largest foreign exchange earner, contributing to a large percentage of exports. Tourism, which is dependent on the quality of national parks and wildlife reserves, is an important contributor of foreign currency earnings and employment; this among other things makes environmental and climate security highly strategic parameters for Tanzanian stability.

Environmental and Climate Security in Tanzania

In the course of enumerating the facets of environmental and climate security in Tanzania it was important to reveal the environmental threats. The fact that environmental threats do not respect national boundaries, and no single State or group of States can successfully cope with the environmental threats, calls for a much broader perspective to widen the understanding towards environmental and climate security in the country and region.

The stability of Tanzanian security depends mainly on the availability of favourable climate conditions that offer reliable food supply throughout the year for people to be food secure. The connection between environmental and climate security always poses ruthless threats to human survival from the standpoint of environmental dynamics. Since the beginning of the new millennium, the international security environment has changed dramatically; the well-being and security of States and societies encompasses climate change, food and water scarcity, environmental degradation, pandemics, irregular movement of people, and transnational crimes such as cybersecurity. These threats are improving to be more severe and likely to inflict more harm to a greater number of people than conventional threats of inter-State wars and conflicts. As a consequence, the security concerns of States have changed, compelling them to find new and innovative ways to address the new challenges. These, in turn, have had profound implications on the nature of security cooperation among States, as well as global governance.

Environmental and climate security in Tanzania is mainly based on the threatening climate agenda which is likely to set back all forms of economic productions in Tanzania in two main ways: increasing degradation of the natural environment on which so many of its people depend for their livelihoods, and fluctuating rainfall in Tanzania and beyond its borders, reducing the volume of water in all agricultural zones in the country. The water supply in the country also restricts the generation of hydroelectricity on which all forms of industries depend.

Climate has been at the centre of many security analysts in recent times. It is a new security threat in modern times, such that the change in the climate that is being observed is monitored by the Intergovernmental Panel on Climate Change (IPCC). This is a group of scientists from across the world which, under the coordination of the United Nations, produces Reports assessing global knowledge and evidence about climate change.

Climate change has already caused a shortage of water resources in various areas of Tanzania and Africa at large. Water will become increasingly scarce in the years to come. The emerging environmental and ecological security paradigm focuses heavily on the broad array of challenges presented by Nature. Ecological security grows out of the continually evolving relationships between human societies and an ever-changing physical environment that sustains all forms of life. A central assumption inherent in this new way of thinking about security is that threats to well-being are just as likely to come from Nature as they are from other people. This includes environmental degradation, water shortages and pollution, health problems including high rates of infant mortality, respiratory illnesses and typhoid.

The fact is that all countries including those in Africa, see security threats arising from destabilisation of commercial markets, kleptocratic alliances with governments and security forces, and the manner in which criminal and illegal activity 'undermines the stability of nations, subverting government institutions through corruption and harming citizens worldwide'. Climate change is usually presented as a potential threat multiplier, overstretching the societies' adaptive capacities and creating or exacerbating political instability and violence, possibly to the extent of inter-State and even intra-State conflict. The triggers are assumed to include competition for resources, access to environmental services, and potentially destabilising mass migration flows although those assumptions are subject to geopolitical environment.

According to the Intergovernmental Panel on Climate Change (IPCC), changes in climate are more apparent now and are already having negative effects on the society and economy of developing and emerging countries. The effects of these changes threaten not only human security in many regions worldwide, but also peace and stability. Environmental issues formed part of the political trends during various periods in Tanzania's history and hence posed a number of challenges to Tanzania's authority in the form of grassroots opposition to environmental degradation and exploitation; inter-ethnic competition for land, water and other resources. In all areas, poverty and environmental degradation are linked in a vicious downward spiral in the region. Trans-border environmental problems are developing into trans-border conflicts among East African countries; hence a direct link between environmental degradation, scarcity of resources, competition and conflict for access to scarce resources. To prevent conflict, there needs to be regional environmental cooperation.

Need for taking action to enhance Environmental and Climate Security in Tanzania

Following the need to continuously assess global knowledge and evidence about climate change, the IPCC is responsible for the task. The changes in the climate that are being observed are monitored by the IPCC which comprises a group of scientists from across the world which, under the coordination of the United Nations, has observed an alarming rate of climate change impacts since the high level of carbon release in the atmosphere.

As countries have developed and economies and populations have expanded, more and more greenhouse gases have been released into the atmosphere. The shared prosperity among international actors covers foreign policy which attempts to reconcile domestic interests with external circumstances taking into account the available means, resources, and institutions for doing so. State actors operate between institutions that continually constrain them while managing the tensions between domestic and international society. So do the climate change efforts. This calls for the need for taking action to enhance environmental and climate security in Tanzania.

Actions for Climate injustice in Tanzania: The fact that everyone on earth will be affected by climate change, the countries and communities that experience the most severe impacts are in the developing world, including Tanzania. This is due to their location, their economic status and the burdens that they already bear including hunger, poverty and disease. This calls for a much wider multilateral and international partnership among various actors of the North and South in managing unjust climate practices.

In the course of proposing action for unjust climate practices in Tanzania, the striking of a balance between the countries of the North and South is important. If the poor countries try to develop in the same way as the rich countries, their industrialisation will release more destructive outcomes. This is to say that the countries responsible for releasing the largest amounts of greenhouse gases into the atmosphere are also the richest and the most industrially developed.

The top five greenhouse gas emitting countries are China, the United States, India, Russia and Indonesia, leaving underdeveloped countries already suffering from numerous problems to withstand the prevailing non-traditional security threats in different dimensions. Less developing countries are experiencing an acute shortage of fresh water and consequently lacking clean drinking water for human consumption. This shortage also causes death of millions in the population. The climate-driven economies in less developed countries leave food production and power production initiatives under siege since the consequences of climate change are challenging the existing initiatives on the ground. This, among other things, calls for more reforms in the ongoing multilateralism strategies in the world.

This has to reflect in the implementation of the countries' foreign policies which is dependent on a State's size, population, geographical location, resources, the State's level of economic and technological development, societal structure and forces which comprise social classes, ethnic composition and cultural and psychological factors at work in the society, contingency and situational factors including political and economic crises, coups d'etat, elections, strikes, large-scale violence, military action and war, intensity of national social drivers and reactions in the State system including the decision making machinery of the government, and finally leadership, which refers to the way in which State power is used by current office bearers and State actors in implementing foreign policies. It is high time that integration of climate change mitigation and governance strategies begins to take place.

Climate change related issues in Tanzanian Context: The climate change agenda indeed needs close international collaboration and partnership since the related disasters are shared internationally. Tanzania shares more international water resources (6 lakes, 5 rivers and 7 aquifers), than any other country in Africa. This is more than any other nation in Africa in comparison. A larger part of the country's international borders are water bodies. The Ruvuma river forms a border with Mozambique, Lake Tanganyika with the Democratic Republic of the Congo, Zambia and Burundi, Lake Nyasa and the Songwe River with Malawi, the Kagera River with Rwanda, Uganda, and Lake Victoria with Uganda and Kenya (URT, 2014).

Tanzania has been protecting its coastal and marine resources through a multilateral approach. The country has used a variety of tools including the establishment of Marine Protected Areas, implementation of Sustainable Development Goals and other policies relevant for marine environment conservation, protection and sustainable use. These natural protected resources hold a useful portion of livelihood support mechanisms for a majority of developing countries including Tanzania (URT, 2000). This results in more adoptable climate change mitigation initiatives including the following multilateral inclusive Conventions and Treaties:

- *United Nations Convention on the Law of the Sea (UNCLOS) 1982*

UNCLOS provides that some ocean areas are under national jurisdiction while others are beyond the jurisdiction of any single State, i.e., are open to all States, whether coastal or landlocked. Beyond the limits of national Exclusive Economic Zones (EEZs) or in the high sea, UNCLOS recognises high seas freedoms of navigation, overflight, cable laying, fishing, and scientific research, etc. The Government of Tanzania implemented this Convention through the parliament as the Territorial Sea and Exclusive Economic Zone Act 1989, stating that the Exclusive Economic Zones shall not extend beyond 200 nautical miles from the baseline from which the breadth of the territorial sea is measured (URT, 2007).

- *The Convention for the Protection, Management and Development of the Marine and Coastal Environment of the Eastern African Region (Nairobi Convention, 1985)*

The Nairobi Convention was adopted in 1985 and came into force in 1996. The principle objective of the Nairobi Convention was to establish close cooperation to protect and improve the state of wild fauna and flora and natural habitats in the East African region through the establishment of specially protected areas in the marine and coastal environment. Article 10 of the Nairobi Convention requires all Parties to the Convention to take appropriate measures to protect and preserve rare or fragile ecosystems as well as rare, depleted, threatened or endangered species and their habitats. The Convention was amended and adopted in April2010, hence being an active Convention to raise attention of climate change towards action (URT, 2007).

The need for Devising Multilateral Approach to Non-Traditional Security Challenges: Climate change Mitigation and Governance

The rapid economic development taking place in the world leading to the unsustainable extraction of energy resources, can result in environmental problems such as land degradation, pollution, deterioration of aquatic systems, and climatic changes. Unsustainable extraction of energy resources can lead to negative environmental problems such as degradation, deterioration of aquatic systems, climate change, and pollution. Statistics are available on coal and natural gas production. Uranium production has not started, although the Government is considering using it in power generation by 2040, after building enough capacity for its use (Machiwa, 2010).

Although generation mix might contribute a solution to access issues, the efficient use of energy resources will also need to be enhanced in order to ensure sustainable development. Use of non-renewable energy resources such as oil and gas in one way or another will continue to contribute to environmental pollution. Therefore, further additions of renewable resources, such as geothermal, hydro, wind and solar in the generation mix will be helpful in minimising environmental pollution and contributing to the building of a green economy. We can therefore see that non-traditional security issues cannot be allowed to lag behind in our policymaking and dialogue at the regional and global levels.

Conclusion and Recommendations

Conclusion

The call for acknowledging the role of multilateralism in solving the world's challenges, particularly those related to non-traditional security, has to be given a chance when we try to understand security studies in different realms – it might be in the fields of academic research, policy advice or pedagogic practice. The fusion may allow the growing understanding of what is working and what is not. The theory proposed will then be used in the larger political context of the contemporary geopolitical changes. This among others will effectively help to facilitate the harmonization of methods for compilation of environment statistics and information which is in line with international standards, specifically, the Framework for the Development of Environment Statistics. This will enable timely environmental management in the multilateral context. This includes holding all countries accountable for the related climate change consequences and making all multilateral frameworks work for the need of holding global mechanisms accountable for the task of striking a balance among all forms of non-traditional security challenges which need collective efforts. The fact that national solutions and initiatives are often inadequate, the non-traditional security threats require regional and multilateral cooperation, calling upon countries from all regions to join hands in devising climate change mitigation and governance strategies and policy options.

Recommendations

Based on the study's findings, it is hereby urged that:

(i) It is high time to incorporate non-traditional security challenges in the countries' national foreign policies.

(ii) In the course of reforming multilateralism strategies in the era of Indo-Pacific, it is high time to widen the participation of both public and private sector actors in the realisation of foreign policy implementation to foster and align Indo-Pacific interests in the African region.

(iii) It is urged that multilateral approaches should be reformed and devised to accommodate all forms of recently reported non-traditional security challenges in the entire spectrum of the international relations space.

NOTES

1 Y. Kim and S. Blank, "Non-Traditional Security (NTS) in Central Asia: Contending Paradigms and Current Perspectives", *The Korean Journal of International Studies*, 10(1), 2012, pp. 123-152.

2 Hans Günter Brauch, "Securitizing Global Environmental Change Handbook for the Anthropocene", Berlin: Springer, 2009; Stefan Elbe, "Should HIV/AIDS Be Securitized? The Ethical Dilemmas of Linking HIV/AIDS and Security", *International Studies Quarterly*, 50(1), Mar., 2006, pp. 119-144; Rita Floyd, "The Environmental Security Debate and Its Significance for Climate Change," *The International Spectator* 43(3), 2008, pp 51–65. https://doi.org/10.1080/03932720802280602

3 B.H. Khan, "Non-Conventional Energy Resources", TATA McGraw Hill, 2009.

Ensuring Water, Health, Food, Energy Security and Technology

CHAPTER 19

Ensuring Water, Health and Food Security: Role of Multilateral STI Ecosystem

Umar Ibrahim Gaya

Introduction

The Indo-Pacific region, recognised with 60 per cent of the global GDP, is uniquely-placed as a global centre of both economic dynamism and challenge. However, depending upon the member country, there is imminent challenge for sustainable management of water, sanitation and well-being, as well as food security threats. Interestingly, these challenges posed by all other sustainable development goals (SDG) are directly or indirectly related to health while the corresponding mechanisms for addressing SDG challenges may be preventive, detective or control-based, with an imperative of the preventive approach. This chapter analyses the perspective of impact of leveraging multilateral science, technology and innovation (STI) in ensuring water, health and food security for the benefit of human well-being in both the Indo-Pacific region and its partners from the G20. It emphasises joint partnership and collaboration, and seizing opportunities at both bilateral and multilateral levels in exploiting the economic opportunities and ties that are associated with the STI in addressing the challenges of food, heath and water in the insecure countries. These may include multilateral projects, goal-setting, action frameworks, capacity building and resource sharing that can strengthen preparedness and response in therapeutic challenges, vaccines development, design of diagnostic tools, water treatment technologies, and food security challenges through agriculture. Ultimately, the pursuance of these goals can lead to other socio-economic benefits such as technological catching-up, especially for the less developed countries.

The Indo-Pacific comprises 18 South Asian countries (Laos, Malaysia, Singapore, Thailand, Timor Leste, Vietnam, Myanmar, the Philippines, Indonesia,

Brunei, Bangladesh, Bhutan, Cambodia, Maldives, Nepal, India, Sri Lanka, and Pakistan), six East Asian (People's Republic of China, Republic of Korea, Taiwan, Mongolia, Japan, Democratic People's Republic of Korea), two Australasian (Australia and New Zealand) and 14 Pacific Island countries. These countries shared the following strategic commonalities as of 2022:[1]

(a) A record 60 per cent of the global GDP.
(b) The region's largest economies, controlled by five countries of the Indo-Pacific – the Peoples' Republic of China, Japan, India, the Republic of South Korea and Australia.
(c) Currently, the combined GDP of the top five mentioned above, equals US$29.3 trillion. It should be noted that the whole European Union (EU) has a combined GDP of US$17.2 trillion[2]
(d) Economic activity worth $47.19 trillion
(e) Geography: 65 per cent of the world's Oceans and 25 per cent of its landmass.
(f) Over half the world's people, including 58 per cent of the youth.

Notwithstanding these advantages, there are numerous strategic challenges affecting the region. These include 50 per cent of global greenhouse gas emissions, 65 per cent of the world's population, 37 per cent of the world's poor, heightening instability and tensions, China's dominance, and climate change.[3] In 2021, the Inter-Governmental Panel on Climate Change (IPCC) has proved beyond reasonable doubt that climate change is widespread, rapid, and intensifying more than previously predicted.[4]

Globally, countries' actions are presently sustained through 17 titles of the 2030 Agenda for Sustainable Development Goals (SDGs). Arguably, the world cannot be a better place without constant mitigation of the potential and existing impact of such sustainable challenges, which include water, health, and food insecurity. While SDG6 ensures clean water and sanitation for all, SDG3 aims to ensure good health and well-being for all at all ages.[5] On the other hand, SDG2 promises to end hunger, achieve food security and promote sustainable agriculture.

In line with UN sustainable development goals, the science, technology and innovation (STI) concepts have been major tools for the improvement of well-being, predicting our future and guiding for possible solutions to our existing problems. The coordination framework for implementation of UN SDGs may be unilateral, bilateral, plurilateral or multilateral. Multilateral methods are in the forefront of effectiveness because they are more inclusive, multi-polar, more collaborative and meditative. We intend to treat the role of multilateral STI in ensuring the water, health and food security in the context of the Indo-Pacific, and the countries from Africa, specifically Nigeria.

Developing STI Solutions for Mitigating SDG 6,3,2 Challenges

Addressing Water Insecurity

In the next three decades, the global population is forecast to increase by 2 billion people, thereby creating demands for new innovations, sustainable infrastructure, green fuel, food, new medicines, safe drinking water and adequate sanitation.[6] Earlier this year, the UN Secretary-General was ambitious about water security, as he said that "The UN 2023 Water Conference in March must result in a bold Water Action Agenda that gives our world's lifeblood the commitment it deserves". Consequently, at the UN Water Conference in March 2023, the water agenda was adopted as a step towards speedy implementation of SDG6.

Recently, five climate-based water security risks have been enumerated as namely the household/rural, urban, environmental, economic and resilience-to-water-related risks.[7] Household or rural security risks include the drying of springs, decline of groundwater, and increased demand for water in extreme weather conditions. Similarly, the urban water risks include groundwater decline, inter-annual variation in supply, and increasing urban floods and intensities. Environmental risks include effects of exacerbated pollution, loss of biodiversity, water temperature regime changes affecting water quality, and floods. Water loss through evaporation, competition for scarce resources and increased risks to water due to floods, constitute risks to economic security. Floods, cyclones and droughts, due to their gradual onset, result from resilience to water related risks.

Water source conservation and groundwater management and revival of community actions are imperative to improve household water security, rainwater harvesting. Rainwater harvesting systems (RWHs) have usually served as an alternative water resource in the event of climate crises. The catchment area and population would dictate the modelling of a rainwater tank, daily water savings, rainwater tank capacity, operation system parameters and investment risks.[8] Ultimately, rainwater harvesting is surely a practice that can contribute to the greening of society, dealing with water scarcity in rural and urban areas. Other important water security practices include storm water management, water-sensitive urban design, and water-use efficiency.

To enhance economic water security, water-use efficiency, water accounting, water allocations, water valuation, and water footprint assessment are the usual practices. On the other hand, resilience to water related risks can be improved through disaster-resilient housing and infrastructure, integrated disaster risk management and planning. On the other hand, environmental water security can be improved by environmental flow awareness and monitoring, wastewater treatment and recycling. Wastewater treatment increases the availability of water for household use. In the Indo-Pacific dyes are important, non-biodegradable water pollutants and advanced oxidation processes (AOPs) which rely on light have been recently proposed as emerging technologies for the total mineralisation of such environmentally unfriendly, recalcitrant pollutants.[9]

The AOPs rely on in situ generation of highly reactive chemical species produced by using solar light.[10] The most attractive feature of AOPs is that this highly potent and strongly oxidising species allows the conversion of a wide range of chemical contaminants into benign mineral substances. Photolysis is a common example of advanced oxidation method of water treatment, which is applied in most beverage industries where water is irradiated by light for the benefit of disinfection and decontamination.

Photo-Fenton is another advanced oxidation method, which relies on powerful in situ-generated hydroxyl radicals to degrade organic pollutants. The Fenton reagent is a chemical system consisting usually of iron (II) salts or oxide, and hydrogen peroxide (H_2O_2). There is also a Fenton-like reagent where iron is replaced by another metal. Various Fenton or Fenton-like systems have been utilised for the removal of basic dyes from aqueous environments. The Fenton methods has been shown to be improved by augmenting sonication to the pollutant reaction system.[11]

Photocatalysis is perhaps the most popular advance treatment process. It is based on the illumination of semiconducting material in a water-based medium with the option of using different forms of light.[12] There are many semiconductors in use, but the basic material that has served as standard is titanium dioxide. This material has been found to be chemically inert in the polluted environment, and light responsive, thus deriving an effective decontamination at relatively lower cost. In addition, light-titanium dioxide-based photo-oxidative degradation can combined with either physical or chemical operation for the purpose of efficiency improvement.[13] Consequently, there is a rise in the hyphenated methods, which paved the way for the growing number of novel water treatment technologies for overcoming high treatment costs.[14] The choice of method depends on the composition of water in terms of the class of the organics and the pollutant level.

Coupled photocatalytic methods of operation have proven their efficacy in air and water purification. For instance, there has been a practice of coupling biological treatment with photocatalysis degradation for the removal of organic contaminants to reduce operational cost on the single photocatalytic process. The mineralisation time was shortened compared to the single biological treatment and the electrical cost was saved compared to the photocatalysis.[15] It is reported that hydrogen peroxide-based sound-enhanced photocatalytic degradation is efficient in the complete mineralisation of popular herbicide waste, the propyzamide.[16] The application of photocatalytic membrane reactors designed to combine slurry with membrane filtration is a solution to the problem of separation of photocatalyst in aqueous systems.[17]

Photocatalytic treatment of pollutants can be assisted by a combination of electron-scavenging inorganic additives such as ozone,[18] hydrogen peroxide, sulphite and bromate added to trap electrons and generate more ·OH.[19] Where ozone is used as the additive it adds some attractive features for organic contaminant removal which include relatively higher scavenging effect, ability to decrease the rate of de-excitation of electrons and elimination of residues.[20] The combined ozononation-photocatalysis provides a double benefit, which can be shared for disinfection and removal of recalcitrant organic contaminants even in large-scale operations, and for recalcitrant pollutants.[21]

How the STI Mitigates Health Challenges

Among the global goals, SDG3 is crucial as it is associated with Public Health aims to reduce the global maternal mortality ratio, end the epidemics of AIDS, tuberculosis, malaria and other communicable diseases, and in general reduce illness and mortality globally. Almost all of the other 16 SDGs are related to health. The advantages of STI in health can be summed up in the following manner:[22]

(a) *Telemedicine:* Remote access to specialists and tests is created on tele-sets that eliminate quacks. For example, EKG for cardiologists can be done using mobile phones.

(b) *Mobile health (mhealth):* Mobile phones is suitable for use in the provision of health services to areas where technological developments are lacking, especially in conflict areas.

(c) *Electronic medical records:* Electronic medical records are good for a mobile and non-mobile population, such as conflict-affected communities.

(d) *Wireless health devices:* These devices are available for operation where there is no internet service.

(e) *Cloud-based storage systems:* Cloud-based storage systems have improved the quality of medical service. Kenya saw an improvement of 42% in missing medical data through cloud computing.

The STI is vital to preventive, detective and corrective health approaches. Multifaceted institutional strengthening, establishment of high-quality scientific infrastructure, planning and campaign have the potential to prevent diseases. Similarly, the STI can promote the capacity for detection in vaccines manufacturing, climatic risks assessments, and in-situ digital detections. The STI can promote the capacity of a community to deal with undesirable health events, for example, COVID-19.

Combating Food Insecurity Issues

The 2007 Asian economic crisis affected a number of countries and was a wake-up call for the Indo-Pacific. Thailand for example, had to introduce the concept of Self-Sufficiency Economy Philosophy (SEP) towards participatory and sustainable development in agriculture.[23] Prior to this, at the 1996 World Food Summit, food security was defined as: "When all people, at all times, have physical and economic access to sufficient safe and nutritious food that meets their dietary needs and food preferences for an active and healthy life". Differently and simply put, the United States Department of Agriculture (USDA) defines food insecurity as the "Lack of consistent access to enough food for every person in a household to live an active, healthy life".

The four types of food security are food availability, accessibility, utilisation and stability. Excessive inadequacy of any of these pillars in a community could lead to fragility, conflict and clashes. It is therefore imperative to take stock of progress and monitor improvement effectively. The FAO has developed strategies to measure the progress of SDGs that focuses on four main areas.[24] The first strategy is the development of national statistical plans that agree with the SDG Indicator Framework. The second supports the implementation of new, cost-effective data collection tools, and the third supports the upgrade of existing data collection tools, to produce food and agriculture data as well as relevant SDG indicators. The last strategy seeks to improve analysis and use of SDG indicators in decision-making. However, the organisation found that the ability of countries to report even their basic national data on the socio-economic and environmental dimensions of food and agriculture is still low.

Fundamentally, one thing that is lacking about food security is the academic research on hunger.[25] Moreover, there has been no established link between specific SDGs, and the outcomes of adopted agricultural technological products is lacking in developing countries. In sum, the enhancement of food security can change the game in the current debate on food availability for sustainable development. The adoption of crop protection products of multinational brands (CMBs) rather than sub-standard crop protection products, may translate as a responsible farming practice if assuming the use of crop protection products is inevitable.[25] In order to meet the global demand for SDG2, decreased yield and productivity must be addressed by building a resilient, sustainable and innovative system[26] Some of STI-based methods for achieving these goals include:

(a) *Industry 4.0 technologies:* The fourth industrial revolution has given us autonomous decision-making tools such as artificial intelligence, the internet of things, big data analysis, remote sensing, machine learning, robotics, block chain technology, and digital twins. As these technologies can improve productivity, transparency, and visibility, they accordingly increase the resilience of the agricultural and food supply chain.[27]

(b) *Smart precision and farming technology:* Smart precision and farming technology like farming robot, unmanned tractors and autonomous vehicles can replace intensive manual labour which in turn can improve the productivity, adaptability, and resilience of the agro ecosystem and associated farming community.[28]

(c) *Ecological agricultural intensification:* Utilising ecological processes based on efficient management and improved inputs, to raise crop productivity per unit area, can increase food availability.[29]

(d) *Farm and crop diversification:* Diversification strategies implemented at the field, farm, and landscape levels, result in greater production to satisfy the global food demand.[30]

(e) *Resilience farming method:* Conventional farming knowledge and techniques can enhance resilience of modern farming in extreme regimes.[31]

Scientific Multilateralism and Supporting Bodies

Multilateral global channels have been in existence, and they continue to increase due to the need to double efforts in meeting the sustainable development goals. There are several multilateral institutions which serve to promote multilateral initiatives and cooperation on SDG matters, and these include the following:[32]

(a) The Green Environment Fund (GEF): Provides funds for the protection of the global environment and environmentally sustainable development, under for example, the Least Developed Countries Fund (LDCF), the United Nations Framework Convention on Climate Change (UNFCCC) and the Special Climate Change Fund (SCCF).[33]

(b) The Economic Community of West African States (ECOWAS).

(c) The Global Climate Facility (GCF) invests in low emission and climate-resilient development.

(d) The African Development Bank (ADB) contributes to poverty reduction and economic and social development in the least developed African countries, by providing concessional funding for programmes, technical assistance for studies and capacity building activities.

(e) Brazil, India, China, South Africa (BRICS): Promotes peace, development and cooperation.

(f) Quadrilateral Security Dialogue (Quad): Strategic security dialogue between Australia, India, Japan, and US

(g) India-Brazil-South Africa (IBSA): South-South cooperation for least developed nations

(h) Shanghai Cooperation Organisation (SCO): Focuses on security-related concerns. Turkey, Egypt, Cambodia, Kuwait, Kingdom of Saudi Arabia, China, India and Pakistan are members.

(i) Association of Southeast Asian Nations (ASEAN): Facilitates free flow of skilled labour, goods, capital, services and investments.

(j) Community of Latin American and Caribbean States (CELAC) for intergovernmental dialogue and agreement.

(k) Conference on Interaction and Confidence-Building Measures in Asia (CICA): A multinational forum for enhancing cooperation towards promoting peace, security and stability.

The ASEAN too has come to the forefront as one of the most dynamic regions in the global economic and security dimensions, with China, India, Japan, South Korea and Taiwan playing a vitally significant role. However, there has been a shortage of multilateral organisations that promote the role and focus of science, technology and innovation in addressing the global challenges. The BRICS operated through the existing frameworks of its member countries as follows:

(a) *Brazil:* National Council for Scientific and Technological Development (CNPq).

(b) *Russia:* Foundation for Assistance to Small Innovative Enterprises (FASIE) and Ministry of Science and Higher Education (MSHE).

(c) *India:* Department of Biotechnology (DBT) and Department of Science and Technology (DST).

(d) *China:* Ministry of Science and Technology (MOST) and the National Natural Science Foundation of China (NSFC).

(e) *South Africa:* Department of Science and Innovation (DSI), National Research Foundation (NRF), Water Research Commission (WRC), Technology Innovation Agency (TIA) and the South African Medical Research Council (SAMRC).

For the first time we propose the Gaya Fusion Model (GFM), a model that seeks to ensure the smooth implementation of policies and action plans. Figure 1 shows the features of this model. It comprises three components (the people, directions and the system) and shows how the co-existence of any two can create a positive synergy in the implementation of action plans. However, for effective implementation, the fusion of the three sets is required. Even though the union of any two is required, but for an effective result all three must co-exist sufficiently. Wherever in the implementation one of the components dominates, it will be difficult to achieve a meaningful result. It is perhaps for this reason that even after having summits, establishing action plans (2012-2016) and development banks, the BRICS method has been described as having "lagging States" and a suggestion to seek new ways has been made.[34] The ASEAN Plan of Action on Science Technology and Innovation (APASTI –2016-2025) was different. It is a strategy document adopted by the Ministers on 6November 2015 which could perhaps agree with the Gaya Fusion Model and if implemented well, could be an efficient concept.

In the APASTI, the people component is basically a plan to ensure deep awareness of the STI, while on the directions it proposed an innovation-driven economy with deep STI enculturation and a system of seeding and sustaining STI by leveraging ICT and the resources of our talented young, women and private sectors.[35] It invoked an active R&D collaboration, technology commercialisation and entrepreneurship and a network of centres. It also plans an enhanced STI management system to support ASEAN innovation reaching global markets and that promotes innovation, integration and narrowing of development gaps.

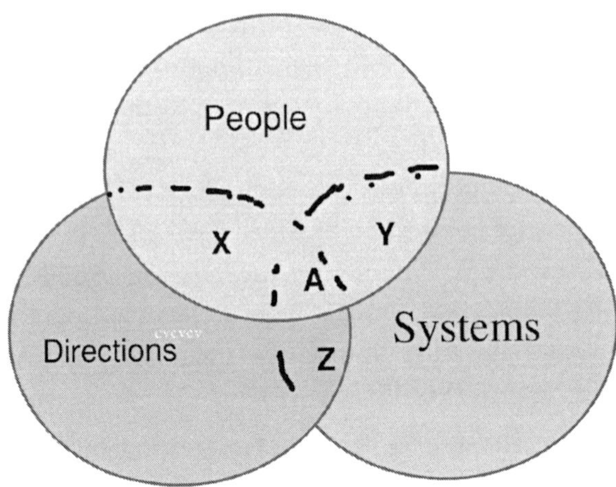

Fig. 1: The Gaya Fusion Model. Where A shows an effective implementation framework and X,Y, Z show the people-directions, people-system and system-directions intersections.

The 2012 UN Conference on Sustainable Development ("Rio+20") called for a technology facilitation mechanism option in its communique. This led to the initiation of Inter-agency Working Groups on a Technology Facilitation Mechanism (IAWG), comprising the United Nations Department of Economic and Social Affairs (UN DESA), United Nations Environment Programme (UNEP), United Nations Industrial Development Organization (UNIDO), United Nations Conference on Trade and Development (UNCTAD), United Nations Educational, Scientific and Cultural Organization (UNESCO), International Telecommunications Union (ITU), World Intellectual Property Organization (WIPO), and the World Bank Group. This group was mandated to do the following:[36]

(a) Map the existing technology facilitation initiatives including support for policy formulation and strengthening of technological capabilities and innovation systems.
(b) Identify areas of synergy and of possible cooperation within the UN system on technology-related work.
(c) Develop options for a possible online knowledge hub and information-sharing platform.
(d) Cooperate with relevant stakeholders on building STI capacity building.

Consequently, the technology facilitation mechanism (TFM) was launched at Adis Ababa in September 2015, for multilateral ecosystems. It has three components for SDGs. The first is a United Nations Inter-agency Task Team on STI, comprising ten member groups from civil society, private sector and scientific community. There is also a collaborative Multi-stakeholder Forum on STI. The last component is an online platform as a gateway for information on existing STI initiatives, mechanisms and programmes. This action agenda was faulted on the need for more commitment, enabling environment, including innovative, cross-sectoral policy and funding.[37]

Africa's Potentials for Multilateral Cooperation in STI

The Science, Technology and Innovation Strategy for Africa 2024 sees the significance of joint partnership and collaboration at both bilateral and multilateral levels to deal with global challenges.[35] Africa's goal for investment in STI stands at 1 per cent of the GDP. Nigeria (as well as a few other African countries) have met the 1 per cent GDP requirement as shown in Table 1[38] and has additional advantages such as population (211 million), GDP (US$ 520), and being Africa's largest oil and gas producer, 10th in the world. It has also attended the BRICS expansion dialogue in May 2022. Barrack Obama once said "If Nigeria does not get it right, Africa will really not make more progress".[39] Nigeria is an OPEC member and a member of African Continental Free Trade Agreement (AfCFTA), which reduces tariffs on intra-African trades to zero.

Table 1: The STI Opportunity taking Potential based on GDP

Country	*GDP (US$)*	*1% of GDP (US$)*
Nigeria	520,000,000,000	52,000,000,000
South Africa	335,000,000,000	33,500,000,000
Algeria	209,000,000,000	20,900,000,000
Egypt	246,000,000,000	24,600,000,000
Angola	123,000,000,000	12,300,000,000

Source: The Science, Technology and Innovation Strategy for Africa 2024

It is well known that the last global pandemic has revealed the risks in critical science, technology and innovation. The top five Indo-Pacific countries have the opportunity of driving partnership in technological catch-up in STI of the least-developed countries within and outside their group in the areas of medicine, vaccine production, and advanced manufacturing in order to have capacity for rapid response especially in the event of global problems such as health pandemics.

For example, the Global Innovation Index (GII) of Nigeria in 2022 was 114, which is far lower than that of India.[40] Such variation in innovation indices can hurt the efficiency in the delivery of STI and multilateral cooperation. Generally, different countries have different opportunity-taking indices (OTI) which reflect the use of scientific resources to establish new technologies.[40] The OTI is a ratio between the country's share of the world's scientific publications, represented by ISI data (as a proxy for national scientific production) and the resulting technological products. The opportunity-taking index of Taiwan is 0.99327 while Hungary correlates negatively (-0.53389). The OTI of the US, Japan, Korea, Canada, and Taiwan exceeds 0.9. The improvement in well-being has been shown by several means, commensurate with technological advancement. This assists in focussing on the narratives in the areas of STI change in least-developed countries.

Conclusion

In the current global scenario, where the significance of STI cannot be overstressed, the future of developing countries in security dimensions is contingent on their performance vis-a-vis the major actors in global economy. As the Indo-Pacific undergoes transformational changes, dependency on members and non-members has been stressed especially in terms of the role of science, technology and innovation. While some African countries have reasonable GDPs whose component would have aided sustainable actions and multilateral partnerships with the Indo-Pacific, it seemed less due to the incongruity of the polarity and compatibility. This raises the question of adopting the use of the Genuine Products Index (GPI) rather than the GDP, so that the all-important influencing factors are incorporated in multilateral terms. In connection with sustainable health, greater partnership in STI is recommended, especially to transfer the resource persons, not the patients, or connect/support them using emerging digital health systems. Lastly, the Gaya Fusion Model, a reasonable model for the effective implementation of multilateral coordination frameworks, is described.

NOTES

1 "Canada's Indo-Pacific Strategy", at https://www.international.gc.ca/transparency-transparence/indo-pacific-indo-pacifique/index.aspx?lang=eng#a1_1 (Accessed 17 March 2023). and (2) "Indo-Pacific Strategy of the United States", Quad Leaders' Summit, White House, Washington, February, 2021, pp. 1-18.

2 https://european-union.europa.eu/principles-countries-history/facts-and-figures-european-union_en (Accessed 17 March 2023).

3 World Health Organization (WHO), SDG 3: Ensure Health Lives and Promote Wellbeing

for All at All Ages, (2017) Retrieved from: http://www.who.int/sdg/ targets/en/ (Accessed 03 April 2024).

4 "Climate Change 2022: Impacts, Adaptation, and Vulnerability Working Group II Sixth Assessment Report", *Technical Summary*, TS.C4, Intergovernmental Panel on Climate Change, 2022, p. 96.

5 World Health Organization (WHO), SDG 3: Ensure Health Lives and Promote Wellbeing for All at All Ages, (2017) Retrieved from: http://www.who.int/sdg/ targets/en/ (Accessed 19 March 2024).

6 "Module 5: Technology, Innovation, and the SDGs. Youth Workers 4 Global Goals (YW4GW)-Capacity Building in the Field of Youth", A European Union Sponsored publication, May 12-13, New York, 2020, pp. 1-20.

7 Hemant Ojha, Nicholas Schofield, "Climate Change and Water Security in the Indo-Pacific Region: Risks, Responses, and a Framework for Action", Canberra: Australian Water Partnership, Sydney, Australia, 2022, pp. 1-114.

8 D.A. Kakoulas, S.K. Golfinopoulos, D. Koumparou, D.E. Alexakis, "The Effectiveness of Rainwater Harvesting Infrastructure in a Mediterranean Island", *Water*, 14(5), 2022, p. 716.

9 M. Zahoor, A. Arshad, Y. Khan, M. Iqbal, S.Z. Bajwa, R.A. Soomro, I. Ahmad, F.K. Butt, M.Z. Iqbal, A. Wu, W.S. Khan, "Enhanced Photocatalytic Performance of CeO_2–TiO_2 Nanocomposite for Degradation of Crystal Violet Dye and Industrial Waste Effluent", *Applied Nanoscience*, 8, 2018, pp. 1091-1099.

10 V.D. Potle, S.R. Shirsath, B.A. Bhanvase, V.K. Saharan, "Sonochemical Preparation of Ternary rGO-ZnO-TiO2 Nanocomposite Photocatalyst for Efficient Degradation of Crystal Violet Dye", *Optik* (Stuttg). 208, 2020, pp. 164555.

11 A. Hassani, C., Karaca, S., Karaca, A., Khataee, O., Açışl, B., Yılmaz, "Enhanced Removal of Basic Violet 10 by Heterogeneous Sono-Fenton Process Using Magnetite Nanoparticles", *Ultrasonics Sonochemistry*, 42, 2018, pp. 390-402.

12 N. Mintcheva, S. Yamaguchi, S.A. Kulinich, Hybrid TiO2-ZnO "Nanomaterials Prepared Using Laser Ablation in Liquid, Materials (Basel)", 13(3), 2020, p. 719.

13 V. Augugliaro, M. Litter, L. Palmisano and J. Soria, "The Combination of Heterogeneous Photocatalysis with Chemical and Physical Operations: A Tool for Improving the Photoprocess Performance", *Journal of Photochemistry and Photobiology* C: Photochemistry Reviews, 7, 2006, pp. 127–144.

14 F. Azeez, E. Al-Hetlani, M. Arafa, Y. Abdelmonem, A.A. Nazeer, M.O. Amin, M. Madkour, "The Effect of Surface Charge on Photocatalytic Degradation of Methylene Blue Dye Using Chargeable Titania Nanoparticles", *Scientific Reports*, 8, 2018, 7104.

15 D. Suryaman, K. Hasegawa and S. Kagaya, "Combined Biological and Photocatalytic Treatment for the Mineralization of Phenol in Water", *Chemosphere* 65, 2006, pp. 2502–2506.

16 J. Yano, J-I. Matsuura, H. Ohura and S. Yamasaki, "Complete Mineralization of Propyzamide in Aqueous Solution Containing TiO2 Particles and H2O2 by the Simultaneous Irradiation of Light and Ultrasonic Waves", *Ultrasonics Sonochemistry*, 12, 2005, pp. 197–203.

17 S. Mozia, M. Tomaszewska, A. W. Morawski, "A New Photocatalytic Membrane Reactor (PMR) for Removal of Azo-dye Acid Red 18 from Water", *Applied Catalysis B: Environmental*, 59, 2005, pp. 131–137.

18 M. Pera-Titus, V. García-Molina, M.A. Baños, J. Giménez and S. Esplugas, "Degradation of Chlorophenols by Means of Advanced Oxidation Processes: A General Review", *Applied Catalysis B: Environmental*, 47, 2004, pp. 219–256.

19 M. Faisal, M.A. Tariq, M. Muneer, "Photocatalysed Degradation of Two Selected Dyes in UV-irradiated Aqueous Suspensions of Titania", Dyes and Pigments, 72, 2007, pp. 233-239.

20 M.D. Hernández-Alonso, J.M. Coronado, A.J. Maira, J. Soria, V. Loddo, V. Augugliaro, "Ozone Enhanced Activity of Aqueous Titanium Dioxide Suspensions for Photocatalytic Oxidation of Free Cyanide Ions", *Applied Catalysis B: Environmental* 39, 2002, pp. 257–267.

21 A.A. Mofidi, J.H. Min, L.S. Palencia, B.M. Coffey, S. Liang, J.F. Green, "Task 2.1: Advanced Oxidation Processes and UV Photolysis for Treatment of Drinking Water", Metropolitan Water District of Southern California, La Verne, California, California Energy Commission, Sacramento, California", 2002, pp. 1-93.

22 Y.M. Asi., C. Williams, "The Role of Digital Health in Making Progress Toward Sustainable Development Goal (SDG) 3 in Conflict-affected Populations", *International Journal of Medical Informatics*, 114, June, 2018, pp. 114-120.

23 O.F. von Feigenblatt, M. Cooper, P. Pardo, "Sufficiency Economy Philosophy (SEP): Thailand's Emic Approach to Governance and Development as Evidence of an Asian Value-Oriented Inclusive Leadership Management Philosophy," *Strategic Analysis*, 46(4), 2022, pp. 430-440.

24 P. Gennari, J. Rosero-Moncayo, F.N. Tubiello, "The FAO Contribution to Monitoring SDGs for Food and Agriculture", Correspondence to the Editor, *Nature Plants*, at https://doi.org/10.1038/s41477-019-0564-z (Accessed May 10, 2023).

25 A. Sianes, A. Vega-Muñoz, P., Tirado-Valencial, Antonio ArizaMontes. "Impact of the Sustainable Development Goals on the Academic Research Agenda. A Scientometric Analysis," *PLoS ONE*, 17(3), 2022, e0265409.

26 M. Bilal, B. Brümmer, J. Barkmann, "A Discussion on the Outcomes of Adopted Agricultural Technological Products and Specific Sustainable Development Goals: Evidence from Pakistan", *Cogent Economics & Finance*, 10, 2022, pp. 213-264.

27 K. Kumareswaran and G.Y. Jayasinghe, "Systematic Review on Ensuring the Global Food Security and Covid 19 Pandemic Resilient Food Systems: Towards Accomplishing Sustainable Development Goals Targets," *Discover Sustainability*, 3, 2022, p. 29.

28 A. Mishra, E. Bruno, D. Zilberman, "Compound Natural and Human Disasters: Managing Drought and COVID-19 to Sustain Global Agriculture and Food Sectors", *Sci Total Environ*, 754, 2021, pp. 142-210.

29 C.B. Pandey, M.K. Garu, R.K. Goyal, "Climate Change and Agrofroestry: Adaptation, Mitigation, and Livelihood Security", New India Publishing Agency, New Delhi, 2018, pp. 1-565.

30 H. Lakhran, K. Sandeep, R. Bajiya, "Crop Diversification: An Option for Climate Change Resilience", *Trends Biosci.*, 10(2), 2017, pp. 516–518.

31 M.A. Altieri, C.I. Nicholls, A. Henao, M.A. Lana, "Agroecology and the Design of Climate Change-Resilient Farming Systems", *Agronomy for Sustainable Development*, 35(3), 2015, pp. 869–890.

32 "Multilateral Organizations: Scaling up our Impact," *International Fund for Agricultural Development*, https://www.ifad.org/en/multilateral-organizations, (Accessed May 10, 2023).

33 "Mission and Strategy, African Development Bank Group", at https://www.afdb.org, (Accessed May 10, 2023).

34 P. Jha, A. Chakraborty, "BRICS in the Contemporary Global Economy: Prospects and Challenges," OXFAM India, *Working Papers Series*, OIWPS-XVII, 2013, pp. 1-14.

35 "ASEAN Plan of Action on Science, Technology and Innovation" (APASTI), 2016-2025, The ASEAN Secretariat Jakarta, 2017, pp. 8-15.

36 "Module 5: Technology, Innovation, and the SDGs. Youth Workers 4 Global Goals (YW4GW)-Capacity Building in the Field of Youth." A European Union Sponsored Publication, May 12-13, New York, 2020, pp. 1-20.

37 Module 5: Technology, Innovation, and the SDGs. Youth Workers 4 Global Goals (YW4GW)-Capacity Building in the Field of Youth. A European Union Sponsored publication, May 12-13, New York, 2020, pp. 1-20.

38 The Science, Technology and Innovation Strategy for Africa 2024.

39 Chekwube Nzomiwu, "US, Nigeria's Faulty Election and Africa's Progress", *Vanguard*, https:/ /www.vanguardngr.com/2023/03/us-nigerias-faulty-election-and-africas-progress/ (Accessed 14 march 2023).

40 E. de Motta e Albuquerque, "National Systems of Innovation And Non-OECD Countries: Notes About a Tentative Typology", *Revista de Economia Política*, 19(4):35-52, 1999, pp. 545-566.

CHAPTER 20

Strengthening Multilateralism for Peace and Sustainable Development

Diana Benoit

Today's complex and multifaceted global challenges call for strengthened multilateralism that can adapt to the new realities of the 21st century. Current challenges such as health crises, violent conflict, climate change, poverty and inequality continue to exert compelling pressure on the multilateral system to combine efforts and effectively tackle present and future obstacles. The emergence of dominant actors in global politics and a novel paradigm in international relations present opportunities for new or renewed strategic cooperation in key priority sectors.

The Significance of Multilateralism

In today's world, the multitude of complex global challenges demand a strengthened multilateralism that can effectively address and adapt to the evolving realities of the 21st century. The COVID-19 pandemic, with its far-reaching implications, has exacerbated the fragility of health, social and economic structures in various parts of the world.[1] Simultaneously, violent conflicts, climate change, poverty and inequality continue to exert immense pressure on the multilateral system, compelling nations to unite their efforts to tackle these issues.[2] To confront these challenges effectively, there is a need to reinforce global governance structures and establish a multilateral approach that is fit for the purpose. A multilateral approach provides a platform for countries to come together, share resources, expertise and best practices and jointly develop strategies to tackle these pressing issues. It encourages the active participation and engagement of all nations to ensure that no voice is left unheard and that collective action can be taken for the benefit of all. Collective actions play a pivotal role in supporting both national and global development goals. The challenges we face today, whether they are economic, social or environmental in nature, require a collaborative and coordinated approach. Individual nations alone often lack the resources, expertise and capacity to address these challenges comprehensively.

A strengthened multilateral system is essential for fostering greater cooperation and collaboration among nations. It allows for the pooling of diverse perspectives, knowledge and experiences, leading to more effective problem-solving and decision-making processes.[3] By promoting dialogue, negotiation and compromise, a multilateral approach facilitates the development of inclusive and sustainable solutions that consider the interests and needs of all the stakeholders involved.[4] Strengthening multilateralism involves enhancing the capabilities and capacity of multilateral institutions to coordinate and cooperate on a global scale. Multilateral institutions play a vital role in addressing emerging global challenges and responding to shifts in global power dynamics.[5] Institutions facilitate global collaboration, enabling nations to collectively tackle global challenges and mitigate the negative consequences that may arise from pursuing individual interests in areas such as climate change, conflicts, disease control and financial stability.[6] This entails reforming and innovating existing mechanisms to make them more agile, efficient and inclusive.

The interconnectivity of economies, trade networks and supply chains has become more evident than ever. The disruption caused by the pandemic, coupled with regional and international conflicts, highlights the imperative of collaborative endeavours to support national and global development goals. It is essential to recognise the emergence of dominant actors in global politics and explore new avenues for strategic cooperation in key priority sectors. Moreover, effective and sustainable multilateralism necessitates the active participation of actors from all levels of society. Inclusive multilateralism implies incorporating diverse perspectives and ensuring the representation of marginalised groups and civil society organisations.[7] By fostering a global culture of multilateralism based on inclusivity, transparency and accountability, we can build a foundation for democratic decision-making processes and sustainable development.[8]

Collective action can be understood and approached from various perspectives.[9] One perspective views it as a coordination challenge, focusing on factors such as incentives, disincentives, transaction costs and institutional frameworks within the field of institutional economics and public choice. Another perspective sees it as a political issue, highlighting the political dynamics and behaviour among actors with differing and sometimes conflicting interests, such as the formation of coalitions to either support or oppose policy changes. In order to maintain a global collective effort, it is fundamental to establish commitments that are binding –formally or informally – because the participants involved in such collective action must collaborate and contribute together over an extended period.[10] By pooling resources and efforts through collective actions, nations can achieve far greater impact and effectiveness in advancing their development goals. Collaboration in areas such as trade, investment, technology transfer and capacity building fosters mutual benefits and contributes to inclusive and sustainable development.[11] It allows countries to tap into a broader network of support and expertise, accelerating their progress towards national development goals.

Collaboration among nations allows for the sharing of best practices, innovative ideas and lessons learned, enabling faster progress and avoiding unnecessary duplication of efforts. It is important to recognise that collective actions are not limited to governmental efforts alone. Non-governmental organisations, civil society, private sector and other stakeholders also play a crucial role in supporting collective actions and contributing to national and global development goals.[12] Their participation brings diverse perspectives, innovation and resources to the table, enhancing the effectiveness and inclusivity of collective endeavours. In addition, collective actions have the power to address global challenges that transcend national boundaries. Issues like climate change, transnational crime and pandemics require joint efforts to be tackled effectively. The Climate Action Network (CAN), comprising 430 environmental non-governmental organisations from diverse regions around the world, operates regional offices in Africa, Europe, Latin America and South and Southeast Asia. The primary goal of this network is to coordinate the strategies of its members on climate change, fostering information exchange and striving to formulate joint position papers for significant international events.[13] Such a network illustrates that by working together nations can devise global strategies, establish international frameworks and implement coordinated measures that aim to mitigate these global challenges. The exchange of information, technologies and expertise enables countries to learn from each other's experiences and develop a more holistic approach towards sustainable development.

21st Century Multilateral System

Evolution and Current State

Multilateralism is described "as an approach encouraging actors (states but also non-state entities) to collaborate to identify common problems (including global public goods and bads), to design methods to provide public goods, finance the provision or prevention and monitor the outcomes of common actions".[14] It stands as a central and interconnected norm within diplomatic culture, accompanied by principles such as the limited use of force as a final recourse for self-defence, ongoing bilateral dialogue between officially recognised representatives, transparent and open dialogue whenever feasible and the importance of maintaining civility and tact in diplomatic discourse.[15] The multilateral system has undergone significant evolution over time, shaped by changing global dynamics and the complexities of international relations. The existing framework of multilateralism originated in the aftermath of the Second World War, characterised by the emergence of a world order predominantly shaped and dominated by liberal Western powers, with the United States at the forefront of its design.[16] Multilateralism now serves as a platform for identifying areas of shared interest among nations with differing viewpoints, achieved through negotiations and finding common ground. This reflects the evolving reality that the composition of countries necessary for effective collective responses is changing.

The current state of the multilateral system is marked by both achievements and challenges. On one hand, multilateral cooperation has successfully contributed to addressing numerous global issues. It has facilitated international agreements on climate change, nuclear non-proliferation and human rights, among others. The system has also been instrumental in providing platforms for diplomatic negotiations and resolving conflicts.[17] On the other hand, the multilateral system faces numerous challenges that test its effectiveness and relevance. The rise of nationalism and protectionism in some countries has strained international cooperation and hindered progress on key global issues. Since the late 1990s, a new role for multilateralism has arisen, characterised by a growing emphasis on inclusivity and the incorporation of diverse perspectives to achieve a consensus on shared norms of conduct.[18] Additionally, the system's decision-making processes have been criticised for being slow, cumbersome and lacking inclusivity. Power imbalances among member states and the influence of dominant actors have raised concerns about equitable representation and decision-making within multilateral institutions. The multilateral system has evolved from being influenced by a small group of affluent countries with similar viewpoints to a framework shaped by compromises among nations with diverse global perspectives. This transformation began with Russia joining the G-8 in 1998, followed by the establishment of the G-20 as the primary global economic management group and culminating in the consensus on the Sustainable Development Goals agreed upon by all United Nations member states.[19]

Multilateral Framework Challenges

The rapid pace of globalisation, technological advancements and emerging global challenges have presented new complexities for the multilateral system.[20] Issues such as cyber threats, terrorism, pandemics and the digital divide require innovative approaches and strengthened collaboration among nations. In response to these challenges, efforts are being made to reform and adapt the multilateral system to better address contemporary realities.[21] One of the key challenges is the slow and complex decision-making process within multilateral institutions. The involvement of numerous stakeholders with diverse interests and perspectives often leads to protracted negotiations and compromises. This can hinder timely and effective responses to pressing global challenges, particularly when urgent action is required. Another challenge lies in the power imbalances among member states within the multilateral system. Some countries, particularly major powers, wield disproportionate influence and can shape the agenda and outcomes in a manner that aligns with their national interests. This imbalance can undermine the principle of equitable representation and decision-making, affecting the legitimacy and effectiveness of the multilateral framework.

Transparency and accountability are additional areas of concern. The opacity surrounding certain decision-making processes and the limited mechanisms for holding actors accountable can erode trust and legitimacy. Ensuring greater transparency and strengthening accountability mechanisms is essential for promoting the credibility and integrity of the multilateral system. Occasionally, civil society organisations have managed to acquire and disclose unofficial versions of G8 declarations as a means to exert pressure for increased transparency in G8 proceedings.[22] Inclusivity is another area where the multilateral system falls short. While efforts have been made to include non-State actors and civil society organisations, there is still a need for greater participation and representation from marginalised and underrepresented groups. Ensuring the inclusion of diverse perspectives and voices is necessary for a more inclusive and equitable global governance system. Addressing these challenges and shortcomings in the existing multilateral framework requires collective effort and commitment from member states.[23] Reforming decision-making processes, promoting transparency and accountability, addressing power imbalances and enhancing inclusivity are key areas that need to be prioritised. Strengthening the framework's responsiveness to emerging challenges and embracing innovation will also contribute to its effectiveness and long-term sustainability.

Adapting To Global Trends

Adapting to new realities and emerging global trends is essential for the multilateral system to remain effective and relevant in addressing the complex challenges of the modern world. The global landscape is constantly evolving, shaped by technological advancements, shifting power dynamics and emerging issues that require innovative approaches and collaborative efforts. This acknowledgment reflects the understanding that addressing contemporary challenges often surpasses the capabilities of individual governments to tackle alone, prompting the need for collective responses and collaborations.[24] One of the key areas where adaptation is crucial is in addressing the impact of technological advancements. Rapid developments in areas such as artificial intelligence, automation and digital connectivity have transformed various aspects of society and the economy. The multilateral system must stay abreast of these changes and find ways to harness the potential benefits while mitigating the risks and challenges they pose. The emerging digital technologies significantly enhance good governance by facilitating better public access to information, increasing awareness of decisions and policies among the public, improving communication to share experiences and enabling greater participation of the public in political processes.[25] This may involve establishing new frameworks for digital governance, cybersecurity and data privacy to ensure the responsible and inclusive use of technology.

Furthermore, adapting to emerging global trends involves recognising and responding to changing power dynamics. The rise of new economic powers, regional alliances and non-State actors has reshaped the global landscape. The multilateral system needs to reflect these shifts and ensure the representation and inclusion of diverse voices and perspectives. As strategic competition intensifies, international institutions will undergo transformations. For instance, the United States and China are expected to utilise multilateral organisations both competitively, by strengthening ties with specific allies through avenues like development financing and cooperatively, by fostering global collaboration, particularly in areas such as climate change.[26] Reforming institutions to enhance the participation of emerging powers and recognising the changing nature of global governance are necessary steps in this process. Addressing emerging global challenges also requires the multilateral system to adopt a proactive and anticipatory approach. Issues such as climate change, pandemics and migration are increasingly interconnected and require holistic, long-term solutions. The multilateral framework should foster collaboration among nations, facilitate knowledge-sharing and encourage joint efforts to prevent and mitigate these challenges. Economic decision-making should be guided by the consequences of climate change, which hinder growth, development and equal opportunities.[27] By mobilising resources, an inclusive and transformative approach to addressing climate change can address existing inequalities and enhance our ability to withstand the impacts of climate-related events.[28]

Challenges for Multilateral Institutions

The institutional framework of global governance is built upon the fundamental principle of multilateralism.[29] Multilateral institutions play an important role in addressing global challenges by fostering international cooperation, promoting consensus-building and coordinating collective action. The notion of enhancing peace and international cooperation through the incorporation of a more institutionalised multilateral aspect alongside traditional bilateral diplomacy gained significant traction after the First World War, particularly with the emergence of proposals for a League of Nations.[30] These institutions serve as platforms where countries can come together to discuss, negotiate and develop solutions to complex global problems that transcend national boundaries. One key role of multilateral institutions is to facilitate dialogue and collaboration among nations. They provide a forum for diplomatic discussions, enabling countries to exchange ideas, share experiences and build common understanding. By bringing together diverse perspectives and expertise, these institutions create opportunities for finding innovative and sustainable solutions to global challenges. Prior to this, the prevailing belief was that the likelihood of war and conflict could be diminished by promoting continuous diplomatic dialogue and communication between sovereign states, even those in hostile relationships, primarily through bilateral exchange of diplomatic missions in respective capital cities.[31]

Multilateral institutions also play a vital role in promoting global norms, rules and standards. Through conventions, treaties and agreements, these institutions establish frameworks that guide international behaviour and promote cooperation. Multilateral diplomacy serves as a platform for negotiating global agreements that aim to enhance the global condition. Two notable examples are the Nuclear Non-Proliferation Treaty that prohibits the acquisition and exchange of nuclear weapons and associated technologies among non-nuclear weapon states; and the United Nations Convention on the Law of the Sea has established universally agreed-upon regulations governing the utilisation of the Earth's oceans.[32] They help create a sense of shared responsibility and accountability among member states, encouraging them to adhere to common rules and principles for the greater benefit of the international community. In addition to their operational role, multilateral institutions contribute to global governance by providing a platform for addressing systemic issues and promoting collective decision-making.[33] They help bridge the gap between national and international interests, allowing countries to find common ground and work towards shared objectives. By fostering dialogue and negotiation, these institutions enhance global governance mechanisms and strengthen the rule-based international order.

Multilateralism and Small States

Opportunities for Sustainable Development

Multilateralism holds significant importance for small States in navigating the complex landscape of International Relations. The global community initially acknowledged the unique circumstances of small States during the United Nations Conference on Environment and Development (UNCED) held in Rio de Janeiro in 1992.[34] One significant outcome of the UNCED Conference was the formulation of Agenda 21, an ambitious action plan that advocated for innovative strategies to foster sustainable development in the twenty-first century. According to this agenda, Small Island developing States and islands supporting small communities[35] "are a special case both for environment and development. They are ecologically fragile and vulnerable. Their small size, limited resources, geographic dispersion and isolation from markets, place them at a disadvantage economically and prevent economies of scale".[36] For small States, multilateralism offers an opportunity to participate in decision-making processes on equal footing with larger and more powerful nations; build alliances and form coalitions with like-minded nations; and raise global awareness about their unique contributions, experiences and perspectives. By engaging in multilateral forums, small States can have a say in shaping global norms, rules and policies that affect their security, economy and overall well-being. This equal participation fosters a sense of ownership and empowerment, enabling small States to advocate for their specific concerns and needs.

In addition, multilateralism provides small States with access to critical resources, technical assistance and capacity-building support. Many multilateral institutions offer programmes and initiatives specifically designed to assist small States in areas such as trade, development, health, education and climate change adaptation. The majority of funding has been supplied thus far by international sources of public finance, encompassing grants and loans from global and regional development banks, other institutions dedicated to development finance, as well as bilateral and multilateral donors.[37] Developed nations have committed a substantial financial pledge to support initiatives targeted at combating climate change. Some of these major multilateral climate funds include Adaptation Fund, Green Climate Fund, Special Climate Change Fund and Strategic Climate Fund.[38] Additionally, the small States have achieved positive outcomes in attracting blue financing to facilitate sector-specific and cross-sectoral planning, as well as policy coordination. They have also successfully garnered blue investments in sustainable fisheries development, conservation, aquaculture, water and waste management and efforts to address the deterioration of marine ecosystems.[39]

Seychelles as a Multilateral Actor

Seychelles, as a small island nation, has achieved notable recognition and made significant contributions diplomatically to international politics. Through its proactive engagement and focused initiatives, the country has garnered a reputation for its accomplishments and leadership in various issues. Small States should adopt the best practice of collaborating with regional and international partners when addressing national security concerns. Seychelles serves as an exemplary case that has entered and adhered to various bilateral and multilateral agreements.[40] These agreements not only aim to strengthen partnerships but also prioritise the enhanced monitoring and protection of its territorial sea and Exclusive Economic Zone. For instance, it nurtures a strong partnership with its neighbouring countries in the Indian Ocean Africa region. As an active member of the Indian Ocean Commission, Seychelles actively contributes to the promotion of inter-island trade, facilitation of shipping services, conservation of tuna resources, development of renewable energy and the advancement of tourism.[41] It holds memberships in the Common Market for Eastern and Southern Africa and the Southern Africa Development Community; and over the past decade, it has maintained a close collaboration with the World Bank and the International Monetary Fund in order to advance economic liberalisation efforts.[42]

One of the country's notable achievements is its championing of the blue economy. Recognising the immense potential of its marine resources, Seychelles has pioneered the concept of the blue economy, promoting sustainable development and conservation of oceanic resources.[43] By implementing policies that balance economic growth with environmental protection, it has become a global model for harnessing the benefits of the ocean while preserving its ecosystems. The country has also been instrumental in innovative financial mechanisms such as blue bonds and debt-for-nature swaps. These ground-breaking approaches have attracted international attention and support for financing marine conservation and sustainable development projects. Its ability to develop and implement such innovative financial instruments has positioned the nation as a leader in finding innovative solutions to environmental challenges. In terms of its commitment to combating piracy in the Indian Ocean, Seychelles has actively participated in international efforts and regional partnerships to ensure the safety of sea trade routes. Its proactive approach, including capacity-building programmes, sharing of expertise and cooperative initiatives, has contributed significantly to the decline of piracy incidents in the region.[44]

Furthermore, Seychelles has actively been engaged in global initiatives addressing climate change. As a vulnerable island nation facing the impact of rising sea levels and other climate-related challenges, Seychelles as a nation has been a vocal advocate for climate action. Various representatives have participated in international negotiations, highlighting the urgent need for mitigation and adaptation measures. Like other small States, it faces similar climate change risks, including changes in rainfall patterns resulting in flooding and landslides, prolonged periods of drought, rising sea temperatures, alterations in acidity levels and harm to marine ecosystems, more intense storms and storm surges and long-term sea-level rise.[45] The country's commitment to renewable energy and its efforts to transition to a low-carbon economy have highlighted its determination to address climate change and protect its natural resources. It has also demonstrated leadership in promoting sustainable tourism. Recognising the importance of tourism as a major contributor to its economy, Seychelles has embraced sustainable practices to preserve its unique natural and cultural heritage; and it has become a model for the development of responsible and sustainable tourism.

Blue Economic Growth

Seychelles has been at the forefront of implementing innovative initiatives that address critical challenges and promote sustainable development. Collectively, initiatives such as blue bonds, debt-for-nature swaps and anti-piracy efforts demonstrate the country's proactive approach to addressing complex challenges and advancing sustainable development. By leveraging innovative financial mechanisms, engaging in debt restructuring for conservation purposes and actively participating in efforts to combat piracy, Seychelles highlights its commitment to environmental preservation, economic growth and regional security. These initiatives not only benefit the archipelago but also contribute to global sustainability goals and foster cooperation among nations in tackling shared challenges.

The United Nations presented a Concept Paper which provided a broad definition of the 'Blue Economy' as an ocean-based economy that aims at "the improvement of human well-being and social equity, while significantly reducing environmental risks and ecological scarcities".[46] Seychelles has employed the concept of the Blue Economy as a framework for shaping its foreign policy and domestic governance, offering an insightful case study to explore the underlying ideas and perspectives associated with it.[47] The country has emerged as a prominent champion of the blue economy,[48] portrays its commitment to sustainable development and the responsible use of oceanic resources. While the term 'blue economy' is interpreted in various ways, in this context, it refers to the collection of economic sectors and associated policies that collectively determine the sustainability of utilising oceanic resources. The World Bank and United Nations Department of Economic and Social Affairs illustrates the blue economy as a concept that "seeks to promote economic growth, social inclusion and the preservation or improvement of livelihoods while at the same time ensuring environmental sustainability of the oceans and coastal areas".[49] This concept recognises the immense economic potential of the ocean while emphasising the need for environmental conservation and the protection of marine ecosystems. In its role as a champion of the blue economy, Seychelles has actively pursued policies and initiatives aimed at harnessing the benefits of its vast maritime territory while ensuring the long-term health and sustainability of its marine environment. The nation has established extensive protected areas, including marine parks and reserves, to safeguard its diverse marine ecosystems.

The World Bank defines bonds as "a debt instrument issued by governments, development banks or others to raise capital from impact investors to finance marine and ocean-based projects that have positive environmental, economic and climate benefits".[50] Blue bonds have been proposed as a financing mechanism to support the development of the blue economy, addressing the fiscal limitations confronted by small States.[51,52] Seychelles pioneered the issuance of the world's inaugural sovereign bond explicitly designated as 'Blue' and this innovative use-of-proceeds bond is specifically intended to fund sustainable ocean activities.[53] They represent a ground breaking financial mechanism that enables the country to raise funds specifically for marine conservation and sustainable ocean-related projects. These bonds attract investment from both public and private sectors, emphasising the economic value of preserving and sustainably utilising marine resources. By leveraging a concessional loan of $5 million from the Global Environmental Facility and securing a $5 million guarantee from the World Bank, Seychelles strategically aimed to achieve a price point for the blue bond that would satisfy investor expectations while enabling effective deployment of the debt financing for its development initiatives.[54] Through strong cooperation with civil society organisations, governments can leverage bond issuance as a viable approach to secure the necessary funding for advancing sustainable initiatives in the blue economy. By leveraging the potential of blue bonds, Seychelles demonstrates its commitment to the blue economy concept, highlighting the importance of responsible management and conservation of the marine environment.

Seychelles has gained global recognition through its notable accomplishments, including a successful debt swap for conservation and climate change adaptation in 2015, as well as the issuance of the pioneering blue bond in 2018.[55] These initiatives have significantly contributed to the implementation of the blue economy roadmap, further elevating the country's international prominence. The Seychelles Conservation and Climate Adaptation Trust (SeyCCAT) serves as the prominent blue economy initiative of Seychelles.[56] This trust fund, established in 2015 through a collaboration between the Government of Seychelles, Nature Conservancy and philanthropists including Leonardo DiCaprio, manages funds generated from a debt-for-nature swap. The swap involved the reduction of Seychelles' sovereign debt by $21.6 million and was facilitated with the support of the United Kingdom, France, Belgium and Italy. In these arrangements, Seychelles works with international partners to exchange a portion of its debt for commitments to invest in nature conservation and sustainable development projects. The debt-for-nature swap and the subsequent establishment of SeyCCAT in Seychelles has been presented as an embodiment of the blue economy concept. Over time, SeyCCAT's responsibilities have expanded to encompass the management of blue bonds issued by the Seychellois government?. These bonds raised $15 million, which are allocated to financing marine and ocean initiatives.[57] This innovative approach not only helps alleviate the burden of debt but also directs resources towards environmental protection and sustainability. Debt-for-nature swaps highlight Seychelles' commitment to balancing economic development with the preservation of its natural resources.

The Seychellois government has also played a vital role in anti-piracy efforts, particularly in the Indian Ocean region. Recognising the threat posed by maritime piracy to international trade and security, Seychelles has actively participated in regional and international collaborations to combat piracy. Its strategic location garners substantial international support and enhances its relationships with key regional and global stakeholders due to the presence of piracy and its broader strategic implications. Following significant containment of piracy from 2012 onwards, the country emerged as a prominent player in countering piracy in the Western Indian Ocean, earning recognition as a reliable partner to international actors and an influential voice in the broader discourse on maritime security.[58] Through cooperative initiatives, capacity-building programmes and the prosecution of pirates, Seychelles has contributed significantly to the decline of piracy incidents in the region. These anti-piracy efforts highlight Seychelles' commitment to maritime security and its willingness to collaborate with other nations to ensure the safety of sea trade routes.

The presence of institutional frameworks in the maritime sector offered a level of adaptability in addressing the specific issues at hand. An illustration of this is the highly acclaimed regional law enforcement centre located in Seychelles, which received substantial support from international donors in terms of personnel and equipment.[59] Moreover, Seychelles demonstrated its standing when the Contact Group on Piracy off the Coast of Somalia (CGPCS) was seeking a regional chairperson after the European Union's tenure from 2012 to 2014. The country volunteered for the position and its candidacy received unanimous endorsement at the 17th Plenary of the CGPCS.[60] As the primary multilateral mechanism for steering and coordinating the global response to Somali piracy, Seychelles as the regional chairperson was entrusted with chairing upcoming Plenaries, leading international community efforts and ensuring consensus among the group's over 80 participants, including States and international organisations.

Conclusion

In conclusion, this article calls upon policymakers, international organisations and civil society to prioritise and support reformed multilateralism efforts. It emphasises the urgency of addressing power imbalances, promoting equity and enhancing the representation of small States in decision-making processes. While traditional multilateralism has played a significant role in global governance and cooperation, it is important to recognise its shortcomings and address them to strengthen its effectiveness. An analysis of the limitations of traditional multilateralism highlights the need for reforms to enhance efficiency, inclusivity, flexibility, accountability and stakeholder engagement within multilateral institutions. By addressing these shortcomings, multilateralism can better respond to emerging global challenges and promote sustainable peace and development for small States and beyond. Reformed multilateralism offers a promising framework for addressing the needs and concerns in the pursuit of sustainable peace. By promoting inclusivity, cooperation, and the recognition of the unique challenges faced by these States, reformed multilateralism can contribute to a more equitable and effective global governance system. It provides an avenue for small States to actively participate in decision-making processes, advocate for their interests, and foster international cooperation to overcome their challenges and build a more peaceful and sustainable future.

Through strengthened collaboration, capacity building, and stakeholder consultations, Multilateral Development Banks and International Financial Institutions can contribute to a more inclusive and context-specific approach to development assessment. To promote more equitable and accurate assessments of development needs, Multilateral Development Banks and International Financial Institutions should stop using Gross Domestic Product (GDP) per capita as a sole benchmark for assessing development. Instead, a more comprehensive set of indicators should be adopted to reflect the multi-dimensional nature of development. This approach aligns with the recognition that GDP per capita fails to capture important aspects such as income distribution, social development and environmental sustainability. By revising the Multilateral Vulnerability Index and introducing broader criteria, the countries' eligibility for concessional finance can be assessed more effectively. This revision should include factors such as environmental vulnerability, economic diversification, exposure to external shocks and social resilience. Such a comprehensive characterisation would provide a more accurate assessment of a country's development needs and eligibility for concessional finance.

NOTES

1 Ji Youn Yoo, et al., "Comparative Analysis of COVID-19 Guidelines from Six Countries: A Qualitative Study on the US, China, South Korea, the UK, Brazil, and Haiti," *BMC Public Health*, 20 (1), 2020, p. 2.

2 Emmanuel Chiwetalu Ossai, "COVID-19 and Peace in Conflict-Affected Areas," *Encyclopedia*, 2 (4), 2022, pp. 1678-1687.

3 Kishore Mahbubani, "Multilateral Diplomacy," in Kishore Mahbubani (ed.), *The Asian 21st Century*, Springer Singapore, Singapore, 2022, p. 1681.

4 Bruce Jenks and Homi Kharas, "Toward a New Multilateralism," *Brookings*, 29 April 2016, https://www.brookings.edu/articles/toward-a-new-multilateralism/ pp. 1-6.

5 Ngaire Woods, *Governing the Global Economy: Strengthening Multilateral Institutions*, International Peace Institute, 2018, p. 2.

6 Ibid, p. 3.

7 Bruce Jenks and Homi Kharas, no. 4, p. 40.

8 Kathryn J. Bowen et. al., "Implementing the 'Sustainable Development Goals': Towards Addressing Three Key Governance Challenges-Collective Action, Trade-Offs, And Accountability," *Current Opinion in Environmental Sustainability*, Volumes 26–27, June, 2017, p. 91.

9 Ibid.

10 Aleksander Surdej, "Multilateralism and International Governmental Organizations: Principles and Instruments," *Transforming Government: People, Process and Policy*, 14(3), 2020, p. 339.

11 Kathryn J. Bowen, et al., no. 8, p. 91.

12 Knut G. Nustad, "The Development Discourse in the Multilateral System", in Morten Boas, Desmond McNeill (eds.), *Global Institutions and Development*, Routledge, London and New York, 2004, p. 155.

13 Jan Aart Scholte, *Building Global Democracy? Civil Society and Accountable Global Governance*, Cambridge, Cambridge University Press, p. 234.

14 Aleksander Surdej, no. 10, p. 345.

15 Geoffrey Wiseman, "Norms and Diplomacy: The Diplomatic Underpinnings of Multilateralism," in J. P. Muldoon, J. F. Aviel, R. Reitano and E. Sullivan (eds.), *The New Dynamics of Multilateralism: Diplomacy, International Organizations, and Global Governance, United States*, Routledge, 2011, p. 5.

16 Yuen Yuen Ang, "Reinventing Multilateralism: What to Do, What to Study, and Why," *Global Perspectives*, 4(1), 2023, p. 1

17 Julia C. Morse and Robert O. Keohane, "Contested Multilateralism," *The Review of International Organizations*, 9(4), 2014, pp. 385-412.

18 Bruce Jenks and Homi Kharas, no. 4, p. 11.

19 Ibid.

20 Ibid., p. 18.

21 Ngaire Woods, no. 5, p. 3.

22 Jan Aart Scholte, no. 13, p. 193.

23 Bruce Jenks and Homi Kharas, no. 4, p. 18.

24 Bruce Jenks and Homi Kharas, no. 4, p. 6.

25 Jan Aart Scholte, no. 13, p. 162.

26 Ngaire Woods. "Multilateralism in the Twenty-First Century," *Global Perspectives*, 4(1), 2023, p. 7.

27 Aditi Mukund and Namrata Kabra, *Towards Inclusive Climate Multilateralism: An Opportunity for the G20*, Task Force 7 Towards Reformed Multilateralism: Transforming Global Institutions and Frameworks, 2023, p. 5, https://kuberneininitiative.com/wp-content/uploads/2023/10/T20_PolicyBrief_TF7_729_ClimateMultilateralism.pdf

28 Jan Aart Scholte, no. 13, p. 187.

29 Aleksander Surdej, no. 10, p. 345.
30 Geoffrey Wiseman, no. 15, p. 7.
31 Geoffrey Wiseman, no. 15, p. 7.
32 Kishore Mahbubani, no. 3, pp. 232-233.
33 Miles Kahler, "Regional Challenges to Global Governance," *Global Policy*, 8(1), 2017, p. 100.
34 Martin J. Bush, *Climate Change Adaptation in Small Island Developing States*, John Wiley & Sons, United Kingdom, 2018, p. 19.
35 Herein referred to as small States.
36 "Agenda 21," at https://www.un.org/en/conferences/environment/rio1992 (Accessed 21 March2023).
37 Cyrus Rustomjee, "Financing The Blue Economy In Small States," CIGI Policy Brief, 78, May 2016, p. 2.
38 Martin J. Bush, no. 34, pp. 152 -153.
39 Cyrus Rustomjee, no. 37, p. 2.
40 Diana Benoit, "Ocean-based Sustainable Development: Challenges and Opportunities for Seychelles," *Journal of Indian Ocean Studies*, 29(3), 2021, p. 217.
41 Country Watch, "Seychelles Country Review," Country Report, 2022, p. 75.
42 Ibid, p. 77.
43 Diana Benoit, no. 40, p. 215.
44 Christian Bueger and Anders Wivel, "How Do Small Island States Maximize Influence? Creole Diplomacy and the Smart State Foreign Policy of the Seychelles," *Journal of the Indian Ocean Region*, 14(2), 2018, pp. 177-178.
45 Martin J. Bush, no. 34, p. 207.
46 Lee Ki-Hoon, Junsung Noh and Jong Seong Khim, "The Blue Economy and the United Nations' Sustainable Development Goals: Challenges and Opportunities," *Environment International*, 137, 2020, p. 1.
47 Liam Saddington, "Geopolitical Imaginaries in Climate and Ocean Governance: Seychelles and the Blue Economy," *Geoforum*, 139, 2023, p. 1.
48 Dominique Benzaken, et al., "Good Governance for Sustainable Blue Economy in Small Islands: Lessons Learned From the Seychelles Experience," *Frontiers in Political Science*, 4, 2022, p. 13.
49 World Bank and United Nations Department of Economic and Social Affairs, *The Potential of the Blue Economy: Increasing Long-term Benefits of the Sustainable Use of Marine Resources for Small Island Developing States and Coastal Least Developed Countries*, World Bank, Washington DC, 2017.
50 World Bank, Sovereign Blue Bond Issuance, "Sovereign Blue Bond Issuance: Frequently Asked Questions", 2018 at https://www.worldbank.org/en/news/feature/2018/10/29/sovereign-blue-bond-issuance-frequently-asked-questions, (Accessed 21 March2023).
51 Antaya March, Pierre Failler and Michael Bennett, "Challenges When Designing Blue Bond Financing for Small Island Developing States," *Journal of Marine Science*, 2023, p. 1.
52 Benjamin S. Thompson, "Blue Bonds for Marine Conservation and a Sustainable Ocean Economy: Status, Trends, and Insights from Green Bonds," *Marine Policy*, 144, 2022, p. 1.
53 Nathalie Roth, Torsten Thiele and Moritz von Unger, "Blue Bonds: Financing Resilience of Coastal Ecosystems. Key Points for Enhancing Finance Action," *Blue Natural Capital Financing Facility: Technical Guidelines*, Prepared for IUCN GMPP, 2019, p.15.
54 Antaya March, Pierre Failler and Michael Bennett, no. 51, p. 1.
55 Dominique Benzaken et al., no. 48, p. 4.

56 Liam Saddington, no. 47, p. 2.

57 Ibid.

58 Christian Bueger and Wivel Anders, no. 44, p. 179.

59 Katja Lindskov Jacobsen and Jessica Larsen, "Piracy Studies Coming of Age: A Window on the Making of Maritime Intervention Actors," *International Affairs*, 95(5), 2019, p. 1047.

60 Christian Bueger and Wivel Anders, no. 44, p. 179.

CHAPTER 21

Intellectual Property in an Era of Great Technology Competition

Mohammed Soliman

The United States and China are two of the world's largest economies, and both are vying for technological dominance in the 21st century. With this competition comes a heightened focus on intellectual property (IP) protection, which has become an increasingly contentious issue between the two countries. This chapter explores the concept of intellectual property and its role in US-China technology competition. It provides an overview of the various types of intellectual property, the challenges faced by companies operating in China, the efforts made by both countries to protect intellectual property, and the potential implications of US-China technology competition on global intellectual property rights.

The Source of Technology Competition between the United States and China

Competition between China and the United States in the technology sector has been intensifying over the past few years. Both countries invest heavily in research and development and compete for dominance in critical areas such as artificial intelligence (AI), 5G networks, and quantum computing. This competition is not only crucial for economic reasons but also has national security implications.

There are several factors driving technology competition between China and the United States. One of the main factors is economics. Both countries recognise the importance of technology in driving domestic economic growth and creating jobs. They are investing heavily in research and development to create new technologies that can realise economic growth in a highly competitive international market.

The second primary driver of this competition is national security. Both countries view technological dominance as critical in maintaining national security. They recognise the strategic value of technologies such as AI, 5G, and quantum computing and are investing heavily in these areas to ensure that they maintain a technological advantage over their rivals.

A third driver of the present technology competition is ideology. The Chinese government sees technology as a critical enabler of its political goals, including expanding its influence globally and shaping the international order to reflect its worldview more closely. The United States, for its part, recognises the importance of technology in *preserving* the current international order, which it primarily designed. These differing worldviews – the US seeking to protect the post-Second World War liberal international order and China aiming, for example, to embed rigid respect for national sovereignty – are driving the competition in the technology sector.

Areas of Competition

Of the several areas of competition between China and the United States in the technology sector, one of the most significant is artificial intelligence.[1] China has made significant progress in AI in recent years, setting a goal of becoming a world leader in the field by 2030. The United States is also investing heavily in AI and has a significant lead in the development of underlying technology, such as computer chips.

Another area of the competition is 5G networks.[2] 5G networks are critical for enabling the next generation of technologies, such as autonomous vehicles and the Internet of Things. China has made significant progress in rolling out 5G networks and aims to be the global leader in this area. The United States has been slower to adopt 5G but is also investing heavily in the development of the technology.

A third area of competition is quantum computing. Quantum computing has the potential to revolutionise computing by enabling faster and more powerful processing. China has significantly advanced its ability to develop quantum computing technology and as with the previous two areas of competition, has set a goal of becoming a world leader in the field. The United States, for its part, is making significant investments in quantum computing and has led in demonstrated technical capability in every major approach to quantum technologies. Despite this leadership, the United States lags behind China in terms of the development of the underlying technology and more specifically, quantum sensing, which is "the use of quantum physics to improve the capabilities of a wide variety of types of sensors."[3]

Consequences of Technology Competition

The present technology competition between China and the United States has significant consequences for both countries as well as for the rest of the world. One of the most significant consequences is economic[4]. The technology sector is a key driver of economic growth and job creation worldwide. The country that becomes the leader in key technologies such as AI, 5G, and quantum computing will have a significant advantage in terms of global economic competitiveness.[5]

Technology competition also has national security implications. Technologies such as AI and 5G are seen by both the US and China as critical for maintaining military and intelligence superiority.[6] Therefore, the nation that develops these technologies at a greater and more advanced rate will have a significant advantage in terms of national security.

US-China technology competition also has broader geopolitical implications. Both countries are vying for global influence, and technology is a key tool in this competition[7]. Whoever becomes the lead producer and operator of key technologies will have a significant advantage in terms of shaping the global narrative, projecting power, and influencing other countries. One major factor that will shape the outcome of this highly strategic technology competition is intellectual property.

Overview of Intellectual Property and Intellectual Property Rights

Intellectual property refers to creations of the mind, such as inventions, literary and artistic works, designs, and symbols, which are used in commerce. Accordingly, intellectual property rights (IPRs), as per the definition in the World Trade Organisation's Agreement on Trade-Related Aspects of Intellectual Property Rights (TRIPS), are "the rights given to persons over the creations of their minds"[8] that "usually give the creator an exclusive right over the use of his/her creation for a certain period of time." Several types of IPRs exist within these areas, including copyrights, patents, trademarks, and trade secrets. These IPR types are divided into two broad categories[9]: artistic and industrial.

Artistic IPRs, in the form of copyrights, aim to uphold the rights of authors of literary and artistic works, as well as computer programmes, and give the owner the exclusive right to reproduce, distribute, and display the work. Copyrights last for the life of the author/creator plus 70 years.

Industrial IPRs – the area more relevant to US-China technology competition – is characterised as the protection of distinctive signs, such as trademarks and geographical indications, and involves protections that stimulate innovation, design, and the production of technology, such as invention-protecting patents, industrial designs, and trade secrets. Patents are granted to inventors for new and useful processes, machines, articles of manufacture, or compositions of matter. They give the inventor the right to exclude others from making, using, selling, or importing the patented invention for a limited period – usually 20 years – from the filing date of the application. Trademarks are symbols, words, or phrases that identify and distinguish goods and services of one party from those of others. They protect the owner's exclusive right to use the mark and prevent others from using identical marks in the same market. Trade secrets refer to confidential information that gives a business a competitive advantage. Examples of trade secrets include customer lists, manufacturing processes, and marketing strategies. Trade secret protection is granted to businesses that take reasonable steps to keep the information secret.

Challenges Faced by Companies Operating in China

China is the world's second-largest economy and a major player in the global technology industry. However, intellectual property protection in China has been a contentious issue for many years. Foreign companies operating in China have faced several challenges when it comes to protecting their intellectual property, including:

1. Lack of Enforcement: Despite having laws that protect intellectual property, enforcement has been a major issue in China.[10] Intellectual property infringement is widespread, and many companies have reported difficulty in enforcing their rights.
2. Weak Legal System: The legal system in China has been criticised for being weak, opaque, and subject to political influence. This has made it difficult for foreign companies to protect their intellectual property in Chinese courts.[11]
3. Counterfeiting: China has long been known as a hub for counterfeit goods. The production and sale of counterfeit goods can be detrimental to a company's brand and reputation and can also lead to lost revenue.
4. Forced Technology Transfer: The Chinese government and Chinese firms have used various strategies to acquire intellectual property from US companies and innovators. Some foreign companies operating in China

have reportedly been forced to transfer technology to their Chinese partners as a condition of doing business in the country through licensing agreements[12]. Other attempts at facilitating technology transfer are made through foreign direct investment, venture capital investments, joint ventures, human and cyber espionage, and talent acquisition[13]. Forced technology transfer can lead to the loss of competitive advantages and damages the integrity of intellectual property.

5. Cybersecurity Concerns: Cyber attacks targeting intellectual property have become major concerns for companies operating in China.[14] These attacks can lead to the theft of trade secrets and other confidential information.

Efforts Made by Both Countries to Protect Intellectual Property

Intellectual property is a critical issue in technology competition between the United States and China.[15] Both countries have different approaches to IP protection, and this has become a contentious matter in their bilateral relations. Below, this chapter explores the US' approach to IP in the context of technology competition with China, its implications, and its potential consequences.

The United States' IP Strategy

The US has a robust system of IP protection designed to encourage innovation and promote economic growth. The system includes patents, trademarks, copyrights, and trade secrets. The US Government has prioritised strengthening IP protection both domestically and internationally.[16] This priority is two-fold: first, it looks to set precedents and standards for international regulatory practices to accommodate compliant innovators and firms domestically and internationally. Second, it seeks to curb China's ambitions to confront the US' IP strength and capture larger technological markets.

One of the most significant steps the US government has taken to strengthen IP protection is the establishment of the US Patent and Trademark Office (USPTO).[17] The USPTO is responsible for granting patents and trademarks to inventors and businesses. It also provides resources and support to help inventors and businesses protect their IP. The US government has also taken steps to strengthen IP protection through legislation. One of the most significant pieces of legislation in this area is the America Invents Act (AIA),[18] which was signed into law in 2011. The AIA introduced several significant changes to the US patent system, including a move from a first-to-invent system to a first-inventor-to-file system.

The US government has also taken steps to strengthen IP protection through international agreements. One of the most significant international agreements in this area is the Agreement on Trade-Related Aspects of Intellectual Property Rights – known as TRIPS[19] – which was signed in 1994. TRIPS requires member countries to provide a level of IP protection that is consistent with international standards.

Implications of the US Approach to IP amidst Technology Competition with China

The US approach to IP protection has significant implications for technology competition with China. One of the most significant implications is that it has created a level playing field for US businesses. US businesses can invest in R&D with confidence, knowing that their innovations will be protected by strong IP laws. This has helped to promote innovation and economic growth in the US. However, the US approach to IP protection has also created tensions vis-a-vis technology competition with China. The US has often accused China of engaging in IP theft and infringement, significantly contributing to the trade war between the two countries.[20] The US government's hardline the position on IP protection[21] has become a major sticking point in its bilateral relations with China.

The US government has accused China of engaging in several IP-related practices that are harmful to US businesses. These include forced technology transfer, cyber espionage, and counterfeiting.[22] The US government has also accused China of violating international IP standards, such as those set out in TRIPS. The US government, across administrations, also generally enjoys bipartisan support for its stance and policies regarding China and IP protection[23] and has taken several steps to address these concerns. One of the most significant steps has been the imposition of tariffs on Chinese imports. These tariffs are designed, in part, to pressure China to improve its IP protection regime and to cease engaging in practices that harm US businesses.[24]

Potential Consequences of the US Approach to IP during Technology Competition with China

The US approach to IP protection amidst technology competition with China has potential consequences for both countries and the rest of the world, namely the Global South. The first and one of the most significant consequences is economic. IP protection is critical for promoting innovation in both domestic and international technology sectors, key drivers of economic growth and job creation. The trade war between the US and China has already significantly impacted the global economy,[25] and continued tensions in this area could lead to further economic disruption. The US' approach to IP protection also has national security implications. Technologies such as AI, 5G, and quantum computing are critical for maintaining military and intelligence superiority.[26] IP theft and infringement could give China an unfair advantage in these areas and threaten critical US national security elements. Tightened international regulations surrounding IP protection could also have adverse impacts on innovation and technology emerging from the developing world.

China's IP Strategy

China's approach to IP protection has evolved significantly over the years. In the early years of its economic development, China did not have a strong system of IP protection.[27] This led to concerns among foreign businesses that their innovations would be stolen or copied. As a result, many foreign businesses were reluctant to invest in China. However, in recent years, China has taken steps to strengthen its IP protection regime. The Chinese government has introduced several laws and regulations to protect IP, including patents, trademarks, copyrights, and trade secrets. The Chinese government has also established specialised IP courts to handle IP-related disputes.

One of the most significant steps taken by the Chinese government to strengthen IP protection is the establishment of the State Intellectual Property Office (SIPO). The SIPO, an appendage of China's State Administration for Market Regulation[28] formed in 2018, is responsible for granting patents and trademarks to inventors and businesses. It also provides resources and support to help inventors and businesses protect their IP. China has also moved to strengthen IP protection through international agreements.[29] China joined the World Trade Organisation (WTO) in 2001 and has agreed to adhere to the terms of the TRIPS agreement.[30] TRIPS requires member countries to provide IP protection that is consistent with international standards.

Implications of China's Approach to IP Protection in Technology Competition with the United States

China's approach to IP protection has significant implications in technology competition with the United States. One of the most significant implications is that it has created a more level playing field for foreign businesses operating in China.[31] Foreign businesses in China can invest in R&D with more confidence, knowing that their innovations will be protected by stronger IP laws. This has helped to promote innovation and economic growth in China.

China's IP protection policies also have implications for China's domestic industries. China has historically been reliant on foreign technology, particularly from the United States. However, as China has become more technologically advanced, it has started to develop its own domestic industries. Stronger IP protection has helped to encourage this trend,[32] allowing China to develop its own technological capabilities.

Potential Consequences of China's Approach to IP Protection during Technology Competition with the United States

China's approach to IP protection during technology competition with the United States has potential consequences for both countries and the rest of the world. The technology sector is a key driver of US economic growth as well as the US job market.[33] China's approach to IP protection has direct and indirect consequences for the US economy and further geopolitical consequences for the US' global standing.

In the immediate term, the strengthened IP protection introduced by the Chinese government could attract innovators to join Chinese firms and invite foreign companies to operate in China, dampening the inflows of such innovation to the US. China's increased regulatory standards will also allow for Chinese firms to challenge US firms in the global market and to the extent where possible, enter US markets. The trade war between the United States and China has already significantly impacted the global economy, and continued tensions in this area could lead to further economic disruption and curb the US' global economic standing.

Domestic improvements to China's IP protection regulations could also play a role in enhancing the attractiveness of Chinese foreign direct investment (FDI) opportunities in other countries. By addressing the reputation that Beijing has shouldered via Washington's accusations of IP theft, increased Chinese FDI in key regions could deprive the US of opportunities to extend their own strategic reach through economic and technological partnerships.

Potential Consequences of China-US Intellectual Property Competition on Global Innovation

Competition between China and the United States over IP protection has significant implications for the future of global innovation. As the two largest economies in the world, their actions have far-reaching consequences for the global economy, particularly in the technology sector. Below, the chapter explores the potential consequences of China-US IP competition on global innovation.

- **Stifling Innovation:** One potential consequence of the China-US IP competition is that it could stifle innovation. IP protection is critical for promoting innovation because it incentivises inventors and businesses to invest in R&D. However, if IP protection is weak or inconsistent, it can discourage innovation by reducing the barriers for competitors to copy or steal inventions.[34] China-US IP competition has led to accusations of IP theft and infringement on both sides.[35,36] These accusations have created uncertainty for inventors and businesses, particularly those operating in both countries. This uncertainty can discourage investment in R&D, as inventors and businesses may be reluctant to disclose their innovations or invest in new technologies fearing that they could be stolen or copied.
- **Reducing Collaboration:** Another potential consequence of China-US IP competition is that it could reduce collaboration between inventors and businesses in the two countries. Collaboration is critical for innovation because it allows inventors and businesses to share knowledge, resources, and expertise. However, if IP protection is weak or inconsistent, it can make collaboration more difficult[37] by creating concerns about the protection of intellectual property. China-US IP competition has already led to a decline in collaboration between the two countries. For example, many Chinese researchers have faced increased scrutiny and restrictions when seeking to collaborate with US researchers.[38] This has led to a decline in joint research projects and reduced opportunities for knowledge sharing and innovation.[39]
- **Distorting Markets:** China-US IP competition could also distort international markets by creating barriers to entry for some businesses. IP protection is critical for promoting competition because it allows inventors and businesses to protect their innovations and compete on a level playing field. However, if IP protection is weak or inconsistent, it can create barriers to entry[40] for businesses that do not have the resources to protect their innovations. China-US IP competition has already led to accusations of unfair competition on both sides. The United States has accused[41] China of engaging in forced technology transfer and intellectual property theft, which has created barriers for entry of US businesses seeking to operate in China. At the same time, China has

accused the United States of unfairly restricting Chinese businesses from accessing certain technologies and markets.

- **Inhibiting Technological Progress:** China-US IP competition could also inhibit technological progress by creating a more fragmented global technology landscape. IP protection is critical for promoting technological progress because it provides incentives for inventors and businesses to invest in R&D. However, if IP protection is weak or inconsistent, it can lead to a proliferation of similar technologies and create barriers to innovation. China-US IP competition has led to increased fragmentation in the global technology landscape.[42] For example, China has developed its own domestic industries in response to concerns about reliance on foreign technology.[43] This may lead to a more fragmented global technology landscape, with different countries and regions developing their own technologies and standards.

To promote global innovation, it is important for both countries to work together to establish a strong and consistent system of IP protection, that promotes competition, collaboration, and technological progress.

Potential Consequences of China-US Intellectual Property Competition on the Global South

The competition between China and the United States over intellectual property (IP) protection has significant implications for the Global South, a geographic zone which includes developing countries in Africa, Asia, and Latin America. As the two largest economies in the world, the actions of China and the US have far-reaching effects on the global economy, particularly in the technology sector. Below, this chapter explores the potential consequences of the China-US IP competition on the Global South.

1. **Access to Technology:** One potential consequence of China-US IP competition is that it could limit access to technology for developing countries in the Global South. If IP protection is too strong or inconsistent, it can create barriers to access for developing countries that do not have the resources to invest in R&D or protect their own innovations. China-US IP competition has led to increased fragmentation in the global technology landscape.[44] This has created a more complex and challenging environment for developing countries that are seeking to access new technologies. For example, some US companies have restricted access to certain technologies[45] in response to concerns about

IP protection. At the same time, Chinese companies have developed their own technologies, which may not be compatible with existing global standards.

2. **Imbalanced Trade Relations:** Another potential consequence of China-US IP competition is that it could exacerbate imbalanced trade relations between developed and developing countries.[46] IP protection is critical for promoting competition because it allows inventors and businesses to protect their innovations and compete on a level playing field. Inconsistent or overly strong IP protection can create barriers for developing countries that do not have the resources to protect their own innovations.
3. **Limited Economic Growth:** China-US IP competition could also limit economic growth in developing countries by creating barriers to innovation and technology transfer. Despite being a critical tool for promoting technological progress, IP protection can lead to a proliferation of similar technologies and create barriers to innovation. China-US IP competition has created a more complex and challenging environment for developing countries to acquire new technologies. This has limited their ability to innovate and develop new industries, which can have significant implications for economic growth and development. China-US IP competition has also solicited a more restrained digital trade agenda[47] and an increased sensitivity to knowledge sharing from the US, as well as Chinese enthusiasm towards new international IP standards. Consequently, these trends provide an uneasy outlook on the ability of developing nations to innovate and manufacture their own technologies and could very well hinder the Global South's pursuit of digital sovereignty.

Potential Solutions to Mitigate the Impacts of US-China IP Competition on the Global South

To address the potential consequences of China-US IP competition on the Global South, it is important for both countries to work together to establish a strong and consistent system of IP protection that promotes competition, collaboration, and technological progress. Some potential solutions include:

- Encouraging collaboration between inventors and businesses in the Global South and the developed world to promote knowledge sharing and innovation.
- Developing a more balanced and inclusive system of IP protection that takes into account the needs and concerns of developing countries.

- Encouraging greater investment in R&D and technology transfer in the Global South to promote innovation and economic growth.
- Developing a more transparent and predictable system of IP protection that promotes greater certainty and predictability for inventors and businesses.

Potential Solutions to Consequences of China-US Intellectual Property Competition

The competition between China and the United States over intellectual property protection has significant implications for the global economy, particularly in the technology sector. To address these challenges, there are several potential solutions that both countries can consider:

- Strengthening international intellectual property norms and standards: One solution is to establish stronger international norms and standards for intellectual property protection. This could include promoting greater transparency and predictability in intellectual property protection, ensuring fair access to technology, and improving coordination and cooperation between countries on intellectual property protection.
- Encouraging collaboration and knowledge sharing: Another solution is to encourage greater collaboration and knowledge sharing between inventors and businesses in both developed and developing countries. This could involve promoting greater access to technology and technical expertise, encouraging the sharing of best practices in intellectual property protection, and supporting joint ventures and partnerships between businesses in different countries.
- Supporting technology transfer and innovation: A third solution is to support greater technology transfer and innovation in the Global South. This could involve providing funding for research and development, supporting the development of local innovation ecosystems, and encouraging greater investment in new and emerging technologies.
- Establishing alternative dispute resolution mechanisms: Another potential solution is to establish alternative dispute resolution mechanisms for intellectual property disputes. This could involve establishing independent arbitration panels, promoting mediation and conciliation, and providing support for capacity building in intellectual property law and dispute resolution.

- Promoting greater awareness and education: Finally, promoting greater awareness and education regarding intellectual property issues could help to address some of the challenges associated with China-US intellectual property competition. This could involve promoting greater awareness of intellectual property rights and obligations, supporting capacity-building and training programmes, and developing public awareness campaigns to promote a greater understanding of intellectual property issues.

Conclusion

The competition that has pitted China and the United States against each other over intellectual property protection has significant consequences for the global economy. The Global South, in particular, bears such burdens, as the process by which developing countries are provided with technology, capacities, and knowhow by Chinese and US firms will come under increased pressure. The potential consequences of this competition include limited access to technology, the exacerbation of imbalanced trade relations, and obstructed economic growth. Considering the cyclical relationship of global disorder and intellectual property competition – circumstances of disorder exacerbate IP competition which in turn creates further decoupling – global and domestic economies are facing a downward spiral that erodes bilateral and multilateral relationships and restricts innovation.

To address the potential consequences of this competition, it is important for both the US and China to work together to establish a strong and consistent system of intellectual property protection that promotes collaboration, innovation, and economic growth for all countries. By promoting greater transparency, encouraging collaboration and knowledge sharing, supporting organised technology transfer and innovation, establishing alternative dispute resolution mechanisms, and promoting greater awareness and education, it may be possible to mitigate some of the negative consequences of China-US intellectual property competition and strive for a more inclusive and equitable global economy.

With this being said, the barriers that challenge these solutions are formidable, from political to logistical barriers. Potential shifts in geopolitical tensions and global economic pressures, such as a possible Chinese invasion of Taiwan or a global crisis that impacts supply chains similar to the Covid-19 Pandemic, will produce new sets of region-specific issues that necessitate technology sharing as a form of cross-regional economic integration. As IP warfare continues to wage on, the ability of innovations emerging from US and Chinese firms to address emerging issues will be hindered. If effective solutions to great power competition over intellectual property conflicts cannot be adopted, it could exacerbate the circumstances of global disorder that characterises today's international landscape. The US' standing as the foremost leader in technological innovation, as well as its broader economic might, is threatened by an enhanced Chinese IP protection strategy that goes unchecked.

As the developing world takes steps to pursue digital sovereignty, a race is ensuing between great economic and technological powers to provide their own technologies and investments to sponsor digital transformations for decades to come. The IP conflict between the US and China is not only a specific policy issue for both countries but also lurks within every available arena for great power competition. The US' response to China's IP approach will also define conventions of international regulation-setting and illustrate a shift that will be felt in nearly every domestic and global sector.

NOTES

1 Jessica Brandt, Sarah Kreps, Chris Meserole, Pavneet Singh, and Melanie W Sisson, "Succeeding In the AI Competition with China: A Strategy for Action," Brookings Institution, September 2022, at https://www.brookings.edu/wp-content/uploads/2022/09/FP_20220930_us_china_tech.pdf (Accessed 2 April 2023).

2 Nicol Turner Lee, "Navigating the U.S.-China 5G Competition," *Brookings Institution*, April 2020, at https://www.brookings.edu/wp-content/uploads/2020/04/FP_20200427_5g_competition_turner_lee_v2.pdf (Accessed 2 April 2023).

3 Parker, Edward, Daniel Gonzales, Ajay K. Kochhar, Sydney Litterer, Kathryn O'Connor, Jon Schmid, Keller Scholl, Richard Silberglitt, Joan Chang, Christopher A. Eusebi, and Scott W. Harold, "An Assessment of the U.S. and Chinese Industrial Bases in Quantum Technology," *RAND Corporation*, 2022 at https://www.rand.org/content/dam/rand/pubs/research_reports/RRA800/RRA869-1/RAND_RRA869-1.pdf (Accessed 27 March 2023).

4 "Intellectual Property Rights (IPR) and International Trade", *Congressional Research Service*, 7 February 2022, at https://crsreports.congress.gov/product/pdf/IF/IF10033 (Accessed 30 March 2023).

5 Sara Hsu, Ja-Ian Chong, Rorry Daniels, Shirley Martey Hargis, John Lee, "Finding Firmer Ground: The Role of High Technology in U.S.-China Relations," *The Carter Center*, 7 February 2023, athttps://www.cartercenter.org/resources/pdfs/peace/china/finding-firmer-ground-the-role-of-high-technology-in-u.s.-china-relations.pdf (Accessed 30 March 2023).

6 Michael Raska, "Strategic Competition for Emerging Military Technologies: Comparative Paths and Patterns," in *PRISM*, 8(3), 2020, pp. 64-81.

7 Graham Allison, Kevin Klyman, Karina Barbesino, Hugo Yen, "The Great Tech Rivalry: China vs the U.S.," *Belfer Center for Science and International Affairs* at the Harvard Kennedy School, December 2021, at https://www.belfercenter.org/sites/default/files/GreatTechRivalry_ChinavsUS_211207.pdf (Accessed 1 April 2023).

8 "What Are Intellectual Property Rights?", *World Trade Organization*, at https://www.wto.org/english/tratop_e/trips_e/intel1_e.htm (Accessed 30 March 2023).

9 Ibid.

10 "China Commercial Guide - Protecting Intellectual Property," *International Trade Administration*, 7 April 2023, at https://www.trade.gov/country-commercial-guides/china-protecting-intellectual-property (Accessed 7 April 2023).

11 Daniel Rechtschaffen, "How China's Legal System Enables Intellectual Property Theft", *The Diplomat*, 11 November 2020, at https://thediplomat.com/2020/11/how-chinas-legal-system-enables-intellectual-property-theft/ (Accessed 7 April 2023).

12 Sean O'Connor, "How Chinese Companies Facilitate Technology Transfer from the United States," *U.S.-China Economic and Security Review Commission*, 6 May 2019, at https://www.uscc.gov/sites/default/files/Research/How%20Chinese%20Companies%20Facilitate%20Tech%20Transfer%20from%20the%20US.pdf (Accessed 11 April 2023).

13 Michael Brown and Pavneet Singh, "China's Technology Transfer Strategy: How Chinese Investments in Emerging Technology Enable a Strategic Competitor to Access the Crown Jewels of U.S. Innovation," *Defense Innovation Unit*, January 2018, at https://nationalsecurity.gmu.edu/wp-content/uploads/2020/02/DIUX-China-Tech-Transfer-Study-Selected-Readings.pdf (Accessed 11 April 2023).

14 "Findings of the Investigation into China's Acts, Policies, and Practices Related to Technology Transfer, Intellectual Property, and Innovation under Section 301 of the Trade Act of 1974," *Office of the U.S. Trade Representative*, 22 March 2018, at https://ustr.gov/sites/default/files/Section%20301%20FINAL.PDF (Accessed 7 April 2023)

15 Jon Bateman, "Countering Unfair Chinese Economic Practices and Intellectual Property Theft," in U.S.-China Technological Decoupling: A Strategy and Policy Framework, *Carnegie Endowment for International Peace*, 25 April 2022, at https://carnegieendowment.org/files/Bateman_Countering_Unfair_Economic_Practices.pdf (Accessed 29 March 2023).

16 Congressional Research Service, no 4.

17 "General Information Concerning Patents", *United States Patent and Trademark Office, United States Patent and Trademark Office* at https://www.uspto.gov/patents/basics/general-information-patents#:~:text=Functions%20of%20the%20United%20States%20Patent% 20 and%20Trademark%20Office&t ext=The%20role%20of%20the%20USPTO,corporate %20products%2C%20and%20service%20identifications (Accessed 2 April 2023).

18 "Leahy-Smith America Invents Act, Public Law 112-19," *U.S. Patent and Trademark Office*, 16 September 2011, at https://www.uspto.gov/sites/default/files/aia_implementation/20110 916-pub-l112-29.pdf (Accessed 12 April 2023).

19 "Agreement on Trade-Related Aspects of Intellectual Property Rights", Annex 1C of the Marrakesh Agreement Establishing the World Trade Organization, *World Trade Organization*, 15 April 1994, at https://www.wto.org/english/docs_e/legal_e/27-trips.pdf (Accessed 9 April 2023).

20 Jon Bateman, no. 15.

21 Office of the Spokesperson, "Briefing on Limiting the CCP's Ability to Steal U.S. Technologies and Intellectual Property," *U.S. Department of State*, 2 June 2020, at https://www.state.gov/briefing-with-senior-state-department-officials-on-u-s-limiting-thepeoples-liberation-armys-ability-to-use-nonimmigrant-visa-programs-to-illicitly-acquire-u-stechnologies-an? (Accessed 30 March 2023).

22 "How China's Economic Aggression Threatens the Technologies and Intellectual Property of the United States and the World," *White House*, 18 June 2018, at https://trumpwhitehouse.archives.gov/wp-content/uploads/2018/06/FINAL-China-Technology-Report-6.18.18-PDF.pdf (Accessed 30 March 2023).

23 Gerald F. Seib, "Amid Polarization, Bipartisanship Emerges on China, Big Tech," *The Wall Street Journal,* 10 June 2019, at https://www.wsj.com/articles/amid-polarization-bipartisanship-emerges-on-china-big-tech-11560177194 (Accessed 13 April 2023).

24 Kevin J. Hickey, Nina M. Hart, Brandon J. Murrill, Kevin T. Richards, "Intellectual Property Violations and China: Legal Remedies," *Congressional Research Service*, 7 September 2022, at https://sgp.fas.org/crs/row/R46532.pdf (Accessed 7 April 2023).

25 Pablo D. Fajgelbaum, Amit K. Khandelwal, "The Economic Impacts of the US-China Trade War," *Annual Review of Economics*, 14 (1), 28 April 2022, pp. 205-228.

26 Michael Raska, no. 6.

27 Katrin Muehlfeld, Mei Wang, "Intellectual Property Rights in China – A Literature Review on the Public's Perspective," *Frontiers in Sociology* 7:793165, 12 April 2022, at https://www.frontiersin.org/articles/10.3389/fsoc.2022.793165/full (Accessed 29 March 2023).

28 "China's New State Administration for Market Regulation: What to Know and What to Expect," Ropes & Gray, 3 April 2018 at https://www.ropesgray.com/-/media/Files/alerts/2018/04/20180402_China_LS_Alert.pdf?la=en&hash=5464384AF9D02E3C43F676EB57CE491528BEFBE0 (Accessed 3 April 2019).

29 Katrin Muehlfeld, Mei Wang, no. 27.

30 Kristin Brandl, Izzet Darendeli, Ram Mudambi, "Foreign Actors and Intellectual Property Protection Regulations in Developing Countries," *Journal of International Business Studies,* 50, 826–846, 1 July 2019.

31 Ivy Liang, "Developments in Protection of Foreign Intellectual Property Protection in China," *Gowling WLG*, 4 August 2020, at https://gowlingwlg.com/en/insights-resources/articles/2020/foreign-intellectual-property-protection-in-china/ (Accessed 4 April 2023).

32 Yukon Huang, Jeremy Smith, "China's Record on Intellectual Property Rights Is Getting Better and Better," *Foreign Policy*, 16 October 2019, at https://foreignpolicy.com/2019/10/16/china-intellectual-property-theft-progress/ (Accessed 4 April 2023).

33 "U.S. Economic Contribution of the Consumer Technology Sector," PricewaterhouseCoopers LLP (PwC), April 2019, at https://cdn.cta.tech/cta/media/media/resources/research/pdfs/2019_pwc_cta_economic-contribution-of-the-consumer-technology-sector.pdf (Accessed 13 April 2023).

34 Jonathan F. Lee, "Innovation, Intellectual Property, and the Role of External Forces," Paper presented at the Tenth Annual Conference on Innovation Economics, Chicago, Illinois, 2017, Northwestern Pritzker School of Law, Chicago, Illinois, 2017, at https://wwws.law.northwestern.edu/research-faculty/clbe/events/innovation/documents/lee_innovation_intellectual_property_role_of_competition.pdf (Accessed 4 April 2023).

35 Joe McDonald, "China Accuses Washington of Cyberspying on University," *AP News*, 5 September 2022, at https://apnews.com/article/technology-china-united-states-beijing-hacking-0bbe609d2b35e767a6082ca630d1ca3f (Accessed 9 April 2023).

36 "China Denies Accusations of Stealing US Intellectual Property," *Bloomberg Law*, 22 November 2018, at https://news.bloomberglaw.com/ip-law/china-denies-accusations-of-stealing-u-s-intellectual-property (Accessed 9 April 2023).

37 Ilaria Mazzocco, Qin Mei, "How U.S.-China Tensions Have Hurt American Science," Big Data China: CSIS Trustee Chair in Chinese Business Economics & Stanford Center on China's Economy and Institutions, 9 December 2022, at https://bigdatachina.csis.org/how-u-s-china-tensions-have-hurt-american-science/ (Accessed 11 April 2023).

38 Caroline Wagner, Xiaojing Cai, "Changes In Co-Publication Patterns among China, The European Union (28) and The United States of America, 2016-2021," 15 February 2022,

at https://arxiv.org/pdf/2202.00453.pdf (Accessed 9 April 2023).

39 Remco Zwetsloot, "US-China STEM Talent Decoupling: Background, Policy, and Impact", *Johns Hopkins University Applied Physics Lab*, October 2020, at https://www.jhuapl.edu/assessing-us-china-technology-connections/publications (Accessed 11 April 2023).

40 Joel R. Reidenberg, Jamela Debelak, "Report on Analysis of the Economic/Legal Literature on Intellectual Property (IP) Rights: A Barrier to Entry?" *Report presented at the Eighth Session of the Committee on Development and Intellectual Property*, November 2011, Geneva, *World Intellectual Property Organization*, 16 January 2012.

41 Sean O'Connor, no. 12.

42 Diego A. Cerdeiro, Rui Mano, Johannes Eugster, Dirk V Muir, Shanaka J Peiris, "Sizing Up the Effects of Technological Decoupling," *International Monetary Fund*, Working Paper No. 2021/069, 12 March 2021.

43 Bates Gill, "China's Quest for Greater Technological Self-Reliance," *Asia Society*, 23 March 2021, at https://asiasociety.org/australia/chinas-quest-greater-technological-self-reliance (Accessed 11 April 2023).

44 Diego A. Cerdeiro, Rui Mano, Johannes Eugster, Dirk V Muir, Shanaka J Peiris, no. 42.

45 Gerald F. Seib, no. 23.

46 Hilary McGeachy, "US-China Technology Competition: Impacting a Rules-Based Order," The United States Studies Centre at the University of Sydney, May 2019, at https://publicsectornetwork.com/wp-content/uploads/2020/01/US-China-technology-competition-impacting-a-rules-based-order.pdf (Accessed 15 April 2023).

47 Hilary McGeahy, no. 46.

Bibliography

Ayoob, Mohammed, "Security in the Third World: the worm about to turn?", *International Affairs*, 60(1), 1984.

Baldwin, David, "The Concept of Security", *Review of International Studies*, 23(1), 1997.

Baldwin, Richard "The World Trade Organization and the Future of Multilateralism", *The Journal of Economic Perspectives*, 30(1), Winter 2016, pp. 95-115

Buzan, Barry, *People, States, and Fear. An Agenda for International Security Studies in the Post-Cold War Era*, Colchester, ECPR Press, 2009.

Buzan, Barry, *People, States, and Fear: The National Security Problem in International Relations*, Brighton, Wheatsheaf Books, 1983.

Buzan, Barry; HANSEN, Lene, *The Evolution of International Security Studies*, Cambridge, Cambridge University Press, 2009.

Cox, Robert W. "Multilateralism and World Order", *Review of International Studies*, 18(2), April 1992, pp. 161-180

Dunn Cavelty, Myriam; MAUER, Victor, "Introduction", in DUNN CAVELTY, Myriam; MAUER, Victor (eds.), *The Routledge Handbook of Security Studies*, London, Routledge, 2010.

Goodrich, Leland M., "U.S. Foreign Policy: Shield of the Republic by Walter Lippmann", in *The American Political Science Review*, 37(5), 1943.

Guilhot, Nicolas (ed.), *The Invention of International Relations Theory: Realism*, the Rockefeller Foundation, and the 1954 Conference on Theory, New York, Columbia University Press, 2011.

Hampson, Fen Osler Paul Heinbecker, 'The "New" Multilateralism of the Twenty-First Century', *Global Governance*, 17(3), July-Sept. 2011, pp. 299-310

HUGHES, Christopher W.; LAI, Yew Meng (eds.), *Security Studies. A Reader*, London, Routledge, 2011.

Jokela, Juha, *Global Governance and Effective Multilateralism, The G-20: A Pathway To Effective Multilateralism?* Challiot Paper, European Union Institute for Security Studies (EUISS), 2011

Lippmann, Walter, *US foreign policy: Shield of the Republic*, Boston, Little Brown and Company, 1943.

Malin, James C.U.S., "Foreign Policy: Shield of the Republic by Walter Lippmann; America's Foreign Policies, Past and Present by Thomas A. Bailey", *Pacific Historical Review*, vol. 12, no. 4, 1943.

Mcdonald, Matt, "Constructivism", in Paul D. Williams, Matt McDonald (eds.), *Security Studies. An Introduction*, London, Routledge, 2018, 3rd edition.

Peoples, Columba and Vaughan-Williams Nick, *Critical Security Studies. An Introduction*, London, Routledge, 2021, 3rd edition.

Price, Richard "Hegemony and Multilateralism", *International Journal*, 60(1), Winter, 2004/2005, pp. 129-150

Ruggie, John Gerard "Multilateralism: the Anatomy of an Institution", *International Organization*, 46(3), 1992, pp. 561-598

Smith, Edward, "The Traditional Routes to Security. Realism and Liberalism", in Peter Hough, Andrew Moran, Bruce Pilbeam, Wendy Stokes (eds.), *International Security Studies. Theory and Practice*, London, Routledge, 2021, 2nd edition.

Smith, Graham M., "Into Cerberus' Lair: Bringing the Idea of Security to Light", *British Journal of Politics and International Relations*, 7(4), 2005

Sumner Benson, Mary, "U. S. Foreign Policy: Shield of the Republic by Walter Lippmann; Collective Security: The Why and How. by Joseph H. Ball", *The Far Eastern Quarterly*, vol. 3, no. 3, 1944.

Williams, Robert E. Jr, "The Invention of International Relations Theory: Realism, the Rockefeller Foundation, and the 1954 Conference on Theory, Edited by Nicolas Guilhot", *Ethics and International Affairs*, 26(2), 2012.

Wolfers, Arnold, "Discord and Cooperation. Essays on International Politics", Baltimore, John Hopkins Press, 1962.

Wolfers, Arnold, "National Security as an Ambiguous Symbol", *Political Science Quarterly*, vol. 67, no. 4, 1952.

Wolfers, Arnold, "The Pole of Power and the Pole of Indifference", *World Politics*, vol. 4, no. 1, 1951.

Index

5G, 21, 170, 186, 188, 329-31, 335

ACFTA, 210
Advanced Oxidation Processes, 300
AfCFTA, 121, 307
Africa, 1-4, 6, 9, 24, 33-34, 36, 63, 73-75, 90, 98, 111, 116, 118, 121-23, 129-30, 132-33, 135, 162-63, 176, 203-08, 231, 273, 277, 282, 284, 286, 289, 291-92, 299, 304-05, 307, 314, 320, 338
Africa's Ezulwini Consensus, 130
African Development Bank (ADB) , 4, 134, 145, 167, 242, 245-46, 304
Agalega, 109, 126
AI, 13, 55-56, 134, 170, 185, 329-31, 335
AIIB, 10, 139
America Invents Act, 333
Andersen, Inge, 252
Annan, Kofi, 272
Anti-Dumping Duties, 200
António Guterres, 5, 73
APEC, 63, 180-81
Aral Sea Region, 255
Arctic, 3, 54, 259
ASEAN, 2, 4, 7, 11, 28, 61-64, 69, 154-57, 163, 175, 178, 181-83, 191, 193, 200, 246, 304-05
ASEAN Free Trade Area, 62
ASEAN-India Comprehensive Strategic Partnership, 175
ASEAN-India Joint Cooperation Committee, 175
ASEAN-India Plan of Action, 175
ASEAN-India POA, 175
Asia, 1-3, 20-21, 33, 105, 116, 130-31, 133, 166, 170, 180, 236, 244, 248, 338
Asia Europe Meeting, 154
Asia, Multilateralism, 247
Asian Age, 2
Asian Century, 2
Asian Development Bank, 2, 4, 134, 147, 242
Asian Security Conference, 28
Asia-Pacific, 1, 61
Asset Purchase Agreement, 169
Australia, 4, 10, 109-11, 135, 172, 175, 178, 183, 188, 298, 304

Bangladesh, 10, 134, 162, 191-201, 246, 298
Bangladesh Standards and Testing Institution, 200
Bank of Mauritius (BoM), 123
Banking Crisis, 96
BBIN, 196, 200, 245
BBIN-MVA, 200
Beijing, 102, 105, 336
Belgium, 323
Bhutan, 195-96, 198, 244-45, 298
Black Lives Matter, 49
Blue Bonds, 321, 323
Blue Dot Network, 4
Blue Economy, 322
Blue Pacific, 4
Brazil, 33-34, 76, 90, 173, 176, 192, 204, 304
Bretton Woods, 7-9, 94, 98-103, 106-07, 133-34
Brexit, 33
BRI, 3, 111, 155-56, 160-62
BRICS, 1, 7, 9, 33, 37, 101-02, 104, 106-07, 123, 130, 173, 176, 304-05, 307
Bridgetown Initiative, 83
Brunei, 135, 298
Build Back Better World, 4

Bush, George W., 94
Buzan, Barry, 220

Cambodia, 59, 61, 298, 304
Canada, 166, 178, 308
Capital Adequacy Frameworks, 140
Carr, Edward Hallett, 32
CCL, 76, 77
CECPA, 109-10, 116, 119-20
CELAC, 7, 304
Central Asia, 160, 162, 254, 294
Chagos Islands, 125
Chagos, 110, 125-26
Chandrayaan-3, 172
Change Management Team, 273
Chile, 178, 273
China, 1-4, 9, 21, 33-34, 58, 80, 97, 99-101, 105, 109-11, 117-23, 125-26, 131, 136, 140, 153, 156-63, 166, 168, 170, 172-73, 175-78, 180-82, 186, 191, 205, 210, 215, 225-26, 228-34, 246-47, 252, 291, 298, 304-05, 317, 329-42
China's IP Strategy, 335
China-Central Asia-West Asia, 162
China-Indochina, 162
China-Mongolia-Russia, 162
China-Russia Relations, 233
China-US Intellectual Property Competition on Global Innovation, 336
China-US Intellectual Property Competition on Global South, 338
China-US Intellectual Property Competition, Potential Solutions to Consequences, 340
Christine Lagarde, 100
CICA, 7, 304
CIS Tourism Development Strategy, 258
Climate Action Network, 314
Climate Change Adaptation Initiative, 247
Climate Technology, 256
Cloud-based Storage Systems, 302
Coast of Somalia, Contact Group on Piracy off, 324
Cold War, 21, 30-34, 37, 40-48, 50-55, 58, 60-61, 64, 94, 98-99, 101, 105, 157, 160, 203, 222, 244, 282-83
Common Effective Preferential Tariff, 62
Commonwealth of Independent States (CIS), 101, 254-61
  Model Laws
    On Environmental Disaster Zones, 257
    On Environmental Safety, 257
    On Industrial Safety of Hazardous Production Facilities, 257
    On Prevention of Major Accidents Associated with Emissions/Discharges of Hazardous Substances and Limitation of Their Possible Consequences, 257
    On Radiation Safety of Population, 257
    On Safe Handling of Pesticides and Agrochemicals, 257
    On Safety of Activities Related to Genetically Modified Organisms, 257
Completely Knocked Down (CKD), 170
COP21, 269, 275
COP26, 255
COVID-19, 1-2, 4-5, 21, 73, 78, 80-82, 89, 96, 104, 129-30, 132-33, 153, 158-59, 162, 203, 207-08, 271, 302, 312
CPTPP, 175, 178
Cybersecurity, 129, 188, 288, 317, 333
da Silva, Luiz Inácio Lula, 106
David, Charles-Philippe, *War and Peace: Contemporary Approaches to Security and Strategy*, 33
De-dollarisation, 102, 123
Delivering Public Goods, Deploying Niche Diplomacy, 62
Deutsch, Karl, 32
Digital Initiatives Bank, 256
Doi Moi, 59
DSSI, 78, 84
DTAA, 109, 111-13, 115-16, 119
East Asia, 1, 155, 177, 243-44
Ecological Agricultural Intensification, 303
Egypt, 106, 176, 304, 307
Electronic Medical Records, 301
Equity-to-Loans Ratios (E/L), 140
Europe, 2, 4, 21, 30, 33, 41, 61, 77, 97-98, 105, 130, 154, 157, 160, 162, 175, 210, 228, 270, 314
European Union (EU), 3-4, 33, 96-97, 105, 156, 178, 246, 268, 298, 324

EV, 168-69
Exclusive Economic Zone , 126, 292, 320
Expanded Partnership for Quality Infrastructure, 4
Exposure Exchange Agreements, 146

FAO, 240, 302
Farm and Crop Diversification, 303
FDI, 45, 117, 167-68, 173, 176, 180, 192, 336
Financial Stability Board, 77
Fintech, 122
Flexible Credit Lines, 77
Flood Management and Mitigation Programme, 247
FOIP, 161, 163, 174-75
Food Safety and Standards Authorities of India, 200
Four Nations Initiative (4NI), 273
France, 110-11, 140, 171, 204, 241, 267, 275, 277, 323
French Development Agency, 268
FSAP, 76-77
FSF, 76-77
FTA, 110, 118-23, 178, 180
Fukuyama, Francis, 32

G7, 4, 73, 76, 89, 101, 163, 166, 174, 177, 182-83, 255
G7 Plus, 183
G8, 316
G10, 183
G20, 1, 7, 10, 12, 28, 33, 37, 73-74, 76-78, 83, 86-90, 97, 107, 144, 148, 163, 165-67, 174, 177, 182, 297
GATT, 34, 197
Gaya Fusion Model, 305
GDP, 2, 12, 43-46, 79, 95, 131, 135, 165-66, 173, 176, 204, 207, 288, 297-98, 307-08, 325
General Capital Increases, 144
Genuine Products Index, 308
Germany, 68, 100, 140, 161, 171, 173
GFA, 73-78, 83, 85-86, 89-91
GHG, 79, 89, 266
GIFT, 112
Global Challenges Funding, 88
Global Climate Facility, 304
Global Environment Facility, 277, 304
Global Innovation Index, 308
Global North, 11, 73-74, 85, 89-91, 100, 249
Global South, 3-7, 11, 28, 67-70, 73-74, 83, 89-91, 96, 100, 102-05, 115, 130, 165, 173-74, 178, 233, 249, 334, 338-41
Global Water Partnership, 242
Globalisation, 17, 49, 137, 156, 208
GPGs, 79, 89-90
Graduation Discussion Income, 144
Greater Mekong Sub-region, 246
Green Jump, 256

Health Silk Road, 4
Hegemonic-War Cycle, 26
Herz, John H., 220
Highly Indebted Poor Countries, 75
HIV/AIDS, 285
Hobsbawm, Eric, 94
Hyper-Complexity, 17
Hyper-Connectivity, 17
Hyper-Transparency, 17
Hyper-Vulnerability, 17
Hyundai Motor India Engineering, 169

IBRD, 139-46
IBSA, 7, 304
ICT, 41, 46, 49, 112, 154, 159, 184, 207, 305
IDWSSD, 240
IFIs, 73-75, 90, 99, 102, 134, 245
ILO, 5, 7, 133
IMF, 5, 73-78, 80, 82, 84-87, 89-90, 98-101, 103, 107, 131, 134-37, 207
Impacts of Climate Change on Madagascar, 264
India, 1-10, 28, 34, 68-70, 90, 97, 105, 109-17, 119-26, 130-31, 134-36, 156-57, 162-63, 165-78, 182-88, 191-201, 204-07, 209, 215, 232-34, 245-46, 248, 252, 275, 278, 291, 298, 304-05, 308
India-ASEAN, 183
India-Brazil-South Africa (IBSA), 304
India-Japan, 183
Indian Bureau of Indian Standards, 200
Indian Ocean, 9, 54, 68, 109-12, 114, 126, 162, 172, 178, 188, 220, 264, 267-68, 277, 320-21, 324

Indian Ocean Region, 178, 188
Indian Science and Technology Foundation, 185
India-Pakistan War, 195
India-ROK Summit in Framework of G20, 182
India-US, 183
Indonesia, 10, 90, 106, 131, 135, 156, 161-62, 170, 193, 291, 297
Industry 4.0 technologies, 303
International Relations (IR), 17-18, 27, 31, 40, 52-56, 153, 157, 203, 319
International Relations Studies, 35
International Solar Alliance, 245, 275
International Telecommunications Union, 306
Investment, 45
IORA, 68, 178, 188
IOs, 237-38
IP, 13, 329, 333-42
IPCC, 266, 274, 289-90, 298
IPEF, 135
IPRs, 331-32
Iran, 23-26, 34, 106, 156-57, 176
Israel, 171
IT, 55, 166, 184, 255-56
IWRM, 241, 243

Jaishankar, Dr. S., 6
Japan, 1-4, 68, 100, 109, 131, 135, 140, 153, 156-57, 160-63, 166, 172-75, 177, 180-81, 183, 298, 304, 308
Japan-India Free and Open Indo-Pacific Initiative, 174
JCPOA, 21

Kenya, 274, 277, 292, 302
Kia 2.0 Strategy, 169
Ki-moon, Ban, 273
Korea Display Industry Association, 171
Korea Science and Engineering Foundation, 185
Korea-ASEAN Strategic Partnership, 182
Korea-China Strategic Partnership, 180
Korea-Japan Strategic Partnership, 181
Korea-US Strategic Partnership, 180
Kyrgyzstan, 254-55

Latin America, 2-3, 6, 73-75, 101, 106, 162, 314, 338
LDCs, 79-80, 82, 90, 201, 268, 272, 275
Least Developed Countries Fund, 304
Like-Minded Group of Developing Countries, 67
Limitation of Benefits, 112-13
Line of Credit (LoC), 114-16
Long-Term Capital Management, 76

Madagascar, 11, 109-10, 263-71, 275, 277-78
    Climate Change Mitigation and Adaptation Measures, 265
    Environmental Multilateral Instruments, 268
Malaysia, 2, 135, 193, 297
Maldives, 244, 298
Mandaviya, Mansukh, 5
Maritime Asia, 161
Maritime Route, 110
Maslow, *Hierarchy of Needs,* 215
Mauritius, 9, 109-26, 206, 267, 277
    Instant Payment System, 124
    Renminbi Clearing Centre, 123
Mauritius-China Economic Relationship, 117
McKinsey, 2
MDBs, 10, 73-74, 77, 80-82, 84-90, 133-34, 139-48
Meckling, John, 236
Mediterranean Sea, 162
Meishermer, John, 32
Mekong River Commission, 246
Mercantilism versus Mind-Centrism, 55
Middle East, 41, 98, 101, 126
Middle-Income Countries, 143
Militarisation, 252
Millennium Challenge Corporation, 4
Miller, Alexei, 103
Minerals Security Partnership, 174
Ministry of Defence, 186
Ministry of Science and Higher Education, 305
Ministry of Science and Technology, 305
Mobile Health, 301
Modi, Narendra, Indian Prime Minister, 1, 114, 165-67, 173, 175-76, 186, 188
Mongolia, 47, 162, 298
More Friends, Fewer Enemies, 59
Morgenthau, Hans, 32

Moscow, 94-95, 101-03, 105, 156
MoU, 169, 171-72, 185
Mozambique, 36-38, 109-10, 207-08, 277, 287, 292
    Channel, 264
    Higher Institute of International Relations, 34
Multi-Axis Pluripolarity, 55-56
Multi-Dimensional Pluripolar architecture, 56
Multilateral Debt Relief Initiative, 75
Multilateral Diplomacy, 59, 62-64
Multilateralism, 1, 5, 8, 11-12, 15, 30, 35, 37, 40, 58, 64-66, 129, 133, 137, 208, 215, 223-24, 228-29, 236, 247, 270, 278, 303, 312, 315, 319
    Limits, Tackling Climate Change, 270

Napoleonic Wars, 30, 270
National Action Plan to Combat Climate Change, 266
National Coast Guard, 116
National Environment Policy for Sustainable Development, 269
National Payments Corporation of India, 124
NATO, 95, 101, 204, 228
NDB, 10, 139
Neo-Marxist, 100
Nepal, 192, 195-96, 198, 244-46, 298
Net Security Provider, 109, 112
New Delhi, 102, 165, 171, 177, 195, 240
New Zealand, 135, 178, 255, 298
Nigeria, 299, 307-08
Non-Aligned Movement, 60
Non-Performing Loan, 140
Non-Traditional Security Challenges, 284
Northern Mozambique, 110
North-South, 67, 156-57, 277
NRF, 185, 305
NTS, 11, 12, 282-83, 294

Observatory of Economic Complexity, 205
Oil Spill, 110
Old Multilateralism, 215, 223, 227-30, 234
One Earth, One Family, One Future, 6
Open-Ended Working Group on UNSC Reforms, 5
Opulence versus Discontent, 42

P5, 5
Pan African Payment and Settlement System, 123
Paris Call for Action, 274
Pascha, W., 155
Pax Mongolica, 53
Pax Romana, 53
Pearl Harbour, 219
Persian Gulf, 99-100, 162
Pluripolar, Multi-Axis World Architecture, 54
PNA, 266-67
PNLCC, 266, 269
Politicisation, 252
post-Cold War, 21, 41, 51-52, 54-55, 157, 203
Precautionary Credit Lines, 77
Preferred Creditor Status, 142
Private Non-Guaranteed, 80
Public and Publicly Guaranteed, 80
Public-Private Partnerships (PPP), 210, 242

QR Codes, 124
QUAD, 4, 7, 178, 187
Quality Infrastructure Investment, 163

R&D, 122, 169-71, 184, 186, 305, 334-35, 337-38, 340
Rainwater Harvesting Systems, 299
Ramgoolam, Sir Seewoosagur, 111
Rapid Credit Facility, 84
Red Sea, 162
REDD+ mechanism, 267
Regional Comprehensive Economic Partnership, 178
Regional Payment and Settlement System, 123
Renminbi Clearing Centre, 122
Republic of Korea, 10, 135, 165-66, 298
Resilience farming Method, 303
Resilience, 4, 7, 78, 87, 131, 135, 166, 209
Resilient Semiconductor Supply Chains, 185
Response of Politicians, 51
Revisionism, 8, 17, 26-27
RFI, 84, 186-87
RST, 78, 84, 87, 90
Rules of Origin, 119-21

RuPay card, 124-25
Russia, 21, 33-34, 58, 76, 78, 94-97, 99, 101-07, 129, 153, 157-60, 162, 166, 171, 173, 176-77, 204, 208, 228, 233, 252, 254, 291, 305, 316
Russia-Ukraine War, 129, 153, 157-59, 162, 208, 233

SAARC, 68, 244-45
SADC, 36, 38, 123, 210
SAGAR, 4, 111-12
Sandler, Tod, 156
SASEC, 191, 245
Saudi Arabia, 99, 105-06, 176, 304
SBM, 114, 124
SBMIDCL, 115
SCO, 7, 28, 104, 106, 256, 260, 304
SCRI, 4, 7, 131, 135
SDGs, 3, 5, 9, 73-74, 78-79, 80, 83-90, 133, 139, 144, 147, 165, 176, 242-43, 297-98, 301-03, 307
SDRs, 77-78, 84-88, 90
Second World War, 21-22, 30, 34-35, 37, 53, 55, 65, 73, 97-98, 101, 129, 160, 203, 270, 315, 330
Securitisation, 109, 146, 251-54
Selective Capital Increases, 144
Self-Sufficiency Economy Philosophy, 302
SeyCCAT, 323
Seychelles, 126, 267, 277, 320-24
SEZs, 200-01
Shock, Lehman, 77
shuttle diplomacy, 181
SIJORI, 193
Singapore, 2, 131, 135, 193, 297
Singer, J. David, 32
Six Ts, 21
SLL, 142-43
Small Island Developing States, 275
Smart Precision and Farming Technology, 303
Socialist Bloc, 61
South Africa, 34, 90, 111, 123, 176, 273, 277, 304-05, 307
South Asia, 1, 3, 162, 172, 191, 231, 236, 243-46, 248-49
South China Sea, 126, 131, 161-62
South Korea, 166-72, 175-84, 187-88, 298, 304
South Korea-India Cooperation in G20, 177
South Korea-India Cooperation in QUAD Plus, 187
South Korea-India Defence and Security Cooperation, 186
South Pole, 172
Southeast Asia, 1, 3, 11, 101, 162, 231, 236, 243, 246, 248-49, 314
Southern Indian Ocean, 126
South-South, 12, 67, 132, 204, 264, 275-78, 304
Special Strategic Partnership, 183
State Intellectual Property Office, 335
STI, 12, 297-99, 301-03, 305-08
Stockholm International Peace Research Institute, 171
Sweden, 273

Taiwan, 180-81, 298, 304, 308, 341
Tanzania, 277, 282-92
    Actions for Climate Injustice, 290
    Climate Change Issues, 291
Technical and Financial Partners, 266
Technical Cooperation among Developing Countries, 276
Technology, 21
Telemedicine, 301
Tenets, 22
Terriff, Terry, *Security Studies Today*, 216
Territory and Water, 22
Terrorism, 22, 176, 284
Thailand, 135, 246-47, 273, 297, 302
the Philippines, 135, 297
Trade, 5, 8, 10, 21, 44, 100, 118-19, 121-23, 131-33, 139, 151, 178, 180, 182, 195, 203, 205-06, 246, 271, 306-07, 331-32, 334-35, 339
Trade in Services, 122
Trans-Atlantic Mono-Axis, 53
TRIPS, 331, 334-35
True Multilateralism, 215
Trump, Donald, 175, 180
Trust, 22
Turkey, 106, 160, 304
Typhoons, 225

UAE, 105, 176
Ukraine, 21, 78, 94-96, 103, 133, 153, 157-60, 162, 166, 204, 208, 228
UN, 3, 5-6, 11, 22-25, 53, 55, 61, 63-64, 67, 73-74, 79, 83, 85-86, 89, 99, 102, 106, 110, 125, 130, 133, 136, 231, 240-42, 249, 251-54, 270-77, 298-99, 306
UN FCCC, 253
UN Human Rights Council, 251
UN Intersecretariat Group for Water Resources, 240
UN Security Council (UNSC), 5, 23, 25, 135, 188, 251
UN Water Conference, 240, 299
UNCED, 241, 319
UNCTAD, 79, 80, 133, 306
UNEP, 263, 268, 270-71, 274, 277-78, 306
UNESCO World Heritage Committee, 63
UNFCCC, 266, 268-69, 271, 274-75, 304
Unified Payments Interface, 124
United Kingdom (UK), 110-11, 126, 140, 171, 194, 204, 255, 323
United Nations, 4-6, 8, 23, 25, 33-38, 58, 60-61, 63-64, 66, 73, 75, 86, 125, 130-32, 135, 160, 225, 240-41, 252, 255, 263, 266, 268-70, 273-74, 276, 289-90, 292, 304, 306-07, 316, 319, 322
United Nations Economic and Social Council, 63
United States, 5, 21, 32-34, 58, 74, 77, 94-99, 101, 103, 140, 158, 168, 172, 175, 177, 180, 204-05, 224, 226, 228-29, 255, 291, 302, 315, 317, 329-31, 333, 335-38, 340-41
    Department of Agriculture, 302
    IP Strategy, 333
US Patent and Trademark Office, 333
US Treasury Bills, 103
US' anti-Russian Sanctions Policy, 105
US-China, 99, 180, 331, 335, 341-42
    IP Competition on the Global South, Potential Solutions to Mitigate, 339
    Technology Competition, 329
US-India Comprehensive Global and Strategic Partnership, 173
USSR, 33, 102
Uzbekistan, 255

Vasudhaiva Kutumbakam, 6, 165
Vietnam, 2, 8, 58-67, 69, 135, 170, 246, 297
Virtual Payment Address, 124
Vostro Account, 124-25

Waltz, Kenneth, *Theory of International Politics*, 31
Warsaw Pact, 53
Washington, 9, 75, 94-97, 99-06, 336
Washington Consensus, 75, 100, 103
Water Research Commission, 305
West, 24, 34, 95, 130
    Economic Crisis, 96
Western Indian Ocean, 324
Westphalian, 53
WHO, 5, 7, 132, 136, 240, 274
Wireless Health Devices, 302
Wolfers, Arnold, *Discord and Collaboration: Essays on International Politics*, 216
World Bank, 5, 34, 38, 73-77, 80-81, 85, 90, 98, 100, 133-34, 136, 140, 143, 146-47, 173, 192, 242, 306, 320, 322-23
World Bank Group, 81, 140, 306
World Intellectual Property Organization, 306
World Water Council (WWC), 242
WTO, 5, 7-8, 49, 62, 98, 100, 107, 131-33, 136, 174, 271, 335

Yellow Vests, 49
Yunnan, 247

Zakaria, Fareed, *The Post-American World*, 157
Zambia, 123, 204-07, 209-10, 292